Books by Beth Lindsay Templeton

POVERTY

Loving Our Neighbor:
A Thoughtful Approach for Helping People in Poverty

Understanding Poverty in the Classroom:
Changing Perceptions for Student Success

A Coat Named Mr. Spot

Angelika's Journal:
What You Can Do About Poverty and Homelessness

INSPIRATIONAL

Conversations on the Porch:
Ancient Voices–Contemporary Wisdom

More Conversations on the Porch:
Ancient Voices—Contemporary Wisdom

Refrigerator Prayers for Ordinary People:
Conversations with God about the Details of Life

PERSONAL GROWTH AND CHALLENGES

Uncharted Journey:
On the Challenges of Getting Older and Other Transitions

The Sacred Year

MISCELLANEOUS

The Christmas Strawberry…and Other Stories

George's War: Then and Now

Grace-full Love
by the Week

Beth Lindsay Templeton

Greenville, S.C.

Grace-full Love *by the* Week

Copyright © 2023 Beth Lindsay Templeton

All rights reserved. No part of this book may be used or reproduced by any means, graphic, electronic, or mechanical, including photocopying, recording, taping or by any information storage retrieval without the written permission of the publisher except in the case of brief quotations embodied in critical articles and reviews.

Unless otherwise noted, scripture quotations are from the *New Revised Standard Version of the Holy Bible*, text copyright 1990 by Graded Press. Published by Thomas Nelson Publishers for Cokesbury: Nashville. Italics are by the author.

Often used in text:

- Eugene H. Peterson, *The Message: The Bible in Contemporary Language*, NavPress: Colorado Springs, Colorado, 2002.
- *The Contemporary English Version*, American Bible Society, Thomas Nelson Publishers, Nashville, 1995.
- *The Inclusive New Testament*, Priests for Equality, Brentwood, MD, 1996.

All other references are provided in the text.

Published by:

FpS

1175 Woods Crossing Rd., #2
Greenville, S.C. 29607
864-675-0540
www.fiction-addiction.com

ISBN: 978-1-952248-96-2

Cover & Book Design
by United Writers Press

Cover art courtesy of Angela Sudermann

Printed in the United States of America

This book contains 52 weeks of devotionals, each focusing on a single biblical passage. You may elect to skip around. You may choose to start on any day of the week, although weekdays are provided at the top of each page. You may decide to read the devotionals in a traditional way, beginning in a new calendar year on January 1 and continuing through a year. For those in the last group, the date associated with each week appears below beside the week number, passage, and page numbers. Finally, the devotionals loosely relating to liturgical seasons are noted in the final column.

Week	Begins	Passage	Page	Seasons
1	Jan 1	John 1: 1-5, 9-14, 16-18	2	
2	Jan 8	Luke 3: 15-22	10	
3	Jan 15	Psalm 139	18	
4	Jan 22	Matthew 4: 1-11	26	
5	Jan 29	John 3: 1-17	34	
6	Feb 5	Psalm 23	42	
7	Feb 12	Mark 12: 28–34	50	
8	Feb 19	Luke 12: 13-21	58	
9	Feb 26	Mark 10: 17-31	66	
10	Mar 5	Matthew 18: 1-7, 10	74	
11	Mar 12	Matthew 6: 9-10; Ephesians 5: 1-2, 15; 6: 1-9	82	Lent and Easter
12	Mar 19	John 11: 1-44	90	
13	Mar 26	Luke 19: 29-42	98	
14	Apr 2	Mark 16: 1-8	106	
15	Apr 9	Luke 24: 13-35	114	
16	Apr 16	John 20: 19-29	122	
17	Apr 23	Matthew 28: 16-20	130	
18	Apr 30	1 Samuel 1: 1-18	138	
19	May 7	Nehemiah 2: 17-18, 12: 27, 43	146	
20	May 14	Luke 24: 50-53, Acts 1: 1-11	154	
21	May 21	Acts 2: 1-21	162	
22	May 28	Psalm 131	170	
23	Jun 4	Exodus 15: 1-16; Isaiah 43: 1-4	178	

Week	Begins	Passage	Page	Seasons
24	Jun 11	Ephesians 2: 1-10	186	
25	Jun 18	John 14: 1-7	194	
26	Jun 25	John 15: 1-8	202	
27	Jul 2	Mark 7: 24-30; Matthew 15: 21-28	210	
28	Jul 9	Luke 15: 1-10	218	
29	Jul 16	Acts 10: 1-33	226	
30	Jul 23	Jonah 3: 1 -4: 4	234	
31	Jul 30	Joshua 1: 1-9	242	
32	Aug 6	Ezekiel 37: 1-14	250	
33	Aug 13	Amos 5: 21-24	258	
34	Aug 20	Matthew 5: 1–12	266	
35	Aug 27	Psalm 103: 1-14	274	
36	Sep 3	Letter to Philemon	282	
37	Sep 10	Ephesians 2: 1-10	290	
38	Sep 17	Acts 5: 1–11	298	
39	Sep 24	Isaiah 6: 1-8	306	
40	Oct 1	2 Timothy 3: 14-4: 5	314	
41	Oct 8	Luke 4: 16-30	322	
42	Oct 15	Matthew 20: 1-16	330	
43	Oct 22	Genesis 12: 1-9	338	
44	Oct 29	Genesis 16: 1-15; 21: 8-21	346	
45	Nov 5	Genesis 22: 1-14	354	
46	Nov 12	Genesis 25: 19-34	362	
47	Nov 19	Genesis 45: 1-15	370	
48	Nov 26	Psalm 85	378	
49	Dec 3	Luke 1: 68-79	386	Advent and Christmas
50	Dec 10	Luke 1: 46-55	394	
51	Dec 17	Psalm 80: 1-7, 17-19	402	
52	Dec 24	Luke 2: 1-7	410	
Final Day	Dec 31	Luke 2: 21-40	418	

Preface

Through the years, I've used a variety of devotional books. I have used some of them for several years. Others make it only a few weeks or months.

One book that I've continued to use suggests reading the same passage every day for a week in addition to different scripture passages each day. I discovered that reading the same passage for a week often opened the verses for me in wondrous ways. I would notice something on Thursday that moved me in new ways, even though I had already read the passage for several days.

So when I decided to write a devotional book, I followed that pattern, using the same passage for seven days. This gives a flow to the days as well as providing an opportunity for the passage to open to the reader in new ways.

I hope you will be enriched with these daily readings.

Blessings,
Beth

Grace-full Love
by the Week

Week 1
John 1:1-5, 9-14, 16-18

1 In the beginning was the Word, and the Word was with God, and the Word was God. 2 He was in the beginning with God. 3 All things came into being through him, and without him not one thing came into being. What has come into being 4 in him was life, and the life was the light of all people. 5 The light shines in the darkness, and the darkness did not overcome it.

…

9 The true light, which enlightens everyone, was coming into the world.
10 He was in the world, and the world came into being through him; yet the world did not know him. 11 He came to what was his own, and his own people did not accept him. 12 But to all who received him, who believed in his name, he gave power to become children of God, 13 who were born, not of blood or of the will of the flesh or of the will of man, but of God.
14 And the Word became flesh and lived among us, and we have seen his glory, the glory as of a father's only son, full of grace and truth.

…

16 From his fullness we have all received, grace upon grace. 17 The law indeed was given through Moses; grace and truth came through Jesus Christ. 18 No one has ever seen God. It is God the only Son, who is close to the Father's heart, who has made him known.

Week 1
Sunday

John 1:1-5, 9-14, 16-18

In the beginning was the Word, and the Word was with God, and the Word was God. He was in the beginning with God. All things came into being through him, and without him not one thing came into being. ...In him was life, and the life was the light of all people. The light shines in the darkness, and the darkness did not overcome it (John 1:1-5).

This language is moving, but very philosophical. The Gospel writer of John struggled with ways to communicate with both Jewish and Greek Christians. In the Jewish mind, LOGOS, "word," was more than a mere sound. It was something which had an independent existence and...actually did things. For example, "And God SAID, Let there be light." And there was light.

We too understand that words have power. Affirming words can make a child who grows up in poverty believe that he or she has worth. A kid who lacks for no material wishes can believe that he or she is worthless when told that repeatedly. A good wife can believe that she deserves the abuse she receives because her husband tells her she does. Words can make us believe our prejudices. Words can blind us to the blessings right in front of us. We understand that words can create good or evil. Jesus *spoke* to disciples, crowds, and religious leaders, and things happened.

Prayer for the Day: *God of all good things, help me pay attention to my words today. May they be healing, not hurting. Amen.*

John 1:1-5, 9-14, 16-18

**Week 1
Monday**

The gospel writer chose the word LOGOS: word, action, reason, and wisdom. Let's look at verse 5 in the first stanza: *The light shines in the darkness and the darkness did not overcome it.* This is such a beautiful thought. Darkness does not overcome.

Wisdom teaches that darkness never understands the light. Hatred does not understand love. Ugliness and despair do not understand beauty and hope. The powers of darkness, hatred, and greed do not value the ideas of justice, peace, and beauty for all people. But light, love, beauty, hope, justice, and peace will triumph. Don't we need this message now? Darkness does not overcome light.

Prayer for the Day: *God of Light, help me hold onto your promise that darkness does not win. Amen.*

Week 1
Tuesday

John 1:1-5, 9-14, 16-18

Dr. Martin Luther King, Jr. said, "The ultimate weakness of violence is that it is a descending spiral, begetting the very thing [violence] seeks to destroy. Instead of diminishing evil, it multiplies it. Through violence you murder the hater, but you do not murder hate. In fact, violence merely increases hate…Darkness cannot drive out darkness; only light can do that. Hate cannot drive out hate; only love can do that."

The powers of darkness tried to overcome Jesus, even by killing him, but they could not destroy him. We can live in hope even when we feel as if we are drowning or dying. We can live with hope even in the midst of a pandemic. We *must* live with hope. We can know that even though all evidence points to destruction and downfall, the ultimate outcome is in God's, our Creator's and Redeemer's, hands. Christians believe in resurrection. Darkness does not overcome the light.

Prayer for the Day: *God of Hope, thank you for love that drives out hate. Amen.*

John 1:1-5, 9-14, 16-18

Week 1
Wednesday

Have you wondered if you would have been a follower of Jesus if you had lived when he walked the earth? You may not have known anything at all about him because you were so busy simply living your life. You may have been one of the Pharisees who were threatened by this man. How would you have known that Jesus was the Christ? How could you have known? Even though Jesus performs signs and miracles throughout the Gospel of John, his actions are followed by understanding and confusion, faith and doubt. His own did not know him.

We can know God because God comes to each of us in ways that are uniquely given for each one of us. For some like Moses, God's coming is a bush that does not burn; for others, it is a cloud as when the Hebrews left Egypt and wandered in the wilderness. For some it is a still small voice, and for others, it can be an angel, with or without wings. God may come to us in a friend's comment or insights from a dream. We may read a book or a quote or a posting on social media. We may watch a show or hear music that resonates deeply within our spirit. God comes to us in ways that each of us most needs so we can find wholeness and meaning.

Prayer for the Day: *Most present God, help me listen for your voice throughout this day. Amen.*

Week 1
Thursday

John 1:1-5, 9-14, 16-18

Our passage reminds us that in Christ we are in a new kind of world. We are related to God, not by flesh or blood as we are with our parents and siblings and children. We are related to God because of God's love which became flesh in Jesus. Therefore, through God, we are related to all our fellow human beings as siblings. We share the same holy parentage through Jesus Christ. We are a new race—one in God.

Wouldn't it be wonderful if we lived and cared for others as if we believed that we were related to everyone in the world? To live and care for others as if we believed we are related to everyone in the world no matter their skin color, their education level, their nationality, their religion, their political persuasion, their sexual orientation, or any of the many other categories that we use to divide our world into us and them. We are all God's children and that makes us all brothers and sisters to each other. We are bound to each other through God's love.

Prayer for the Day: *God of Beginnings, open my eyes to see and my heart to embrace ALL my brothers and sisters. Amen.*

John 1:1-5, 9-14, 16-18

**Week 1
Friday**

The Word became flesh and lived among us (John 1:14). Isn't this amazing! God became human. For the only time in the history of the world, we humans could touch God. We could smell God, we could eat with God, we could talk with God, we could even play with God. The Greek understanding is that the Word pitched a tent among us. Jesus went camping. Pitching a tent lends itself to a picture of temporary residence—that the Messiah was on a journey. And it also points back to the tent where God's glory was present with the Israelites in their wilderness wanderings. And this God, this Jesus, is now with us, traveling with us now and forevermore.

What does this mean for us? It means that we can see God in ways that we never could before. Do you yearn to know God, to know what God wants from you, to know how you are to be God's loving child? Well, here is the answer: Look at Christ. Look at how he served, how he loved, how he challenged his culture and popular truths, and what and whom he valued.

Are we willing to see this Christ who is revealed in scripture rather than as we tend to create him in our own versions of the gospel? Can we have faith in Jesus the Christ as he is rather than in the sweet, passionless image that we often have of him? To really know Christ, the Word, the Creator, is to know God. To know Christ in our lives is to acknowledge that Christ, the creator of the world, is more than we can ever grasp.

Prayer for the Day: *God who came to us in a human body, help me to see you in all your humanness so I can understand more who I am to be. Amen.*

Week 1
Saturday

John 1:1-5, 9-14, 16-18

We see the Word in grace and truth. Jesus *showed* us what truth is. Many of us think in pictures or need tangible experiences to know something. We do not know what an apple is unless we see a picture of it or better yet hold an apple in our hands. We cannot describe the taste of an apple to its fullest. We must take a bite of it and savor it in our mouths to know the truth of the apple. God became someone, a human being, that we could recognize and relate to. In Christ, we know the truth of God. We know the savory experience of walking the way of Christ.

Not everyone knows Christ. Even his disciples were confused more often than not. Our passage says not everyone accepts Christ. But…the good news is that Christ lived and still lives among us with grace and truth. We have seen God because we have seen God's son, Jesus the Christ, in our midst. How does that happen? *We* know Christ and *others* know Christ by how we live and work and worship and play. We can scarcely get our minds around this. No wonder the gospel writer used such philosophical language. Trying to explain the fullness of Christ in our lives and our world is beyond challenging. Barbara Brown Taylor sums this passage up when she says: "We are words about the Word before we ever say a word." (*Day1.org*, January 5, 2020)

Prayer for the Day: *God of Light and Grace and Truth, help me be your Word today. Amen.*

Week 2
Luke 3:15-22

15 As the people were filled with expectation and all were questioning in their hearts concerning John, whether he might be the Messiah, 16 John answered all of them by saying, "I baptize you with water, but one who is more powerful than I is coming; I am not worthy to untie the strap of his sandals. He will baptize you with the Holy Spirit and fire. 17 His winnowing fork is in his hand to clear his threshing floor and to gather the wheat into his granary, but the chaff he will burn with unquenchable fire."

18 So with many other exhortations he proclaimed the good news to the people. 19 But Herod the ruler, who had been rebuked by him because of Herodias, his brother's wife, and because of all the evil things that Herod had done, 20 added to them all by shutting up John in prison.

21 Now when all the people were baptized and when Jesus also had been baptized and was praying, the heaven was opened, 22 and the Holy Spirit descended upon him in bodily form like a dove. And a voice came from heaven, "You are my Son, the Beloved; with you I am well pleased."

Week 2
Sunday

Luke 3:15-22

To understand Luke's version of the baptism of Jesus, we need to look at the passages that come before and after. At the end of the second chapter of Luke, we find Jesus astounding the teachers in the Temple. Then the gospel is silent, as are all the gospels, about the next 30 years of Jesus's life until John the Baptist shows up. Luke spells out with great detail John's message of repentance and moral living. John the Baptist was such an expounder of repentance for the forgiveness of sins, the people began asking if he was the Messiah. Then in the Gospel of Luke, John is arrested. Jesus is baptized, followed by a list of people in Jesus's genealogy. Luke's version of the genealogy has no women, some of the men mentioned were unknown and maybe scoundrels, and Luke's last two listings were son of Adam and son of God. The only other genealogy of Jesus is in the Gospel of Matthew. That one begins with Abraham and ends with Mary's husband, *Joseph*, not son of Abraham and son of God. After the baptism and genealogy, Luke tells of the temptation of Jesus in the wilderness.

In this week's scripture reading, we learn that the people were filled with expectation. We read that all were questioning in their hearts concerning John, whether he might be the Messiah.

The times were turbulent. Israel was an occupied territory. Taxes were heavy. The people yearned for the coming of the Messiah to save them from their tribulations. Listen to some of the characteristics described in Psalm 18 about the deliverer they expected: *The earth reeled and rocked; the foundations also of the mountains trembled and quaked, because God was angry…The Lord thundered in the heavens and the Most High uttered his voice. And he sent out his arrows, and scattered them* (Psalm 18:7-14). This is who the people were expecting to save them from their oppressors. Could that be John?

In our times, we experience taxes, political and climate-related turbulence, wars, and family challenges. You might ask yourself, "Do I put my faith in political systems and political parties, or do I put my faith in God?" Who…or what…do I seek as a Messiah?

Prayer for the Day: *God of deliverance, help me keep my mind, heart, eyes, and ears open for your action in my life and in my world. Amen.*

Luke 3:15-22

**Week 2
Monday**

There must have been some heated discussions about the Messiah. Could it be John? Or could it be Jesus? In the Gospel of John, some disciples of John the Baptist actually defected to Jesus. One of those was Andrew, Simon Peter's brother. Luke cleared up the question of whether John the Baptist might be the Messiah when he told about John being arrested after he challenged Herod the ruler.

With John's arrest, he was now off the stage for Luke just about the time Jesus entered with his ministry. But—and now here's one of those tricky Biblical details—if John was in jail, who baptized Jesus? Do we need to agonize over this point? No. The other gospels make it clear that John the Baptist baptized Jesus. Unfortunately, Matthew and Mark then had to deal with the sticky theological question, "Well, then, what sins did Jesus have to repent of since that is why people were baptized by John?"

Jesus's repentance is a non-issue for Luke. John is not the Messiah because he's in jail. Jesus is the Messiah. Luke made it very clear from the beginning of his gospel that Jesus was the Messiah. Hear again just a few lines of Mary's song in Luke: *He has brought down the powerful from their thrones, and lifted up the lowly; he has filled the hungry with good things, and sent the rich away empty* (Luke 1:52-53).

Prayer for the Day: *Jesus, my redeemer, help me hear your Truths without getting bogged down in the details…in every aspect of my life. Amen.*

Week 2
Tuesday

Luke 3:15-22

We move to Luke 3:21—*Now when all the people were baptized, and when Jesus also had been baptized...*Jesus was one of an ordinary crowd of ordinary people being baptized. From this first moment of his public ministry, Jesus identified with us. He aligned himself with us. That's pretty amazing. He waited in line with the rest of us. He claimed no special privileges. He was with us waiting to be baptized. When Jesus waited in line with the rest of the people, he affirmed that each of us is a child of God, known by God even before we were created. When Luke follows the baptism of Jesus with his version of the genealogy, he reinforces the fact that Jesus was connected with all of humanity all the way back to Adam.

The late John Leith, seminary professor and theologian, "liked to say that every human life is rooted in the will and intention of God: In baptism the child's name is called because our faith is that God thought of this child before the child was, that God gave this child an identity, an individuality, a name, and a dignity that no one should dare abuse. Human existence has its origin not in the accidents of history and biology, but in the will and the intention of the Lord God, creator of heaven and earth" (Robert M. Brearley, "Pastoral Perspective," Luke 3:15-17, 21-22, *Feasting on the Word, Year C, Vol 1*, p. 240). Jesus aligned himself with this God-given identity for all of us when he waited in line to be baptized with the rest of the people there.

Prayer for the Day: *God of wonder, I can hardly grasp that you chose to become one of the common people. You chose to become like me. Thank you for this wondrous gift. Amen.*

Luke 3:15-22

Week 2
Wednesday

And when Jesus had also been baptized and was praying... (Luke 3:21). None of the other gospel renditions of this event have Jesus praying. Jesus prayed. Ernest Hest reminds us: "Throughout his Gospel, Luke shows us Jesus praying. Jesus prays before he calls his disciples (6:12), before asking them who he is (9:18), at the time of his transfiguration (9:29), before teaching his disciples how to pray (11:1), on the night of this arrest (22:41), and at his death (23:46)" (Ernest Hess, "Homilectical Perspective," *Feasting on the Word, Year C, Vol 1*, p. 239).

What does this say about us? What does this say about the church? That we are to pray. How come we so often move to prayer as our last solution rather than our first? Here is Jesus at the inauguration of his public ministry and he is praying. Prayer. Talking things over with God. Listening for God's guidance. Being open to God's wisdom and grace. Seeking God's courage for us. Prayer.

Prayer for the Day: *Most holy God, help me to pray, especially when I do not know the words. Will your Holy Spirit pray for me then? Amen.*

Week 2
Thursday

Luke 3:15-22

Another curious detail appears in Luke's telling of the baptism of Jesus: *And the Holy Spirit descended upon him in bodily form like a dove* (Luke 3:22). Neither Matthew, Mark, nor John indicate that the Holy Spirit descended on Jesus *in bodily form*. The reality of this spiritual experience was tangible... in bodily form. It was not just a feeling or just a thought. It was real—a true in-breaking of a new age. Luke describes Jesus eating fish in Chapter 22 after the resurrection. When the disciples saw Jesus eat, they knew that he wasn't a ghost! When a dove descended on Jesus, we know this really happened. We know the Holy Spirit was very much involved in what was happening.

Prayer for the Day: *Loving God, birds are so special. Help me see birds as messengers from you and then to hear what you have to offer to me. Amen.*

Luke 3:15-22

Week 2 Friday

The final and maybe most important thing of this baptism happened next. "A voice came from heaven, *'You are my Son, the Beloved; with you I am well pleased'*" (Luke 3:22). These words are reminiscent of a couple of different Old Testament passages. Psalm 2:7: *"I will tell of the decree of the Lord; He said to me, 'You are my son; today I have begotten you.'"* This particular psalm points to the kingship of God when it says "*He who sits in the heavens laughs; the Lord has [the kings of the earth] in derision…[He will]terrify them in his fury, saying, 'I have set my king on Zion, my holy hill'*" (Psalm 2:4-5). The second half of the Holy Spirit's comment harkens back to Isaiah 42:1, which says, *Here is my servant, whom I uphold, my chosen, in whom my soul delights. I have put my spirit upon him.* The Isaiah chapter goes on to talk about God's chosen as the one who brings justice. *See, the former things have come to pass, and new things I now declare* (Isaiah 42:9).

Dr. Fred Craddock reminds us that the beautiful words, "You are my Son, the Beloved; with you I am well pleased" bring together both "sovereignty [Psalm 2] and service [Isaiah 42]" at this, the beginning of Jesus's earthly ministry (*Luke: Interpretation*, John Knox Press, 1990, p. 51). Wouldn't you love to hear someone say these words to you: "You are my beloved; with you I am well pleased"? Maybe there is someone to whom you want to say these words. Maybe the church needs to learn to say these words more to all the people who are hungry for meaning and care and affirmation and love and grace in their lives. You are my beloved; with you I am well pleased.

Prayer for the Day: *Beloved God, help me know that I am beloved so I can share with another their own belovedness. Amen.*

Week 2
Saturday

Luke 3:15-22

It seems that when we choose to live with Jesus in our lives, to walk the way that Jesus calls us to walk, to follow Jesus as the way, the truth, and the life, that we are to identify with all people, just as Jesus did. Jesus waited and was baptized with all the other people. He did not choose to be with only certain people. Luke tells us that *all* the people there had been baptized and then it was Jesus's turn.

And just as Jesus depended on God through prayer, so we, too, can bring more prayer into our own lives. When we pray, we have more a sense of being in God. Paul says that in God we live and move and have our being. Prayer seems to be the main way that we connect with God in order to experience love, grace, peace, wisdom, and guidance.

Jesus heard God's words as affirmation of his calling. Can we, too, listen for God to call us beloved so we can walk in the path that God has laid out for us? As we connect with the baptism of Jesus and remember that we, too, have been baptized, can we affirm our own God-given purpose and then live it out with God's help?

Prayer for the Day: *God who is Father, Son, and Holy Spirit, remind me of my baptism. Lace my life with prayer, identification with all your beloved children, and your grace, peace, and welcome as your beloved child. Amen.*

Week 3
Psalm 139

1 O Lord, you have searched me and known me.

2 You know when I sit down and when I rise up; you discern my thoughts from far away.

3 You search out my path and my lying down and are acquainted with all my ways.

4 Even before a word is on my tongue, O Lord, you know it completely.

5 You hem me in, behind and before, and lay your hand upon me.

6 Such knowledge is too wonderful for me; it is so high that I cannot attain it.

7 Where can I go from your spirit? Or where can I flee from your presence?

8 If I ascend to heaven, you are there; if I make my bed in Sheol, you are there.

9 If I take the wings of the morning and settle at the farthest limits of the sea,

10 even there your hand shall lead me, and your right hand shall hold me fast.

11 If I say, "Surely the darkness shall cover me, and night wraps itself around me,"

12 even the darkness is not dark to you; the night is as bright as the day, for darkness is as light to you.

13 For it was you who formed my inward parts; you knit me together in my mother's womb.

14 I praise you, for I am fearfully and wonderfully made. Wonderful are your works; that I know very well.

15 My frame was not hidden from you, when I was being made in secret, intricately woven in the depths of the earth.

16 Your eyes beheld my unformed substance. In your book were written all the days that were formed for me, when none of them as yet existed.

17 How weighty to me are your thoughts, O God! How vast is the sum of them!

18 I try to count them—they are more than the sand; I come to the end—I am still with you.

19 O that you would kill the wicked, O God, and that the bloodthirsty would depart from me—

20 those who speak of you maliciously and lift themselves up against you for evil!

21 Do I not hate those who hate you, O Lord? And do I not loathe those who rise up against you?

22 I hate them with perfect hatred;

I count them my enemies.

23 Search me, O God, and know my heart; test me and know my thoughts.

24 See if there is any wicked way in me, and lead me in the way everlasting.

Week 3
Sunday

Psalm 139

The psalms express raw feelings of extreme praise and exultation and of abject anger and hatred. We find comfort in words in our holy scripture that we could have said if only we were that eloquent.

O Lord, you have searched me and known me. You know when I sit down and when I rise up; You discern my thoughts from far away. You search out my path and my lying down, and are acquainted with all my ways. Even before a word is on my tongue, O Lord, you know it completely (Psalm 139:1-4).

WOW!!! God knows us in every millisecond of our lives. God knows us when we are passive or reflective, as when we are sitting down, and knows us when we are active, as when we rise up. God even knows what we are thinking. God knows what we are saying. The psalmist seems to say that God knows our unconscious or subconscious thoughts, even before we are aware of them. What is hidden to us, God can discern.

Have you ever voiced aloud or in your heart a question, a frustration, a challenge, a thanksgiving to God? Then were you later astounded at responses that came to you "out of the blue?" The book just jumped off the shelf at you in the store. A guest on a television show spoke to your heart. You found the answer to the questions you did not even know you were asking. God knows our thoughts even before we do!!!

We are not automatons or robots. God waits for us to ask and then leads us to amazing insights that are perfect for us at that specific time and place.

Prayer for the Day: *Searching God, thank you for staying with me even when I am not aware of you. Amen.*

Psalm 139

**Week 3
Monday**

You hem me in, behind and before, and lay your hand upon me. Such knowledge is too wonderful for me; it is so high that I cannot attain it (Psalm 139:5-6).

God is in your past, and in your future, behind and before. Whatever has happened in the past in your life, good or bad, God was there. Let that sink in…God was there in everything that has happened to you in the past. Where there was pain, grief and suffering, God was there…maybe even hurting alongside of you. And because you are here, God obviously helped you get through the experience. And because God was with you in the past, God knows the possible lessons that you can learn from the past and can walk with you as you deal with whatever you must. *And* God will be with you in the future. Isn't that comforting?

God is leading you into whatever your future is. God is leading you to a future that you cannot even begin to fathom. What dreams can you dream? God is there. No wonder the psalmist exclaimed that "Such knowledge is too wonderful."

Prayer for the Day: *Creator, I am in awe of you and your love for me and the entire world. Help me reflect that love in my own living and connecting with others. Amen.*

Week 3   **Psalm 139**
Tuesday

Where can I go from your spirit? Or where can I flee from your presence? If I ascend to heaven, you are there; if I make my bed in Sheol, you are there. If I take the wings of the morning and settle at the farthest limits of the sea, even there your hand shall lead me, and your right hand shall lead me, and your right hand shall hold me fast. If I say, "Surely the darkness shall cover me, and the light around me become night," even the darkness is not dark to you; the night is as bright as the day, for darkness is as light to you (Psalm 139:7-12).

The inescapable God. What wonderful picture imagery. We can't get away from God, no matter how much how much we want to and no matter where we are. If we feel as if we are living in a mountain top experience with God or if we feel at the depths of isolation and abandonment from God, the loving, holy God is there.

The magnificent sunrises on the coast can remind us of the wings of the morning. Slowly the rays of light wing their way across the sky. Slowly, slowly they spread further and further until finally the entire sky and land are bright and glorious. The psalmist says that in God's hands, this is how our lives look. Wings of the morning…isn't that a wonderful picture?

When little kids hide, they stick their heads under the covers but forget their rear ends are poking out. They believe they are hidden…but they are not. The psalmist is reminding us that we hide like little kids do…but God sees us and knows where we are.

Prayer for the Day: *Comforting God, you hold me tight even when I'd rather you didn't. Thank for never letting me go from your loving grace, especially when I cannot claim it. Amen.*

Psalm 139

**Week 3
Wednesday**

The next verses eloquently point out that God knew you from the very moment of your existence.

For it was you who formed my inward part; you knit me together in my mother's womb...My frame was not hidden from you, when I was being made in secret, intricately woven in the depths of the earth (Psalm 139:13).

A dad told his daughter that she was the twinkle in his eye even before he knew she was coming into his life. How much more would this twinkle be with God? God knew us even before our conception. How can this be? We cannot know the answer, but we can be glad that it is so.

This first part of the psalm ends with: *How weighty to me are your thoughts, O God! How vast is the sum of them! I try to count them—they are more than the sand; I come to the end—I am still with you* (Psalm 139:17-18).

There is no way we can begin to imagine how deeply and how thoroughly God knows us. We must acknowledge that we don't even know ourselves very well. So how indeed can God know us? We concur with the psalmist that God's thoughts are indeed weighty.

Prayer for the Day: *Birthing God, your ways are beyond my knowledge and imagination. Help me fall into your steadfast and everlasting love even when I do not understand it. Amen.*

Week 3
Thursday

Psalm 139

If the psalm would just end there, we could stop and feel wonderful and warm and cozy. But if we stop there, we begin to be comfortable with a faith that may be shallow and flat.

We move into hate and vengeance with verse 19: *O that you would kill the wicked, O God, and that the bloodthirsty would depart from me.* James L. Mays helps us know that vengeance in the Psalms is "not personal revenge. The term does not mean vindictive revenge; it refers to [God's] action [as ruler] to do justice and restore order where the regular and responsible institutions of justice have failed" (James L. Mays, *Psalms: Interpretation*, Westminster John Knox Press, 1994, p. 212).

Clinton McCain helps even further: "The psalms of vengeance are acts of nonviolence. By entrusting vengeance to God in prayer, [the writers of the psalms] refuse to take vengeance into their own hands. Thus the cycle is broken by these prayers" (J. Clinton McCain, Jr. "Old Songs for New Millennium: A Study of Psalms, Lesson 5," *The Presbyterian Outlook*, Dec. 6-13, 1999).

And so, the psalmist wishes aloud for God to kill the wicked. The psalmist claims hatred for people who hate God. God's enemies are the psalmist's enemies.

Prayer for the Day: *God, I really want to enact revenge. I do not want to hand over to you my feelings of hate and fear. Help me, O Redeemer and Comforter. Amen.*

Psalm 139

Week 3
Friday

We can delude ourselves that, of course, God's enemies are mine. And maybe the reverse is also true. My enemies are God's enemies.

When we deceive ourselves into our rightness as far as God is concerned, when we deceive ourselves into our sure knowledge of God's mind in any given situation, when we set ourselves up as judge for God, when we set ourselves up as prosecutor and executor for God, we have elevated ourselves to God's level and we have sinned greatly. God may know us, but we cannot… we cannot in any shape, form, or fashion…claim that we know God as well or as deeply as God knows us.

We can honestly give God our anger and our hatred. According to Old Testament scholar, Walter Brueggemann, "that may be the only way we can move to forgiveness. It may be that genuine forgiveness is possible only when there has been a genuine articulation of hatred" (Brueggemann, *Psalms*, p. 77). People who journal confess that some of their pages have serious sections of letting God have it. And who better to give our anger to than God, the God who has known us from the time we were being created in secret?

However, let's make sure that we are not blaming our anger or our hatred on other people simply because they do not agree with us. We may delude ourselves saying: "If they do not agree with me then they certainly must not agree with God and therefore God must strike them down. God must kill them, God must make them go away."

But that person, that one whom we have claimed as enemy also has verses 1-18 undergirding him or her. God knows. God has searched and known that other person, too. We are all part of the future that God is leading us to. When we believe we have insider knowledge from God and we call for vengeance because we are right (!!!), we may discover that the vengeance falls on *our* heads rather than on the other person's.

Prayer for the Day: *God of Justice, help me release my desires for revenge to you and then trust you for my own good. Amen.*

Week 3
Saturday

Psalm 139

This psalm closes with: *Search me, O God, and know my heart; test me and know my thoughts. See if there is any wicked way in me, and lead me in the way everlasting* (Psalm 139:23-24). It depends on how you read these words as to the meaning you may glean from them. One way to read them is in the tone of "If I'm lying, I'm dying…I'm okay, God. Just look at me and you can see. I'm your person, God. Just look for yourself. So, God, whenever I pronounce your word of judgment, then, God, hop to because I have spoken and you know me, God."

On the other hand, *Search me, O God, and know my heart; test me and know my thoughts. See if there is any wicked way in me, and lead me in the way everlasting* can be read as, "God, this is what I think, but please, I beg you, search me and show me the errors of my ways and the fallacies of my thinking. Where I am judgmental, show me and help me change as you want me to. Search me. Lead me to see and change where I harbor greed or injustice or vindictiveness or grudges. Show me where I work from prejudices and assumptions. Unsettle me where I am blind to the ways I hurt other people. See if there is any wicked way in me, and lead me in the way everlasting.

Prayer for the Day: *O God, search me and know me. Lead me in the way everlasting. Amen.*

Week 4
Matthew 4:1-11

1 Then Jesus was led up by the Spirit into the wilderness to be tempted by the devil. 2 He fasted for forty days and forty nights, and afterwards he was famished. 3 The tempter came and said to him, 'If you are the Son of God, command these stones to become loaves of bread.' 4 But he answered, 'It is written,

> "One does not live by bread alone, but by every word that comes from the mouth of God."'

5 Then the devil took him to the holy city and placed him on the pinnacle of the temple, 6 saying to him, 'If you are the Son of God, throw yourself down; for it is written,

> "He will command his angels concerning you," and on their hands they will bear you up, so that you will not dash your foot against a stone."'

7 Jesus said to him, 'Again it is written,

> 'Do not put the Lord your God to the test.'"

8 Again, the devil took him to a very high mountain and showed him all the kingdoms of the world and their splendour; 9 and he said to him, 'All these I will give you, if you will fall down and worship me.' 10 Jesus said to him, 'Away with you, Satan! for it is written,

> 'Worship the Lord your God, and serve only him.'"

11 Then the devil left him, and suddenly angels came and attended him.

Week 4
Sunday

Matthew 4:1-11

The context of this story is that Jesus has just been baptized. He is in the process of moving from his private life of the previous 30 years into his public ministry. His life is being redefined and he is wrestling with mighty and significant questions. The Spirit has led him into this discernment process and the devil seems to be God's agent.

Whether you believe in an incarnate devil with horns and a tail, we do know that demonic forces are alive and well. Sometimes we name the devil social media because it numbs us from our true calling as people who know and share God's love in the world. Sometimes the devil is called addiction. At other times, it is called greed or prejudice or judgmentalism. Sometimes the devil is named raw ambition or fear. Whatever we now call the devil, God allows us to wrestle with the tests that the devil puts in front of us. The Spirit is right there with us, having led us into this opportunity for growth.

This is at the beginning of Jesus's public ministry, and he was working out for himself what it means to be the Son of God, what it means to be the Chosen One. He fasted and wrestled with the questions posed by the devil. This was *not* a debate that lasted only a few sentences with closure assured by quoting scripture verses from Deuteronomy. This was a testing process that took 40 days of fasting and agony.

Jesus the man wrestled with the question about being the Son of God throughout his ministry. Later in the Gospel of Luke (9:18), Jesus asked his closest associates, "Who do *you* say that I am?" The challenges of being the Messiah—as God defined that task—seemed to be an ongoing process. Even at the end, Jesus wrestled with this calling when he asked that the cup be removed from him but once again, Jesus said, "Not my will, but thine."

As ordinary human beings, we find this testing of Jesus very reassuring. If the Son of God had these kinds of questions about what it meant to be the Messiah, then Jesus was truly human and not some superhero disguised as a mere mortal. When Jesus wrestles with how to define himself and his life work, we can relate. We likely have known a kind of wrestling, a time of redefinition, a period of discernment. This wrestling helps us encounter the holy God and become more of the person you, I, we were created to be.

Prayer for the Day: *God, lead me not into temptation but if it is necessary for my growth, be with me in the process. Amen.*

Matthew 4:1-11 Week 4
Monday

So...the devil says to Jesus, "*If* you are the Son of God..." We might hear this comment as "If you are a Christian...If you are a good person..." The devil taunts, "If you are who you say you are, who you intend to be, then..."

So, the first test issued was to turn stones into bread. This test may have been real for someone who was fasting but not very rational because one comes off the fast slowly, with small liquid meals, and certainly not a loaf of bread. But to push this test further, the question could be, "Are you relevant?" "Do you produce something the world values?" "Are you addressing the needs of your community?"

When Jesus is struggling with what it means to be the Son of God, then what better way is there to prove that than by bringing about a world where the widows and orphans were cared for? Making bread was certainly a tangible sign that he could take care of God's people. After all, the Hebrews who wandered in the desert for 40 years were fed manna by God. Surely the Son of God would be able to do the same thing.

When you are struggling with what it means to be a child of God, what kinds of testing do you endure to prove that you are relevant? Do you preach on the street corner? Do you give money and yourself to missions (as important as that is) to *prove* that you are a Christian? Do you know the words of the faith... but not the worth of the faith in your life? Do you prove you are saved by knowing up and down your doctrines and scriptures? Do you try to make your ecclesiastical pronouncements bread for your soul?

Prayer for the Day: *Creator, Redeemer, Sustainer, I want to be relevant. Help me be so in your way, not mine. Amen.*

Week 4
Tuesday

Matthew 4:1-11

Jesus told the devil that we do not live by bread alone but by the word of God. We do not live by being able to quote scripture by chapter and verse, even though that is a handy skill to have. We live by being infused with the word of God. As Jeremiah says, *I will put my law within them, and I will write it on their hearts; and I will be their God, and they shall be my people* (31:33). When we know the word of God as well as we know the stories of our own family, then we begin to understand how Jesus was wrestling. How does one prove that one is the Son of God? By living the word. By putting flesh on the love and grace and discipline of God. Not by special tricks to prove one's relevance.

If we *could* turn stones into bread, what have we proven? Only that we can turn rocks into bread. We have not proven that we have worth as a child of God. What rocks are challenging you?

Jesus wrestled mightily with this. What does it mean for him to be the Son of God? How does he live as the Son of God? It would be easier to turn stones into bread than take the road Jesus took to show us how to live. Jesus determined through his wrestling that he would not be the Messiah as defined by cultural expectations…to provide a land of plenty just for the asking. God was guiding him in truer, more authentic directions.

Prayer for the Day: *Son of God, help me live your word. Nurture me to embody your love and grace and discipline.*

Matthew 4:1-11

Week 4
Wednesday

The devil did not stop with the testing. Once again… "*IF* you are the Son of God…." The devil raised the odds. He took Jesus to the top of the Temple in Jerusalem. And the crafty devil used Jesus's own methods for this test. He quoted scriptures to Jesus: "It is written: *He will command his angels concerning you,*" (Psalm 91:11) and "*On their hands they will bear you up, so that you will not dash your foot against a stone*" (Psalm 91:12).

How tempting that might have been to Jesus. He was the Chosen One who had grown up within the Jewish understanding of the Messiah who would bring peace and prosperity. Many in his time thought that the Messiah would clear the land of all the foreign occupiers. How cool would it have been to descend upon Jerusalem on a cloud? What better way to announce the kingdom of God? What an opportunity to be spectacular?

Is this a temptation that you struggle with? To be spectacular? Do you want your children to believe that you are the best mommy or daddy in the world? Are you the best daughter or son-in-law? Preachers struggle with the desire to be one of the top ten preachers in the country. Are you spectacular? Are you the most sought-after lawyer, health care provider, artist, or pet groomer? Do you make the best cup of coffee ever?

Jesus says, "No, this is not the kind of Chosen One that I will be. I will not be spectacular. I will not jump because that is not who I am in the Spirit with God as my father" Jesus, too, quotes scripture (Deuteronomy 6:16) saying: "*Again it is written, 'Do not put the Lord your God to the test.'*"

Prayer for the Day: *Loving God, I confess that I routinely test you. Forgive me and build up my trust in you. Amen.*

Week 4
Thursday

Matthew 4:1-11

Some of the spectators at the crucifixion also challenged Jesus, saying, *If you are the Son of God, come down from the cross* (Matthew 27:40). The religious officials retorted, *He saved others; he cannot save himself. He is the King of Israel; let him come down from the cross now, and we will believe in him* (Matthew 27:42). This is a direct challenge to put God to the test. The officials defined how *they* wanted God to be revealed. God obviously had other ideas about demonstrating God's sovereignty, love, and power.

And, when we're honest, don't we really keep testing God? Please, God, please give me a parking space. Please God, show your love by healing my loved one. Please God, please God prove to me that you are indeed God. Intervene for me and then I will believe!

Some people pray for signs. And sometimes, they receive them. But Jesus is saying that signs alone will not prove anything real and substantial about God just like jumping off the pinnacle of the Temple will not prove that Jesus is the Chosen One. Jesus wrestled with the test to prove what he knew in his deepest self he was.

Jesus knew that quarrying the scriptures for a verse to support someone's opinion or way of thinking was not what God was about. Jesus quoted Deuteronomy saying, "Do not put the Lord your God to the test." Jesus could have been spectacular, and he could have requested that God help him show he was the Messiah by jumping from the top of the Temple and landing with the smoothest landing anyone had ever seen. What a soul wrenching challenge to deny the call to be spectacular!

Prayer for the Day: *God of Wonder, do you get very angry when I want to be spectacular in the way the world defines that rather than how you do? Amen.*

Matthew 4:1-11

Week 4
Friday

The devil was very persistent. The reward offered to Jesus in the next test was not the devil's to give…all the kingdoms of the world. All Jesus had to do was to worship the devil. If Jesus was truly the Savior of the World, then the devil's offer sounds reasonable. How easy it would be to accomplish the task of being Lord of the world. All one had to do was worship anything other than God.

This challenge is very difficult for us. We worship so many other gods. We worship family, careers, material items, political parties, our country, and our technology. We expect to reap security and affirmation and power and glory through these gods that we follow. What's the problem? We understand this test that Jesus was facing.

And Jesus was truly tested because he allowed the devil to dialogue with him and to lead him to a very high mountain. Jesus did not avoid the temptation but faced it head on. Maybe that's the only way he could be clear about being the Chosen One. If he avoided a test, a temptation, he might wonder when it would come again. For this time in the wilderness… to which the Spirit led him…, Jesus did not hide from the tests. He went along with the devil to the top of the Temple and to the top of the mountain. He engaged with the challenges and emerged stronger and clearer about his public ministry. He said, "Away with you Satan! For it is written, 'Worship the Lord your God, and serve only him.'"

Prayer for the Day: *Sovereign God, help me name all the idols in my life that I worship and put them away to worship only you. Amen.*

Week 4
Saturday

Matthew 4:1-11

We may discover that we have fallen into the trap of worshiping other gods. We are to worship the Lord our God and serve only him.

We can think about the tests we face as followers of *this* Messiah who did not allow the world to define what his Messiahship would look like. Just as the Spirit was with Jesus during this time of testing, so the Spirit is with us as we enter our own wildernesses when we try to discern what faith means to us and how we want to live in, through, and with that faith.

Jesus faced his testing and did not turn stones to bread or jump off the Temple so that he could prove he was the Messiah. Jesus did not worship the devil so that all the kingdoms of the world and their splendor would be his. He did not succumb to the definitions of Messiahship that were being placed before him in the wilderness.

And yet…and yet… Jesus did the feed the multitudes. He did say he was the bread of life. The kingdoms of the world are his through his life, death, and resurrection. He showed repeatedly over and over that he was the Son of God by healing, teaching, and forgiving. The world worships him. Everything he wrestled with at the beginning of his ministry became his in due course but in the way and time that the Holy Lord determined.

Jesus taught us to pray, "Lead us not into temptation" because he knew personally what a struggle and challenge some of those tests can mean for us. We can abide in the deep knowledge that the Spirit is with us in those times. We can listen for God's word rather than be seduced by the world's definitions. We can hold tight to our Lord who walked difficult paths and is with us now and forevermore.

Prayer for the Day: *God of discovery, help me discern the traps I fall into when I allow someone or something to become the focus of my worship. Amen.*

Week 5
John 3:1-17

1 Now there was a Pharisee named Nicodemus, a leader of the Jews. 2 He came to Jesus by night and said to him, "Rabbi, we know that you are a teacher who has come from God; for no one can do these signs that you do apart from the presence of God.' 3 Jesus answered him, 'Very truly, I tell you, no one can see the kingdom of God without being born from above.' 4 Nicodemus said to him, 'How can anyone be born after having grown old? Can one enter a second time into the mother's womb and be born?' 5 Jesus answered, 'Very truly, I tell you, no one can enter the kingdom of God without being born of water and Spirit. 6 What is born of the flesh is flesh, and what is born of the Spirit is spirit. 7 Do not be astonished that I said to you, "You must be born from above." 8 The wind blows where it chooses, and you hear the sound of it, but you do not know where it comes from or where it goes. So it is with everyone who is born of the Spirit.' 9 Nicodemus said to him, 'How can these things be?' 10 Jesus answered him, 'Are you a teacher of Israel, and yet you do not understand these things?

11 'Very truly, I tell you, we speak of what we know and testify to what we have seen; yet you do not receive our testimony. 12 If I have told you about earthly things and you do not believe, how can you believe if I tell you about heavenly things? 13 No one has ascended into heaven except the one who descended from heaven, the Son of Man. 14 And just as Moses lifted up the serpent in the wilderness, so must the Son of Man be lifted up, 15 that whoever believes in him may have eternal life.

16 'For God so loved the world that he gave his only Son, so that everyone who believes in him may not perish but may have eternal life.

17 'Indeed, God did not send the Son into the world to condemn the world, but in order that the world might be saved through him.

Week 5   **John 3:1-17**
Sunday

This passage begins with Nicodemus coming to visit Jesus in the night. You visit friends, relatives, and neighbors in the night. What's the big deal? The big deal is that Nicodemus is talked about in the Gospel of John, the gospel that focuses on dark and light. The gospel that begins with *All things came into being through him.... What has come into being in him was life, and the life was the light of all people. The light shines in the darkness, and the darkness did not overcome it* (John 1:3-5). Nicodemus is in the dark, not fully committed to the Way of Jesus. He's not fully ready to declare his faith or even to have it change his life. He comes in the dark.

Nicodemus is a Pharisee and a Jewish leader. He shows up again in John's gospel (John 7:50) when he half-way defended Jesus to the chief priests and pharisees by saying, *Our law does not judge people without first giving them a hearing to find out what they are doing, does it?* He was quickly told that no prophet comes from Galilee. Later Nicodemus reappears when he and Joseph of Arimathea prepare the body of Jesus for burial (19:38-42). In all of Nicodemus' appearances, he seems at best to be in the shadows if not fully in the dark. He seems to be a "kind-of" follower of Jesus.

Nicodemus says to Jesus, *Rabbi, we know you are a teacher who has come from God; for no one can do these signs that you do apart from the presence of God* (John 3:2).

Prayer for the Day: *God of light, help me live in your light rather than my darkness. Help me be more than a "kind-of" follower of you. Amen.*

John 3:1-17

**Week 5
Monday**

Nicodemus seems to truly want to know Jesus, but cannot let go of his preconceived notions of how the world works when he says, "*How can these things be?* (John 3:9). After Jesus talks about the necessity of being born from above, Nicodemus retorts, *How can anyone be born after having grown old? Can one enter a second time into the mother's womb and be born?* (John 3:4). Such a caricature of what Jesus was actually conveying.

And yet, in our culture, being born again has been greatly distorted and removed from its rich meaning. People may ask, "Are you born again?" meaning "Are you the kind of Christian I am?" It seems that if you've not been born again, often meaning you cannot state the date and time you accepted Jesus as your Lord and Savior, when you made a private deal between God and you, then you're not a real Christian.

This misunderstanding of being born again, as prevalent as it is, cheapens the profound meaning of the biblical witness. The current questions of "Are you born again?" imply that the individual *decided* to join the Jesus movement. The implication is that you or I are in control of this relationship with the triune God…because we made a decision. But think about it. Did we decide to be born the first time, being pushed into the world by our mother? No. So when we are born again, is it our choice? No. God pushes us out into the world. God's spirit brings us to begin life anew. Being born again is a powerful way of talking about *transformation* that is at the center of the Christian life.

Prayer for the Day: *God of new birth, is it true? You really choose me? It's not a transaction? You love me that much? WOW! Amen.*

Week 5
Tuesday

John 3:1-17

Paul alludes to this birth imagery when he says, "In God we live and move and have our being." What is the only way we live and move and have our being in another being? When we're in the womb. Isn't that a powerful way of thinking about our lives in God. To be totally nourished, protected, cared for by a loving God. The same God that allows us transformation. H.A. Williams says that being born again is a "radical transformation of our lives, a new beginning which is like being born again." (*Tensions* by H.A. Williams) New, with limitless possibilities.

And being born again is not simply a once in a lifetime event. Being born from above happens every morning. We come from the darkness, knowing that who we were yesterday does not have to be the person we are today. We enter the light of day with the possibility of transformation awaiting us.

Sometimes you are aware of God doing mighty things in your life. Sometimes God does not seem to be at work at all in you. Maybe you are just living and moving while waiting on a major symbolic birthing event. Or maybe the transformation is subtle, but you look back and know that God has been active in your life.

Prayer for the Day: *Birthing God, you have brought me to life in you and you continue to nurture me all my days. Help this reality move deep inside me. Amen.*

John 3:1-17

Week 5
Wednesday

Here's the verse that you may have memorized as a child and, of course, in the King James Version. *For God so loved the world, that he gave his only begotten Son that whosoever believeth in him shall not perish but have everlasting life* (John 3:16).

"For God so loved the world." What do you understand "the world" to refer to? Is *world* a positive or a negative term? Is it the creation of Genesis 1? Is it the *world* as defined by culture, economics, wars, politics, human beings? Is *world* everyone we love? Or is *world* everyone we love to hate? Is the *world* just you and me, or is it everyone and everything created by God?

In scripture, we find a God who loved the world and the people in it. This God provided laws to help people know how to live with each other and pay homage to this awesome deity. This God sent prophets to help wake people up to their foolish and destructive ways. This God loves the world as it is in all its messiness and yearns for us to be partners in this love and care for all creation, for everyone, including those who are not like us. "God so loved the world."

Prayer for the Day: *God, do you really love the entire world? Everyone? Even those I cannot stand? I'm going to have to meditate on this one. Amen.*

Week 5
Thursday

John 3:1-17

That he gave his only Son often is used as the idea of giving Jesus to the cross. But that limits the gift. God's gift of his only Son happened in a stable in Bethlehem and every day of Jesus's ministry, including the cross. God loves the world so much that God was willing to become one of us. God showed us through Jesus that he really gets us. God knows our fatigue, our frustration, our desire, our hunger, our laughter, our tears, all those things that make us human. God loves us so much that God in Jesus chose to join in.

To help us grasp the enormity of this gift, imagine that you really are fascinated with and love fish, not to eat but to watch and relate to. You sit at the edge of the lake and talk and talk to the fish. You run to the water's edge first thing in the morning and again at dusk just before darkness descends. You are passionate about these fish. You get angry and frustrated when people pollute the lake. You love these fish so much, you become a fish. You give up your air breathing lungs and your feet. You give up hair, home, and hamburgers. You become a fish. This is how much you love fishes.

God loves us so much that he gave his Son. God became one of us.

Prayer for the Day: *Gift-giving God, I forget to say thank you enough. So, for now, THANK YOU! Amen.*

John 3:1-17

Week 5
Friday

"*So that everyone who believes in him...*"

Have you had someone knock on your door and ask if you're born again or if you've been saved? Did they also inform you if you simply affirm several statements, that's all there is to it? They ask you to believe with your mind. But being born again, being a follower of Christ's way is not a mental consent to certain propositions. Believing is about loving God. The old English meaning of believing was more like belove-ing. It's not about affirming certain doctrines and creeds, as important as those are to people of faith. When you believe in God, you belove God. You give your heart to God. You enter into at a new way of being because God gives you a new way of living in this world. God beloves you. God beloves me. And you and I belove God. Beloving Jesus means giving our heart, loyalty, fidelity, and commitment to Jesus. This is a new way of life.

"*May not perish but have everlasting life...*"

In John's gospel, eternal life is often present life...not necessarily a blessed afterlife. John 17:3 states: "*And this is eternal life, that they may know you, the only true God, and Jesus Christ whom I have sent.*" The verbs are present tense. And think about it, if we belove God with our heart, soul, mind, and strength, then don't we experience life beyond what we could imagine? Yes, we still experience grief, loss, doubt, pain and...we experience strength, tranquility, and gentleness as well. We experience life in its fullness, abounding life with all its darkness...and light, death...and life.

"Living life in the age to come" is of course living in a future blessedness where God will wipe every tear, death will be no more, mourning and crying and pain will be no more (Rev. 21:4). But living in a life to come also means living in this life as if God were already ruler. As if God's desire for justice and caring for one another and loving our neighbor and seeing God in every single person on the face of this globe were fact rather than mere glimpses of truth and grace. And we do that when we belove God, when we give our heart to God, when we experience new birth of transformation, of beginning over and over and over again.

Prayer for the Day: *Beloved, I want to belove you. I want to belove others. Because you created all of us, I want to embrace all of us but that's very hard to do. You know how "they" are. Oh my God...that's what you're talking about, isn't it. Wanting for EVERYONE justice and caring. Amen.*

Week 5
Saturday

John 3:1-17

Marcus Borg says, "[I]n John, this verse [3:16)] is not about believing a set of statements about Jesus now for the sake of heaven later. It is about beloving Jesus and beloving God as known in Jesus, in the incarnation, and entering into the 'life of the age to come' now. It is not about people going to hell because they don't believe. It is about the path into life with God now" (Marcus Borg, *Speaking Christian*, p. 161).

If this understanding does not resonate with your own deeply held beliefs, that's okay. If the way you understand today's passage comforts you, calls you into a life of discipleship, opens your heart to deep abiding love, that's wonderful. Blessed are you.

We are pulled to embrace God's will. We are nudged to obey God's call. We are embraced to receive God's power. We are strengthened to reflect God's peace. We are to give our heart to, belove, a God who wants us to be born again, to be transformed into a new life of love and care for God's entire world. God loves this world so much that God became one of us so we could finally get what being in relationship with God looks like and feels like and sounds like. And that kind of life is LIVING in capital letters. Living in the light. Living as a new person created by and in God.

Prayer for the Day: *Nudging God, help me get what living in relationship with you looks and feels like. I want that for my life. Amen.*

Week 6
Psalm 23

1 The Lord is my shepherd, I shall not want.
2 He makes me lie down in green pastures; he leads me beside still waters;
3 he restores my soul. He leads me in right paths for his name's sake.
4 Even though I walk through the darkest valley, I fear no evil; for you are with me; your rod and your staff—they comfort me.
5 You prepare a table before me in the presence of my enemies; you anoint my head with oil; my cup overflows.
6 Surely goodness and mercy shall follow me all the days of my life, and I shall dwell in the house of the Lord my whole life long.

Week 6
Sunday

Psalm 23

Imagine that you've joined a casual work acquaintance at your favorite gathering spot. Seemingly out of the blue, your friend says, "At work, some of the folks were talking about a special event that was happening at one of their churches. They seemed excited about the event and their church. I never really heard any of them talk about God but since they are involved in their church, I assume they believe in God. I hear stuff on television about God but somehow much of that does not resonate with me. I know you are active in your church. Do you actually believe in God? If you do, why?"

Internally your chin drops to the floor, but you manage to keep an interested look on your face. Your mind is running in circles wondering what to say. The first words out of your mouth are: "Yes, I am a church member and yes, I believe in God."

Your conversation partner says, "Yeah, but why?"

You reply, "That's a harder question. I cannot give you an outline of rational reasons of why I believe in God. It seems that God just is part of my life. I did not intentionally say one day, "I believe in you, God." I just knew that God is with me. God sought me out rather than I sought God. I trust God. I know that may sound like woo-woo but God is with me and loves me and guides me. It's simply a fact of my life. I try to live more and more into that reality of God's grace and love and mercy and guidance. Some days I actually manage to do that!"

Prayer for the Day: *Magnificent God, thank you for being in my life. Help me share that reality with others when the occasion may arise. Amen.*

Psalm 23

**Week 6
Monday**

Our conversation continued about my belief in God.

"Okay. Can you tell me more?"

At that point, you remember that when you were at a funeral recently, you picked up a pocket-size card with the 23rd Psalm printed on it. You pull it out of your backpack and briefly look it over. Then you say, "This psalm, the twenty-third psalm, is from the hymnbook and poetry book of the Bible. It describes the God I know.

"See here, where it says that God is my shepherd? Well, that must mean that I'm kind of like a sheep. I don't know a whole lot about sheep, but I know that they are not considered to be especially smart, and they get lost. I guess that kind of describes me, too. But God is my shepherd. Shepherds really took care of their sheep. They looked and looked for sheep that wandered away. I like that, knowing that God will find me even when I wander away from the best ways for me to live a full and fulfilling life. Then the psalm describes that the shepherd provides abundant food (green grass) and still waters that are places for me to hydrate safely. So, God provides abundantly for my basic physical needs: food and water and rest. That's what good shepherds do for sheep like me."

"Okay, I think I get that."

Prayer for the Day: *Good shepherd, I know that I get lost sometimes. I am comforted that you will find me and bring me back to the rest of the flock. Amen.*

Week 6
Tuesday

Psalm 23

I continued with: "And then it says, *"God restores my soul."* I understand this to say that God repaired and continues to repair my whole being, everything I am, the totality of me so I can be whole. I know that this is an ongoing project for God because you know me. Look at me. But I am comforted that all this repair can happen because God is doing it. I don't have to fix myself all by myself."

"The words on this card say, *"Even though I walk through the valley of the shadow of death. I fear no evil."* What I get from this is that God is with me even when life is the pits. You remember when a couple of months ago I walked around hardly ever smiling? I never spent time with you or any of my other friends. I didn't even respond much to texts or Snapchat. I felt like I was in total darkness, in a place of a death shadow. It doesn't matter now why I felt that way. I just felt totally alone. When I finally began to emerge from that dark and scary place, I realized that God had been there with me. Even being able to get out of bed happened because God helped me…even though I didn't know it at the time. One day, you passed me in the hall. You were wearing your covid mask, but I could see your eyes smile at me. That was a gift from God, and you did not even know you did it. The checkout person at the grocery store actually chatted with me and I felt like I was not invisible. God was with me during my journey through the shadow of death. The evil and things I feared did not overtake me. God was with me through you and other people who reached out to me in ways unknown to you and them."

Prayer for the Day: *Guiding God, thank you for helping me grow beyond those dark places of life, even though I'd like for you to act more quickly sometime!!! Amen.*

Psalm 23

Week 6
Wednesday

I kept sharing: "The psalm talks about God's rod and staff comforting me. These are tools of the shepherd's trade, and God knows how to use them to protect me. I am not always aware of God's protection. After all, I'm a sheep but God knows what is needed and when that is needed.

"Then the psalm says that God feeds me even though enemies are nearby. Part of me pictures this as my sitting in a large banquet hall that looks like the Hogwarts' school dining room with a table laden with lots of food. On the perimeter of the room are ghastly faces staring at me. But the more I've thought about this, the more I see it this way: God is a gracious host who once again provides abundantly for me. And even when people, events, possibilities that I fear seem very close, God can step in and provide for me and protect me. I find comfort in God's protection even though I know that people still have guns and knives and anger that can do me in. Nevertheless, it is God's intent to protect me and love me.

"And God's generosity continues even with pouring oil on my head and filling my cup to the brim. Now I know that we do not often anoint people unless you count dumping a cooler of Gatorade on the head of the coach as anointing. When I read about anointing, I think of when I go to my massage therapist and she uses essential oils as she massages my temples and my neck. If God's anointing is even half as good as what she does, then WOW!"

Prayer for the Day: *Protecting God, thank you for the many many ways you show your love to me. Amen.*

Week 6   **Psalm 23**
Thursday

The psalm continues with *"Surely goodness and mercy shall follow me all the days of my life."* Somewhere I learned that this line can actually mean, "**Only** goodness and mercy will pursue me as I walk the totally right ways that God is leading me to." I like the thought of being pursued by goodness and mercy. God must really want me to be abundantly cared for! And God will help me walk in God's ways, in right ways, in ways that take account of other people and all of life and not just me.

"And then it closes with living in God's house for my entire life. I don't think this is so much a literal house even though I know that people who struggle to hold onto their homes or who are even homeless would like to live in God's literal house. I think this is a house where everyone has basic life needs met abundantly. Where true justice abounds. Where love is an active verb which means choosing to love even when that is not easy. You know—*that* kind of place.

"So, this describes who I think God is. But that's just part of it. I figure that if God is this way toward me then I have some responsibility to honor that."

Prayer for the Day: *God, you created me, you are with me in my troubles, and you comfort me no matter what is happening. May I be this for someone else as a way to honor you. Amen.*

Psalm 23

Week 6
Friday

"Shall I continue?"

"Sure. I've been listening this long. What's another few minutes? Anyway, I've never had anyone explain this to me like you do."

"Okay. I figure that God loves me like a shepherd loves the sheep and provides abundantly for all this sheep's needs. Well, sometimes I don't think my needs are getting met. But then I look around and realize that there are lots of people who have greater needs than I do…needs that are not getting met. People are hungry. They are homeless. They are mistreated. They are hated just for being alive. I wonder why God is not leading them beside still waters? Where are their green pastures? And then one day it dawned on me. That may be how God wants me and all these other sheep to live. *We* are to become the good shepherds for other sheep. We are not to just sit back and become fat sheep. We are to provide green grass (you know, the real kind of grass, not the kind you smoke) for people who do not have stable sources of food. We don't necessarily have to provide them the food. We can create situations and opportunities where they can count on having food all the time for themselves and their families. We are to provide places where people's souls, their entire beings can thrive and blossom."

Prayer for the Day: *God of abundance, enliven my heart to the ways I can care for others, so I can be the kind of shepherd to them that you are to me. Amen.*

Week 6
Saturday

Psalm 23

"We are to protect others from their enemies. You know … the enemies who call them awful names just because of their skin color or their language accents. The enemies who proclaim them lazy and then do not provide employment for them along with transportation to get to work and safe childcare for their children while the parent labors. Those kinds of enemies."

"Hmmm. I've never thought of enemies in that way. I always think of murderers and thieves. I don't consider people who use their power and status in ways that harm others as enemies."

"Well, that could be enemies."

"I've begun to think that the *way* God leads people to green grass is through us. We become God's hands and feet. We are the rod and staff. We anoint with love and care about other people. God works through us. God does not wave a magic wand.

"I know that I experience God deep inside myself. I guess that's my soul. I know that God acts to let me know I'm loved and cared for but even that happens through other people. I figure that's just God working through them for me."

"And while we're talking, I sometimes think of this psalm as being a guiding document for Jesus. Do you know about Jesus? He is God, too. I cannot explain about him being God and being human, so we won't even go there today. Anyway, Jesus said he was the Good Shepherd. Jesus fed people. He provided for people. He talked about having life in God's house. I remember seeing a picture of Jesus when I was a child. He was holding a lamb. That was being a good shepherd, wasn't it? And Jesus told us to love our neighbors as ourselves as well as love God with our entire heart, soul, mind, and strength. That's kind of what I think we learn from this psalm…to care for others just as God, just as Jesus cares for us.

"This kind of thinking sometimes blows my mind! Is this what you wanted to hear?"

"Well, you certainly gave me a lot to think about. I think I was originally asking for a simple yes or no but I'm so glad that you went into all this for me."

Prayer for the Day: *Jesus, Good Shepherd, help me be a caring shepherd in my life, my family, my church, my community, and my world. Amen.*

Week 7
Mark 12:28-34

28 One of the scribes came near and heard them disputing with one another, and seeing that he answered them well, he asked him, "Which commandment is the first of all?"

29 Jesus answered, "The first is, 'Hear, O Israel: the Lord our God, the Lord is one; 30 you shall love the Lord your God with all your heart, and with all your soul, and with all your mind, and with all your strength.' 31 The second is this, 'You shall love your neighbour as yourself.' There is no other commandment greater than these.'"

32 Then the scribe said to him, "You are right, Teacher; you have truly said that 'he is one, and besides him there is no other'; 33 and 'to love him with all the heart, and with all the understanding, and with all the strength', and 'to love one's neighbour as oneself'—this is much more important than all whole burnt-offerings and sacrifices."

34 When Jesus saw that he answered wisely, he said to him, "You are not far from the kingdom of God." After that no one dared to ask him any question.

Week 7
Sunday

Mark 12:28–34

Those who have been followers of Jesus's way for a long time may find these commandments quoted by Jesus very familiar...maybe *too* familiar. If you have been instructed in the church, you *know* you are to love God with all your heart, soul, and mind and your neighbor as yourself. You have heard this all your life. Suppose, though, just suppose that you had never heard this teaching. Is it possible for you to try to hear it as something brand new or something you have never heard before? As you hear these words as if for the first time: *"You shall love the Lord your God with all your heart, and with all your soul, and with all your mind."* Now you are being pulled into something... maybe even a very complete way of living. You are being pulled into the wonder of God's Word.

You are to love God with your heart. Biblical love is not based on feeling, on the sentiments of Valentine cards, or the flutter of the heart when in the presence of someone. In the Hebrew way of thinking, the heart is the center of will. To love with your *heart* is to *choose* to love, to address the need of being connected with God who is greater than you can dream and who is as close as your own breath. You choose to love God in order to act on our passion for God's guidance, grace, truth, and wisdom. You choose to love.

Now choosing is not something you do once, and it is done forever. You sometimes must choose daily or every hour because there will be plenty of opportunities for you to choose to place your allegiance elsewhere. Other challenges for worship and adoration will come to you regularly. Television commercials entice you to adore bathroom cleaners or cars or injury lawyers. You are bombarded with requests for your allegiances and priorities. Choosing to love God is a daily responsibility and joy.

Prayer for the Day: *Beloved God, help me to choose to love you and your world. Amen.*

Mark 12:28–34   **Week 7 / Monday**

Biblical love is commitment to another, no matter how good or bad, no matter how endearing or obnoxious. Biblical love is action, not feeling, a way of choosing rather than a way of reacting. When you love God, you love because you *choose* to love, not because you are feeling close or warm or fuzzy. *Certainly*, there are times when you feel positively overwhelmed by your good and gracious God. There are other times, though, when your *decision* to follow Christ's way is the only sense you have of being connected to the Source of your life. You discover that at times you must remind yourself that you have committed your life to being faithful and loving—because you certainly don't feel that way!

Love is a need of life itself. Love is that sense of connectedness when the "is-ness" of one person recognizes the "is-ness" of another person. In the holy sense, then, love of God addresses your need for an intimate relationship with the creator of the vastness beyond ourselves, to connect you with the One who cares for you more deeply and more completely than any human you know, and to fulfill your deep search for meaning and completeness beyond your wildest imagination. Love of God is committing to the One who yearns to be engaged with you and then committing to love others and thereby experiencing all the joy and wonder…and confusion… that communion entails.

Prayer for the Day: *God of love, help me commit to love others and thereby experience all the joy and wonder…and confusion… that communion entails. Amen.*

Week 7   **Mark 12:28–34**
Tuesday

You commit with your *heart*...and you commit with your *soul*. What in the world does this mean? Theologians throughout the centuries have discussed and argued about what the soul is, when it is created, and where it is located. For today, you can think of soul as your life force, your energy, or your spirit. The soul is where your enthusiasm resides, where your hope lives, and where your joy bubbles. You can love God with your laughter, your tears, your visions, and your frustrations. You can love God with your anger, your commitments, your courage, and your fears. You can love God with your soul.

Prayer for the Day: *God my creator, I want to love you with my soul. Help me figure that out and embrace it. Amen.*

Mark 12:28–34

Week 7
Wednesday

You commit to God with your *mind*. You actually think about holy things. You question. You challenge. You study. You read. You discuss. You dialogue. You doubt. You do not pronounce that you know all, that you have the final, last word, or that you have inner knowledge which gives you the power to rule the world, your community, your church, or your family. You love God with your mind, always seeking to learn more about what it means to be a faithful person, what it means to be a disciple of Jesus, or what it means to follow in Jesus's footsteps. In loving God with your mind, you acknowledge that you may have a bit of the truth; someone else might have another bit; and someone else has yet another bit. Together you all will get closer to the truth, but you will never arrive at the whole truth about your loving God.

Job thought he knew the right and wrong ways of the world until God responded with *Do you give the horse its might? Do you clothe its neck with mane?* (Job 39:19). After being given many other examples of how God's knowledge and ways are vaster than you can ever conceive, Job answered, *I know that you can do all things, and that no purpose of yours can be thwarted...I have uttered what I did not understand, things too wonderful for me, which I did not know* (Job 42:2–3). Therefore, you journey with God through committing your mind to this Holy One.

Prayer for the Day: *Holy One, thank you that I do not have to shut down my mind as I grow in my relationship with you. Help me to use it with wisdom and vigor. Amen.*

Week 7
Thursday

Mark 12:28–34

When you love God with your heart, mind, and soul, you commit with your whole being.

Someone who is just exploring faith and hearing all this for the first time might say, "That all sounds very good, but how can I love God when I cannot see God?" That's actually a very good question.

In Jesus's life and ministry, he demonstrated how you can show your love for God. The most famous passage for how that happens is Matthew 25:31–46 when Jesus says (verses 35–36, 40) that when you feed hungry people, you feed *him*. When you clothe naked people, you clothe *him*. When you give a thirsty person something to drink, you quench *Christ's* thirst.

Prayer for the Day: *Jesus, thank you for showing me how to love. Help me practice with your guidance. Amen.*

Mark 12:28–34

Week 7 Friday

You demonstrate to yourself and to the world that you truly love God with your heart, soul, and mind by loving your neighbors. You love the people who need your love. You love people who hurt in all manner of ways—emotionally, physically, spiritually, or economically. This is not always simple, is it? You can easily love those people who are most like you, who think like you do, who value what you value, or who are enjoyable to be with. You find it harder to love people who make you angry, threaten you, or degrade what you find most important. You *really* find it hard to love people who are lazy, make your life difficult, stink, or make you feel small.

Many churches have signs out front that say, "All are welcome." When a church displays this greeting, the members want to be hospitable. They really believe that anyone can come into their fellowship and experience the warmth and support they each receive there for themselves. Their sense of welcome is sincerely grounded in their belief in Christ's invitation to come to him.

However, if Clarence, a man who had not bathed in days and who was babbling nonsense entered, would members truly welcome him? Love is action, not feeling. Would *you* be able to welcome Clarence? Would you be able to invite him to sit with you? Would you offer him your hand when he looks so nasty? When you decide to love him, will you reach out to him no matter what? Might you take him to a shower facility after the service? Loving him means being willing to be his friend or advocate. Loving him means patting his shoulder or holding his hand … if that will comfort him. Loving him means choosing to love … not feeling warm, loving feelings.

Prayer for the Day: *Most gracious God, help me be bold when opportunities to share love come my way. Amen.*

Week 7
Saturday

Mark 12:28–34

There is a great deal in the Bible about loving our neighbor. The Samaritan traveler helped the victim of robbery alongside the road even though he could just as easily have ignored that person. Jesus reached out repeatedly to people who were blind, to women with long-term illnesses, to those who needed a good meal, and to lepers who were despised by society. Jesus showed over and over how to love your neighbor. You too have neighbors who are despised because of illness (mental or physical), sexual orientation, color of skin, quality of speech, accent, or general attitude. You know *what* you as a faithful person are called to do. Sometimes you just have trouble doing it. Sometimes you do not *will* to actively care about the welfare of others.

But Jesus taught that in caring for others, you care for him. He even gave you a measuring rod for how to think about loving your neighbors. He said to love them as you love yourself. This was not original with Jesus. He was quoting Leviticus 19:18, which says, *You shall not take vengeance or bear a grudge against any of your people, but you shall love your neighbor as yourself: I am the* LORD.

Jesus reminded his followers that loving neighbors means that you take their needs as seriously as you do your own. If you believe that you should be listened to, then you listen to others. If you believe that you deserve respect, then you respect others—as hard as that might be. If you value decent, affordable homes for your family, can you value decent, affordable homes for other people as well and then work to make them a reality? This loving your neighbor as yourself gets played out in many different ways. You can meditate on the areas in your life in which you are not loving yourself and certainly not loving your neighbors as yourself.

You love God when you love your neighbor. You love your neighbor when you love yourself. You love yourself when you love God. As you love totally with your focus on God, neighbors, and yourself, you will experience the fullness of being a follower of your Lord, Jesus Christ. You can revel in that joy while you grow more and more into the wonderful person that God is creating you to be. May God be with you as you live into that kind of total love.

Prayer for the Day: *Tender, passionate God, help me love totally… you, myself, and others. Amen.*

Week 8
Luke 12:13-21

13 Someone in the crowd said to him, "Teacher, tell my brother to divide the family inheritance with me."

14 But he said to him, "Friend, who set me to be a judge or arbitrator over you?"

15 And he said to them, "Take care! Be on your guard against all kinds of greed; for one's life does not consist in the abundance of possessions."

16 Then he told them a parable: "The land of a rich man produced abundantly. 17 And he thought to himself, 'What should I do, for I have no place to store my crops?' 18 Then he said, 'I will do this: I will pull down my barns and build larger ones, and there I will store all my grain and my goods. 19 And I will say to my soul, Soul, you have ample goods laid up for many years; relax, eat, drink, be merry.' 20 But God said to him, 'You fool! This very night your life is being demanded of you. And the things you have prepared, whose will they be?'

21 So it is with those who store up treasures for themselves but are not rich towards God."

Week 8
Sunday

Luke 12:13-21

Have you cleaned out things in garages, sheds, and basements and then someone entered the home and remarked, "I thought you said you'd been cleaning out"? Do you lament that you accumulate so much stuff that you actually need storage units and closet organizers?

In this week's passage, a brother asks Jesus to give a legal ruling over an inheritance dispute—a common request of a rabbi. Rabbis were expected to be knowledgeable about the law and to give rulings accordingly for arbitration and justice using the property and inheritance laws in the first five books of the Bible, especially in Numbers and Deuteronomy.

But this situation was different. The petitioning brother already knew what outcome he was looking for. He was seeking justice as he defined it. "Tell my brother to divide the family inheritance with me."

Does this sound familiar? "Mama, make him give me back my toy." "Chairperson, do it my way because I am right." "Government leader, help me pressure others into granting rights I believe are mine." "When I count my blessings, I come up short so give me what I believe is mine."

Jesus, make the problem go away, and I am telling you how to do it to my satisfaction.

But Jesus replies, "Friend, who set me up to be a judge or arbitrator over you?"

Dr. Kenneth Bailey in his commentary *Through Peasant Eyes* (p 61) writes: "There is obviously a broken relationship between this man and his brother. The man wants the broken relationship finalized by total separation. But Jesus insists that he has not come as a 'divider'. The obvious alternative is 'reconciler.' He wants to reconcile people to one another, not finalize divisions between them."

But reconciliation would require the petitioner to look at himself differently. Reconciliation may require that we see ourselves in different ways. We may have to change how we relate with the person we have a dispute with. We may have to change our relationship to property. We may have to consider established law in a different way. How easy is it for us to do those things?

How many families have divided themselves over who gets Mama's ring. Churches have been ripped apart by fights over property, about who has the power to choose the color of the carpet, about who can and cannot be a minister, about whose theology is correct, or about how the money is spent. By refusing to help two brothers separate because of things, because of property, Jesus is pointing to a healthier way to be together.

Prayer for the Day: *God of Reconciliation, help me remember that things are not more important than people. Amen.*

Luke 12:13-21   **Week 8 / Monday**

Stanza 1, Verse 15 is the first wisdom saying: *Take care! Be on your guard against all kinds of greed; for one's life does not consist in the abundance of possessions.*

What in the world do people think when they keep accumulating stuff? Do we think that the more possessions we have, the happier we will be? Do you think that if you have an abundance of things, you will have an abundant life? Some may even believe the bumper sticker that says, "He who dies with the most toys, wins." You may have known people that when they died, their friends …THEIR FRIENDS… said, "If they could have figured out how to take it with them, they would have."

This passage is NOT teaching how to better care for your things. This passage is talking about desire—desire that can never be satisfied. Of course, you need a certain minimum of material goods. But a greater abundance of goods does not mean a greater abundance of life.

If you lost every material possession you own, have you lost anything that makes your life worth living? That's a pretty sobering question, isn't it? And yet you likely spend much of your time and energy either getting, cleaning, repairing, or worrying over your things—which have absolutely no impact on your sense of living an abundant life.

Prayer for the Day: *Life of all who live, help me claim what is truly worth living for and what is not. Amen.*

Week 8
Tuesday

Luke 12:13-21

Verse 16 describes goods given. *The land of a rich man produced abundantly.* The man was already rich because he was described as "rich." Where did the rich man's excess wealth come from? Sun, soil, and rain joined to make him wealthy. He is careful and conservative. There is no indication that he grabbed his wealth or that he cheated someone for it. "There is nothing here of graft or theft; there is no mistreatment of workers or any criminal act" (Fred Craddock, *Luke: Interpretation*, Westminster John Knox Press, p. 163). He is *not* unjust. He's simply a fool, according to the parable. It seems the rich man made no special effort. He just had a great crop so now he needed to figure out what to do with this surplus that he did not earn.

We move to stanza two, verse 17: The Problem. *And he thought to himself, "What should I do, for I have no place to store my crops?"* The bumper crop, given by God, is now referred to as "my crop." An ancient theologian, named Ambrose, had a wonderful suggestion for where the excess crops could be stored…the mouths of children who were hungry.

Kenneth Bailey points out something that only someone who had lived and worked in the Middle East would have noted. He said that the leading men in the village always worked out their issues in group, sitting around "at the gate" discussing for hours the topic at hand. The elder community involved "group thinking." In our parable, the man does his thinking alone. His conversation is with himself. Bailey suggests that he obviously has no one else to discuss his "problem" with. Does he trust no one?

With the rich man discussing the problem with only himself, Jesus is drawing a "picture of the kind of prison that wealth can build" (Craddock). The man is not opening himself up to the possibilities or alternative options that other people might have, people with different approaches and opinions. Craddock suggests that "he lives completely for himself, he talks to himself, he plans for himself, he congratulates himself." He lives in a vacuum.

Prayer for the Day: *Giver of all good and perfect gifts, give me people to help me discern how to best use the many gifts you bless me with. Amen.*

Luke 12:13-21

**Week 8
Wednesday**

Stanza Three, verse 18, The Present Plan: I will do this—I will pull down my barns and build larger ones, and there I will store all my grain and my goods. The prophet Jeremiah talked about tearing down and building up (Jeremiah 1:10) as a way of following God's will. However, the rich fool uses the same language, not to be God's man, but to be self-indulgent. He looks at God's good gifts to him now as "my crops, my barns, my goods."

You delude yourself with: "The blessings I enjoy are ones that I earned. My health is because I take care of myself. This is my church. My riches are mine. Mine, mine, mine." Sometimes you and I sound like two-year-olds who have just learned that word and concept…MINE.

Prayer for the Day: *God of compassion, help my heart to be compassionate by reminding me that everything comes from you to be used for the glory of your world and with love for all creation. Amen.*

Week 8   **Luke 12:13-21**
Thursday

Stanza Four, verse 19: The Future Plan. *"And I will say to my soul, 'Soul, you have ample goods laid up for many years; relax, eat, and drink, be merry.'"* The word "soul" in Hebrew means "the whole person." The rich fool seems to think that his total needs can be met by material surpluses well preserved for his own exclusive use.

William Barclay tells the story about a "conversation between [an] ambitious [young man] and an older man who knew life. [T]he young man [said], 'I will learn my trade.'

'And then?' said the older man.

'I will set up in business.'

'And then?'

'I will make my fortune.'

'And then?'

'I suppose that I shall grow old and retire and live on my money.'

'And then?'

'Well, I suppose that some day I will die.'

'*And then?*' came the last stabbing question" (William Barclay, *Luke*, 165).

Prayer for the Day: *God of life and death, show me the way of abundant life that is not defined by things. Amen.*

Luke 12:13-21   **Week 8 / Friday**

Stanza Five, verse 20: "But God said to him, 'You fool! This very night your life is being demanded of you. And the things you have prepared, whose will they be?'" Finally, someone gets through to the man and that someone is God Almighty. It is fascinating that God does not accuse him. God does not ask, "What have you done for others?" or "Why have you failed to help those in need?" or "Why are there no friends or family to receive your wealth?" God [simply] thunders: "Look at what you have done to yourself! You plan alone, build alone, indulge alone, and now you die alone!" (Bailey, 67).

Psalm 49:16-17 (CEV) speaks to the emptiness that is echoed in God's question. It says: *Don't let it bother you when others get rich and live in luxury. Soon they will die and all their wealth will be left behind.*

God says, *And the things you have prepared, whose will they be?* (Luke 12:20). The question is open-ended. We do not know what the rich man's response was. We each have to answer the question for ourselves. *This very night your life is being demanded of you. And the things you have prepared, whose will they be?*

In verse 21 there is a second wisdom saying: *So it is with those who store up treasures for themselves but are not rich toward God."*

Prayer for the Day: *God of abundance, I want to define wealth as my relationship with you rather than the things I have. But I need help to do this. HELP! Amen.*

Week 8
Saturday

Luke 12:13-21

Can you think about how you are rich? Can you think about what it means to be rich toward God? The rich fool tried to find his happiness by conserving rather than by giving. He spent his energy on things rather than on worshiping God and serving others. He did not acknowledge that his surplus was a free gift from God. He focused on himself and put his trust in things and in his own abilities to build.

But what else might it mean to be rich toward God? St. Francis is alleged to have said, "What you are looking for is what is looking." We are hoping that our things will make us feel secure and wanted and loved. But things don't do it. They are not looking for us. But God is seeking us. Our families are looking. Our friends are looking. Our church family is looking. Are you spending too much time maintaining things and too little time maintaining your sons/daughters, friends, parents, grandparents, and grandchildren?

What you are really looking for is not things. You are looking for God, for family, for friends, for love, for faith, for compassion.

The God-shaped hole in your heart will not be filled with bigger and bigger barns. Your deep hunger will not be filled with so much stuff that you need extra storage units or special boxes. The God-shaped hole in your heart will only be filled with God and all that God means to you. God's grace and love and mercy are the values on which to spend your time and energy. God's grace and love and mercy that are reflected in your friends and families are your true blessings.

Where shall we store the gifts given to us by God? We shall store them in the outstretched arms of God for the building up of the people of God—for all of God's children and all of God's creations.

Prayer for the Day: *God of blessings, let me count my blessings and not my things. Amen.*

Week 9
Mark 10:17-31

17 As he was setting out on a journey, a man ran up and knelt before him, and asked him, "Good Teacher, what must I do to inherit eternal life?"

18 Jesus said to him, "Why do you call me good? No one is good but God alone. 19 You know the commandments: You shall not murder; You shall not commit adultery; You shall not steal; You shall not bear false witness; You shall not defraud; Honour your father and mother."

20 He said to him, "Teacher, I have kept all these since my youth."

21 Jesus, looking at him, loved him and said, "You lack one thing; go, sell what you own, and give the money to the poor, and you will have treasure in heaven; then come, follow me."

22 When he heard this, he was shocked and went away grieving, for he had many possessions.

23 Then Jesus looked around and said to his disciples, "How hard it will be for those who have wealth to enter the kingdom of God!" 24 And the disciples were perplexed at these words.

But Jesus said to them again, "Children, how hard it is to enter the kingdom of God! 25 It is easier for a camel to go through the eye of a needle than for someone who is rich to enter the kingdom of God."

26 They were greatly astounded and said to one another, "Then who can be saved?"

27 Jesus looked at them and said, "For mortals it is impossible, but not for God; for God all things are possible."

28 Peter began to say to him, "Look, we have left everything and followed you."

29 Jesus said, "Truly I tell you, there is no one who has left house or brothers or sisters or mother or father or children or fields, for my sake and for the sake of the good news,
30 who will not receive a hundredfold now in this age—houses, brothers and sisters, mothers and children, and fields, with persecutions—and in the age to come eternal life. 31 But many who are first will be last, and the last will be first."

Week 9
Sunday

Mark 10:17-31

Jesus loved this rich man! Jesus loved him even when he knew that there was something lacking in the man's life. Jesus loved him even though he was a man who lived by the law and not by grace. Jesus loved him even when Jesus knew he was not perfect. Jesus loved him no matter what his condition, no matter what he could or would do or what he had done in the past...good or bad. Jesus loved him no matter what the rich man's illusions were about himself. Jesus loved him. There are plenty of instances of Jesus's having pity or being filled with compassion. In the Gospel of Mark, there is no other individual in the entire gospel for whom this is said: Jesus loved him. So before you go too far in shaking your head about the rich man and how tight-fisted he was, remember that Jesus loved him. And when you realize that Jesus may be asking of you similar things which you find difficult, you can remember that Jesus loves you—even when you cannot, on your own, fulfill his request or instruction.

Prayer for the Day: *Ever loving God, thank for you loving me even when I do not merit it. Amen.*

Mark 10:17-31

**Week 9
Monday**

Jesus asked this man to follow him. The only other individuals in Mark to whom Jesus directly said, "Follow me," were Peter, Andrew, James, John, and Levi, son of Alphaeus…all of whom were in the twelve. Most people with whom Jesus interacted in the gospel of Mark were told not to follow but to go—to go in peace (hemorrhaging woman), to go home (blind man at Bethsaida). It seems that Jesus was asking this rich man to become one of his disciples, to join him on the journey, to spend time with him, to learn from him on a day-to-day basis.

If that is the case, it makes sense for Jesus to ask him to give away his money to the poor. The other disciples had left their livelihoods to be with Jesus. Peter in fact said in verse 28, *Look, we have left everything and followed you.* The disciples had renounced their previous lives. A rich man might have many distractions if he were still concerned with managing his acquisitions, keeping tabs on his portfolio, dealing with his labor force issues, going to all the meetings People who are fortunate to have stock portfolios know from the ups and downs how nerve-wracking owning stocks can be. Jesus knew that life on the road with him did not allow for such distractions.

Prayer for the Day: *Source of knowledge, show me what I'm holding onto so that I cannot be fully present to you. And then help me to know what to do next. Amen.*

Week 9
Tuesday

Mark 10:17-31

Sometimes this passage is used to promote the idea that you must give away your possessions to be a follower of Jesus. And when that prescription is presented, you may agree with Kahlil Gibran's rich man who retorted in the book titled *Jesus, the Son of Man*: "But he possessed nothing; therefore, he knew not the assurance and the freedom of possessions, nor the dignity and the self-respect that lie within…Now had I heeded Him and given my possessions to the poor, what would have befallen my slaves and my servants and their wives and children? They too would have become beggars at the gate of the city or the portico of the temple. Nay that good man did not fathom the secret of possessions. Because He and His followers lived on the bounty of others. He thought all men should live likewise… The ant that stores food for the winter is wiser than a grasshopper that sings one day and hungers another" (p 148).

Gibran's character's arguments sound hauntingly familiar. You may have heard people say, and maybe you have said or thought it yourself, "If I give away everything, then I become a drag on society just like those I am supposed to help."

This passage can lend itself to instilling guilt and could play well for stewardship sermons and to raise funds for non-profits. Faithful people *do* wrestle with the tentacles which possessions have on them and some feel guilty when not giving sacrificially. You may respond that hearing the challenge to give from your relatively vast wealth is certainly a call to demonstrate your faith. You know that sharing your resources is a spiritual discipline. You know that giving to poor people is essential for their wellbeing. You know that giving to the church is a no-brainer so that God's purposes can be fulfilled within the walls of the congregation as well as out in the world. Even though you know all that, you are uncomfortable when you hear these words of Jesus: *You lack one thing; go, sell what you own, and give the money to the poor, and you will have treasure in heaven.* Then he said, *It is easier for a camel to go through the eye of a needle than for someone who is rich to enter the kingdom of God.* And so you squirm or you tune out.

Prayer for the Day: *Generous God, help me not run away from wrestling with how to use my resources as a faithful and responsible person. Amen.*

Mark 10:17-31

**Week 9
Wednesday**

As you wrestle with this passage, remember that riches in and of themselves were not necessarily distasteful to Jesus. He spent time with Zacchaeus and did not ask him to give away all his possessions. However, Zacchaeus did re-prioritize his wealth. Jesus chastised the Pharisees for setting aside their wealth as *corban*, as dedicated to God, so that they could neglect their financial responsibility for their parents. In Mark 4, Jesus even says that *"for those who have, more will be given; and from those who have nothing, even what they have will be taken away."* Jesus was buried in the tomb provided by Joseph of Arimathea, a man of wealth. It seems that Jesus did not see poverty (voluntary or otherwise) as a virtue in and of itself.

Jesus *was* passionate about caring for those whom others ignored or looked down upon. You may remember the woman who gave all she had from her little pittance of money. You remember Jesus's powerful judgment phrase about the hungry and the naked and those in prison and the thirsty and the stranger. You remember how he reached out to the untouchables of his time: lepers, women, children.

So Jesus cared about poor people but he was not laying down an eleventh commandment when he said, "Go, and sell what you own, and give the money to the poor." This passage is not really about giving away one's possessions—as important as it is to let loose the ties our things have on us.

Prayer for the Day: *So God…how do I think about my money and possessions. If it's not ALL or NOTHING, then what is it? What is my lesson here? Amen.*

Week 9
Thursday
Mark 10:17-31

When Jesus listed some of the commandments, the rich man said he kept them. He did not murder, he did not commit adultery, he did not steal, he did not bear false witness, he did not defraud. He honored his father and his mother.

Look at his specific list. Notice all the things he did not do. It's rather like when young boys who may claim: "I did not kick the dog, I did not punch my brother, I did not make a mess." But all the "did nots" did not necessarily mean that they were boys who were perfect or innocent. The rich man seemed to understand that the things he did not do were not enough. He wanted to know what he *could* do...to inherit eternal life...to assure his everlasting reward.

This is the point.... What must I do to inherit eternal life?

Jesus did not but might have pointed out one other commandment which the rich man did not, in fact, mention that he was keeping: "You shall have no other gods before me." Maybe on one level the rich man needed to meditate on what other gods he was worshiping—possessions, status and influence, power, community leadership, family (Dr. Ralph F. Wilson, *Jesus Walk*, Luke 18:18-23, internet). Or maybe he needed to consider: "You shall not make for yourself an idol." Maybe he was seeing his own perfection, his own image as his idol. Maybe when he ran up to Jesus and knelt before him and called him, "Good Teacher," just maybe he was hoping that he would get the pat on the head and be told that he had just received, as Paul Minear called it, the "ticket of admission" to eternal life (Paul S. Minear, *Mark, The Layman's Bible Commentary*, p. 102)

Prayer for the Day: *Rock of my life, keep me aware of where you are leading me to grow. Help me not get stuck in thinking how good I am, especially when I compare myself to others. Amen.*

Mark 10:17-31

Week 9
Friday

Don't we all keep a mental list of our own reasons of why we are good Christians? Of how we are faithful? Of how we really are more faithful than the person who is sitting down the row from us? Don't we all, in some way, believe that we are stacking up resources for our admission ticket? We even laugh when someone does good and say, "You will have stars in your crown," indicating on some deep level that we actually believe we earn our way into the presence of God?

Certainly the disciples seemed to have thought that the rich man should have been given that ticket to eternal life. They said, *Then who can be saved?* Here we had a "model citizen: decent, law-abiding, charitable, and religious" (Douglas A.R. Hare, *Mark: Interpretation*, p. 228). His being rich certainly fit the common wisdom that wealth indicated God's blessings. Remember Job? When he lost everything, his friends tried to figure out how he had angered God which they believed he obviously did since he lost family and fortune. Then and now in popular culture, wealth equals God's blessings.

Our rich man, who wanted to know the one last thing he could do to guarantee that he would have life eternal was told to do the one thing which he seemingly could not do. He was told to sell all he had and give it to the poor. Even knowing all this, Jesus loved him because as Jesus said, *For mortals it is impossible, but not for God; for God all things are possible.* Jesus told the rich man to do something which the man found impossible. In his being appalled at the final instruction, this almost disciple had the opportunity to recognize that life with God is a gift. It is not earned. This bears repeating: Life with God is a gift. It is not earned.

Prayer for the Day: *Giving God, thank you for my life with you. Let me never take it for granted. Amen.*

Week 9
Saturday   **Mark 10:17-31**

The man who almost became a disciple was shocked and went away grieving. He missed out on an even closer relationship with Jesus when he did not get the profound truth that eternal life is a gift. There is nothing you can do to earn it. You *can* model the kingdom of God in the here and now by what you choose to do with your resources.

You can wonder what the rich man did next. Did he go about being even more stringent in keeping the law, hoping against hope that he could rack up enough brownie points for eternal life? OR did he read about starving children in Africa and remember Jesus's words and write a very generous check, hoping that was enough to meet the impossible obligation? Did he "calm down, [think] about what Jesus had said, going over and over it in his mind? [Realizing] he hadn't been given a time limit, [he began giving, slowly at first and then more and more until]...he gradually discovered the rewards of giving to be greater than the rewards of wealth..." (Fletcher Farmer, March 2000, *Ministry of Money*, Issue 123).

Did he finally realize that the gift of eternal life was already his and, in gratitude, begin sharing his wealth? Did the "almost" disciple become a true follower of Christ?

Prayer for the Day: *God, if I was this almost disciple whom Jesus loves, how would I respond? Amen.*

Week 10
Matthew 18:1-7, 10

1 At that time the disciples came to Jesus and asked, "Who is the greatest in the kingdom of heaven?"

2 He called a child, whom he put among them, 3 and said, "Truly I tell you, unless you change and become like children, you will never enter the kingdom of heaven.

4 "Whoever becomes humble like this child is the greatest in the kingdom of heaven. 5 Whoever welcomes one such child in my name welcomes me.

6 "If any of you put a stumbling-block before one of these little ones who believe in me, it would be better for you if a great millstone were fastened around your neck and you were drowned in the depth of the sea. 7 Woe to the world because of stumbling-blocks! Occasions for stumbling are bound to come, but woe to the one by whom the stumbling-block comes!"

…

10 "Take care that you do not despise one of these little ones; for, I tell you, in heaven their angels continually see the face of my Father in heaven."

Week 10
Sunday
                                Matthew 18:1-7, 10

Shortly after Jesus says to the disciples *"From that time on, Jesus began to show his disciples that he must go to Jerusalem and undergo great suffering at the hands of the elders and chief priests and scribes, and be killed, and on the third day be raised"* (Matthew 16:21), the disciples wonder who will be the greatest in the kingdom of heaven.

Are the disciples clueless? Here their master, their teacher, tells them that he must suffer and be killed, and the disciples are wondering who will be the greatest in the kingdom of heaven? Are they still thinking that the kingdom that Jesus is talking about is a kingdom established after Rome is kicked out of the region and they have a new kingdom where they are the rulers? The rule makers? The establishers of order? Are they picturing a kingdom like the one that David established so many centuries earlier? A kingdom that no longer exists? Had Jesus still not been able to get through their preconceived notions? Did they truly believe that they would no longer be who they used to be: fishermen, tax collectors, or even students of the rabbi? Did they believe their proximity to the person they believed was the Messiah would put them in seats of honor? Was their appetite for prominence blinding them to the light that was before them? After all this time, were they still consumed by darkness? Did they not hear the part about suffering and death?

Prayer for the Day: *God of life and death, help me let go of my need to "be first," "be best," "be on top," I know that in you I am already all of those things…just maybe not in the way the world defines them. Amen.*

Matthew 18:1-7, 10

**Week 10
Monday**

Have you ever played a version of the game when you tell your siblings that Mom loved you best? When asked by grandchildren which of her two sons (their fathers) she loved best, the grandmother always responded, "The one I'm with at the time."

It is human nature to want to know you have value to another. You want to know that you are number one or if not number one, then at least number two. This helps explain prejudices. People may need to put down another person or an entire group of people just to make themselves feel that they have value. When you compare yourself to others, you are always in trouble. You may either assess that you are better than another or the other is better than you. Either way you lose your sense of your own uniqueness because of who you actually are…not because of how you think you are when standing beside someone else.

Douglas Hare says it seems to be a special device "that people are continually trying to lord it over one another: the rich over the poor, the intelligent over the simple, adults over children…whites over [people of color, Americans over everyone else, Christians over people who profess other faiths.]" (Douglas Hare, *Matthew: Interpretation*, p. 209). On and on it goes.

Prayer for the Day: *God of mercy, help me claim that I am 100% great…in your eyes, no matter how I think I compare with anyone else. Amen.*

Week 10
Tuesday

Matthew 18:1-7, 10

So who is the greatest in the kingdom of heaven? In Mark's telling of this episode, he has the disciples arguing over this question. Jesus hears them arguing and then asks them what they are arguing about. What happens then? They are silent. Jesus has caught them competing for power, wealth, and prestige. They, too, are engulfed with the powers and temptations of the world. Have they have not yet grasped the fullness of Jesus's teaching? Did they, too, leap to examples of Jesus's power when he healed, gathered large crowds, and fed people? Did they truly not understand that their beloved Messiah would suffer and die? Did they not take into themselves that the kingdom Jesus talked about was primarily an internal change, not an exterior claim? Jesus's kingdom was one where love ruled, not imperial power.

Harry Adams reminds: "It is sad for a person to be so consumed with what others think about him [or her] to be so insecure about what people think… that [the person] must seek public recognition of [personal] importance" (Harry B. Adams, *Feasting on the Word*, B-4 p 96).

The disciples were on a journey with Jesus to Jerusalem, the seat of power. Even when Jesus kept telling them about his impending death, they fought that knowledge. Peter actually rebuked Jesus earlier (Matthew 16:22) for saying these things. He proclaimed that *this must never happen to you*. At that time, Jesus said to Peter: *Get behind me, Satan! You are a stumbling block to me; for you are setting your mind not on divine things but on human things* (Matthew.16:23).

Prayer for the Day: *Lord God, help me release my need to know what other people think of me. Actually…that's none of my business, is it? Amen.*

Matthew 18:1-7, 10

**Week 10
Wednesday**

Addressing this frustrating questioning about who is the greatest, Jesus teaches, he calls a child to come to him. This action seems out of place considering the seriousness of the question/the argument. A "child"?

Children in that day were considered only property. They were on the same level as a slave. Sharon H. Ringe tells us that Matthew's audience "would have heard the word 'child' as referring to someone like the servant who served meals to everyone else in the household, in that both were seen as without 'honor' or high social standing. A child did not contribute much of anything to the economic value of a household or community, and a child could not do anything to enhance one's position in the struggles for prestige or influence. One would obtain no benefit from [offering] to the child hospitality or rituals of honor or respect that one might offer to someone of higher status or someone whose favor one wanted to [obtain]. Children and servants were of equally low social status" (*Feasting on the Word, B-4*, p. 97).

Jesus tells the disciples that they must become as a child to enter the kingdom. Forget being in charge; become a child just to enter.

They might have been thinking…you mean we have to become a nobody? A child? Someone with no power, no prestige, no authority, no status. Say what??? They must join the lowest of the low in a very stratified society?

Prayer for the Day: *God of the child, you came into the world as a child. Help me remember how special that is and claim that humility for myself. Amen.*

Week 10
Thursday

Matthew 18:1-7, 10

Jesus says the disciples must become humble like a child. For many in that time, humility was not a virtue but a vice. It "smacked of a servility appropriate to slaves, women, and children but indecent among free men" (Douglas Hare, *Matthew: Interpretation*, p. 210). For Jesus, being humble became great. The picture just got turned upside down.

To welcome, to offer hospitality to someone, was to receive that person as a valuable person, no matter how lowly he or she seemed to be. Jesus went on to say that welcoming this child was the same as welcoming Jesus himself. What a serious challenge, shocking even, that Jesus said a child was an example for living in the kingdom of God. This idea opposed what was socially acceptable.

But then Paul jumps into the picture. Listen to what he says in 1 Corinthians 1:26-31: *"Consider your own call, brothers and sisters; not many of you were wise by human standards, not many were powerful, not many were of noble birth. But God chose what is foolish in the world to shame the wise; God chose what is weak in the world to shame the strong; God chose what is low and despised in the world, things that are not, to reduce to nothing things that are, so that no one might boast of the presence of God. [Paul says God] is the source of your life in Christ Jesus, who became for us wisdom from God, ... in order that, as it is written, 'Let the one who boasts, boast in the Lord.'"*

Prayer for the Day: *God, strength of the weak, when I look down upon those I consider weak, open my eyes so I will see them as your special person whom you love dearly. Amen.*

Matthew 18:1-7, 10

Week 10
Friday

Jesus tells the disciples that if they put a stumbling block before a child, it would be better for them to be cast into the sea with weights around the neck. Jesus is *very* serious about this. So...where are you putting stumbling blocks for those whom Jesus cherishes?

The obvious answer is to look at children in your family as well as youth in your church, school, or community. Even when there are great teachers, coaches, and mentors for kids, remember that children and teens are the responsibility of everyone. Does every young person find school, church, or their community to be a welcoming place for them no matter what their individual challenges may be? What children are being left out? Are you and your group falling short in some way? Are there children in your community who cannot participate because there is no one reaching out to bring them in, welcome them, nurture them?

A church leader was asked to help a congregation negotiate conflict that was brewing there. The pastor of the church understood from initial interviews that the congregation wanted to bring youth into the church. The pastor took them at their word and began an outreach program that connected with community youth. A number of them even chose to come to worship. But there was a problem. A woman on the conflict management team commented that she did not understand why these kids could not dress the proper way for church. The pastor left not too long after that. Some in the congregation did not welcome a child in Christ's name.

Where else may you be a stumbling block?

You may be a stumbling block when you neglect sharing the good news of your triune God's love and grace and mercy and justice and compassion for all with people with whom you interact.

You may be a stumbling block when you puff yourself up and claim that you are important because of what you do, how much money you give, what positions in life and the church you hold. When you bring focus on yourself without acknowledging that you are who you are because of God's breath in your lives, you can cause others to stumble.

You may be a stumbling block when you condone laws, public policies, and attitudes that do not honor the blessedness of those without power, prestige, status, or position.

Prayer for the Day: *Lord God, I do not want to be a stumbling block. Help me discover where I am and then lead me to different ways of being and thinking. Amen.*

Week 10
Saturday　　　　　　　　　　　　　　　　　　　**Matthew 18:1-7, 10**

Then Jesus said something that gives pause. He said, *Take care that you do not despise one of these little ones; for, I tell you, in heaven their angels continually see the face of my Father in heaven* (Matthew 18:10). Do you love the thought of having a guardian angel? William Barclay explained that "in the time of Jesus the Jews had a very highly-developed angelology. Every nation had its angel; every natural force, such as the wind and the thunder and the lightning and the rain had its angel. They even went the length of saying... that every blade of grass had its angel. So, then, they believed that every child had his guardian angel [meaning that through the angels] they always have the right of direct access to God" (Barclay, *Matthew*, p. 180). You may not fully embrace all this but it certainly gives you something to ponder.

In her poem "The Way to Jerusalem is Cluttered," Ann Weems writes: "The way to Jerusalem / is cluttered / with bits and pieces of our lives/ that fly up and cry out, / wounding us as we try / to keep upon this path / that leads to Life. / Why didn't somebody tell us / that is would be so hard? / In the midst of the clutter, / the children laugh / and run after stars. / Those of us who are wise / will follow; / for the children will be the first / to kneel in Jerusalem" (Ann Weems, *Kneeling in Jerusalem*, Westminster/John Knox Press, Louisville, Kentucky, 192, p. 42).

Prayer for the Day: *God, help me embrace your kingdom rather than the kingdoms of media, cultural values, and even my own fantasies. Help be become childlike. Amen.*

Week 11
Matthew 6:9-10; Ephesians 5:1-2, 15; 6:1-9

Matthew 6

9 Pray then in this way: Our Father in heaven, hallowed be your name. 10 Your kingdom come. Your will be done, on earth as it is in heaven.

Ephesians 5

1 Therefore be imitators of God, as beloved children, 2 and live in love, as Christ loved us and gave himself up for us, a fragrant offering and sacrifice to God.
...
15 Be careful then how you live, not as unwise people but as wise...

Ephesians 6

1 Children, obey your parents in the Lord, for this is right.
2 Honour your father and mother—this is the first commandment with a promise:3 so that it may be well with you and you may live long on the earth.
4 And, fathers, do not provoke your children to anger, but bring them up in the discipline and instruction of the Lord.
5 Slaves, obey your earthly masters with fear and trembling, in singleness of heart, as you obey Christ; 6 not only while being watched, and in order to please them, but as slaves of Christ, doing the will of God from the heart.
7 Render service with enthusiasm, as to the Lord and not to men and women, 8 knowing that whatever good we do, we will receive the same again from the Lord, whether we are slaves or free.
9 And, masters, do the same to them. Stop threatening them, for you know that both of you have the same Master in heaven, and with him there is no partiality.

Week 11
Sunday

Matthew 6:9-10; Ephesians 5:1-2, 15; 6:1-9

Speaking of God as Father also infers that God is the householder of the world. In a patriarchal society, the head of the household was spoken of as male. So, what does a good household look and feel like?

House imagery has been used in scripture to help us understand God and our relationship to God.

In the Gospel of John (14:2), Jesus said, *In my Father's house are many dwelling places. If it were not so, would I have told you that I go to prepare a place for you?* The first words in this statement are "in my Father's house." This is clearly a statement that God is a householder...and a householder that encompasses all other houses.

St. Teresa of Avila in the sixteenth century wrote about the interior castle. Here is the opening of her book of explanation: "*While* I was begging our Lord to-day to speak for me, since I knew not what to say nor how to commence this work which obedience has laid upon me, ...I thought of the soul as resembling a castle, formed of a single diamond or a very transparent crystal, and containing many rooms, just as in heaven there are many mansions.... What, do you imagine, [she asks] must that dwelling be in which a King so mighty, so wise, and so pure, containing in Himself all good, can delight to rest?"

She goes on to describe in great detail the various rooms and applies them to the Christian walk and how we can grow in faith and maturity. Her castle encompasses for some the entire picture of growth in Christian maturity.

Prayer for the Day: *Strength of my life, thank you for this day. Help me stay connected with you today. Amen.*

Matthew 6:9-10; Ephesians 5:1-2, 15; 6:1-9

Week 11
Monday

Now let's turn to the phrase from the Lord's Prayer: "Hallowed be thy name." You repeat these words… that you've said over and over… and may not really give much thought to their meaning. "Hallowed be thy name." What in the world does "hallowed" mean anyway? The dictionary says it means to make holy; to set apart from common. The prayer asks that God's name be set apart from anything common, ordinary, or the status quo. God's name is the shorthand description for who God is, what God does, past, present, and future. We pray that nothing about God's world, God's presence, or our connection with all that is God is part of the status quo. It is not common. Therefore, "to ask God to make God's name holy, is to ask God to make the world into a good household, [a healthy household, a place where everyone thrives, where everyone becomes the person that he or she is created by God to be]." "Hallowed be thy name" is actually a parallel to "Your kingdom come… on earth, as it is in heaven" (Marcus Borg).

God's good household on earth…thy kingdom come on earth. So, another way of thinking about the kingdom of God is to think about the household of God.

It may be easier to get your head around the idea and questions raised by thinking about the household of God rather than the kingdom of God. Maybe you can relate to a household. Kingdoms may be harder.

Prayer for the Day: *Our Father, who art in heaven, hallowed be thy name. Thy kingdom come, thy will be done, on earth as it is in heaven. Give us this day our daily bread; and forgive us our debts as we forgive our debtors; and lead us not into temptation but deliver us from evil. For thine is the kingdom and the power and the glory, forever. Amen.*

Week 11   Matthew 6:9-10; Ephesians 5:1-2, 15; 6:1-9
Tuesday

Let's look at this household room by room.

A household has a kitchen. In God's household, this kitchen uses the foods of the earth in ways that nourish everyone. Food is not contaminated. It is not empty of nutrition yet loaded with calories. The meals prepared are balanced for what bodies need for health, strength, and growth. The workers in this kitchen prepare enough food for everyone in the household…from the highest-ranking person there to the lowest. Those who have less status in the household are actually fed a bit better because they are responsible for so much of the daily activities of the household… people like maids, childcare workers, gardeners, essential workers. Because they are valued, they are well fed. No one gets scraps or the leftovers that others don't want. The kitchen staff make sure that everyone in the household is fed well so that they each can fulfill their call by God.

In the dining room, the great feast is joyous and full of conversation. Jesus often talked about life with him as being at a great feast. In the dining room, everyone is welcomed at the table. Just as Jesus welcomed tax collectors, women, and betrayers to his table, we, too, in the household of God, welcome all to the table. There is no US and THEM at the table. Everyone is welcomed no matter their skin color, nationality, mental ability, or economic status. Each makes sure that table mates are satisfied. Each includes others in significant conversation. Each goes out of his or her way to make sure everyone else has a satisfying dining experience. No one is pampered too much and no one is neglected.

Prayer for the Day: *God of abundance, I know that people in my world do not have adequate food. Help me find my own unique way to help address that need. Amen.*

Matthew 6:9-10; Ephesians 5:1-2, 15; 6:1-9

**Week 11
Wednesday**

In the nursery, all children are taken care of. One is not left out while others get to go to preschool. All children have access to small classes, adequate educational supplies, and extracurricular activities. Children are affirmed, not put down or bullied. They are safe and do not fear abuse, abandonment, or violence. They know that their home is stable and that they are loved. They do not have to assume responsibilities beyond their years. They do not have to protect their siblings from hunger, abuse, or neglect. Children get to play with abandon. They are taught skills and attitudes that promote their place in God's household. They learn to value what is important and ignore all the rest. They are healthy because they have medical services available when needed.

In the bedroom, everyone has a safe and comfortable place to sleep. No one sleeps on the floor or in a corner. When nightmares come, each person is comforted. The room is comfortable…not too hot and not too cold. The bed is soft for those who like soft and firm for those who like firm. People get enough sleep but not too much. They awaken rested and ready for the next day in the household of God.

The bathroom, too, in the household of God, is not common, not just okay. The bathroom provides people who are weary in body a tub to soak and relax in. There are foot soaks for those in the household who are on their feet all day. There are soothing lotions for those with scabs, ailing skin, or who need a healing touch as someone lathers the creams and oils on their damaged bodies. The towels are extravagant. No one has to use dirty clothes to dry their bodies or use public places to relieve themselves. Everyone can take care of their bodily functions in a pleasant and safe place. And because everyone can get clean, no one sniffs at them and walks away. And shampoo abounds for sweet smelling hair.

Prayer for the Day: *Oh, my God, how unlike my world is for what you intend. Help me find my place in your household. I want to be a good resident. Amen.*

Week 11
Thursday

Matthew 6:9-10; Ephesians 5:1-2, 15; 6:1-9

The living room is large and gracious. Everyone there finds a comfortable place to be. When there are disagreements, the living room provides a place to work out differences. It creates an environment for acceptance, joy, and peace. People know that the living room helps nurture what is important in life. After all, it is called a living room, not a fighting ring, a killing place, or an ignoring situation. No one feels invisible or unwanted in the living room. People play games, sing songs, laugh, cry, do creative activities, and enjoy being with each other. Here they celebrate the joy of being in the household of God.

The library/study is important for people to continue to grow in mind. It's a place where people ask questions and grapple with what it means to be a member of God's household. It's the room where people continue to wrestle with what it means to be hallowed, to be set apart, to be holy, to not be common, to not accept the status quo. The library has resources from all kinds of thinkers—thinkers on the left of any issue and thinkers on the right and thinkers in the middle. Discussions in the library are vibrant. Eventually people come to a place where they can allow for a diversity of thought and action and know that is part of being in the household of God.

These are just some of the rooms in the house.

When we go outside, the buildings are well cared for. The land is valued and not used as an unending resource. The air is cared for. Plants and animals thrive because nothing is hindering their growth and survival. The earth is not seen as a commodity. It is set apart as holy because is it part of God's household. The dirt, water, and air are treated as holy, as essential aspects of the care of the householder. The outdoors are not for making someone or something rich but for the health and well-being of all the plants and animals and people in God's household.

Prayer for the Day: *O God, what are we all doing when we ignore your creation, when we take it for granted, when we do not understand its holiness? Forgive me for my part in this. Amen.*

Matthew 6:9-10; Ephesians 5:1-2, 15; 6:1-9

Week 11
Friday

You have been considering how the Household of God might be if...if...if everyone grasped that vision and committed to being good residents in this household. You have a picture of how the world would be if more people would take seriously what faith, trust in God could look like if people strive to live as God's followers, if people truly followed the way of Jesus.

But there's yet another aspect of God's household. In Ephesians, there's a householder's list for those who live in the household. Scholars seem to believe that the writer of Ephesians, maybe Paul, maybe not, used a common household table to instruct people of faith, followers of Jesus, how to be good residents in God's household.

Chapters 5 and 6 in Ephesians sound rather like a letter written by a father to his son as his son headed off to college. The head of the household might write: *Therefore be imitators of [Me], as beloved children, and live in love, as [I] loved you...Be careful then how you live, not as an unwise person but as wise... So do not be foolish, but understand what the will of your Father is* (Ephesians 5:1, 15, 17).

Prayer for the Day: *Loving God, I want to be an imitator of you. Help, please. Amen.*

Week 11
Saturday
Matthew 6:9-10; Ephesians 5:1-2, 15; 6:1-9

In Ephesians, there are instructions for specific members of the household. Some of these instructions might be samplers hanging on the walls of the household of God, strategically placed as reminders for all residents.

Children, obey your parents in the Lord (Ephesians 6:1).

Fathers, do not provoke your children to anger, but bring them up in the discipline and instruction of the Lord (Ephesians 6:4).

Finally, be strong in the Lord and in the strength of God's power (Ephesians 6:10).

Two questions for you to consider:

1. Is my own household a model of the household of God?
2. Am I committed to being the kind of person who yearns to live in God's household and does whatever is in my power and calling by God to bring the possibility of this holy household to my community, my country, and my world?

Prayer for the Day: *Father God, help me meditate on these questions and live into the answers I desire. Amen.*

Week 12
John 11:1-44

1 Now a certain man was ill, Lazarus of Bethany, the village of Mary and her sister Martha. 2 Mary was the one who anointed the Lord with perfume and wiped his feet with her hair; her brother Lazarus was ill. 3 So the sisters sent a message to Jesus, "Lord, he whom you love is ill." 4 But when Jesus heard it, he said, 'This illness does not lead to death; rather it is for God's glory, so that the Son of God may be glorified through it.' 5 Accordingly, though Jesus loved Martha and her sister and Lazarus, 6 after having heard that Lazarus was ill, he stayed two days longer in the place where he was. 7 Then after this he said to the disciples, "Let us go to Judea again."

8 The disciples said to him, 'Rabbi, the Jews were just now trying to stone you, and are you going there again?' 9 Jesus answered, "Are there not twelve hours of daylight? Those who walk during the day do not stumble, because they see the light of this world. 10 But those who walk at night stumble, because the light is not in them." 11 After saying this, he told them, "Our friend Lazarus has fallen asleep, but I am going there to awaken him." 12 The disciples said to him, "Lord, if he has fallen asleep, he will be all right." 13 Jesus, however, had been speaking about his death, but they thought that he was referring merely to sleep. 14 Then Jesus told them plainly, "Lazarus is dead. 15 For your sake I am glad I was not there, so that you may believe. But let us go to him." 16 Thomas, who was called the Twin, said to his fellow-disciples, "Let us also go, that we may die with him."

17 When Jesus arrived, he found that Lazarus had already been in the tomb for four days. 18 Now Bethany was near Jerusalem, some two miles away, 19 and many of the Jews had come to Martha and Mary to console them about their brother. 20 When Martha heard that Jesus was coming, she went and met him, while Mary stayed at home. 21 Martha said to Jesus, "Lord, if you had been here, my brother would not have died. 22 But even now I know that God will give you whatever you ask of him." 23 Jesus said to her, "Your brother will rise again." 24 Martha said to him, "I know that he will rise again in the resurrection on the last day." 25 Jesus said to her, "I am the resurrection and the life. Those who believe in me, even though they die, will live, 26 and everyone who lives and believes in me will never die. Do you believe this?" 27 She said to him, "Yes, Lord, I believe that you are the Messiah, the Son of God, the one coming into the world." 28 When she had said this, she went back and called her sister Mary, and told her privately, "The Teacher is here and is calling for you."

29 And when she heard it, she got up quickly and went to him. 30 Now Jesus had not yet come to the village, but was still at the place where Martha had met him.

31 The Jews who were with her in the house, consoling her, saw Mary get up quickly and go out. They followed her because they thought that she was going to the tomb to weep there.

(cont'd next page)

Week 12
Sunday

John 11:1-44

The Gospel story of Lazarus is amazing. Jesus raises Lazarus from the dead...Lazarus, who was in the tomb for four days. Even though this is a story full of signs and meaning, it is told only once and that is in the Gospel of John. The other three gospels, Matthew, Mark, and Luke, do not mention the raising of Lazarus at all. Nor do they even hint at such a miracle. Luke tells a story of Mary and Martha when Jesus visited them, but their brother Lazarus is not there in name or in person. Luke *does* use the name Lazarus in his telling of the rich man and the poor man, but the Lazarus of Luke is not the Lazarus of John.

Whereas the other gospels use the cleansing of the Temple when Jesus threw out the money changers as the defining moment toward crucifixion, John uses this powerful story to lay the groundwork for the charges made against Jesus at his trial. Some scholars have wondered if the raising of Lazarus really happened since the story does not appear anywhere else. Other theologians see the story as a powerful way of seeing a fuller picture of Jesus, as a way to deepen our understanding of Jesus and his impact and message for us. There is also a powerful personal challenge for each of us with this story.

Prayer for the Day: *God of wonder, open my mind and heart so I may see the depths of this story so it will become part of my faith journey. Amen.*

---

32 When Mary came where Jesus was and saw him, she knelt at his feet and said to him, "Lord, if you had been here, my brother would not have died." 33 When Jesus saw her weeping, and the Jews who came with her also weeping, he was greatly disturbed in spirit and deeply moved. 34 He said, "Where have you laid him?" They said to him, "Lord, come and see." 35 Jesus began to weep. 36 So the Jews said, "See how he loved him!" 37 But some of them said, "Could not he who opened the eyes of the blind man have kept this man from dying?"

38 Then Jesus, again greatly disturbed, came to the tomb. It was a cave, and a stone was lying against it. 39 Jesus said, "Take away the stone." Martha, the sister of the dead man, said to him, "Lord, already there is a stench because he has been dead for four days." 40 Jesus said to her, "Did I not tell you that if you believed, you would see the glory of God?" 41 So they took away the stone. And Jesus looked upwards and said, "Father, I thank you for having heard me. 42 I knew that you always hear me, but I have said this for the sake of the crowd standing here, so that they may believe that you sent me." 43 When he had said this, he cried with a loud voice, "Lazarus, come out!" 44 The dead man came out, his hands and feet bound with strips of cloth, and his face wrapped in a cloth. Jesus said to them, "Unbind him, and let him go."

John 11:1-44

Week 12
Monday

The first thing to notice about Jesus in this passage is that he demonstrated that he would act as he saw fit to act, without adhering to any outside pressure from anyone. Jesus did not come immediately when Mary and Martha sent word to him that Lazarus was ill. Even though there is no indication that they specifically requested Jesus to come, it is clear that they expected him to come right now. Are you like Mary and Martha? You know there are certain people in your life that all you have to do is let them know you are scared or hurting or joyful and, because of their love for you, you know they will be with you in whatever way they can. And when it comes to Jesus, you want him to act *when* you want him to act, and *how* you want him to act, and *on your demand*. Here Jesus says of his slowness in action: *This illness does not lead to death; rather it is for God's glory, so that the Son of God may be glorified through it.... Lazarus is dead. For your sake, I am glad I was not there, so that you may believe* (John 11:4, 14).

Another way that Jesus demonstrated that he was acting according to his own time was when Jesus decided it was *indeed* finally time for him to go to Bethany to Mary, Martha, and Lazarus. The disciples sought to dissuade him. They were afraid the Jews would try to stone him, to kill him. But Jesus went anyway. Possibly he knew that Bethany was the next necessary step toward his journey to the cross. His frightened disciples followed him on his God-given path.

Another insight about Jesus from our passage is his understanding of resurrection. After Martha met him on the road and chided him for not being there, he assured her that she would see her brother again. She replied from the accepted Jewish point of view of immortality, that she knew Lazarus would rise again on the last day (Job 14:10-11, see 1-13). But Martha thought of resurrection as something that would happen much later.

Prayer for the Day: *Life of the universe, when I ask you to do something on my timetable, remind me that my time is not your time. Help me live into your time. Amen.*

Week 12 — Tuesday
John 11:1-44

Jesus offered more than a comfort-less belief in a resurrection in some far off last day. He said, *I am the resurrection and the life. Those who believe in me, even though they die, will live, and everyone who lives and believes in me will never die* (John 11:25-26). Jesus says that he is where death ends and life begins. Everlasting life begins now and in him.

In faith, you have everlasting life now—RIGHT NOW—immediately!!! What a comfort to hold onto. When you are living in those crucifying events of your life—divorce in your family, illnesses of spouses, children, or friends, difficult people in your life, pandemics, political unrest, war, death, fear....Jesus offers you life *now*, leads you out of the tombs you find yourself in, sends you people to help you loosen the bindings of death that you are trapped in. Gail O'Day reminds that "through our faith in Jesus, death loses its power and gains new power. The victory over death that resurrection represents is available in the present moment in the person of Jesus, not simply in some distant future" (Gail R. O'Day, *Women's Bible Commentary, John*, 298).

There is a quote which goes something like this, "What would you do if you knew you could not fail?" The resurrection, as Jesus showed, lets you know that you cannot fail. You have abundant life *now* and you will continue to have abundant life. When you are tempted to say, "Oh sure, that's easy for you to say. You do not know my life. My life is not abundant," you are not living into your resurrection faith. Even though there may be much evidence to the contrary, you can claim, if you only choose to do so, the abundance you have.

Prayer for the Day: *God of abundance, help me claim the overflowing blessings I already have. Amen.*

John 11:1-44

Week 12
Wednesday

Poverty workers hear people say, "Thank God, I'm still here. I thank God for people who help me." What a faith, demonstrating deep belief that Jesus is their resurrection and life.

Similarly, Martha responded through her confession of faith. *Yes, Lord, I believe that you are the Messiah, the Son of God, the one coming into the world* (John 11:27). Mary knelt and cried, *Lord, if you had been here, my brother would not have died* (John 11.32). The roots of the Greek word used indicate that Jesus's distress was so deep that his body trembled. Maybe the pain was so great that an involuntary groan came from his heart (E.V. Rieu as mentioned in *Barclay, John*, Vol 2, p. 97).

This kind of pain was unbelievable to the cultural understanding of God in the first century. Greeks believed the primary characteristic of God was *apatheia*, a total inability to feel any emotion at all. They believed in an isolated, passionless, and compassion-less God. The Son of God weeping, shaking, and groaning from his heart was almost beyond belief.

Remember this picture of Jesus convulsed in pain and crying for people he loves. Jesus cries that way for you, as well.

Jesus is willing to go where others will not. He gets involved with gross situations. He will not shrink from stink and horror. Lazarus had been in the tomb for four days. It was not going to be a pleasant sight or smell, and Jesus ordered the stone removed.

There are situations in your life, family, church, community that stink. You have times when life is bleak and dark. You may have thought at times that there is no way out; there is no hope or healing or forgiveness or joy. You, like Mary, know what the grave contains. And you don't want any part of it.

Because your Lord is willing to go into the stink, the bleakness, your despair, you can let go of the limits that you place on what is possible in order to embrace the limitless possibilities offered by Jesus. You can struggle to let go of the way death defines your life and claim the new life, the new possibilities of life in Jesus Christ.

In his willingness to be in the pain and stench, Jesus simply prays, *Father, I thank you for having heard me. I knew that you always hear me, but I have said this for the sake of the crowd standing here, so that they may believe that you sent me* (John 11:41-42). And then Jesus screams at Lazarus to come out.... AND HE DOES.

Prayer for the Day: *God of life, I want to fully embrace the life you are leading me in. Amen.*

Week 12
Thursday

John 11:1-44

For many years, a painting of the raising of Lazarus hung in the offices where I worked. It was a sixteenth century oil painting that was given to one of the employees. He chose to keep it in the office since the building was heat controlled and had a security system. The painting was huge, about four feet by six feet.

The painting was typical of the sixteenth century. The women all had bared bosoms. The artist obviously used the same model for all the women. Lazarus himself was a youth about 14-16 years of age. He stood in the hole of the grave up to his knees. On his head was a wreath of laurel leaves. He stood there in his birthday suit with a quizzical look on his face.

And this is why this painting is wrong. Lazarus did not come out of the grave looking like a fresh-faced youth. He came out bound by the grave cloths.

Jesus called Lazarus out of the grave. But who actually gave Lazarus freedom? Who actually unbound Lazarus? The people did. The community around Lazarus unbound him and let him go. Jesus called the dead person to life, but Jesus did not finally let him go. Jesus told the community to release the person.

Prayer for the Day: *Okay, God, you mean that I—and other people around me—am called to unbind people who are bound by all of society's ills. Whoa! Amen.*

John 11:1-44

**Week 12
Friday**

You worship a creator who works in God's own time. You worship a Christ who showed that resurrection living is about the here and now and not simply some distant future event. You worship a Spirit who feels deeply and groans with you. Your Lord and Savior, Jesus Christ, is willing to go into the awful parts of your life. And so, you are called to partner with this loving, amazing God. There are people in your midst who respond to Jesus's call to new life. They may leave jobs that crush their spirits, they may remove themselves from killing relationships, they may decide that they are giving up habits that are life destroying. When they do these things, they are coming forth from the things that are binding them. You have a part to play in their new lives as well. You can't sit back and say, "If things are not working out for them, they must not have a strong enough faith. They must be weak if they can't make the changes in their lives which everyone knows they should make." This passage points out that you may need to help unwrap their grave cloths. You may need to offer that encouraging word. You may need to simply sit with someone while he/she considers the next steps.

Jesus may give your friends or family a powerful glimpse of limitless possibilities, but they may need help with the unbinding. They may need your assistance in walking free and light. In the power of Christ's resurrection and life you can pray, listening for God's word which is essential. You, too, may need help with unbinding for a new life. You can ask for help from a community of faith as you struggle to unbind yourself from your limiting thoughts, ways of doing things, and beliefs.

Prayer for the Day: *God of freedom, help me be about unbinding… myself and others as they want my help. Amen.*

Week 12
Saturday

John 11:1-44

What would have happened to Lazarus if nobody had unbound him? His hands and feet were wrapped with cloths. His face was wrapped. He might not have been dead, but was he alive? Was he free? If there had been no one to unwrap him, he might as well have gone back into the grave.

There are all kinds of folks and situations who call for your action. Unbind them. Friends and family are bound with various kinds of distress. Unbind them. People are lonely. Unbind them. People have no hope. Unbind them. There is lack of vision. Unbind them.

Jesus showed that he acted in his own time. He showed us the wonders of resurrection living. He proved to us that he felt deeply and could be powerfully and painfully moved, and that he would enter situations where others may shrink back and be repulsed. And he asked the people around Lazarus and continues to ask you today, to unbind the grave cloths of people who are coming into new life.

Prayer for the Day: *Loving God, am I living the life which Christ is calling me to?*

Week 13
Luke 19:29-42

29 When he had come near Bethphage and Bethany, at the place called the Mount of Olives, he sent two of the disciples, 30 saying, 'Go into the village ahead of you, and as you enter it you will find tied there a colt that has never been ridden. Untie it and bring it here. 31 If anyone asks you, "Why are you untying it?" just say this: "The Lord needs it."' 32 So those who were sent departed and found it as he had told them. 33 As they were untying the colt, its owners asked them, 'Why are you untying the colt?' 34 They said, 'The Lord needs it.' 35 Then they brought it to Jesus; and after throwing their cloaks on the colt, they set Jesus on it. 36 As he rode along, people kept spreading their cloaks on the road. 37 As he was now approaching the path down from the Mount of Olives, the whole multitude of the disciples began to praise God joyfully with a loud voice for all the deeds of power that they had seen, 38 saying,

"Blessed is the king
   who comes in the name of the Lord!
Peace in heaven,
   and glory in the highest heaven!"

39 Some of the Pharisees in the crowd said to him, "Teacher, order your disciples to stop." 40 He answered, "I tell you, if these were silent, the stones would shout out."

41 As he came near and saw the city, he wept over it, 42 saying, "If you, even you, had only recognized on this day the things that make for peace! But now they are hidden from your eyes."

Week 13
Sunday

Luke 19:29-42

The gospels Matthew, Mark, Luke, and John all tell us the story of Jesus the Christ. They share the good news of God in Jesus. They teach about what God believes is important and what is not. They all have wonderful stories. But…it's like reading four different biographies of the same person with each author having different things to emphasize. And…and…they don't all tell the same things. For example, Matthew and Luke have the only narratives about Jesus's birth. But even they are different. Matthew tells the story from men's point of view: Zachariah and Joseph had the dreams and visions. Luke tells the story with Elizabeth and Mary being the lead characters. In Luke there are peasant shepherds, not the learned people, the Magi, found in Matthew.

Another example of the gospel differences is that only Luke tells the parable of the Good Samaritan and the Prodigal Son. Only John has the story of the woman caught in adultery and the washing of feet. Using the oldest found manuscripts of Mark, he does not even have resurrection sightings of Jesus.

Where the stories appear in more than one gospel, there is a tendency to smush them together into just one version. In doing that, what each of the writers wanted to convey may be missed.

Prayer for the Day: *God of truth, your message comes in many different ways. Help me to discern the truths you have for me. Amen.*

Luke 19:29-42 **Week 13 / Monday**

All four gospels tell the story of Jesus's entry into Jerusalem. Imagine now that you are on a game show, and you are quizzed with questions about the entry into Jerusalem. Your references are the gospels of Matthew, Mark and Luke since the story in John has only four verses. Begin!

Did Jesus begin the journey into Jerusalem from Bethphage and Mt. Zion?

Yes.

Did Jesus know the person who owned the colt?

Yes, in Luke. No, in the others.

Did the disciples put their garments on the colt?

Yes.

Did the people shout Hosanna?

Yes, in Matthew and Mark. No, in Luke.

Were the people followers of Jesus or people in the area?

"Crowds" in Matthew, "those" in Mark, disciples in Luke.

What did the people throw down on the street?

In Matthew, they threw down tree branches and garments. In Mark, they put down leafy branches *from the fields* and garments. In Luke, only garments.

Which is the *only* gospel to sing, "Peace in heaven and glory in the highest?"

Luke.

Consider all this so you can forget about what *is not* in the Luke version of the entry into Jerusalem and pay attention to what *is* there. There are no hosannas and no palm branches. There are disciples, not crowds.

Prayer for the Day: *God of the word, I want to hear what your word is saying, not what I think it's saying. Help me pay attention. Amen.*

Week 13   Luke 19:29-42
Tuesday

Luke's telling of the entry into Jerusalem is the third story in his Chapter 19. The first is about Zacchaeus, the story of a little man who, as a tax collector, was an agent of the Roman empire. Jesus met him, and Zacchaeus repented of all the cheating he had done. He said, Lord, I will give to the poor; and if I have defrauded anyone of anything, I will pay back four times as much (Luke 19:8).

Jesus was preparing to enter the very center of religious and political power and here he tells Zacchaeus, the man of the power machine, *Today salvation has come to the son of Abraham* (Luke 19:9).

After the next story, the parable of the pounds, often called the parable of the talents, we have the entry into Jerusalem.

Luke's version seems more somber than the stories in the other gospels. Jesus asked for a colt. Whether he had prearranged this or not is not known. However, by specifying a colt that had never been ridden before, he indicated a sacred purpose. In I Samuel (6:7), only cows that had never borne the yoke could pull the ark of the covenant which symbolized the dwelling of God. When the owners of the colt asked the disciples what they were doing, they replied, "The Lord needs it" and that seemed to be enough.

The disciples put their garments on the colt and set Jesus on it. Only disciples lined the road. They put their garments along the way and sang, *Blessed is the king who comes in the name of the Lord! Peace in heaven, and glory in the highest heaven!* (Luke 19:38).

This cheer: "*Blessed is the king who comes in the name of the Lord! Peace in heaven, and glory in the highest heaven!*" is one that means a lot since it is *here* in the gospel of Luke. Luke tells that when Jesus was born, the angels sang, "*Glory to God in the highest heaven, and on earth peace among those whom he favors.*" The angels called for peace on *earth*. This group of disciples calls for peace in *heaven*.

In the Jewish world, Jerusalem is the place where heaven and earth meet. If peace came in heaven, then, of course, it would come to earth because in Jerusalem, they came together. If peace came on earth in Jerusalem, then of course, it would come to heaven. If peace came to Jerusalem… If peace came to Jerusalem…If peace came to Jerusalem…how contemporary is that?

Prayer for the Day: *God of all the world, I pray for peace in my life, my family, my church, my community, my country, and my world. May it be so. Amen.*

Luke 19:29-42

Week 13
Wednesday

The Pharisees asked Jesus to tell his disciples to stop shouting these things, these blessings, for this king who comes in the name of the Lord; to stop calling for peace and glory in heaven. Who knows for sure why they wanted the people to stop their boisterous chants? Maybe it was fear for their own safety OR fear for Jesus's safety OR because they disagreed with his message. Who knows? Jesus replied, *I tell you, if these were silent, the stones would shout out* (Luke 19:40).

God's message is too powerful to be silenced. Even stones will sing. Truth must be told. It cannot be put down forever. The disciples who were raised in the lessons of the ancient prophets would have known what Jesus was referring to when he said, "The stones will cry out." The disciples would have remembered the prophet Habakkuk (2:9-11): *Alas for you who get evil gain for your houses, setting your nest on high to be safe from reach of harm! You have devised shame for your house by cutting off peoples; you have forfeited your life. The very stones will cry out from the wall, and the plaster will respond from the woodwork.* The disciples would have known that Jesus's statement was shorthand for Don't cut off people. Don't lock people out. Be just. Be in relationship with people who are not like you, who cannot live high on the hill. Be about peace.

Prayer for the Day: *Hope of the earth, sing, sing, sing, shout, shout, shout. Do NOT be silenced. Amen.*

Week 13
Thursday

Luke 19:29-42

Even during the pandemic's social isolation, when people had to be locked out, people had to find ways not to lock out of their lives their friends, family, and even people they did not know. Folks reached out where they could. Many chose not to hoard in order to not cause others to suffer even while taking care of one's own. People acknowledged others' pain and fear. Many held people up in prayer to God. People did not shut down their minds, their hearts, their souls. There were many instances of "stones shouting out!"

The entry story does not end here in the gospel of Luke.

Jesus came into the city, knowing that he was riding into the center of religious and political power, knowing that his message of "passion and compassion completely and irresistibly undermines the world of competence and competition" (Walter Brueggemann, *The Prophetic Imagination*, quoted in *A Guide to Prayer for Ministers and Other Servants*, p. 109). Jesus came into the city knowing that he was on a path of facing the most horrific suffering that a human being could suffer, knowing that his body would break because that's what human bodies do. Even knowing all that, Jesus kept going.

Prayer for the Day: *Jesus, you kept going even in the face of what you knew was coming. Help me have just a bit of that courage and commitment. Amen.*

Luke 19:29-42

**Week 13
Friday**

And Jesus wept. He cried over Jerusalem. He must have loved everything in the city with a love that you nor I cannot even begin to understand. The religious and political leaders needed to silence him. Ann Weems says in her poem, *Fair is Fair:* "The ones in charge of politics wanted to hold onto their crowns/ and the ones in charge of religion wanted to hold onto the keys to the church" (Ann Weems, *Journey to Jerusalem*, "Fair is Fair." P 78). Some of the crowds there for Passover wanted the spectacle of his death. And still he cried. He mourned and moaned, *If you, even you, had only recognized on this day the things that make for peace*! (Luke 19:42).

Can you hear Jesus crying for you? As you face a world with an unknown future, do you experience Jesus's tears? Do you hear Jesus's word for you and then work for peace in community in all its forms? Do you seek ways to facilitate wholeness in your home, your community, your country, and your world? Do you throw up your hands and say, "What can I do?" Do you close your eyes and refuse to see? Do you blame others and thus feel you have absolved yourself of any responsibility? Do you want a world where peace truly does reign, where life is abundant? Do you hear Jesus weeping?

Prayer for the Day: *Oh God of tears, I have no words. Amen.*

Week 13
Saturday

Luke 19:29-42

Coming into Jerusalem, Jesus had to have been...what...? Resigned? Committed? Passionate? It is hard to imagine this as a joyful entrance for Jesus. He knew that his time was drawing to an end. He was just too dangerous to the political power because *his* sense of kingship threatened the kings and vassals of the land. He threatened the religious leadership because he began to replace the codes of purity with codes of compassion. He was a prophet, and the religious leaders certainly did not like his message. Even if the people along the road did not know what was ahead, Jesus did. He knew that Rome killed by crucifixion those who challenged political rule. Jesus knew that calling him Lord threatened the Caesar who was also called Lord, the Son of God. Jesus had been talking about his coming death with his closest disciples for quite a while.

Jesus also knew that he was not the kind of Messiah that many wanted him to be. He did not meet their expectations. He came to offer abundant life. He taught about loving your enemy. He was not a military conqueror. His way was more powerful...the way of justice, mercy, love, grace, peace, and compassion. Yes, at the end of this chapter 19 in Luke, Jesus entered the Temple and drove out those who were selling things there. But no one was killed. He did not have troops with him. He focused on the injustice of the system and the cheapening of God's way for all people to live.

Jesus taught to follow his way...to embrace his truth with your mind, heart, soul, and strength. Will you be silent about what God is doing in your life as an individual and even as part of a community of faith? Will you wait until the stones cry out? Or will you sing of the love, grace, strength, compassion, justice, and truth that you find on occasion because you follow Jesus the Christ? Will you work for peace in all of its manifestations in your life? Will you be a disciple who follows Jesus all the way, or will you be a person who just likes good street theater and then return home to your little, ordinary life that shrivels outside of the Light of Jesus's love?

Prayer for the Day: *O Jesus, my Lord, where am I in this story? Amen.*

Week 14
Mark 16:1-8

When the sabbath was over, Mary Magdalene, and Mary the mother of James, and Salome bought spices, so that they might go and anoint him. 2 And very early on the first day of the week, when the sun had risen, they went to the tomb. 3 They had been saying to one another, 'Who will roll away the stone for us from the entrance to the tomb?' 4 When they looked up, they saw that the stone, which was very large, had already been rolled back.

5 As they entered the tomb, they saw a young man, dressed in a white robe, sitting on the right side; and they were alarmed. 6 But he said to them, 'Do not be alarmed; you are looking for Jesus of Nazareth, who was crucified. He has been raised; he is not here. Look, there is the place they laid him. 7 But go, tell his disciples and Peter that he is going ahead of you to Galilee; there you will see him, just as he told you.' 8 So they went out and fled from the tomb, for terror and amazement had seized them; and they said nothing to anyone, for they were afraid.

Week 14
Sunday

Mark 16:1-8

The dates of Holy Week, the days that honor and remember the entry of Jesus into Jerusalem, the last Passover supper, the trial of Jesus, his crucifixion, and the resurrection depend on the timing of the spring equinox and full moons. Whether this particular reading falls exactly on Holy Week this year is immaterial. The message is powerful whether read and studied in April or October.

The description of the resurrection in the gospel of Mark is one that some people experience as the most real. The verses of today's passage are actually the last words of the gospel. The other verses, chapter 16:8b-20, were added at a much later time. Scholars suppose that scribes somewhere believed that the last portion of the scroll had been ripped off and so they decided to recreate what they believed must have been Mark's intentions. They wanted the Gospel of Mark also to have a resurrection sighting.

But the fact is, in the most ancient manuscripts of Mark, there is no account of anyone seeing the risen Christ. This seems to capture the wonderment, questions, and faith that people confront and live with today. You are expected to believe in the risen Christ and yet, you have not seen him. Add to that, for many people, the resurrection sightings by Jesus's followers are stories that sound more like science fiction rather than aids to salvation, grace, and understanding. When Mary Magdalene sees Jesus and mistakes him for the gardener as depicted in the Gospel of John, some people see, in their mind's eye, Jesus looking as if he is caught betwixt and between the transporter in *Star Trek*. ("Beam me up, Scottie.") John also has Jesus passing through closed doors which sounds rather ghostly and more like special effects and less like encounter with the holy God. You can see why the Mark version of resurrection has power for today.

In Mark, there are no special visitations. The three women are simply told by the man in white that Jesus is not there, that he has been raised, and that he will meet them in Galilee. The man in white is confirming Jesus's promise that he made in Mark 14:28: *But after I am raised up, I will go before you to Galilee.* And the women's reaction to the man's announcement? *They fled...for terror and amazement had seized them, and they said nothing to anyone for they were afraid* (Mark 16:8).

Prayer for the Day: *Jesus, prepare my heart for considering what happened to you during the week called Holy so I can embrace you more fully. Amen.*

Mark 16:1-8

Week 14
Monday

The women left the tomb with terror and amazement. These are real emotions. If you were reared in the church, you may have heard the resurrection accounts so often that you have lost the wonder. You know you are to believe the scriptural accounts and that's all you need. With your familiarity with the story, you have missed something.

Ann Weems says that "the people who heard Jesus were repeatedly amazed." She asks, "Are we today so sophisticated that we are immune to amazement? Can we know that he was crucified…nailed upon the tree, and go about our business of preparing Easter dinner?" Weems asks: "Can we know that he arose from the dead and walked the earth and ate and spoke with his followers and sit unamazed in our chairs as though we cannot hear the WORD OF GOD?…[T]he amazing thing is our lack of amazement in the face of [God's] amazing Amen" (Amazed, *Journey to Jerusalem*, p. 83).

You know that some people have trouble knowing what to do with the story of the resurrection. People wonder, "Do you really believe all that stuff?" Your answer may be "Yes…and…no." Saying "no" acknowledges that talking about the resurrection sounds like sheer foolishness. Even the scriptures point out this fact. Acts 17:32a says, *When they heard of the resurrection of the dead, some scoffed.*

On Easter morning preachers must share with you a story that is unbelievable at best in this world of facts and logic and tell you that this is the most important story that you will ever hear. Terror and amazement.

Prayer for the Day: *God of Easter, help the story become one of terror and amazement for me rather than one I yawn through. Amen.*

Week 14
Tuesday

Mark 16:1-8

Three women—Mary Magdalene, Mary (James's mother), and Salome—went to the tomb to anoint the body since they couldn't do it the day before...on the Sabbath. As they walked along, they wondered aloud how they would get the stone out of the way. Lo and behold, it was already moved. They timidly went in, hoping to find the body but maybe wondering if it had been stolen since it appeared someone had gotten there before them. They found, not the body, but a man in white who gave them instructions to go to Galilee to meet the risen Christ. Likely they screamed before they ran out in terror.

The road the women had been walking was one where a man of compassion and wisdom and grace and guts had been. They had shared his dreams and hopes and eagerly sought the God he showed them. They had purpose and meaning in their lives which was reflected back to them in his eyes. And now those eyes were fixed and glazed over from death. All they could do was to care for his body which he said would be broken for them. What good did that do for them? How would his broken body help them? They wanted him with them. They wanted him to talk to them. They wanted him to listen to them. They did not want him tortured for their sake. They had dreams and plans.

And now here was the guy in white. The white indicated that this was a messenger from God. Notice that this person did not have angel wings and flowing robes and a sweet face and flowing hair curling on his shoulders. It is a guy in white. He told them where they needed to go. He gave them their next instructions.

The women heard. But the last three days had been full of unbelievable happenings. Their emotions and minds were raw from the tragedy. They did not know what to do. So they ran and kept their mouths shut.

Prayer for the Day: *God of power and splendor, how many times do I keep silent after I have encountered your message? Amen.*

Mark 16:1-8

Week 14
Wednesday

"Do you really believe all this stuff?" Why can your answer be yes?

Your answer can be "yes" because of what happened after the crucifixion. Something happened to change the followers of Jesus from a small band of scared people who ran away into a group of fearless proponents of faith in God as Jesus had demonstrated that faith.

Your answer can be yes because of changes you see in your life and in the lives of other people. There's an old story of a man who told his minister that he hadn't understood a sermon in that church for 25 years but that he would never leave the church. The puzzled minister asked for more insight. The man said that "every Monday night, he and few others had been taking the church van to a nearby prison for youthful offenders. 'Sometimes we play ball with the kids,' he said. 'Sometimes we have a little Bible study. Most of all we just get to know them as people. I started doing this because Christians are supposed to do things like that, but now I find that I get a lot from it myself.' He paused for a moment, then continued, 'I have found that you can't prove the promises of God in advance, but if you live them, you find they're true, every one.'" (*The Senses of Preaching*, Tom Long, p. 47)

You can say, "Yes, I believe in the resurrection because there was a man who left his job to follow the call of God upon his heart and took a 73% salary cut to work with unhoused people." Those who knew him said he changed the hearts and minds of people wherever he went because he spoke with passion about the inequities and injustices he saw in the lives and situations of the people with whom he worked. His salary eventually improved, and his life had meaning for many people. He believed in the resurrection because his faith grew deeper and truer than it ever was before.

You believe in the resurrection because the resurrection says that tomorrow is not just like today. Tomorrow can be radically different. He was dead. Now he is alive. How much more different can you get?

Prayer for the Day: *God who conquered death, help me to claim all the ways in my life that I know the resurrection is true. Amen.*

Week 14
Thursday
Mark 16:1-8

If you don't believe in the wonder of the resurrection, then you have no concept that life can be different. You don't understand that no matter how lousy the past has been or how uncomfortable the present, that in God, all things can become new. Can you prove it? No. Do you sometimes want to run away and say nothing? Of course. People look at you as if you're nuts when you live with hope and belief that what you have now is not all there is. Cynicism and pessimism have difficulty holding up long term in the face of resurrection.

Does that mean that life is always easy? That life is always pleasant? That with a life of faith there is no suffering? No, of course not. Life sometimes is painful. There are times when you don't know where to turn. There are times when all you can do is breathe because you don't have to think about it and even breathing may be hard. There are dark times in everyone's life. Some nights you wonder if the sun will ever come up.

Prayer for the Day: *Awesome God, take my life…the dark and the light…and help me know that it is all in your love and grace. Amen.*

Mark 16:1-8

Week 14
Friday

Does believing in the resurrection mean that you don't plan and prepare for the future? Of course not. You were given a brain and God expects you to use your intelligence to the utmost. You are not to suspend good sense when you are a faithful person. But all your plans may not turn out as you thought. The political and religious rulers in Jesus's day planned to deal with the "Jesus problem" by killing him. And you know how their plans turned out.

Does believing in the resurrection mean that you always get a happy ending? No. You do not get happily ever after. In the end, everyone dies. And some people exist in what seems to be living deaths and children die before their time and young adults experience accidents or war that alter their lives forever and old people lose their personalities. You don't always get a happy ending. But you know that you are not living alone. You know that God is there with you. You know that you can find moments of resurrection—faith even in the darkest depths of despair.

Does believing in the resurrection mean that sometimes you step out into, as Charles Hopper calls it, "grace unknown"? ("Incredulous," Alive Now! M/A '91). Yes. When you are catapulted from grief into terror and disbelief as the women at the tomb were, you may walk blindly and hesitantly, not knowing where the path will lead you...yet knowing that you must leave where you are and go to other places—either literally or figuratively. You may have to leave your long-held understandings about family, friends, faith, or future. You may have to look beyond life as you always knew it. You may have to return to where you started just as the disciples were instructed to return to Galilee. Probably Galilee looked vastly different to them when they returned than when they left.

Prayer for the Day: *Lord Jesus, I want to believe. Help my unbelief. Amen.*

Week 14   **Mark 16:1-8**
Saturday

Lois Blanchard Eades says it well: ("Easter Says," *Alive Now!* M/A '87)

> Easter says that day will follow night.
> However dark and merciless that gloom,
> The morning comes, the eastern skies are bright,
> And daylight floods each corner of my room.
>
> Easter says that spring will follow winter,
> That chill and bareness last for just a while.
> The iris blooms; the life-flow soon will enter
> The maple trees; the greening world will smile.
>
> Easter says that joy will follow sorrow;
> For grief walks with us sometimes as we go.
> But tears are for the night; joy comes tomorrow
> And seems the brighter for the pain we know.
>
> Easter says that life will follow death.
> Jesus broke the grip of death! He is alive!
> And certain as the cemetery path,
> Because Jesus lives, my spirit shall survive!

Do you really believe all this stuff? The world is looking, searching for a sign beyond what the New Testament tells. Maybe the only thing you can see is the evidence in lives that are changed or in lives that seem to shout Hallelujah! Maybe that's all you have. Maybe that's all you need. May you move from terror to a resounding "Yes!" Hallelujah! Christ is risen. He is risen indeed.

Prayer for the Day: *Hallelujah God, praise you, praise you. Thanks be to you, my God. Amen.*

Week 15
Luke 24:13-35

13 Now on that same day two of them were going to a village called Emmaus, about seven miles from Jerusalem, 14 and talking with each other about all these things that had happened. 15 While they were talking and discussing, Jesus himself came near and went with them, 16 but their eyes were kept from recognizing him. 17 And he said to them, 'What are you discussing with each other while you walk along?' They stood still, looking sad. 18 Then one of them, whose name was Cleopas, answered him, 'Are you the only stranger in Jerusalem who does not know the things that have taken place there in these days?' 19 He asked them, 'What things?' They replied, 'The things about Jesus of Nazareth, who was a prophet mighty in deed and word before God and all the people, 20 and how our chief priests and leaders handed him over to be condemned to death and crucified him. 21 But we had hoped that he was the one to redeem Israel. Yes, and besides all this, it is now the third day since these things took place. 22 Moreover, some women of our group astounded us. They were at the tomb early this morning, 23 and when they did not find his body there, they came back and told us that they had indeed seen a vision of angels who said that he was alive. 24 Some of those who were with us went to the tomb and found it just as the women had said; but they did not see him.' 25 Then he said to them, 'Oh, how foolish you are, and how slow of heart to believe all that the prophets have declared! 26 Was it not necessary that the Messiah should suffer these things and then enter into his glory?' 27 Then beginning with Moses and all the prophets, he interpreted to them the things about himself in all the scriptures.

28 As they came near the village to which they were going, he walked ahead as if he were going on. 29 But they urged him strongly, saying, 'Stay with us, because it is almost evening and the day is now nearly over.' So he went in to stay with them. 30 When he was at the table with them, he took bread, blessed and broke it, and gave it to them. 31 Then their eyes were opened, and they recognized him; and he vanished from their sight. 32 They said to each other, 'Were not our hearts burning within us while he was talking to us on the road, while he was opening the scriptures to us?' 33 That same hour they got up and returned to Jerusalem; and they found the eleven and their companions gathered together. 34 They were saying, 'The Lord has risen indeed, and he has appeared to Simon!' 35 Then they told what had happened on the road, and how he had been made known to them in the breaking of the bread.

Week 15
Sunday

Luke 24:13-35

You may travel for pleasure. You may visit out-of-town family and friends. Possibly you go to the beach or the mountains for vacations. Do you travel for mission trips or take the trip of a lifetime to another place on the globe? You look forward to these kinds of trips. You are going *to* something, not *from* something.

Cleopas and his traveling companion did not feel this same kind of eagerness on their trip back home. They were traveling *from* something—something that was horribly tragic for them. The man they had been following and on whom they had pinned their hopes for themselves and their homeland had been strung up on a cross on Friday. By Sunday, they knew there was nothing else to do except…go home.

The road is dusty. They are shuffling their feet; their shoulders are drooping; and their heads are hanging almost to their chests. They are speaking softly about what had just happened. They are despondent. They are full of resignation, dismay, and betrayal. They probably feel that sinking, bottomless dread in the pit of their stomachs. They feel almost dead inside.

They are puzzled. Even their own religious leaders would not recognize Jesus as the Messiah spoken of by the prophets. They had handed him over to the Roman political authorities who crucified their beloved Jesus. The wonderful road trip they had begun with Jesus had turned into a walk of despair.

You may know what that journey felt like. You may have experienced a similar kind of dejection. Maybe the death of a spouse or friend meant that life lost its joy. A dearly loved precious son or daughter who carried your aspirations for their lives may have taken a wayward step and you felt that you were eating dust from the road. Maybe you had a beautiful dream for a business or home or career or the church and the dream crumbled before your eyes. Or when you recited your marriage vows, you had hope of happiness, trust, and nurture. But when troubles followed, you experienced the walk of questioning and despondency. Maybe as we get older, the life we anticipated is not the life we are experiencing.

Walking *from* Jerusalem, the seat of the government and the Temple, the seat of power, where things were happening, *to* Emmaus, a small town in the backwaters, had to have been a hard and dreary journey.

Prayer for the Day: *Holy Jesus, there are times when despondency almost overwhelms me. Help me know you are with me in those times. Amen.*

Luke 24:13-35

**Week 15
Monday**

As Cleopas and his companion were walking, someone joined the two guys. The scripture says that *their eyes were kept from recognizing him* (Luke 24:18). William Barclay suggests that Emmaus might have been west of Jerusalem and that at sunset, with the sun in their eyes…they could not recognize Jesus (William Barclay, *The Gospel of Luke, Revised Edition*, p. 294). That's plausible. You may have been in a parking lot somewhere and someone called your name. You could not recognize the person because they were standing where you had to look directly into the sun. Maybe Luke intended to portray the fact that the two guys were just dull because of some holy action of God or because of the shock of recent events. Or maybe they were where you often are—so engrossed in your own stuff, your own problems, your own concerns, that you simply miss those times of divine intervention, those holy coincidences. God's intention is right in front of you. You miss it because you are looking behind yourself or simply looking elsewhere.

For whatever reason, the two men did not recognize their traveling companion. They did not recognize Jesus by sight or by his voice. Jesus asked, "What are you guys talking about while you walk along?"

They stood still, looking sad. Jesus's question was so far out of their reality that they could not even keep walking. They simply stopped on the road…in sadness and amazement. *Are you the only stranger in Jerusalem who does not know the things that have taken place there in these days?* (Luke 24:18).

Prayer for the Day: *Companion God, help me be aware that you are with me today. Amen.*

Week 15
Tuesday

Luke 24:13-35

For Christians looking at the events of 2,000 years ago, it is easy to believe that everyone in Jerusalem must have known about Jesus and about the crucifixion. But when you look at historical and archaeological descriptions of that time, you can acknowledge that probably a lot of people in Jerusalem simply did not know. During Passover, the population in Jerusalem could have risen to half a million people. Crucifixions were rather routine. If people had heard anything at all about Jesus, it probably had more to do with his being a troublemaker than knowing him as the Savior of the World. Remember... Jesus dealt mostly with working people and some religious leaders but certainly not the Romans who were there as government officials. Also, the religious rulers held their judgment court against Jesus in the dark of night. The crucifixion happened within hours. And after the crucifixion, burial was immediate. And all this happened during the feast of Passover when families were gathered to remember and celebrate.

All this is to say that Cleopas and the other person may have felt that everyone should have known what was going on because indeed *their* whole world had caved in. But believing that everyone in Jerusalem knew, in the absence of cable news and social media, showed their extreme anxiety, grief, and bewilderment.

Their next words are filled with sadness: *[We thought everyone knew] the things about Jesus of Nazareth, who was a prophet mighty in deed and word before God and all the people, and how* our *chief priests and leaders handed him over to be condemned to death and crucified him. But we had hoped that he was the one to redeem Israel* (Luke 24:19-21). Can you hear the pain of unrealized dreams and expectations? "But we had hoped that he was the one to redeem Israel."

Prayer for the Day: *O Holy One, there are times when my hopes and dreams are smashed. Help me know that there is still hope even so. Amen.*

Luke 24:13-35 **Week 15 / Wednesday**

Jesus began to teach them their own history. The two guys either did not remember their own scriptures or they misunderstood them. The prophets had foretold that the Messiah would suffer. Psalm 22:1: *My God, my God, why have you forsaken me? Why are you so far from helping me, from the words of my groaning?* Isaiah 53:3: *He was despised and rejected by others; a man of suffering and acquainted with infirmity; as one from whom others hide their faces. He was despised, and we held him of no account.* Zechariah 13:7 *"Awake, O sword, against the shepherd, against the man who is my associate," says the Lord of hosts. "Strike the shepherd, that the sheep may be scattered."*

Jesus illuminates the scriptures once again for Cleopas and the other traveler. He began with Moses. His words may have been very much like those that Paul recorded in II Corinthians 3:12-16: *Since then we have such a hope, we act with great boldness, not like Moses, who put a veil over his face to keep the people of Israel from gazing at the end of the glory. ... Indeed, to this very day whenever Moses is read, a veil lies over their minds; but when one turns to the Lord, the veil is removed.*

But recognition is not yet to be. Isn't that often the way life is? You are hurting and someone comes to you and talks to you and tells you truths. But the talking does not necessarily open your eyes or your heart. Have you ever suffered a grief and a person who cares for you comes and recites scripture passages or gives you comforting phrases or quick words? The words are not necessarily where you find comfort at that moment. Maybe later, but not at first. The words may speak to your brain, but they do not speak to your heart. The words when you are in despair may touch you only on a surface level but not in the depths where you are really hurting. Even Jesus did not bring recognition of the good news with his *words* to the two guys.

Prayer for the Day: *Merciful God, open my eyes, my ears, and my heart so I may hear your words to me in whatever way they come. Amen.*

Week 15
Thursday

Luke 24:13-35

After the three arrived in Emmaus, Jesus intended to continue on his way. He did not choose to intrude further on the companionship of the two people on their sad trip from Jerusalem. But *they* urged him to stay with them because the day was almost over, and Shalom Inns were not part of the landscape. So, Jesus stopped over with them.

And there the story takes a holy turn. Jesus becomes the host when he breaks the bread. In many ways, the story takes on the sense of a ritual of the early church. The word had been preached and now the sacrament was being celebrated. The verbs of the meal are indeed very sacramental: Jesus took the bread, blessed the bread, broke the bread, and gave it to them. Sounds just like the words of Institution: "On the night of his betrayal, Jesus took the bread, and after giving thanks, he broke it and said, 'This is my body which is broken for you. Do this in remembrance of me.'"

And their eyes were opened…not by the words he said but by the actions he took. What joy there must have been in that moment. Their distress and dismay suddenly became joy and hope. With Christ's presence at the table and with sharing of a meal, then every moment is an Emmaus moment—a moving from despair, from no hope to joyful, abounding hope.

Prayer for the Day: *Lord Jesus, be the host at my table today. Amen.*

Luke 24:13-35 **Week 15 / Friday**

Because of Jesus's ordinary actions, the two guys knew that Christ was in their midst. Actions .... not words. When you show the people in your community that you care about them, they experience the love of Christ. When you help provide homes or food for people who have none, you demonstrate the holiness of life. When you *act out* your repentance for people whom you have hurt rather than simply saying, "I'm sorry," the other person experiences the freedom of renewed relationship. When you love wholeheartedly people who are hurting, they know the love of God. Your words cannot convey what your actions do.

When you tell other people that you have changed your life, they cannot believe you until you show by your actions that you have changed. When you profess faith in God, if your actions don't demonstrate that faith, then your message is seen as false. When you say sweet words and use mean actions, your witness to the holy is desecrated. Your actions and your words must go together. The trite phrase "Put your money where your mouth is" highlights this understanding.

And once Cleopas and the other guy knew in whose presence they were eating, they understood. They understood in the blessing, breaking, and giving of the bread. They also understood in remembering. They remembered now the words that they had not really heard or understood before. The teachings of Jesus on the road suddenly made sense to them. They remembered how their bodies responded to the teachings…things they had dismissed before or not paid attention to. They said, *Were not our hearts burning within us while he was talking to us on the road, while he was opening the scripture to us?* (Luke 24:32). Now they got it. They also understood that they now had action to do. They needed to return to Jerusalem and share the good news that Jesus was alive. He had risen from the dead.

Prayer for the Day: *Lover of my soul, let my actions speak louder than my words today. Amen.*

Week 15
Saturday

Luke 24:13-35

The journey *from* Jerusalem had been solemn and sad. The journey back to Jerusalem was enthusiastic and full of joy. In Jerusalem the followers of Jesus were full of amazement and wonder. Peter, too, had seen the risen Christ. And now two guys whom no one had heard of before had broken bread with him.

The teachings of Jesus now took on new significance:

Love one another.

You are the light of the world…Let your light shine before others, so that they may see your good works and give glory to your Father in heaven.

Do not store up for yourselves treasures on earth…

Suffer the little children to come unto me…

Lights, camera, action!

What a story of hope…from despair and bewilderment to joy and hope and action. Even in the bewildering times, life makes sense in the presence of the Christ who suffered, died, and conquered death. It is only through the eyes of Jesus that life makes sense sometimes.

Actions—hope, despair turned into joy—Jesus Christ is Lord. Christ is with us. Hallelujah!

Prayer for the Day: *Holy Teacher, help me hear your lessons for me today and take them to heart…and action. Amen.*

Week 16
John 20:19-29

19 When it was evening on that day, the first day of the week, and the doors of the house where the disciples had met were locked for fear of the Jews, Jesus came and stood among them and said, 'Peace be with you.' 20 After he said this, he showed them his hands and his side. Then the disciples rejoiced when they saw the Lord. 21 Jesus said to them again, 'Peace be with you. As the Father has sent me, so I send you.' 22 When he had said this, he breathed on them and said to them, 'Receive the Holy Spirit. 23 If you forgive the sins of any, they are forgiven them; if you retain the sins of any, they are retained.' 24 But Thomas (who was called the Twin), one of the twelve, was not with them when Jesus came. 25 So the other disciples told him, 'We have seen the Lord.' But he said to them, 'Unless I see the mark of the nails in his hands, and put my finger in the mark of the nails and my hand in his side, I will not believe.'

26 A week later his disciples were again in the house, and Thomas was with them. Although the doors were shut, Jesus came and stood among them and said, 'Peace be with you.' 27 Then he said to Thomas, 'Put your finger here and see my hands. Reach out your hand and put it in my side. Do not doubt but believe.' 28 Thomas answered him, 'My Lord and my God!' 29 Jesus said to him, 'Have you believed because you have seen me? Blessed are those who have not seen and yet have come to believe.'

Week 16   **John 20:19-29**
Sunday

Good ole Thomas, doubting Thomas. He has gotten a pretty bad reputation throughout the years. He is often used as an example of how not to have faith. He is often not held in high esteem as a disciple. He wanted to do that horrid thing of putting his finger in the mark of the nails in Jesus's hand. This *is* the same Thomas who encouraged the disciples to accompany Jesus went he went to Lazarus's tomb with the challenge: *Let us also go, that we may die with him* (John 11:16). Later on, when Jesus made the comment...*I go to prepare a place for you...And you know the way to the place where I am going,* (John 14:2-4). Thomas is the one who retorted, *Lord, we do not know where you are going. How can we know the way?* (John 14:5). Jesus answered Thomas's request for directions with, *I am the way, and the truth, and the life* (John 14:6).

Thomas is one of those people who tend to say the things that others would like to say...except they don't for fear of sounding stupid. "Lord, we don't know the way." "Let's go die with him." Thomas can make the others seem smart.

Prayer for the Day: *Jesus of the Way, sometimes I do not know the way you are leading me. Please help me find it. Amen.*

John 20:19-29

Week 16
Monday

For some reason the gospel writer of John decided that Thomas was an important part of the Jesus story. In fact, if you go along with the best scholarship that believes that the 21st chapter of John is a much later addition to the book, then Thomas is the last person Jesus dialogues within that particular gospel. To make Thomas even more interesting, his exclamation, *My Lord and my God*, of verse 28 completes the John narrative which began with "In the beginning was the Word and the Word was *with* God and the Word was God (John 1:1). "My Lord and my God!" This affirmation could be a very early creed of the church... "My Lord and my God."

If that is the case, then Thomas joins the ranks of such notables as Peter who said: *You are the Messiah, the Son of the Living God* (Matthew 16:16) or of Martha: *Yes, Lord, I believe that you are the Messiah, the Son of God, the one coming into the world* (John 11:27).

So, the problem with Thomas is *not* that he did not have faith. He simply required specific indications to uphold his faith. You might ask, "What's so bad about that?"

Prayer for the Day: *God of Creation, thank you for the gift of this day. May I use it to your glory. Amen.*

Week 16
Tuesday

John 20:19-29

We people of the western hemisphere are thoroughly immersed in the scientific method. We require proof for lots and lots of things. We want spouses to prove they love us by doing special things for us. We do not simply take their word for it. We want demonstrated acts of love. If we hear of a community problem, we want proof that it is a problem.

We love numbers. They often prove whatever it is we are trying to justify. If 51% of people want something, then that side wins. They've proven themselves for victory. If 9 out of 10 people believe something, then that must make it so. Just look at the trouble Galileo had when he demonstrated that the earth revolved around the sun rather than the other way around. The poll numbers just did not support his thesis. If only 1 out of 5 children in America goes to bed hungry, then we can make the case that most children in America are well cared for. We can forget about the other 20% percent. We can prove we are justified in the many ways that we isolate ourselves and refuse to love our neighbor as ourselves. We can prove our ways of life are important. We like proof.

Prayer for the Day: *God of mystery, I confess I like documentation for truths, but I suspect that is not the way you work. Help me embrace a bit more mystery in my life. Amen.*

John 20:19-29   **Week 16 / Wednesday**

Thomas just might become your favorite disciple. What is so wrong with asking for proof? After the gruesome episodes that had just happened with the crucifixion and all, you might have wanted tangible proof as well. Honestly, it does kind of stretch the sense of reality to believe that a dead Jesus was up and about and visiting around! You understand Thomas' request to see for himself. What a rational, reasonable request.

Jesus's response to Thomas' declaration of faith sounds almost as a put down. *Blessed are those who have not yet seen and yet have come to believe* (John 20:29). It comes across that Thomas might not be blessed because he required visible and tangible proof.

If that is what you take away from this passage, then you have missed the point.

Prayer for the Day: *God, have I missed the point? Be with me today as I think about this. Amen.*

Week 16
Thursday

John 20:19-29

After Mary Magdalene came to the tomb and saw that the stone had been removed, she ran back to the disciples and reported what she had seen. Peter and the "one whom Jesus loved" ran back to the tomb. *The one whom Jesus loved...went in, and he saw and believed* (John 20:8). He had faith which needed no proof. That deep knowing came as easily for him as looking in an empty tomb. There are people for whom faith has been that remarkable. They were unbelievers and then something happened—something that they could not explain. They moved from unbeliever to believer in the blink of an eye. The beloved disciple was indeed already a follower of Jesus but his experience at the tomb brought him to the kind of belief to which he committed the rest of his life—without the physical presence of Jesus.

When Mary Magdalene returned, she stood weeping outside the tomb. The one she assumed was the gardener spoke to her. She did not recognize either his voice or his face until he spoke her name, "Mary." She exclaimed, *Rabbouni/Teacher* (John 20:16). She believes in response to a word, her name. Some people need inspiring Bible studies or ringing sermons or powerful spoken prayers to grow into faith. They hear God's word in the voice of a friend or the lyrics of a song. Their spirits are moved to places as yet undiscovered until they hear the word from God from whomever speaks it.

Jesus next appears to the gathered disciples. The disciples saw his hands and his side. They received his blessing of "Peace be with you." And they rejoiced. They saw and believed. People come to faith by witnessing the actions of committed people of faith. They see the courage of someone like Martin Luther King Jr. who lived his life for the way of Jesus that he discovered in the scriptures. They see the commitment of a Mother Teresa who poured out love and compassion on the lowest people in her society. They witness the forgiveness evident in most of the families and members of the Mother Emanuel AME Church in Charleston. They see the way a family raises their children to be responsible, community-minded, caring adults. An important youth leader or a committed and faithful teacher might have inspired you to be where you are today in your faith journey.

And then we have Thomas who came later to his declaration of faith through the possibility of touch and tangible proof.

Prayer for the Day: *God of faith, help me see witness of you in the lives of people around me. Amen.*

John 20:19-29

**Week 16
Friday**

In the twentieth chapter of John, there is someone who believed simply without proof. Another person in the same chapter believed from hearing a word. Yet another believed from seeing. Yet another required tangible proof.

None of these faith experiences is any better or worse than any other. People are led to faith in the manner that is best for them. Your God, the God who created you, knows who you are. This God knows how you learn. This God knows what you need. This God provides for you because you are loved more powerfully and wonderfully than you can even imagine.

What happened after each of these folks proclaimed their belief is the truly amazing part. After believing, they caught a glimpse of the Spirit's movement and claimed that kind of passion for themselves. You know the disciples' belief enlivened them with the Spirit because the passage tells you that is exactly what happened. Jesus gave the Spirit to his closest companions to energize them to carry on his work in the world. Jesus said, *If you forgive the sins of any, they are forgiven them; if you retain the sins of any, they are retained* (John 20:23). Jesus gives this same Spirit to each of us, all the time, in many different ways. This beautiful gift is not for your own importance but so that you may be the messenger of God for those around you and for your world.

You likely have experienced this gift. You may have said the exact right words to someone, and you did not even know that you thought that until it came out of your mouth. Or you visited someone at just the right time for them. Possibly you just knew how to handle an unfamiliar situation and your involvement brought healthy resolution. Maybe you sensed when your family member was open to healing old wounds. You might have realized that the church member who called to ask you to do something in the church was speaking God's call upon your heart and so you said, "yes."

In Jesus's last visit to those closest to him, he equipped them to carry on.

Prayer for the Day: *Loving God, help me not abandon the ways you have equipped me to carry on your work. Amen.*

Week 16 **John 20:19-29**
Saturday

What does this gift of Spirit mean for you? In part, it means that the Spirit nurtures you in your own faith journey. God is as close as the individual atoms in your body and as vast as the worlds beyond the universe. You need that internal strengthening, that still small voice of knowing, that deep sense that you are not on this journey alone. You want to know that intimate relationship with your Creator, Redeemer, and Comforter. The Spirit whispers those words of love and challenge to you. But the gift of the Spirit is more than something *just* for your personal use.

People of faith believe that people are chosen by God to share the Good News of the Gospel in every way that they can. People of God are chosen to be God's hands, feet, voice, ears in the world. Faithful people are chosen for a mighty task within the kingdom of God. Jesus gave to his disciples the Spirit's gifts needed for forgiveness…the gifts of getting deeply and truly involved with people, listening to them, feeling their feelings, hearing their stories, helping them work through whatever they have done, searching with them for ways to make amends, and helping them find their way to the Savior, the only one who can forgive thoroughly and completely.

Jesus came to his disciples in the ways that each of them needed and so you, too, are to approach people in the ways that are best for them to hear the healing words and grace of your Savior.

Thomas required tangible proof. Jesus provided that. Are you willing to search for ways to provide those kinds of tools for people who are striving to grow in their faith? The disciples needed to see the risen Jesus. Are you willing to learn what people yearn to see so their faith can take root and grow? Can you embrace those who want visual contact with sacred moments and holy people? Mary needed to hear her name. She needed a word. Are you willing to speak in a variety of ways? Are you willing to get to know people so that you indeed know their name, know them in their fullness? The beloved disciple just believed. Are you willing to rejoice when someone shares that kind of intuitive sense of the holy without looking at them as if they are crazy?

Good ole Thomas. Jesus loved him and came to him as Thomas needed him to. And when Jesus did that, Thomas professed, "My Lord and my God." If your Lord and Savior Jesus Christ did this for Thomas, then may you be in the manner of Christ for others and for the world.

Prayer for the Day: *Giver of good gifts, may I discover ways to be your hands, feet, eyes, and ears in my world. Amen.*

Week 17
Matthew 28:16-20

16 Now the eleven disciples went to Galilee, to the mountain to which Jesus had directed them. 17 When they saw him, they worshipped him; but some doubted. 18 And Jesus came and said to them, "All authority in heaven and on earth has been given to me. 19 Go therefore and make disciples of all nations, baptizing them in the name of the Father and of the Son and of the Holy Spirit, 20 and teaching them to obey everything that I have commanded you. And remember, I am with you always, to the end of the age."

Week 17
Sunday

Matthew 28:16-20

This passage focuses on the charge that Jesus gave to his disciples as his last act recorded in the Gospel of Matthew. This conversation happened on a mountain (In Luke, the last appearance is in Jerusalem. In the 21st Chapter of John, the last appearance is beside the Sea of Tiberius.) Mountains in scriptural terms are usually places where important things happen. It was on a mountain where Moses received the Ten Commandments. It was on a mountain where Jesus gave the teachings and instructions now called the Sermon on the Mount. It was to the Mount of Olives Jesus went with the disciples after his last supper. And it was on a mountain where Jesus was transfigured with Elijah and Moses before Peter, James, and John. When Matthew locates these last words as being given on a mountain, then he is underlining them with big bold strokes. This charge to disciples then and now is obviously very important!

Jesus and the eleven were on a mountain. Some worshiped and some doubted. What a wonderful relief. Even the disciples, those who walked most closely with Jesus, those who knew him better than anyone else on the face of the earth, some of those disciples doubted. Thank goodness you can know that. Jesus is about to give his last charge to people who both worshiped and doubted. This means that you don't have to have it all together to share in Jesus's commissioning service. You do not have to know everything about the Bible, church teachings, or even about faith. You simply have to be present to hear the charge. You are not expected to carry it out in your own strength. You move in the power of Christ. What a huge load is removed from you.

Prayer for the Day: *Merciful God, help me to be present to you this day. Amen.*

Matthew 28:16-20 **Week 17 / Monday**

Jesus reiterates that you are not working just on your own strength when he says, *All authority in heaven and on earth has been given to me* (Matthew 28:18). Jesus is standing in the long line of the prophets with this bold statement. Daniel 7:13-14 states, *I saw one like a human being coming with the clouds of heaven... To him was given dominion and glory and kingship, that all peoples, nations, and languages should serve him. His dominion is an everlasting dominion that shall not pass away, and his kingship is one that shall never be destroyed.* As the resurrected Christ, Jesus is acting with his full power and Lordship. He is indeed King of Kings and Lord of Lords. In this power, Jesus gives his charge to his disciples in all times and all places. Because of this power, Jesus knows that you can do what he charges you to do. You are operating through this power of Christ, the power that is over all heaven and earth.

The charge: *Go therefore and make disciples of all nations, baptizing them in the name of the Father and of the Son and of the Holy Spirit, and teaching them to obey everything I have commanded you. And remember, I am with you always, to the end of the age* (Matthew 28:19-20).

Did you notice anything missing in this charge? Go therefore, make disciples, baptize, teach to obey, and remember. Go, make, baptize, teach, remember. Where is preach the gospel? Where is profess one's faith prior to baptism? It appears that Jesus is less concerned about what we say than how we live. His commission to us teaches us about living as faithful people.

Prayer for the Day: *My God and Savior, I indeed want to live as a faithful person. Help me be that. Amen.*

Week 17
Tuesday

Matthew 28:16-20

Look at the verbs some more. The first imperative is to *go*. Have you ever traveled to other places? Beforehand you may have seen movies set in the location. You may have watched documentaries. You may have researched online. But every one of those things you could do within the safety of your own home. You never had to leave your living room to see the sights in your chosen venue. But, once you traveled there, you realized that every scene you had ever witnessed paled in comparison to actually being there. Seeing a picture of the inside of a cathedral never brought tears to your eyes like sitting inside that magnificent edifice did. You had to *go*.

This is what Jesus is charging you to do. *To go*. To be engaged in the world, to leave your comfort zones, to interact with others who are beyond your usual world. It was not easy getting to your destination. There were costs with tickets and meals. There may have been hours on planes. But the costs and hours of sitting were worth it. The experience was better than anything you could imagine. Jesus asks you to do what is necessary to step out into this world that he created. And life will be better than you ever expected.

So therefore, you are to go. And what are you to do when you go? You are to make disciples of all nations. The Greek word for all nations is *ethnos*. Notice how similar it sounds to *ethnic*? Greek-speaking Jews used *ethnos* to refer to non-Jewish individuals. *Ethnos* points to people who are not your people. They may not look like you, they may not sound like you, they may not have the same value system. They are the world beyond all that you find comfortable and familiar. It is to these that Jesus is now calling his disciples to go.

You and other faithful people are to go to the entire world, no exclusions, and make disciples.

Prayer for the Day: *Ever living God, I am not planning any major trips any time soon. Therefore, I ask that you open the world to me here, in my own little corner, so I can be a good disciple and help others discover the joy of discipleship. Amen.*

Matthew 28:16-20

**Week 17
Wednesday**

Making disciples. So now how is that done? Jesus tells you. The first thing to do as you minister to/with emerging disciples is to baptize them in the name of the Father and of the Son and of the Holy Spirit. Various churches baptize in various ways and at various times along one's faith journey. Presbyterians and others practice infant baptism, thereby demonstrating the believe that baptism is an act of the Holy Spirit, not an act that follows a decision one makes. Baptists and others practice what is called believer's baptism, where one is baptized upon making a declaration of faith in the Lord Jesus Christ and/or repenting of sin. Some churches proclaim that baptism is a once in a lifetime occurrence. Others believe that people may choose to be baptized multiple times, signifying changes in their faith journey.

Baptism can take the form of sprinkling, pouring, or immersing. No matter the form or frequency, baptism is a sacrament prescribed by Jesus. In baptism, people acknowledge that they are God's beloved child. They are simply loved into the kingdom.

Prayer for the Day: *Father, Son, and Holy Spirit, thank you for the sacrament of baptism with all its layers of meanings. Amen.*

Week 17 — Thursday

Matthew 28:16-20

The next thing to do in making disciples, according to Jesus, is to teach them to obey everything that Jesus has commanded.

Obedience in the Biblical sense is a little different than what you might think of as obedience. You may remember when your parents made you obey them. Usually that meant doing what they wanted you to do whether you agreed with them or not or whether you wanted to or not. Obedience possibly meant that you were to give up a little bit of who you were so that your parents would be pleased.

This is *not* how Biblical writers understood obedience. In the Old Testament, the root word for "obedience" literally means "hear." Hearing God's word means you pay attention to God's activity and you respond with actions of your own. In the New Testament, Jesus said, *Everyone who hears these words of mine and does them will be like a wise man who built his house upon the rock* (Matthew 7:24).

This understanding of obedience may be hard to get your mind around. You may somehow feel you must give up something of your essence when you "obey." Maybe Jeremiah's words will help. "*I will put my law within them, and I will write it on their hearts; [the location of human will] and I will be their God and they shall be my people. No longer shall they teach one another, or say to each other, 'Know the Lord,' for they shall all know me, from the least of them to the greatest*" (Jeremiah 31:31-34).

Obedience then is joyfully and willfully given because Christ's words and example are absorbed into your innermost being. You experience your humanity in its fullness and totality as Christ's words and example are absorbed into your very depths.

Prayer for the Day: *Jesus Christ, help me absorb your words and examples into my innermost being. Amen.*

Matthew 28:16-20

Week 17
Friday

Jesus taught to love your neighbor as he loves you. He taught to reach out to the stranger lying on the side of the road. He taught to have faith that can move mountains. He instructed to feed people who are hungry, to clothe those who are naked, to set the prisoner free. Jesus demonstrated love through healing the brokenness around you. He called followers to a new life, a life as radical as being born anew into a new way of thinking, a new way of being. He turned the world upside down in that the first are last and the last are first. He called disciples to love their enemies. He asked followers to interpret the law in its life-giving spirit, not its letter-of-the-law legalism. He said that his way is life-giving and that a relationship with him is the most important, most intimate thing you can have going for you. He called you to be in community and not to isolate yourself from the life-giving love and grace you have to offer others.

He taught these radical things and now invites you to do them and to teach others this way of life.

Teaching is more than a structured thing. It is more than the classes taught at church or at school. Parents, grandparents, or coaches know that they are constantly teaching—by their actions, by nonverbal body reactions, by words, by the jokes they tell, by the songs they sing, by their interactions, by their silences. You are called by Christ to be a teacher. This is an awesome responsibility. The movies you choose to watch or the music you listen to teach about your values. The television shows you tune into and the social media you follow demonstrate what you love and enjoy. The ways you interact with everyone with whom you come in contact illustrate the depth of your commitments to the God of love. How you spend your free time, how you spend your money, what jobs you choose to undertake—all these teach others about who you are, what you put your faith in, and who or what you worship. Someone said, "Preach the gospel always. When necessary, use words."

Prayer for the Day: *Great teacher, help me teach your ways in all the ways I can. Amen.*

Week 17
Saturday

Matthew 28:16-20

Those things you are to teach, you need to know for yourself. When you know the stories of the Bible as well as you know the stories of your own family, then your witness is truly powerful. You can claim Abraham or Sarah, Esther or Jonah, Peter or Martha, Paul or Lydia as your family members. You can share the truths you learn from their lives. You can evaluate their stories against the stories of Jesus our Lord. You can let God's truth seep into your innermost being so you can teach disciples to hear and embody what Jesus taught as easily as you breathe the air. As a disciple of Jesus Christ, you can continue to feed yourself on the good news of the gospel so you can teach others the realities you know.

A Celtic prayer says, "God to enfold us, God to surround us; God in our speaking, God in our thinking; God in our life, God on our lips; God in our souls, God in our hearts" (*Iona Abbey Worship Book*, p. 189). What a way to live. What a way to teach. What a way to obey.

A fact that you must acknowledge is that you do not always live as Christ might like you to. You might not live as an embodied teacher of Jesus's Way even most of the time. But that is where Jesus's last sentence becomes so life giving for you. He says, *And remember, I am with you always, to the end of the age* (Matthew 28:20). No matter what....

Even when you are a lousy teacher, Jesus is with you. Even when the last thing you want to do is fulfill Jesus's calling in your life, he is with you. When you resist, he is with you. When you ignore, he is with you. When you deny, he is with you.

Another way to translate "to the end of the age" is "all the days." All the days. This seems more immediate, more personal, more in the moment. Each day is a time for you to know that you have the opportunity to live fully in the love and grace of the triune God. You are not alone in your living the Jesus Way.

This Great Commission for disciples of all times and places calls to go, to baptize, to teach, and to remember. No matter how easy or hard it is to go, to baptize, to teach, and to remember as individuals or as a community, Jesus is with his disciples all the days.

Prayer for the Day: *Jesus, help me embrace your great charge deeply inside of me and live it all my days. Amen.*

Week 18
1 Samuel 1:1-18

There was a certain man of Ramathaim, a Zuphite from the hill country of Ephraim, whose name was Elkanah son of Jeroham son of Elihu son of Tohu son of Zuph, an Ephraimite. 2 He had two wives; the name of one was Hannah, and the name of the other Peninnah. Peninnah had children, but Hannah had no children.

3 Now this man used to go up year by year from his town to worship and to sacrifice to the Lord of hosts at Shiloh, where the two sons of Eli, Hophni and Phinehas, were priests of the Lord. 4 On the day when Elkanah sacrificed, he would give portions to his wife Peninnah and to all her sons and daughters; 5 but to Hannah he gave a double portion, because he loved her, though the Lord had closed her womb. 6 Her rival used to provoke her severely, to irritate her, because the Lord had closed her womb. 7 So it went on year after year; as often as she went up to the house of the Lord, she used to provoke her. Therefore Hannah wept and would not eat. 8 Her husband Elkanah said to her, 'Hannah, why do you weep? Why do you not eat? Why is your heart sad? Am I not more to you than ten sons?'

9 After they had eaten and drunk at Shiloh, Hannah rose and presented herself before the Lord. Now Eli the priest was sitting on the seat beside the doorpost of the temple of the Lord. 10 She was deeply distressed and prayed to the Lord, and wept bitterly. 11 She made this vow: 'O Lord of hosts, if only you will look on the misery of your servant, and remember me, and not forget your servant, but will give to your servant a male child, then I will set him before you as a nazirite until the day of his death. He shall drink neither wine nor intoxicants, and no razor shall touch his head.'

12 As she continued praying before the Lord, Eli observed her mouth. 13 Hannah was praying silently; only her lips moved, but her voice was not heard; therefore Eli thought she was drunk. 14 So Eli said to her, 'How long will you make a drunken spectacle of yourself? Put away your wine.' 15 But Hannah answered, 'No, my lord, I am a woman deeply troubled; I have drunk neither wine nor strong drink, but I have been pouring out my soul before the Lord. 16 Do not regard your servant as a worthless woman, for I have been speaking out of my great anxiety and vexation all this time.' 17 Then Eli answered, 'Go in peace; the God of Israel grant the petition you have made to him.' 18 And she said, 'Let your servant find favour in your sight.' Then the woman went to her quarters, ate and drank with her husband, and her countenance was sad no longer.

Week 18
Sunday

1 Samuel 1:1-18

There are times in life when you sense that something new is about to happen. But who knows what the future holds for you or anyone? Your view of time and God's view of time are very different. You are invited to focus on NOW, on what God is asking of you NOW, on how God is engaged NOW, with the understanding that your NOW may or may not be where God will plant you THEN. It is a time of mystery, some fear, and great hope.

Our scripture for today suggests that *place* may be important.

The setting of the story is Shiloh. Shiloh was in Samaria and has been positively identified today with Tel Shiloh in the West Bank. It was the major Israelite worship center before the first Temple was built in Jerusalem. Shiloh was the home of the sanctuary tent that was created during Moses' time to house the Ark of the Covenant with the stone tablets that Moses brought down from the mountain in the wilderness. As the Hebrews wandered for decades before entering the Promised Land, they carried the tent and the Ark with them. This tent sanctuary remained at Shiloh for more than 360 years until the Philistines captured the Ark.

Shiloh was one of the main worship centers before Israel had a king. It no longer functioned after the priest Eli and his sons were killed by God's decree. Shiloh's function was coming to an end as the monarchy established the temple in Jerusalem.

There are times when a change of place is part of your growth. The place may be literal as when you realized that the apartment you lived in shortly after completing your education was no longer useful for your new life. You needed a different location, more room, or maybe even less room.

Place may be figurative. You may remember "Home," but that building no longer exists. You may see it in your dreams, you remember the people who were there, you may even have some pictures. Home may mean happiness and contentment, or it may mean fear and abuse. But it is no longer a literal place. It is a story in your life.

Prayer for the Day: *Holy God, make me mindful of place, when it is right and when it's time to move on. Amen.*

Author Note: I do not know where I first found the categories, beginning with "place," that are discussed in this series of devotionals.

1 Samuel 1:1-18

Week 18
Monday

*P*osition may be important when new things are on the horizon. Elkanah, was head of the household. He had two wives: Hannah and Peninnah. Hannah could not give him children, but Peninnah could. He was happy that he had offspring. It did not seem to bother him that one of his wives, Hannah, had no babies. He made sure that Hannah had more than enough food even though there were times she chose not to eat when the entire family with wives and children went to Shiloh to offer sacrifices. At one of those times when Hannah would not eat and was sad, Elkanah told her that he thought she could think of him as more than ten sons.

Was he being especially loving to his wife by saying this or was he discounting her feelings?

Leadership here has a broad definition. Leaders are in church, government, helping agencies, home, etc. Sometimes they have designated titles. Sometimes they do not. They are simply the people that folks look to for guidance. Some leaders do not listen deeply. They think they know what someone has said, something like Hannah's grief about being childless, and then respond to what they think is obvious or rational but not helpful at all. When Elkanah said, "Don't be sad, you have me," he let his position get in the way of being deeply compassionate with his wife. He listened with only his head, not his heart. He listened from his perspective, not hers.

Listening to the Spirit is important in learning to connect with others with both your head and your heart.

Prayer for the Day: *Holy Comforter, help me listen with my heart and not just my head. Amen.*

Week 18
Tuesday
1 Samuel 1:1-18

Provoking may be important and something new to come forth. Peninnah provokes Hannah. In the story, Peninnah is not a person you might want to be friends with. She is quite happy that she is the mother of Elkanah's sons and daughters and seems to enjoy constantly reminding Hannah of that. As a mother, she has status in the family. She and her children receive more of the family's resources, even though her husband gives the other wife double her share.

You may wonder why provoking is important. It sounds…mean. It implies bullying, looking down upon, being a pain in whatever body part you want to name. There are ugly ways of provoking and healthy ways of provoking.

Sometimes provoking can be a positive stimulus. For example, a minister once consulted with a congregation whose front entrance to the building was almost impossible to find. On more than one occasion, the consultant argued that visitors had to search to find how to get into the worship space. Each time, the committee members explained that the plants making the entrance hard to see were meaningful and had been from when they were planted. Finally, the consultant took the entire committee outside and walked them toward the end of the parking lot and asked, "Where is the entrance?" The consultant provoked them.

When the consultant returned to that church several months later, members had cleared out much of the vegetation, in part because they also finally noticed that many weeds were choking some of those sentimental plants. Not only that, but they also decided to have a person who loved to greet people stand out in the parking lot to welcome everyone to worship.

Had Peninnah not nagged, Hannah might not have known or realized her deeper purpose. Peninnah knew what Hannah most deeply wanted and prodded her rival. Peninnah's prodding brought Hannah to a place of deep prayer and total reliance on God. Peninnah's provoking helped Hannah claim what her loving husband could not. Hannah was able to listen to the voice of God within her deepest soul.

Provoking has a place. The challenge is to provoke in a constructive way. When conflict may arise because of people being challenged, the call is to sit lightly with the conflict and hold each other in the grace of Christ, to love each other through to the vision that God is leading you to.

Prayer for the Day: *Provoking God, you get my attention. Then help me know what to do next. Amen.*

1 Samuel 1:1-18

**Week 18
Wednesday**

A priest / preacher may be important. Eli was the priest of Shiloh, along with his sons Hophni and Phinehas. Later in First Samuel, the story tells that the younger men were stealing the best parts of the sacrifices for themselves and their families. Eli knew this but did nothing about it. That's why they died shortly after God's encounter with the boy Samuel in the night, when God kept calling Samuel and Samuel thought it was Eli.

Eli was not an especially effective pastoral care person. He thought Hannah was drunk as she cried to God to give her a son. He chastised her for making a spectacle of herself. He finally listened to her and sent her on her way with God's blessing. His words must have comforted Hannah because she went to her quarters and ate and drank with her husband. She was no longer sad.

But Eli didn't solve Hannah's problem. Eli turned it over to God when he offered God's blessing. Then Hannah and Elkanah returned home to Ramah to wait and see what would happen.

Leaders will not always create the solutions to your next steps. God will. A leader, minister, or priest may be able to help with a process, but the outcomes belong in God's hands. You may meet with others in a discernment process but will need to listen to the guidance of the Spirit to claim a vision. There may be false starts and stops but with patience and as much non-anxiousness as possible, space can be created to hear and see God's wisdom and guidance.

Prayer for the Day: *Jesus, Great High Priest who has passed through the heavens (Hebrews 4:14), help me always to listen for your voice in the midst of the voices of people who I trust to lead me and others. Amen.*

Week 18 **1 Samuel 1:1-18**
Thursday

Pleading may be important when something new is beginning to hatch. Hannah pleaded with God to give her a son. She exhibited all the symptoms of major grief: lack of appetite, sensitivity to other's opinions of her, weeping, and sadness. Hannah did what so often happens when you believe you've tried everything else, she went directly to God.

Now this in itself is remarkable. She bypassed Eli—he was sitting on a chair outside the door of the temple. But Hannah did not talk with Eli. As the scripture says, *She presented herself to the Lord* (I Samuel 1:10).

Hannah threw herself into prayer. She vowed she would give her God-given son back to God when he reached a certain age. She made a deal with God.

You may relate to deal-making with God. God, if you will just do this for me, then I'll…(fill in the blank).

Prayer for the Day: *Loving God, you know the deepest desires of my heart. Help me to speak them out loud to you. Amen.*

1 Samuel 1:1-18

Week 18
Friday

Do you sense that something new may be going to happen? Hannah then prayed silently. But since Eli thought she was drunk, she must have been praying with a lot of lip moving and body swaying. Possibly her face had squinched eyes and she wrung her hands. Today someone might have thought she was on a bad drug trip. But she's really putting herself into her praying. She's pleading.

Do you have some grief that leads you to plead? A lot of things may have changed for you. You may have lost someone dear to you. You may yearn to hear from someone you used to be close to. You may have lost a job, your health, your sense of stability. You may get impatient with what's happening…or not happening. Not knowing can be scary. But you sense something—something new, something different.

So, Hannah prayed. Oh my, how she prayed.

Prayer for the Day: *Listening God, help me pray, truly pray, especially when I do not know what is happening. Amen.*

Week 18
Saturday

1 Samuel 1:1-18

Place, position, provoking, priest, and pleading may each have their place when God is doing a new thing in your life. Will you look around and see how these things are calling to you? Can you trust God to lead you where you are to go? Can you bring your deepest desires to God and then wait with hope, trust, and confidence that whatever your next new thing is, God is there before you and with you?

Prayer for the Day: *Mighty God, help me pray like Hannah. Amen.*

Week 19
Nehemiah 2:17-18, 12:27, 43

Nehemiah 2

17 Then I said to them, 'You see the trouble we are in, how Jerusalem lies in ruins with its gates burnt. Come, let us rebuild the wall of Jerusalem, so that we may no longer suffer disgrace.' 18 I told them that the hand of my God had been gracious upon me, and also the words that the king had spoken to me. Then they said, 'Let us start building!' So they committed themselves to the common good.

Nehemiah 12

27 Now at the dedication of the wall of Jerusalem they sought out the Levites in all their places, to bring them to Jerusalem to celebrate the dedication with rejoicing, with thanksgivings and with singing, with cymbals, harps, and lyres.

43 They offered great sacrifices that day and rejoiced, for God had made them rejoice with great joy; the women and children also rejoiced. The joy of Jerusalem was heard far away.

Week 19   Nehemiah 2:17-18, 12:27, 43
Sunday

Nehemiah was minding his own business as the cup bearer of King Artaxerxes of Persia. Kimberly Richards reports that "although this sounds like a relatively unimportant job, it is a position of trust and influence. As cup bearer, Nehemiah tasted the king's wine to prevent poisoning, and he guarded the king's chambers" (Kimberly C. Richter, Jim Watkins, Vera White, *Rebuilding: Peacemaking in Nehemiah*, p. 6). Presumably he was living a comfortable life in the king's court with direct access to the king, the seat of power. His brother, Hanani, returned from a trip to Judah and like any polite person, Nehemiah asked him, "How was your trip? Who do we know that is still around?"

Hanani answered, "Those captives who have come back are having all kinds of troubles. They are terribly disgraced (More about how they were disgraced later.) Jerusalem's walls are broken down, and its gates have been burned."

If you were Nehemiah, what would you have done upon hearing this tale of woe? Even though you may like to think you would have jumped right in, is it probable that you would have shaken your head, and muttered, "That's too bad," and gone on with your cup bearer duties which were so important to both the king and to your livelihood and serenity?

Nehemiah reacted differently. He wept and mourned and prayed to God. And after he prayed to God about his deep concern for his countrymen and women, he felt compelled to serve in addressing their needs. Later on, he went before the king and instead of being lighthearted and jovial as he was expected to be as the cup bearer, his face was long and sad. The king noticed his expression and asked, *Why is your face sad, since you are not sick? This can only be sadness of heart* (Nehemiah 2:2).

Nehemiah explained what was going on with his homeland. The place of his ancestors' graves lay in waste and the gates had been destroyed by fire. When the king asked him what he was requesting, Nehemiah asked to go to Jerusalem and take the king's letters of recommendation to all the rulers of the provinces through which he would pass, including a letter requesting timber for rebuilding the wall. The king granted his request. The only thing the king wanted to know was how long Nehemiah would be gone and when he would return.

Prayer for the Day: *Most merciful God, break open hearts so compassion spills out of them. Amen.*

Nehemiah 2:17-18, 12:27, 43   **Week 19 / Monday**

When Nehemiah reached Jerusalem, he did not tell anyone why he was there until after he had surveyed the damage himself. He then pulled together the people and told them that the hand of God had been gracious upon him. He related all the things the king had said. They said, "Let's start building!"

The work was highly organized. In the third chapter of Nehemiah, there is a listing of all kinds of groups and the portion of the wall they reconstructed. One group is listed and then the words, "Next to them" and another group is listed.

But the work did not go without a hitch. Leaders from surrounding provinces were scared that the Jews were fortifying themselves for aggression and so they tried to stop the building—first by accusing Nehemiah of treason, then by making fun of the construction methods, and then by threatening to attack. Nehemiah set guards to protect the builders and reminded the people: "Do not be afraid of them. Remember the Lord, who is great and awesome, and fight for your kin, your sons, your daughters, your wives, and your homes."

Nehemiah arranged for a trumpet to sound a call to arms since the people were spread out and might not hear shouting. He said, "Rally to us wherever you hear the sound of the trumpet. Our God will fight for us."

The wall was completed in 52 days. Quite a feat.

Prayer for the Day: *God of the Ever Returning, raise up a Nehemiah in areas of war and oppression. Amen.*

Week 19
Tuesday

Nehemiah 2:17-18, 12:27, 43

In some ways this story may remind you of the pandemic lock-down that happened in restaurants, schools, churches, and businesses. Rebuilding finally began with starts and stops. Some things will never be rebuilt. There is and was a brokenness among people who disagreed on how to deal with the pandemic both personally and as a country.

But rebuilding goes on where people work together to discern how to define and fulfill the needs of the community. Everyone may not agree. However, the work continues. When people reach out to others, rebuilding happens. Individual lives have been strengthened because of the caring and justice and hope that pops up in various places. Rebuilding is a God-led opportunity.

Prayer for the Day: *God of wholeness, help me find where I can help with rebuilding and give me the courage to get involved. Amen.*

Nehemiah 2:17-18, 12:27, 43

**Week 19
Wednesday**

The story of Nehemiah continues. The returning captives felt they were being disgraced. They cried out against their Jewish kin, the people who were leaders in Jerusalem who had remained and then treated their own citizens no better than the former oppressors had treated them. The returnees said, "We have large families, and it takes a lot of grain merely to keep them alive." Others said, "During the famine we even had to mortgage our fields, vineyards, and homes to them in order to buy grain." Others said, "We had to borrow money from those in power to pay the government tax on our fields and vineyards. We are Jews just as they are, and our children are as good as theirs. But we still have to sell our children as slaves, and some of our daughters have already been raped. We are completely helpless; our fields and vineyards have even been taken from us" (Nehemiah 5:1-6). Isn't this so often how things unfold? People make some progress and then they turn around and become the very people they despise? As you know so well, the fights that happen in churches are often not with other faiths or other denominations but often within their own walls. Christians often spend more time fighting each other than they do fighting anyone else.

On the more personal level, people may have been able to rise above the circumstances in which they were raised and then may look down on people who are still in the situation that they left. They may feel enlightened and put down the people who they perceive to still be ignorant. They may judge other people and are horrified when they themselves are judged. C.S. Lewis in *Mere Christianity* says that the vice that is utmost evil is pride. He elaborates saying, "Unchastity, anger, greed, drunkenness, and all that, are mere fleabites in comparison." He explains that "pride gets no pleasure out of having something, only out of having more of it than the next [person.]" So, a person may fight just to prove he/she is better than, better looking, smarter, richer, more devout. Pride comes in all kinds of attire. And we will fight anyone who challenges our assessments. "Utmost evil" according to Lewis.

Oh, yes, you may be able to relate to the people who were being persecuted by their own people. But you may have to acknowledge that you may also be the persecutor.

Prayer for the Day: *Dear God, help me remember that judgment belongs only to you. Amen.*

Week 19
Thursday

Nehemiah 2:17-18, 12:27, 43

Nehemiah rectified the situation. First, he pledged his own resources to help with food. Then he pleaded, *Let us stop this taking of interest. Restore to them, this very day, their fields, their vineyards, their olive orchards, and their houses, and the interest on money, grain, wine, and oil that you have been exacting from them* (Nehemiah 5:10-11). After he shook out his garment, he added: *So may God shake out everyone from house and from property who does not perform this promise. Thus, may they be shaken out and emptied* (Nehemiah 5:13).

And Nehemiah went even further. He did not take the full allowance of support allotted to him in his role to make sure the people would not be unduly burdened in caring for him and his household. Wow, to have leaders like that—leaders who do not unduly burden the people whom they are trying to help!

Prayer for the Day: *God of this day, in areas where I am leader in my family, church, workplace, or community, help me be a leader who does not burden others but one who truly helps with deep and abiding care and concern. Amen.*

Nehemiah 2:17-18, 12:27, 43 — Week 19, Friday

Nehemiah's purpose is summarized in his words, *Remember for my good, O my God, all that I have done for this people* (Nehemiah 5:19). Personal glory, money, prestige, position were not why he worked so hard. Nehemiah dedicated himself so he would be in the kind of relationship with God that he yearned for. Nehemiah knew he did not *earn* his favor with God. His life to this point already demonstrated that he knew that God was guiding his life. Like a lover who wants to please the beloved, Nehemiah wanted to please God, thereby pleasing himself. Nehemiah wanted to be remembered as a faithful servant who saw his duty and did it.

How would your life be different if you could place your priorities as Nehemiah did? He left security in the king's court, risked his life, and rebuilt a city. His only request was that he would be remembered by God. What might you do to live only to be remembered by God? How would you approach other people and your family if you were trying to please your loving creator? How might you be different if your only motivation was to glorify God with everything you did, said, thought, and fought for?

The wall was completed, and more people returned to Jerusalem. The seventh chapter of Nehemiah relates that 42,360 people returned, not including their 7,337 male and female slaves, 245 male and female singers, 736 horses, 245 mules, 435 camels, and 6,720 donkeys. WOW!

Prayer for the Day: *Gracious God, I want to live so that everything I do glorifies you but I need your help to do this. Amen.*

Week 19   **Nehemiah 2:17-18, 12:27, 43**
Saturday

Nehemiah witnessed tribulations when people returned from years of exile. Those who had stayed behind in the devastation might have had difficulty with people moving in and claiming their land and bringing in their ways learned while in captivity.

To create new life from the ashes, they returned to their sacred scriptures. The priests read from ... the law of God, with interpretation. They helped the people understand the reading (Nehemiah 8:7b-8).

Then they celebrated with a BIG party. Nehemiah said, *Go your way, eat the fat and drink the sweet wine and send portions of them to those for whom nothing is prepared, for this day is holy to our Lord; and do not be grieved, for the joy of the Lord is your strength* (Nehemiah 8:10).

Confession followed. People dressed in sackcloth and threw dirt on their heads to show their sorrow. For three hours they confessed their sins and worshiped the Lord. They agreed how they would live together. For them to return to the roots of their faith they realized that having "foreign wives" (women who worshiped other gods) interfered with rebuilding their country. They decided children could not marry foreigners AND they put away the foreign wives they were already married to and their own children of a mixed marriage. They intentionally honored the Sabbath. They tithed to the temple.

You certainly would not advocate abandoning spouses or your own children, but you might discover changes you want to make, as part of a community of faith, to demonstrate that you intend to live faithfully as God's disciple. You might assure every person, no matter who they are, that he/she/they are eagerly welcomed to be part of your community—that they are indeed part of a family, that they are loved, that their presence and participation is indeed valued, that they will be supported in their growth, that they will be lovingly challenged in their waywardness, and that they too have good ideas. You can grow in God's wisdom so that you discern what you need to hold onto and what you need to do differently so that you can shine God's light everywhere.

After the people in Jerusalem had rebuilt the walls, the real work of rebuilding community began as they studied the scriptures, celebrated, confessed their sins, and committed to living lives worthy of God. The ongoing process is not always easy along the way.

You can echo Nehemiah's words: "[I] pray that God will bless [me] for the good [I] have done."

Prayer for the Day: *God of Nehemiah, help me follow his example as I am able. Amen.*

Week 20
Luke 24:50-53; Acts 1:1-11

Luke 24

50 Then he led them out as far as Bethany, and, lifting up his hands, he blessed them. 51 While he was blessing them, he withdrew from them and was carried up into heaven. 52 And they worshiped him, and returned to Jerusalem with great joy; 53 and they were continually in the temple blessing God.

Acts 1

In the first book, Theophilus, I wrote about all that Jesus did and taught from the beginning 2 until the day when he was taken up to heaven, after giving instructions through the Holy Spirit to the apostles whom he had chosen. 3 After his suffering he presented himself alive to them by many convincing proofs, appearing to them over the course of forty days and speaking about the kingdom of God. 4 While staying with them, he ordered them not to leave Jerusalem, but to wait there for the promise of the Father. "This," he said, "is what you have heard from me; 5 for John baptized with water, but you will be baptized with the Holy Spirit not many days from now."

6 So when they had come together, they asked him, 'Lord, is this the time when you will restore the kingdom to Israel?' 7 He replied, 'It is not for you to know the times or periods that the Father has set by his own authority. 8 But you will receive power when the Holy Spirit has come upon you; and you will be my witnesses in Jerusalem, in all Judea and Samaria, and to the ends of the earth.' 9 When he had said this, as they were watching, he was lifted up, and a cloud took him out of their sight. 10 While he was going and they were gazing up towards heaven, suddenly two men in white robes stood by them. 11 They said, 'Men of Galilee, why do you stand looking up towards heaven? This Jesus, who has been taken up from you into heaven, will come in the same way as you saw him go into heaven.'

Week 20 **Luke 24:50-53; Acts 1:1-11**
Sunday

People of deep faith disagree about how to understand the ascension story. Is it historical? The visual of Jesus floating up into the sky is important to many Christians. Another way to think about the story is that Luke was using poetic language and was painting a picture using theological paintbrushes, not a camera.

The event echoes another Biblical figure who had great impact on the Hebrew people—Elijah, the Old Testament prophet. Elijah was taken into heaven on a whirlwind in a chariot and horses of fire (II Kings 2:9-12). People connected Jesus with the prophet Elijah in very powerful ways. When Jesus and the disciples were going to Caesarea Philippi, Jesus asked them, "*Who do people say that I am? They answered, Some say John the Baptist, and others Elijah, and still others one of the prophets*" (Mark 8:27-35). Another time, on a mountain, Peter, James, and John witnessed Jesus as a dazzling white being standing with Moses and Elijah. The writer of Luke and Acts might have used important imagery from the Elijah story to explain something profound in the lives of Christ's followers.

Luke wrote both the Gospel of Luke and the book of Acts, and yet the time frames are different. In the gospel of Luke, the ascension happens Easter evening, but in Acts, it happens 40 days after the crucifixion and resurrection. Would an incident written by the same person—Luke—have these discrepancies if it was historical—something that could have been captured on camera—rather than symbolic?

Also the number 40 has significance in scripture: Noah experienced rain for 40 days and 40 nights before life was replaced with God's new world; the children of Israel spent 40 years in the wilderness wandering between slavery and the land of promise that was their future; Jesus was tempted for 40 days in the wilderness as he struggled—for a time—between his life before his public ministry and the beginning of that ministry. Forty designates a period of moving from one way of being to a new way of being. The disciples were evolving from one way of living, thinking, and loving—before Jesus's crucifixion—to a new reality in light of Jesus's resurrection. Forty days describes time-between-time. According to the Acts version of the story, Jesus used these 40 days to teach the disciples while he was still with them. He opened their minds to understand the scriptures—that everything written about him in the law of Moses, the prophets, and the psalms must be fulfilled.

Prayer for the Day: *God of inspiration, may this story resonate within me so I too can stand in awe. Amen.*

Luke 24:50-53; Acts 1:1-11

Week 20
Monday

This very picturesque language powerfully shows a message about who Jesus is for you today. With the Ascension, you learn that Jesus's earthly ministry was now truly over. Had he stayed around, he would have been special to a relatively small, insignificant group of people. His gospel would have been in a limited geographical area, not the worldwide reality that it is today. But with today's passages, we get the message that things are changing in powerful ways. We glimpse the Jesus as described in Colossians. Listen to 1:15-20:

> *He is the image of the invisible God, the firstborn of all creation; for in him all things in heaven and on earth were created, things visible and invisible, whether thrones or dominions or rulers or powers—all things have been created through him and for him. He himself is before all things, and in him all things hold together. He is the head of the body, the church; he is the beginning, the firstborn of the dead, so that he might come to have first place in everything.*

In the Gospel's version of the Ascension, this exalted Jesus lifted up his hands, blessed the disciples and while he was blessing them, he withdrew and was carried into heaven. Donald Miller points out that "[Jesus'] departure took place, not after, but while, he blessed them. His parting act of blessing was [and is] a continuous one. The disciples, [indeed all of us] were now [going] to live under his constant benediction" (Donald Miller, *Luke, The Layman's Bible Commentary*, 1959, p. 175).

The action is a little different in the Acts version. Jesus tells the disciples to remain in Jerusalem and to wait for the promise of the Father. The disciples then asked a question that makes one wonder, even after all the events of the crucifixion and resurrection, if they really understood what kind of kingdom Jesus was talking about. Listen carefully to their question: *Lord, is this the time when you will restore the kingdom to Israel?* (Acts 1:6).

Prayer for the Day: *Bless me, Lord Jesus. Amen.*

Week 20
Tuesday

Luke 24:50-53; Acts 1:1-11

In talking about restoring the kingdom to Israel, do the disciples really get that Jesus is talking about a *totally new reality* in God? After all they'd been through, after all Jesus had been through, don't they finally understand that the kingdom of God is not restoring their world to a previous political glory? Did they not listen to Jesus when he taught in the gospel of Mark that *the time is fulfilled, and the kingdom of God has come near; repent and believe in the good news* (Mark 1:15).

Kingdom of God parables often began: "With what shall we compare the kingdom of God?" The answers included very ordinary things: growing seeds, mustard trees, weeds among good plants, treasures hidden in fields, one special pearl, fish nets full of good and bad fish, etc. These were things of ordinary life, among the people. Jesus did not talk about political entities that resembled anything that people knew about governments. John Dominic Crossan and Marcus Borg have suggested that the kingdom of God is what life would be like on earth if God were king—and the rulers of this world *weren't*.

Prayer for the Day: *God of wonder, help me see your kingdom in the midst of the ordinariness of life. Amen.*

Luke 24:50-53; Acts 1:1-11 **Week 20**
                                 Wednesday

The kingdom of God is not a return to anything. It *is* new. It is, as Revelation says, a new heaven and a new earth. The disciples were even trying to pin down the exact time and place of this time of restoration when they asked, *"Lord,* is this the time *when you will restore the kingdom to Israel?" Jesus replied, "It is not for you to know the times or periods that the Father has set by his own authority"* (Acts 1:6-7).

Can you relate to this fogginess demonstrated by the disciples? Folks pray for life to be good and wondrous. People want restoration, not something that is amazingly new. You may want restoration to a former life… not the new life in God's kingdom that God is calling you to. After the death of a dearly loved one, you want *that* person back, not some new life that awaits. Parents of adult children sometimes wish that their children were still young, so that they could pull them on their laps to comfort them, rather than watch them deal with whatever life is throwing at them.

During times of transition, you may resist the steps of loss, letting go, and growth. You may be able to acknowledge that a loss has happened. You may have a harder time acknowledging the letting go and growth parts. You WANT THINGS HOW THEY USED TO BE, NOT HOW THEY ARE NOW. YOU DO NOT WANT WHAT THE FUTURE IS CALLING YOU TO. "Lord, is this the time you will restore the kingdom to Israel?"

Even when you can accept that new life is coming, you want to know *when* that new life is going to happen. With pandemics, storms, shootings, and climate warming, have you wondered, "Is this the end of the world?" You want to predict God's timing. You want certainty and control. You don't want change. You want confirmation that your best guesses about life are right. You want to know the timeline for the next steps. Right? Sure. Okay!

Prayer for the Day: *God of the past, present, and future, help me trust your timing and give me patience…NOW. Amen.*

Week 20   **Luke 24:50-53; Acts 1:1-11**
Thursday

Jesus points the disciples to a time of waiting, not a time of certainty. They wait with hope. Listen to Jesus in the Gospel of Luke, *I am sending upon you what my Father promised; so stay here in the city until you have been clothed with power from on high* (Luke 24:49). In Acts Jesus says, *But you will receive power when the Holy Spirit has come upon you; and you will be my witnesses in Jerusalem, in all Judea and Samaria, and to the ends of the earth* (Acts 1:8)

Jesus told the disciples then and today that he will send the energy, insights, strength, and conviction that they need for the journey. But you must wait for that to happen. You don't even know when, how, or in what form the gift will take. Will Willimon says that "waiting [is] an onerous burden for us computerized and technically impatient moderns who live in an age of instant everything." He says that waiting is "one of the tough tasks of the church.... [and that] our waiting implies that things which need doing in the world are beyond our ability to accomplish solely by our own effort, our programs, and our crusades. Some empowerment is needed" (*Acts: Interpretation*, 1988, p. 21).

Prayer for the Day: *Watchful and caring God, teach me to wait with hope. Amen.*

Luke 24:50-53; Acts 1:1-11

Week 20
Friday

The disciples obviously needed the empowerment that Jesus talked about. *They* were still talking about restoring the kingdom of Israel. And then the next part of the story is almost comical. The disciples are gazing into the heaven where they'd seen Jesus disappear when *suddenly* (the text says) two men in white robes stood by them. Two men appearing is certainly poetical. Remember that Jesus had two people appear with him on the Mount of Transfiguration; two men in dazzling clothes talked with the women at the tomb. Once again there are two men in white robes appearing. They said, "Why do you stand looking up toward heaven?"

"Why do you stand looking up toward heaven?"

What a profound question. Why do you stand looking up at heaven? Do you spend time thinking about what heaven's like, how you will connect with your deceased relatives, if you'll have wings, and even if you are saved? Do you focus so much on what happens after you die that you miss your living here and now? Do you keep looking up at heaven and ignore the earth you walk on, the water you drink, and the plants and animals who need your loving attention?

Do you yearn for the glory of heaven and miss the grace of now? Do you stare into the skies and miss the person standing by you who desperately needs you to pay attention, to care, and to connect?

Why do you stand looking up toward heaven?

Do you look wistfully skyward, wanting to see Jesus… right here, right now? Do you yearn to talk with him directly, to learn from his teachings, and to feel the touch of his hand? Do you seek to hold onto him, to keep him in your small definitions of him rather than releasing him to the glory and majesty of being on the right hand of God? Do you forget that Jesus said that he is right here with you in the person who is hungry, in prison, naked, or thirsty?

Why do you stand looking up toward heaven?

Prayer for the Day: *Merciful God, help me focus on the here and now and not the sweet by and by. Amen.*

Week 20
Saturday   Luke 24:50-53; Acts 1:1-11

Acts 1:12-14 states that the disciples left the Mount of Olives, went to the room where they were staying, and prayed. So they waited with hope and they prayed.

Maybe that is your call today, especially during a time of anxiety in your country and the world. Maybe you are called to hope and pray. You do that knowing that the disciples were soon given the gift of the Holy Spirit who enlivened them, gave them a powerful message to share, and made them witnesses to Judea and Samaria and to the ends of the earth. They moved beyond their little world where Jesus appeared to them sporadically to a deep commitment for bearing witness to this Jesus the Christ who had touched their lives and led them to the kingdom of God. They knew they could no longer wait for people to come to them. They were called to go out beyond their world and share the good news of the person and God who had changed their lives. The Gospel of Luke claimed that they returned to Jerusalem with great joy, and they were continually blessing God.

The time is here to wait in prayer, to wait in hope. You live in Jesus's constant benediction. You wait in joy depending on the promises of Jesus that the power of the Spirit will be yours. In the amazing strength of God's witness in your life, you will witness to the grace, hope, and joy that you find in living as Jesus's own person who walks in his way.

Prayer for the Day: *Eternal One, help me hope and pray. Amen.*

Week 21
Acts 2:1-21

When the day of Pentecost had come, they were all together in one place. 2 And suddenly from heaven there came a sound like the rush of a violent wind, and it filled the entire house where they were sitting. 3 Divided tongues, as of fire, appeared among them, and a tongue rested on each of them. 4 All of them were filled with the Holy Spirit and began to speak in other languages, as the Spirit gave them ability.

5 Now there were devout Jews from every nation under heaven living in Jerusalem. 6 And at this sound the crowd gathered and was bewildered, because each one heard them speaking in the native language of each. 7 Amazed and astonished, they asked, 'Are not all these who are speaking Galileans? 8 And how is it that we hear, each of us, in our own native language? 9 Parthians, Medes, Elamites, and residents of Mesopotamia, Judea and Cappadocia, Pontus and Asia, 10 Phrygia and Pamphylia, Egypt and the parts of Libya belonging to Cyrene, and visitors from Rome, both Jews and proselytes, 11 Cretans and Arabs—in our own languages we hear them speaking about God's deeds of power.' 12 All were amazed and perplexed, saying to one another, 'What does this mean?' 13 But others sneered and said, 'They are filled with new wine.'

14 But Peter, standing with the eleven, raised his voice and addressed them: 'Men of Judea and all who live in Jerusalem, let this be known to you, and listen to what I say. 15 Indeed, these are not drunk, as you suppose, for it is only nine o'clock in the morning. 16 No, this is what was spoken through the prophet Joel:

17 "In the last days it will be, God declares, that I will pour out my Spirit upon all flesh, and your sons and your daughters shall prophesy, and your young men shall see visions, and your old men shall dream dreams.
18 Even upon my slaves, both men and women, in those days I will pour out my Spirit; and they shall prophesy.
19 And I will show portents in the heaven above and signs on the earth below, blood, and fire, and smoky mist.
20 The sun shall be turned to darkness and the moon to blood, before the coming of the Lord's great and glorious day.
21 Then everyone who calls on the name of the Lord shall be saved."

Week 21
Sunday

Acts 2:1-21

Pentecost in the church is a day that is full of mystery. Something strange happened, unexplainable, beyond our imaginations. Whatever it was, it is *Christians'* explanation of how the church began. That's why the day is often called the Birthday of the Church. Church members may wear red, yellow, or orange. Some wave red banners or float red balloons to demonstrate that the Holy Spirit is present…seen in the passage as wind and fire.

So, what happened???

The disciples certainly had been through the wringer. Their leader had been executed in a horrible death. They had either denied him or disappeared when the going got rough. Then Jesus had been resurrected from the dead and their leader had left again to go to heaven.

So now what do they do? Do they call a meeting and begin to strategize? Do they develop policies and procedures? Do they create three-year plans? What would life look like now? What were their next steps? Do they continue life as they knew it? But what life? The one they knew before Jesus came into their presence? Afterwards? But how do they know what to do now that Jesus is no longer here to teach them, to show them, to lead them?

Prayer for the Day: *Father, I understand how the disciples felt. I often don't know what to do. Help me. Amen.*

Acts 2:1-21

Week 21
Monday

The description in Acts is not bland or flat. Something miraculous happened. That's the only way one could explain the existence of the church, the only way that what people-know-now-as-the-Christian-Church could have happened out of that little band of people who had spent time with Jesus. The only way to do justice to the reality of the church then and today is to say that God as the Holy Spirit did something amazing. The disciples did not create the church. God did. Members of congregations did not create their churches. God did. Psalm 127:1 says that *unless the Lord builds the house, those who build it labor in vain*. The reality of the church was and is God's doing.

The disciples and lots of other people had gathered in Jerusalem to celebrate Pentecost, the Festival of Weeks, 50 days after Passover. People presented offerings of new grain to the Lord. They also brought bread, lambs, bulls, and goats. It was a day to commemorate the giving of the Torah, the law, to Moses and the people.

There were lots of people from around the world in Jerusalem world for the Festival of Weeks. So that's where the disciples were gathered. There were only the 12 disciples or the 120 mentioned in the previous chapter. However, in the room where they gathered, a mighty wind rushed through.

Maybe this was the beginning of the Church's birthday party? Really, the birthday actually began way back in Genesis where it says: *In the beginning when God created the heavens and the earth, the earth was a formless void and darkness covered the face of the deep, while a wind from God swept over the face of the waters* (Genesis 1:1). The gathering of disciples seemed to be a bit of a formless void, full of darkness until the mighty wind, the wind of Creation, the breath of the Spirit, filled the house.

Prayer for the Day: *Creator God, I want to be a partner is caring for this world. Lead me, please. Amen.*

Week 21
Tuesday

Acts 2:1-21

Something that looked like tongues of fire appeared. Now you know for sure the people were experiencing the Holy God because God appeared to Moses as a burning bush. The wanderers in the wilderness were sometimes led by a pillar of fire. The appearance of fire means God is present.

Everyone in the house was filled with the Holy Spirit. This is exactly what Luke described in the end of *his* gospel. Luke reports that Jesus said, *Thus it is written, that the Messiah is to suffer and to rise from the dead on the third day, and that repentance and forgiveness of sins is to be proclaimed in his name* to all nations (Luke 24:45). Remember that in Jerusalem people heard the message in their own language, so the good news is proclaimed, so to speak, to all nations. Jesus continues: *You are witnesses of these things. And see, I am sending upon you what my Father promised; so stay here in the city until you have been clothed with power from on high* (Luke 24:49). And so there is a mighty wind and something that looked like tongues of fire coming to the disciples where they were staying.

And somehow, in unexplainable ways, whatever happened in the room where the disciples were gathered moved outside to where there were devout Jews living in Jerusalem from every nation under heaven.

Prayer for the Day: *God who is fire and a still small voice, let me sense your presence in many ways that are calm, amazing, or challenging. Amen.*

Acts 2:1-21

**Week 21
Wednesday**

God's purposes broke into all humanity on the day of Pentecost. There was momentary understanding even in the midst of differences of culture, speech, skin color, and basic assumptions about life. On the day of Pentecost, broken and distorted humanity began to realize that God will bring everyone back together in Jesus Christ as evidenced in the Holy Spirit.

The gift of the Holy Spirit was demonstrated with signs and wonders (people speaking boldly and in languages not their own). The book of Acts proclaims throughout that the Holy Spirit was also evident by healing, economic sharing, and community. The Holy Spirit gave the disciples courage in the face of threat and martyrdom, and as they translated the gospel to the Gentile world. The Spirit provided guidance in major decisions such as commissioning Barnabas and Paul to missionary travel.

Paul explains for us that we know the *Holy Spirit* is at work in our midst when the spirit helps us in our weakness (Romans 8:26), sends spiritual gifts (I Corinthians 12), and reshapes the character and temperament of cooperating believers (Gal 5:22f, David P. Gushee, *Feasting on the Word, Cycle A*). You can know the Holy Spirit is here when you are transformed, when the church is transformed, and when the world is transformed.

This gift of the Holy Spirit on the day of Pentecost was so amazing that other people thought the recipients of this mysterious power were drunk. But this amazing Birthday Gift helped the recipients to receive their authentic voices. They graduated from their fear and wondering about what to do to become people who were empowered to enter an unwelcoming world in order to preach and live the love of Jesus.

Prayer for the Day: *Holy Spirit, let me witness your awesome workings and shout that understanding to all the world. Amen.*

Week 21
Thursday

Acts 2:1-21

The relevant question for you is how will you respond to these party gifts of the Spirit? And more importantly, how will you and others together respond to these gifts? Are you engaged in work of love, peace, and justice? Do you experience fellowship together with others? Are you bold in proclaiming the good news that God loves all of us, creates all of us, calls all of us, and chooses all of us to be God's people? Are you aware that God expects you to share all this with others?

So often, this is where a sermon on Pentecost ends... having told about the recipients of the gift of the Spirit and what they did with that gift. But what happened with the hearers of the languages? What did this mean to each of them?

Imagine you are enjoying the festival of Pentecost and this woman says, "I want to share with you amazing, life-changing news. I just need to ask you a few questions. Just answer yes or no. Here goes:

1. Were you ever rusticated?   yes   no

2. Have you ever had to miss work due to...Contagion?   yes   no

3. Would you describe yourself as being...Assiduous?   yes   no

Would you hear the good news from the woman then? No? Well, what if she asked you if you'd ever lived in the country? Have you been sick? Were you hardworking? Then you could answer the exact same questions.

So often people neglect to communicate with friends, family, co-workers, fellow church members, neighbors in ways they can understand, in ways they need to hear. They use their words, not the other person's words. They end up creating confusion, feelings of insecurity, or even a desire to just forget the entire message they're trying to communicate.

Prayer for the Day: *Jesus, the Word, help me listen to the reality of another so I can communicate with words of understanding. Amen.*

Acts 2:1-21

Week 21
Friday

You likely have heard the spirit's voice coming to you in ways you did not expect. And when you hear these wondrous words of love and care, you rejoice and know that you definitely want to be a child of God in all the ways that comes about.

A woman whose husband died unexpectedly experienced the spirit's voice in amazing, yet ordinary ways. While she was in the ICU waiting room, she noticed that the watch her husband gave her at Christmas had stopped. It ran out of time when her husband was also running out of time. A friend stopped by and heard her exclaim as she looked yet again at the stopped watch. The friend said, "Give me that watch." And within an hour, she returned with a functioning watch. That was the voice of God speaking in a language of love that this grieving woman could understand in that moment.

Another friend asked if she needed a phone charger and drove from her home, about 45 minutes away, to bring a charger to the hospital. Who knew that God's word could come in the language of a phone charger?

There are very powerful ways that to hear the voice of God in language that is very particular to your own particular needs. Probably you have experienced this kind of loving language in your own dialect as well.

Prayer for the Day: *Merciful God, thank you that your word is offered in a myriad of surprising ways. Help me recognize your voice in them. Amen.*

Week 21
Saturday

Acts 2:1-21

This Pentecost celebration calls you to be receptive to what gifts the Holy Spirit gives to you, to be ready to use them even when you're not sure how you're supposed to use them. This Pentecost celebration calls the church to be the church in ways that broaden the amazing message that God loves everyone and yearns for a community of justice, peace, and communion with each other even in differences. This Pentecost celebration calls you to be open to hearing God's voice in unexpected ways, at unexpected times, and in unexpected places. This Pentecost celebration reminds you that as Jana Childers says, the "Spirit does not always arrive as a still, small voice or a faint stirring in the heart. The Holy Spirit's power is not always subtle, fragile, or polite. Even today it can be electric…[chill bump producing, and breathtaking]" (Jana Childers, *Feasting on the Word, Cycle A*).

Where do you as an individual see, experience, and share in the Spirit of God? How will you share this voice?

Prayer for the Day: *Come Holy Spirit, come. Amen.*

Week 22
Psalm 131

1 O Lord, my heart is not lifted up, my eyes are not raised too high; I do not occupy myself with things too great and too marvelous for me.
2 But I have calmed and quieted my soul, like a weaned child with its mother; my soul is like the weaned child that is with me.

3 O Israel, hope in the Lord from this time on and for evermore.

Week 22
Sunday

Psalm 131

Some people are passionate about the psalms. Others may have been raised in the church, gone regularly to Sunday School and been part of the church their entire life. And yet, and yet, they have never connected with the Psalms. You may be one of these.

You may know the academics behind the psalms. You know that some were categorized as psalms of lament, others were triumphal entry psalms. Walter Brueggemann, renowned Old Testament scholar, divides the psalms into three categories: Psalms of Orientation, Disorientation, and New Orientation. You remember that psalms are attributed to King David as the writer, others to King Solomon, and current scholarship even suggests that some psalms were written by an unknown woman. Some psalms were obviously part of the worship liturgy. Some were definitely written for the community while others are for the individual.

You know that many psalms are basically poetry and you don't really care for poetry. There are scholars who will point out, in great detail, the symmetry, the balance, and forward and backward movement of the words and images of a psalm. All this analysis may have done nothing to endear the psalms to you.

Maybe as a child, you memorized the 23rd Psalm and Psalm 121 ("I will lift up my eyes to the hills"). Occasionally a particular psalm might have spoken to you because of something you were going through in your life, but you did not really connect to the psalms in your heart. A minister admitted that the psalms did not sing to her until she began a particular spiritual discipline several years ago. In addition to reading from scriptures as well as Thomas Merton, Henri Nouwen, and excerpts of noted religious thinkers or mystics, she read a psalm every day for a week. She read the same psalm Monday, Tuesday, Wednesday, Thursday, Friday, and Saturday. She was surprised at what she began to discover when she spent that kind of time with just one psalm. She was amazed to read a phrase on Thursday that she'd already read every day that week and all of a sudden, something astounding jumped out at her and captured her heart and imagination. By simply reading, day in and day out, without any of the scholars giving her guidance, she began to realize how pertinent the psalms are for …today.

Prayer for the Day: *God of music and liturgy, open my heart to the wonders of psalms. Amen.*

Psalm 131

Week 22
Monday

Consider Psalm 131 which happens to be one of the shortest psalms in the Bible.

O Lord, my heart is not lifted up, my eyes are not raised too high; I do not occupy myself with things too great and marvelous for me.

But I have calmed and quieted my soul, like a weaned child with its mother; my soul is like a weaned child that is with me.

O Israel, hope in the Lord from this time and forevermore.

When you read the psalm and quickly move on to whatever else is going on in your day, you may say, "Humph! This psalm tells me to know my place, to keep my head down, to accept whatever is dumped on me. I'm not to look up. I'm stupid and can't understand anything!"

Some children are raised that way. As a boy, Ed had a friend named Mark. Mark was a very charming and engaging boy. The two were very close and spent a lot of time at Ed's house. Ed's mother always remarked about how cute Mark was. Finally, after she had once again said how cute Mark was, Ed asked his mother, "Mama, am I cute?" His mom said, "Well, you're cute enough!"

Don't raise your eyes too high. Don't occupy yourself with things too great and marvelous for you.

Put *this* interpretation of verse one aside for now.

Prayer for the Day: *Keeper of my soul, hold me close this day. Amen.*

Week 22
Tuesday

Psalm 131

Verse two talks about a weaned child with its mother. When a child is weaned, he or she can lay in the mother's arms contently without pulling at the mother for food. There is closeness, contentment, and a sense of safety when the child knows that he or she will not go hungry and can rest in the comfort of the mother's embrace without worry.

This imagery—being like a weaned child with its mother—is powerful imagery for how your relationship with God can be. You can rest in the love of God without demanding anything. Just being in relationship with God is sufficient. It is *more* than sufficient. The psalmist says, *My soul is like the weaned child that is with me.* Sit with that for a moment. The contentment, the peace, the safety.

Is this the relationship you yearn for with God? It's powerful imagery, isn't it?

Prayer for the Day: *Mother God, hold me close and safe. Amen.*

Psalm 131 — Week 22, Wednesday

So now return to verse one and interpret it again. If you are content, nurtured, and safe, if you love, love, love being in relationship with your graceful and loving God, then why in the world would you want to look up too high? Why, as the Contemporary English Version says, would you want to be conceited or waste your time on impossible schemes? Why would you want to wrestle with things too great or marvelous for you?

It is not a prohibition...**Don't do this**...it's an acceptance that in God, you don't *need* to do these things.

Because you trust God, you do not need to reach beyond your appropriate bounds. You do not need to push and push for more power, more money, more prestige, more control, or more success. You can accept that you are who you are, you can do what you can do, and you can love others in non-threatening ways just as God loves everyone. You do not have to reach for more affirmation, achievement, and affluence.

But you often don't want to live this way. You want to be God. You want to control others' lives. You delude yourself into believing that you know the mind of God and it is up to you to share that knowledge and DEMAND that others adhere to your insiders' truths. But the psalmist says that he is content being in the mother's arms, in God's arms, trusting, and experiencing wholeness of soul. The psalmist does not need to look up too high or try to figure out how to rule the world. God can take care of that just fine.

Meister Eckhart, German theologian, philosopher, and mystic in the early fourteenth century, wrote: "Blessed are the pure in heart who leave everything to God now as they did before they ever existed."

Prayer for the Day: *Loving God, I often want to be in charge...of everything! Help me release my control to your wisdom and grace. Amen.*

Week 22
Thursday

Psalm 131

When you settle into the arms of God, you snuggle down—not demanding anything, not wanting anything except to be in the loving presence of God. You may like to think that this is how you currently live your life but when you look at your prayers, you may realize that you are not a weaned child at all but a demanding, screaming baby pulling and pulling for God to give you something: Keep my loved one alive. Give me health. Why do you let me suffer? Why do you allow tragedy? Change the world so everyone has basic human needs met. Make my job better. Free my loved one from the demons of addiction. Give us good weather for our picnic. Let me find a parking place close to the restaurant. On and on. We look too high.

This psalm is not about asking questions or wondering about why things are like they are. You *know* that you cannot live without asking questions or wondering why certain things happen. This psalm does *not* require you to be passive, inert, and intellectually unchallenged.

Certainly, there are things in God's intentions and activity that you will never understand. This psalm says you can be okay with that. You will never know or understand. You are not God. Remember that. You... are... not... God.

Prayer for the Day: *Holy God, help me remember that I am not you. Amen.*

Psalm 131

Week 22
Friday

This psalm points to the deep, honest, trusting relationship that is yours to have with God. When you are in that deep communion, you can ask questions and rest in the assurance that you will receive answers when and if the answers are appropriate for you. You don't have to knock the door down. God loves you, cuddles you like a mother cuddles a young child in her lap, and allows you to be who you are without having to try to be someone you are not. You do not have to impress anyone, even yourself. You are God's. You do not have to be totally self-reliant because you have God to rely on. God's certainly got more experience in caring for human beings than you do.

The gospel writer of Matthew (6:25-34) reminds that Jesus reinforced the lessons of this psalm when he said not to worry about what you would eat or drink or what you would wear. He says to strive first for the kingdom of God, for the kind of world that you would live in if everyone followed the commitment to love God with all their hearts, souls, minds, and strength, and their neighbors as self. Jesus could just as easily have said that you can live like a weaned child, resting and secure in the love and care of your God of steadfast love.

Prayer for the Day: *God of steadfast love, you know I'm a worry wart. Help me release that trait to your loving embrace. Amen.*

Week 22
Saturday

Psalm 131

Verse three of this psalm calls people as individuals and as people of God to hope in the Lord from this time on and forevermore. In times of political time of unrest and discord, this call to hope seems particularly appropriate. People do not know what will happen to them and to so many people around the world. Terrorists, fear of the stranger, fires, wide disparity between those who have resources and those who do not, the list goes on and on. You can become despondent and scared.

It seems a particularly good time in your world to live with deep abiding trust in the Lord, your God. Sometimes that is all you can do. And all the time, that is what you are called to do…to trust in the Lord. You are loved by a God who loves you more than the person who loves you most in the world. When it gets right down to it, what more is there to want or need?

You can remember often that you live in the presence of God and draw strength from the knowledge that the one who calls and sends you also sustains you. Praise God.

Prayer for the Day: *All praises to you, God in whom I trust. Amen.*

Week 23
Exodus 15:1-16; Isaiah 43:1-4

Exodus 15
1 Then Moses and the Israelites sang this song to the Lord:
"I will sing to the Lord, for he has triumphed gloriously; horse and rider he has thrown into the sea.
2 The Lord is my strength and my might, and he has become my salvation; this is my God, and I will praise him, my father's God, and I will exalt him.
3 The Lord is a warrior; the Lord is his name.
4 'Pharaoh's chariots and his army he cast into the sea; his picked officers were sunk in the Red Sea.
5 The floods covered them; they went down into the depths like a stone.
6 Your right hand, O Lord, glorious in power—your right hand, O Lord, shattered the enemy.
7 In the greatness of your majesty you overthrew your adversaries; you sent out your fury, it consumed them like stubble.
8 At the blast of your nostrils the waters piled up, the floods stood up in a heap; the deeps congealed in the heart of the sea.
9 The enemy said, "I will pursue, I will overtake, I will divide the spoil, my desire shall have its fill of them. I will draw my sword, my hand shall destroy them."
10 You blew with your wind, the sea covered them; they sank like lead in the mighty waters.
11 'Who is like you, O Lord, among the gods? Who is like you, majestic in holiness, awesome in splendour, doing wonders?
12 You stretched out your right hand, the earth swallowed them.
13 'In your steadfast love you led the people whom you redeemed; you guided them by your strength to your holy abode.
14 The peoples heard, they trembled; pangs seized the inhabitants of Philistia.
15 Then the chiefs of Edom were dismayed; trembling seized the leaders of Moab; all the inhabitants of Canaan melted away.
16 Terror and dread fell upon them; by the might of your arm, they became still as a stone until your people, O Lord, passed by, until the people whom you acquired passed by.

Isaiah 43
1 But now thus says the Lord, he who created you, O Jacob, he who formed you, O Israel: Do not fear, for I have redeemed you; I have called you by name, you are mine.
2 When you pass through the waters, I will be with you; and through the rivers, they shall not overwhelm you; when you walk through fire you shall not be burned, and the flame shall not consume you.
3 For I am the Lord your God, the Holy One of Israel, your Saviour. I give Egypt as your ransom, Ethiopia and Seba in exchange for you.
4 Because you are precious in my sight, and honoured, and I love you, I give people in return for you, nations in exchange for your life.

Week 23
Sunday

Exodus 15:1-16; Isaiah 43:1-4

Note: This week's readings are heavily dependent on Marcus Borg, Speaking Christian, *35-45*

On a television design show, a man slapped his forehead and exclaimed, "I'm gobsmacked," when seeing the reveal of the newly redesigned space. Have you ever heard the phrase before? According to Google, *gobsmacked* means completely shocked, utterly astonished, astounded.

Gobsmacked may be what you feel when you discover that salvation means more than going to heaven when you die.

Wait! What???

Salvation is a very big Christian word. It is a loaded word. For the next several weeks you will unpack salvation in order to learn more about the depth and breadth of this foundational piece for your discipleship and Christian growth.

Prayer for the Day: *Holy God, I guess I'm ready to be gobsmacked. Could that be God-smacked? Amen.*

Exodus 15:1-16; Isaiah 43:1-4

Week 23
Monday

Theologian Marcus Borg relates an experience of facilitating an intergenerational discussion group about salvation. Half were in their twenties and thirties; the other half were in their sixties and seventies. Many were committed and dedicated Christians while others were earnest seekers, considering if there might be something real and important in Christianity. Surprisingly, 80 percent had negative associations with the idea of salvation. Salvation was about going to heaven with the counterbalance of going to hell very alarming.

The discussion group participants understood, especially from their teenage years, that going to heaven meant being saved from their sins. They wondered if they had done enough, been enough, to be allowed to enter the pearly gates. Quite frankly, they were afraid. The Christianity they understood was based in FEAR.

They also understood that only the right kind of Christian got to go to heaven. So there were lots and lots and lots of people excluded from this special journey. Many were "in," but most were "out." Christianity and smugness seemed to be linked in their understanding (Marcus Borg, *Speaking Christian*, 2011, p. 35-36).

We often link eternal life with eternal salvation with going to heaven.

Prayer for the Day: *Rabbi Jesus, teacher, help me broaden my understanding. Amen.*

Week 23
Tuesday

Exodus 15:1-16; Isaiah 43:1-4

Actually, the biblical meanings of salvation, saved, and savior are more than sin and forgiveness, heaven and hell. They speak of transformation on this side of death—personal transformation and even political transformation.

The actual word salvation and its related variations appear almost 500 times in the Bible. Salvation appears 127 times, saved/save/saves/saving about 300 times, savior about 40 times. Only one-third of those are in the New Testament! The Bible book that refers to salvation more than any other is not one of the gospels. It is not in Paul's writings. It is the book of Psalms. Check out Psalm 107 for a great example.

The reality in the Bible is that salvation is seldom about the afterlife. In fact, for most of the centuries covered in the Old Testament, the people of ancient Israel did not even believe in an afterlife! The first clear reference to life beyond death is in the book of Daniel, the last book written in the Old Testament, about 164 BCE. (Thanks to Marcus Borg for this scholarship.)

Prayer for the Day: *Holy Spirit, speak to me in ways that I can absorb beyond what I currently know, believe, and think. Amen.*

Exodus 15:1-16; Isaiah 43:1-4 **Week 23 / Wednesday**

Now for a look at what the Bible *does* say about salvation.

The earliest meaning of salvation is liberation from bondage. One of the major defining stories of the Israelites was their exodus from slavery in Egypt. Throughout the entire Bible there are stories of the mighty acts of God in that process. God raised up Moses. God hardened Pharaoh's heart. God brought the plagues which led to Pharaoh granting permission for the Hebrews to leave. And they left with animals, jewels, and other items of significance. God parted the Red Sea and allowed the former slaves to escape. God guided them as they wandered in the wilderness on their 40-year trek to the Promised Land. God provided them a land to thrive in and named them God's chosen.

With the Exodus, the Israelites were liberated from *economic bondage*: They were no longer slaves, "impoverished, condemned to constant hard labor, given only meager rations" (Borg, 40). They were liberated from *political bondage* where they "had no power, no voice, no say in how the system" (Borg, 41) operated. They were liberated from the *religious bondage* of Pharaoh not allowing them to worship their God.

This sense of salvation, of liberation, is evident in many of the laws they enacted. The year of Jubilee returned property to the original owners, forgave outstanding debts. People did not get to amass the power of the Pharaoh and his minions. The Ten Commandments taught to not steal, kill, covet…things that were ordinary in slavery times. It was many years before the people even had a king because they remembered what life under a Pharaoh was like. Later on, the prophets "Amos, Isaiah, Micah, Jeremiah, and others indicted the monarchy… [as a system] for re-creating Egypt within Israel" (Borg, 41), implementing the kind of oppression that their God had *saved* them from in Egypt.

Salvation meant God's acting to free an entire people from bondage. The Exodus was and is a pivotal understanding of how God frees and takes care of God's own people, of how God saves God's chosen.

Prayer for the Day: *God, do you mean that when I feel in bondage of any kind, being released is one way to understand your saving grace for me? Amen.*

Week 23
Thursday
Exodus 15:1-16; Isaiah 43:1-4

Marcus Borg explains that "the second major framework for shaping the Biblical meaning of salvation is the Jewish experience of the exile in the sixth century BCE. It began when the Babylonians conquered and destroyed Jerusalem and took many of the survivors into exile in Babylon...The exile lasted about 50 years and ended when Persia conquered Babylon and the Persian emperor Cyrus decreed that the exiles could return to their homeland" (Borg, 42).

The second part of the book of Isaiah addressed the exile and the return. Much of the language is familiar because of Handel's Messiah. Just listen to a few excerpts from Isaiah: "'*Comfort ye, comfort my people,' says your God. 'Every valley shall be exalted, and every mountain and hill made low, the crooked way straight, and the rough places plain.*'" Half of the references of savior in the Old Testament are in this part of Isaiah (chapters 40 and following).

"But now says the Lord...Do not fear...I have called you by name, you are mine. When you pass through the waters, I will be with you; and through the rivers, they shall not overwhelm you; when you walk through fire, you shall not be burned, and the flame shall not consume you. For I am the Lord your God, the Holy One of Israel, your Savior...You are precious in my sight, and honored, and I love you...Do not fear, for I am with you" (Isaiah 43:1-5).

Notice that the Israelites experience God's presence on the journey. God says, "I will be with you." They also know God's love: "I have called you by name, you are mine." And they are undergirded by God's assurance. God says, "Do not fear."

This "release from Babylon...[this] journey of return, [embraced by] God's presence and love ...[reinforces] the meaning of savior, salvation, and saved" (Borg, 44). Salvation is also understood as returning from exile, returning home.

Prayer for the Day: *God of deliverance, there are times when I feel I'm in exile from everything I know as normal, from those things that give me comfort and stability, and from people who I have depended on. Bring me home, out of exile. Amen.*

Exodus 15:1-16; Isaiah 43:1-4

Week 23
Friday

The last meaning of salvation to highlight from the Old Testament is from the overwhelming evidence in the Psalms. The word salvation appears over and over in the Psalms. It is mostly about rescue, deliverance from peril and danger. Hear just some excerpts:

The Lord is my light and my salvation; whom shall I fear? (Psalm 27:1)

Restore to me the joy of your salvation (Psalm 51:12)

I thank you that you have answered me and have become my salvation (Psalm 118:21).

Turn, O Lord, save my life; deliver me for the sake of your steadfast love (Psalm 6:4).

Be a rock of refuge for me, a strong fortress to save me (Psalm 31:2).

Save all the oppressed of the earth (Psalm 76:9).

"All of these meanings of salvation in the Old Testament—...liberation from bondage, return from exile, and rescue from peril—continue in the New Testament" especially in the letters of Paul. What the meanings of both the Old and New Testaments "have in common is salvation as 'deliverance,' 'rescue.' To be saved is to be rescued from that which ails [everyone.]." And even more than that, Marcus Borg rejoices in saying that "to be saved is to enter into a new kind of life—a life covenanted with God [which] is the central theme of the Old and New Testaments." To be saved is to live a life transformed. (Thanks to Marcus Borg, *Speaking Christian*, p. 45, for this affirmation of faith.)

Prayer for the Day: *God of salvation, lead me to a transformed life that leads me to new ways that I never could have dreamed of. Amen.*

Week 23
Saturday

Exodus 15:1-16; Isaiah 43:1-4

The Exodus story points us to liberation from bondage. "What bondage in your life do you want transformed?"

Is it economic bondage? Are you struggling with financial obligations because of the economy or because your wants exceed your resources? Do you have plenty but it still does not feel enough? Some yearn for a transformed world where they can earn enough to take care of their families. They dream of adequate childcare, medical help, wages, transportation, housing, education, and safety. They seek God's salvation from the Pharaohs of this world. They want to leave the oppression they experience each day, cross through that Red Sea., and travel to the Promised Land. They seek salvation.

Political or religious bondage may be where God is leading you to a significant transformation in the Here and Now…not in some faraway distant time in the future. Deliverance NOW.

Maybe you are in exile—you feel alone, that everything familiar has disappeared. Nothing is the same or familiar. When you are in exile, you are afraid. You need assurance. You yearn to know that this too will pass, and that God will transform the realities of your life right now. You need a savior right now, not in some far-off distant time. NOW. You call for God, for a savior, for transformation.

Maybe like the psalmists you want to be rescued from peril. You call out to God to rescue you, to lead you, to protect you, to transform you. Your peril may be illness. What does transformation—salvation—in that situation look like for you? The peril may be threats to your safety, to your wellbeing. How do you turn to God your savior for rescue, for safety, for transformation?

Because you are human, you experience bondage, exile, and peril. The message in scriptures is that God is with you, now. God is your salvation NOW. You are in God NOW. God is in you NOW. Your new life is for NOW. Your transformation is possible NOW. Your Christian faith journey is undergirded by a God who is more than you can imagine and yet is as close as your own breath. God is with you NOW to lead you out of Egypt, to bring you home from exile, and to deliver you from peril.

Prayer for the Day: *Praise to you, Father, Son, and Holy Spirit for the hope you fill me with. Amen.*

Week 24
Ephesians 2:1-10

1 You were dead through the trespasses and sins 2 in which you once lived, following the course of this world, following the ruler of the power of the air, the spirit that is now at work among those who are disobedient. 3 All of us once lived among them in the passions of our flesh, following the desires of flesh and senses, and we were by nature children of wrath, like everyone else. 4 But God, who is rich in mercy, out of the great love with which he loved us 5 even when we were dead through our trespasses, made us alive together with Christ—by grace you have been saved—6 and raised us up with him and seated us with him in the heavenly places in Christ Jesus, 7 so that in the ages to come he might show the immeasurable riches of his grace in kindness towards us in Christ Jesus. 8 For by grace you have been saved through faith, and this is not your own doing; it is the gift of God—9 not the result of works, so that no one may boast. 10 For we are what he has made us, created in Christ Jesus for good works, which God prepared beforehand to be our way of life.

Week 24
Sunday

Ephesians 2:1-10

Note: The week's readings pull heavily from Marcus Borg, Speaking Christian, *46-54*

Unfortunately, Christian language can sometimes become a stumbling block. Much "holy" vocabulary is misunderstood by Christians and non-Christians alike—words like salvation, sacrifice, righteousness, redemption, mercy, sin, forgiveness, born again, second coming, God, Jesus, Bible—have been distorted and moved away from their traditional and biblical meanings. If you read any of the writings that debunk Christianity in our contemporary times, they often refer to language and imagery most used by people who tend to believe the Bible is literal in all its language…the world really was created in six days, the only reason we are on the earth is so we can earn our way into heaven, God really loves only Christians as *they* define Christian. Everyone else is going to hell.

The distortion of our Christian vocabulary must sadden God's heart and it certainly cheapens our walk with Jesus. Some of the distortions result from language moving from a picture and story orientation to a literal meaning. One example is when Nicodemus asked Jesus how a person could crawl back into the mother's womb to be born again. Jesus had so much more in mind…not an acknowledgment and acceptance of mental affirmations…but a complete transformation such as one experiences in an actual birth…where what *was* is no more and what *can be* has opened in wonderful, life-giving ways. This new birth imagery unfolds for us the meaning of *in God we live and move and have our being* (Acts 17:28).

A more lighthearted example of how language has been distorted to its literal meanings comes from a story a woman named Emily tells. When she was a girl, she could walk to the Green Stamp store to get large boxes out of their trash bin out back. She dragged these boxes home and turned them into houses, cars, rockets, sleds, and anything else she could dream up. Green Stamps were truly stamps that were green. You received them at the grocery store and sometimes other places of business based on how much you spent. You would glue the stamps into a book and then you could go to the Green Stamp store and redeem your books for various items. Emily says she still has a lamp at her house that she got at the Green Stamp store.

A young boy was approached by a street evangelist who asked very seriously if the young man was saved. The child immediately retorted that "Yes, he was saved. He currently had six-and-a-half books." The evangelist was puzzled with the answer. Then the kid asked, "You want to see them?" The response became clear. Literal language.

Prayer for the Day: *God of wonder, help me embrace wonder rather than exact certitude. Amen.*

Ephesians 2:1-10

Week 24
Monday

The New Testament is full of examples of deliverance and transformation. In his book *Speaking Christian*, Marcus Borg assists in looking at New Testament themes of salvation.

Sometimes the concept of salvation in the New Testament comes from the human predicament of being blind. People with light skin have been blind to the fears, challenges, and heart ache of people with darker skin. People with resources are often blind to the economic realities of those with limited or no resources. Are you blind?

Healing the blind man at Bethsaida reminds that Jesus can save you from your own blindness. He can open your eyes. Listen again to the dialogue between the blind man and Jesus. After putting spit on the man's eyes and laying his hands on him, *Jesus asked, "Can you see anything?" And the man looked up and said, "I can see people, but they look like trees, walking." Then Jesus laid his hands on his eyes again: and he looked intently, and his sight was restored* (Mark 8:22-26).

Jesus seemed to believe that some people who had sight were still blind. He said to pharisees, *You blind guides. You strain out a gnat but swallow a camel* (Mt. 23:24). Where are you blind? In what ways do you need saving from your lack of sight? Jesus proclaimed he was the Light of the World. Barbara Brown Taylor describes in her book, *Learning to Walk in the Dark*, the power of darkness in our lives when she says: "What do I mean by "darkness"?... Just say the word and the associations begin to flow: night, nightmare, ghost, graveyard, cave, bat, vampire, death, devil, criminal, danger, doubt, depression, loss, fear. Fear is the main thing. Almost everyone is afraid of being afraid...It fits the way a shadow fits, because darkness [might we say blindness?] is sticky. It attracts meaning like a magnet, picking up everything in its vicinity that is not fully lit." (4)

Taylor says, "For now, it is enough to say that 'darkness' is shorthand for anything that scares me—that I want no part of—either because I am sure that I do not have the resources to survive it or because I do not want to find out. The absence of God is in there, along with the fear of dementia and the loss of those nearest and dearest to me" (4-5).

Salvation means that Jesus is the Light of the World. Jesus overcomes the dark. Where are you in darkness? Where are you afraid? Where do you need to be transformed into the light? Where do you need sight? Where do you need salvation?

Prayer for the Day: *God of light, bring me out of darkness. Amen.*

Week 24
Tuesday

Ephesians 2:1-10

Marcus Borg says another way of looking at salvation in the New Testament is the movement from death to life. Jesus raised several people from the dead: Jairus' daughter, the son of the widow of Nain, Lazarus. Just as Jesus brought sight to the blind, he brought life to the dead. He even seemed to indicate that there are living people walking around as if dead. Remember when he said, *Let the dead bury their dead?* (Mt.8:22)

Paul, too, speaks of dying and rising with Christ. Hear what he wrote to the Galatians (2:19-20). *For through the law I died to the law, so that I might live to God. I have been crucified with Christ; and it is no longer I who live, but it is Christ who lives in me. And the life I now live in the flesh I live by faith in the Son of God, who loved me and gave himself for me.* Paul is talking about a major transformation in his life, his current life, the here and now. Paul knows that he died to who he used to be…a persecutor of Christians…to life as the apostle who took the good news of Jesus to the Gentiles, greatly beyond the geographic bounds where Jesus walked. Paul was saved to serve Jesus, his Savior, now. Paul's transformation is parallel to the concept of being born again that the gospel of John highlighted.

Are you dead to new ideas? Are you dead because of grief? Because of human relationships that are killing you? Are you dead because you choose to bury yourself in the middle of life itself? Are you dead because of your selfishness? Is your community dead to the beauty of EVERYONE who lives in it, not just those who look, act, think like you? Where are you dead? Where do you yearn for the life that pulls you from the grave of your own ways of living and thinking and being?

Prayer for the Day: *Living God, point me in the ways that I am dead. Amen.*

Ephesians 2:1-10

Week 24
Wednesday

A third way of looking at salvation, as deliverance in the New Testament, according to Borg, is the transformation from infirmity to well-being. He relates that "more stories are told about Jesus as healer than about any other figure in antiquity. But these stories [are] more than factual" (*Speaking Christian*, p. 48). Indeed, even the word "salvation" has Latin roots in the word for "salve, a healing ointment." Healing can refer to our wounds of being human, of being healed from the pains, fears, and burdens we carry simply because we are alive.

A premier example of this is the healing of the bleeding woman who reached and touched Jesus and was healed. Imagine her saying, "I reached out to touch Jesus slowly and with fear, but also with courage and deliberation. And immediately I was healed. It was like a light going through me. And then Jesus truly healed me through and through when he said, *Daughter, your faith has made you well; go in peace.* I, who have had no family or protector, was now called 'Daughter.' Jesus gave me his blessing. Through the encounter, I regained my health—physical, emotional, and spiritual. I reclaimed my place in society as well as a new outlook on life. '*Go in peace,*' he said" (Luke 8:43-48).

You may be literally ill and when you feel better, you may feel as if life is new again. You may feel sick in your spirit and when you emerge from that broken place, you feel reborn. You may feel broken and then you are transformed into wholeness. This is Salvation. This is pure gift from Jesus the Christ.

Prayer for the Day: *Lord Jesus Christ, thank you for my experiences of healing, of emerging from brokenness, of transformation. Amen.*

Week 24   Ephesians 2:1-10
Thursday

The Bible also has political meanings of salvation with two focal points: justice and peace.

Stories and teachings abound addressing the need for economic justice. Acts 2:43-46 states: *Awe came upon everyone, because many wonders and signs were being done by the apostles. All who believed were together and had all things in common; they would sell their possessions and goods and distribute the proceeds to all, as any had need.* The verses remind that no one should have more than is needed and no one has less. After all, it all belongs to God.

This was important in a culture where about 90 percent of the population lived on the margin of subsistence and destitution, according to Marcus Borg (49). The Bible talks of Pharaoh and Herod and Caesar who exploited people, who enslaved, taxed excessively, killed, and controlled. We still need deliverance from them today. Come, Lord Jesus. Save us.

Salvation also enfolds the transformation from violence to peace. Hear these words from John at Patmos in the book of Revelation: *See, the home of God is among mortals. He will dwell with them as their God; they will be God's people and God himself with be with them. God will wipe every tear from their eyes. Death will be no more; mourning and crying and pain will be no more, for the first things have passed away* (Revelation 21:3-4). No mourning. No crying. No pain. ALL the old things are gone…gone…gone. No violence. Peace.

Jesus taught in the Beatitudes: "Blessed are the peacemakers, for they will be called children of God." Peacemakers don't keep the peace. They make it. Salvation is the transformation needed to be able to make peace.

You can glimpse what God's world looks like. You have hints of what salvation of the world feels like. Health, life, light, peace, transformation from what you know now.

Prayer for the Day: *God of justice, open my eyes to where justice is not being served and then embolden me to do what I can about it. Amen.*

Ephesians 2:1-10

Week 24
Friday

So salvation...wow...so much more than going to heaven!
Salvation in the Bible is both personal and political. It is both internal to your life as well as external to your world and culture.

The stories in the Bible proclaim that God wants to deliver you as an individual as well as your world with its political and economic systems from blindness, from death, from infirmity. God yearns for justice and peace. This is salvation.

Prayer for the Day: *Savior, you are giving me LIFE now!!! You are delivering me NOW! Hallelujah! Amen.*

Week 24 — Saturday
Ephesians 2:1-10

Marcus Borg tells about speaking to a mainline clergy conference. He said, "I mentioned in my first lecture that whenever Christianity emphasizes the afterlife as the reason for being Christian, the result invariably is a distortion of Christianity. It becomes a religion of requirements and rewards...It creates an in-group and an out-group" (Borg, 53-54).

[During the question-and-answer period, one minister asked], "If Christianity's not about an afterlife, then what's our product?" (Borg, 54)

Borg said he took the question seriously. His answer was that "our product is salvation as the twofold transformation of ourselves and the world" (Borg, 54).

This answer gives pause. What you can proclaim is not just the afterlife, but that God is about transforming you as an individual and transforming the world in its entirety. Salvation is a deep connection and understanding to the reality of liberation from all that keeps us in bondage. Salvation is about sight, wholeness, healing of the wounds of existence. You and others yearn for a world that is a better place.

You may disagree about how all this happens. But your faith in a saving God allows that salvation can and will happen in ways unknown to you, beyond your wildest imaginations. You can be transformed. Your world can be transformed. Jesus, your Lord and Savior, continues to teach you that this is so and leads you in the process.

Prayer for the Day: *Come, Lord Jesus. Amen.*

Week 25
John 14:1-7

'Do not let your hearts be troubled. Believe in God, believe also in me. 2 In my Father's house there are many dwelling-places. If it were not so, would I have told you that I go to prepare a place for you? 3 And if I go and prepare a place for you, I will come again and will take you to myself, so that where I am, there you may be also. 4 And you know the way to the place where I am going.' 5 Thomas said to him, 'Lord, we do not know where you are going. How can we know the way?' 6 Jesus said to him, 'I am the way, and the truth, and the life. No one comes to the Father except through me. 7 If you know me, you will know my Father also. From now on you do know him and have seen him.'

Week 25 Sunday
John 14:1-7

When you think about salvation and what it really means, you may ponder questions such as: What about Jesus being the Way? What significance does Jesus Christ have? How does understanding that Jesus is the Way open up my understanding of salvation as both personal and political transformation? How do I share my understanding of the good news with anyone else…whether they are Christian, Muslim, Buddhist, Hindu, or no faith at all?

You may think this is pretty radical stuff…wondering about Jesus Christ as the Way. Even someone who is a Christian and claims that Jesus Christ, the triune God, is the center of life can believe that if you do not question all those things that you have heard and talked about all your life, then your faith can become stale and shallow. Christianity then can be used and abused.

Barbara Brown Taylor captures some of this frustration with how faith can be perverted unless you participate in thoughtful wrestling and questioning. In her book, *Speaking of Sin*, she says that the message can get flattened out over time by saying something like this: "All God cares about is whether or not we believe in Jesus. Once our faith has been established, any violence we do to one another in our battles of belief are justified, and any mistakes we make in the flesh are forgiven. All that matters to God is the inner disposition of our hearts" (p. 101). History certainly confirms her assessment.

Jesus and Christian faith and what all this mean have been even more front and center for thoughtful disciples because of the pandemic, attacks on people of color, attacks on people of Asian descent, mass shootings, international war. People of faiths other than certain brands of Christianity have been attacked. For example, people who are Muslim have been beaten or killed. Every religion can be perverted by its followers. So how do you talk with, interact with people who are not Christian and still be true to the gospel of Jesus Christ?

Prayer for the Day: *God of passion, help me understand what it means to walk your way and then to do it. Amen.*

John 14:1-7

Week 25
Monday

During a meeting on interfaith dialogue that was working particularly on Christian-Muslim relations, one comment really stood out. Someone in the group, who had long worked with and among Muslims, said that Muslims welcomed interfaith dialogue, but they respected and expected Christians to be firm in Christian beliefs and not water down their witness as Christians when talking with Muslims about faith matters. He said that this does not mean that Christians try to convert Muslims; Jesus followers simply remain true to their own center as they converse with Muslims, honoring and respecting them and their traditions.

Do you even know what your center is?

Prayer for the Day: *Jesus Christ, my Lord and Savior, I breathe and ask for you to show me my center and help me fully claim it. Amen.*

Week 25 John 14:1-7
Tuesday

Go into all the world and proclaim the good news to the whole creation (Mark 16:15).

There is salvation in no one else, for there is no other name under heaven given among mortals by which we must be saved (Acts 4:12).

I am the way, the truth, and the life. No one comes to the Father except through me (John 14:6).

And yet there are other passages which seem to broaden one's understanding.

In Christ God was reconciling the WORLD to himself, not counting their trespasses against them (II Corinthians 5:19).

Ephesians 1:10 talks about a plan for the fullness of time, to gather all things in him, things in heaven and things on earth.

Amos 9:7 sounds as if there was more than one Exodus, *Listen: Are you not like the Ethiopians to me, O people of Israel, says the Lord. Did I not bring Israel up from the land of Egypt, and the Philistines from Caphtor and the Arameans from Kir?* Other scriptures indicate the love God has for the whole world, for all those "outsiders" who are not part of the "acceptable" groups.

Have you wondered about your proper approach to a doctor or nurse who may be Hindu, or a friend who is Ba'hai? How do you witness to the gospel of Jesus Christ and be true to your Holy God? Some people sound as if they are trying to brainwash the other person, making Jesus sound like a bell hop or a door keeper. Just say the words and you're in, buddy. They sound arrogant as if they are better than anyone else. They may seem threatening, as if they are trying to scare someone into the kingdom. They seem more concerned in right belief or correct doctrine than they are in sharing the wonderful reality of Christ in their lives. Jesus is a big stick that they beat over the heads of anyone who differs from them. They do not even want to have to interact with anyone who is different.

A woman told of an incident in her neighborhood. One day one of the neighbor children who is Ba'hai had on a tee shirt that said, "There is more than one path to wisdom." That same day another child from a fundamentalist Christian family had on a shirt that read, "There is no other name." The mother of the Christian child forbade her child to play with the Ba'hai child.

Prayer for the Day: *God of truth, help me puzzle through this and not believe I already have all the answers. Amen.*

John 14:1-7

**Week 25
Wednesday**

Some Christians focus on being "number one" rather than focusing on the life, death, and resurrection of the God who created the world and everything that is in it. They do not focus on the person of the Holy Spirit who has acted throughout history, nor do they share with others the God who as a human, showed us how to love with compassion and openness.

Some Christians set themselves up as the measuring rod for others. They may ask, "Does this idea in another religion fit my understanding of Christianity?" If so, it is okay. If not, then it is not truth…for them or anyone else. Some Christians dabble in Native Spirituality or Buddhism and pick and choose whatever seems to fit. There is nothing wrong with expanding our knowledge and learning from others and their points of view. Indeed, you may have learned the concept of mindful living by reading Buddhist authors. You may be learning more about honoring the earth and all living things through by learning from indigenous writers or leaders. However, some people seem to lose Jesus in their attempt to be open and accepting of others. Jesus has said that he is the way, the truth, and the life. Marcus Borg reminded that "Way" means journey. So… what is the journey of a Christian? What does that mean as you interact with people of other religious and even other secular systems of truth?

You can find guidance not by looking at doctrine, not by quoting the teachings of the church, but by looking at God. What an amazing thought. You learn what it means to be in relation to God by focusing on God, a triune God: Creator, redeemer, sustainer/ Father, Son, Holy Spirit!

Prayer for the Day: *God of my innermost being, help me focus on you and only you. Amen.*

Week 25
Thursday
John 14:1-7

John of Damascus of the 8th century described the Father, Son, and Holy Spirit, as three dancers, holding hands, dancing around together in joyful freedom. So, for example, the God who created the world and everything and everyone in it is also the Spirit who is everywhere already working in the world and is also the Son, the Logos that was in the beginning and in the end. When you go to someone who is not a Christian, you can know, without a shadow of a doubt, that the Spirit of God is already working in that person's life in whatever way is appropriate for that individual because God created that person. You can simply share your story and the story of your faith and let God do the rest.

When you live your faith this way, when your life shines with Christ's love, when your spirit is enthused by the Holy Spirit, when you are a partner in creating beauty and life, then the other person will initiate the dialog because he/she will see something in your life that is worth talking about. St. Francis of Assisi said, "Preach the word of God wherever you go, even use words, if necessary."

I am the way, the truth, and the life. No one comes to the Father except through me (John 14:6). Even a Hindu scholar has said that John 14:6 is absolutely true. He said, "Jesus is the only way. And that way—dying to an old way of living and being born into a new way of being—is known to all the religions of the world" (Marcus Borg told by Bennett Sims in his newsletter, "Servant Leadership Institute").

This Jesus, this Jesus came to do the will of the Father who sent him. This Jesus, whom you follow, came to announce and inaugurate the kingdom of God. This Jesus, whom you pattern your life after, was a friend of sinners and a friend to unbelieving people who were excluded and rejected by law abiding, morally respectable members of the religious establishment. This Jesus, who died for you, believed that caring for needy, suffering human beings is more important than conformity to requirements of moral and theological orthodoxy. This Jesus, whose story and truths we are to embody, came not to condemn, not to defeat and lord it over his enemies, but to give his life for them and reconcile them to God and to each other. This Jesus who is also your creator and sustainer, is the risen Lord over all principalities and authorities everywhere.

Prayer for the Day: *Come, Lord Jesus, come into my heart. Amen.*

John 14:1-7

**Week 25
Friday**

So what do you do with all this? First of all, you realize that God alone has the right to give the answer. One Christian denomination wrote in a study document: "No one is saved apart from God's gracious redemption in Jesus Christ. Yet we do not presume to limit the sovereign freedom of 'God our Savior, who desires everyone to be saved and to come to the knowledge for the truth.'" (I Tim. 2:4). The document continues: "Thus, we neither restrict the grace of God to those who profess explicit faith in Christ nor assume that all people are saved regardless of faith. Grace, love, and communion belong to God, and are not ours to determine" (Presbyterian Church USA, *Hope in the Lord Jesus Christ*, 11-12).

Isn't this a comfort? No one else, not another person, can decide what is the future for you or anyone else. Have you ever had someone tell you, "You're going to hell!"? They do not know that. Only God has your future. The same denomination declared: "The limits to salvation, whatever they may be, are known only to God. Three truths above all are certain. God is a holy God who is not to be trifled with. No one will be saved except by grace alone. And no judge could possibly be more gracious than our Lord and Savior, Jesus Christ" (Study catechism of the Presbyterian Church, USA, adopted by the 210th General Assembly, question 49).

Prayer for the Day: *God of my life, help me to remember that you are my truth, my knowledge, my peace, my salvation. No person on earth can usurp your role in my life. Amen.*

Week 25   **John 14:1-7**
Saturday

You also remember that you worship a jealous God who wants all your devotion and praise. *You shall have no other gods before me* (Exodus 20:3). And you worship a God who always reached out to others. Dale Bruner, in discussing "I am the way," observed Jesus's remarkable openness of his relationships with all kinds of different people when he wrote: "We are in for some surprises, because this Christ, to whom we are to hold exclusively, is himself very inclusive (Quoted by Terry McGonical, "'My Lord and My God:' The Uniqueness of Jesus in John's Gospel," *Theology Matters, Vol 8, No. 5*. Sept/Oct 2002).

You share your personal story of your relationship with this Jesus the Christ. You tell of what his love and care and teachings and guidance have meant to you. You share where you have been released from a sense of bondage. You claim where you have been brought back from exile in a strange place. You leave old ways of thinking and being and continue to grow into the new life that God holds before you each and every day. Professor Shirley Guthrie gives good guidance when he writes: "We will enter into conversation with people whose faith is different from our own (both outside and inside the Christian community) with honest recognition of the differences that separate us; with great modesty about our own piety, wisdom, and virtue; and with eager willingness to meet our own God in our conversations with them. And we will do it with a boundless generosity of our own that is the very best witness we could possibly make to the crucified and risen Lord who is the way, the truth, and the life" (Shirley C. Guthrie, *Always Being Reformed: Faith for a Fragmented World*, Westminster John Knox Press; Louisville, KY, 1996, p. 76).

Prayer for the Day: *Jesus, my way, my truth, and my life, strengthen me with gentleness when I have opportunity to share relationship with others. Amen.*

Week 26
John 15:1-8

'I am the true vine, and my Father is the vine-grower. 2 He removes every branch in me that bears no fruit. Every branch that bears fruit he prunes to make it bear more fruit. 3 You have already been cleansed by the word that I have spoken to you. 4 Abide in me as I abide in you. Just as the branch cannot bear fruit by itself unless it abides in the vine, neither can you unless you abide in me. 5 I am the vine, you are the branches. Those who abide in me and I in them bear much fruit, because apart from me you can do nothing. 6 Whoever does not abide in me is thrown away like a branch and withers; such branches are gathered, thrown into the fire, and burned. 7 If you abide in me, and my words abide in you, ask for whatever you wish, and it will be done for you. 8 My Father is glorified by this, that you bear much fruit and become my disciples.

Week 26
Sunday

John 15:1-8

A grandmother tells the story of spending time with her 3½-year-old twin grandchildren as they walked around the block of their urban neighborhood. They came to a church with three white crosses planted in the grassy strip between the street and the sidewalk. Her granddaughter touched the cross on the right and asked, "What's this, Mimi?"

She said, "It is a cross."

"What's it for?"

"It shows that this is a Christian church."

Her grandson noted that the middle cross had a white cloth draped around it and he wanted to know what that was. She explained that the white cloth celebrated that Jesus had come back to life after some mean men had killed him. He asked, "What were their names?" She said as she wondered what she had gotten herself into that she didn't know their names (even though Caiaphas, Herod, and Pontius Pilate immediately came to mind).

Then the children noticed the grapevine wreath that was on the middle cross and wanted to know about it as well. Once again, she told them that some mean men had killed Jesus and they had put something like this on his head. Then she moved ahead immediately to the moral of the story. "What this means for you is that Jesus lives in your heart and he's with you all the time."

Her grandson retorted, "I don't want Jesus in my heart. I closed the door yesterday so he couldn't come in."

I'm sinking fast, she thought.

"Well," she said, "when Jesus lives in your heart, you are filled with love for your sister, mama and daddy, me and Papa and lots of other people."

The granddaughter piped up, "I don't want Jesus in my heart."

The grandmother realized that she was going nowhere fast with this conversation, so she just said, "Well, okay. But I want Jesus in my heart so I can love." Then the conversation moved on to the flowers that were just up ahead.

What a lesson these children opened! Jesus said, "Abide in me as I abide in you" and you may say, "I don't want Jesus in my heart." You may rather choose separation from God. You may not want to be connected to the source of life.

Prayer for the Day: *Beloved, I claim for this day I want to be connected to you, the source of my life and of all living beings. Amen.*

John 15:1-8

Week 26
Monday

This passage can be trite, it can be profound, and it can be downright confrontational. The first two verses in themselves are unsettling enough. Jesus said, *I am the true vine, and my Father is the vine grower. He removes every branch in me that bears no fruit. Every branch that bears no fruit he prunes to make it bear more fruit* (John 15:1-2). Did you *hear* what this said? That Jesus himself was pruned because he is the true vine. Do you wonder how Jesus was pruned, or as some commentators translate the word, "How Jesus was cleansed as the plant"?

When you think about it, you realize that Jesus's 40-day experience in the wilderness when he was tempted was certainly a cleansing experience. When the Pharisees and scribes asked him questions, trying to trip him up, he experienced a kind of pruning. When his disciples, his closest friends and confidants, denied him or challenged him, were just plain *dense* by not understanding him, or even abandoned him at his most critical hour a kind of pruning happened. The harshest pruning of all had to be when Jesus was nailed to a cross.

Prayer for the Day: *Father God, I'm not so sure about pruning. But if Jesus experienced it, then maybe...? Amen.*

Week 26
Tuesday

John 15:1-8

This passage says that disciples are the branches on this true vine. This means that pruning will be part of your journey and growth in faith so that you can bear good fruit. But pruning can be painful. Maybe you want to scream, "How can a loving God do this to his own Son, to me?"

Maybe a loving God can do no other than prune you as needed. Have you ever planted seeds and then had a hard time thinning out the seedlings? But if you don't thin the seedlings, the plants will not have the space or nutrients to grow and produce flowers or fruit. Maybe you don't like thinning. Possibly a loving God does not like pruning either but also loves you enough to help you grow strong in your faith so you can bear good fruit. Maybe you need to be pruned of your prejudices or judgmental attitudes. You may need to let go of toxic people in your life. You may still be holding onto the past or even dreams that you outgrew years ago. You might benefit from losing your perfectionism or your busy-ness. Maybe you need to have pruning done on all the excuses you use when you ignore God's call on your life. You might need to be cleansed of your feelings of worthlessness or our feelings of grandeur. Some of this pruning will be excruciating. You might say, like the grandchildren did, "I don't want Jesus in my heart. I don't want God to take away things in me that make me less than the person I am created to be. I don't want to be transformed."

Reba Riley, in her book *Post-Traumatic Church Syndrome*, writes: "This is why being broken [*author changes to pruned*]. This is why being [pruned] is so beautiful: being [pruned] means you have cracks for love and light to shine through, gaps for…[God] to burrow and bloom, space to move from the person you were to the person you will become. Being [pruned] means healing can find you and hope can gush forth like a geyser, flooding every part of you, until you can see why the [pruning] was necessary in the first place; to give birth to you" (Chalice Press, 2016, 335).

Prayer for the Day: *Comforter, help me understand that pruning events come from your love for me. Amen.*

John 15:1-8

Week 26
Wednesday

As a person of faith who believes in a loving God, who worships a God who loves you more than the person who loves you most in the world, you learn in this passage that you carry things, attitudes, and actions that need to be stripped away so that you can grow, blossom, and bring forth good fruit.

Then Jesus gives you your hope in verse three: *You have already been cleansed by the word that I have spoken to you.* Through Christ's teachings and his life, you know what healthy relationship with your triune God looks like—you love and care and follow Jesus's Way. Your Savior has given you everything he had to give in order that you might be part of the healthy vine and produce good fruit. You are a person of the gospel.

Verses four and five give you more to ponder: Jesus says, *Abide in me as I abide in you. Just as the branch cannot bear fruit by itself unless it abides in the vine, neither can you unless you abide in me.* He says, *I am the vine, you are the branches. Those who abide in me and I in them bear much fruit, because apart from me you can do nothing.* Just think about this. Where does the fruit grow? Not on the vine but on the branches. Jesus needs you. Branches are the fruit bearers. You, branch, are the hands, feet, ears, and eyes of Jesus in the world. The way you live your life witnesses to Christ's life-giving support. Bearing fruit makes you happy because that's what healthy branches are created to do.

Is it possible that sometimes you try to bear the wrong kind of fruit? You forget that you're part of a grapevine when you try to produce apples on your branches. You may have had great project in mind, but the project just didn't get off the ground. It did not mature. Maybe you were not paying attention to God's timing, or you may have forgotten who the true vine is.

Jesus is the vine. Your strength to follow this awesome calling of producing good fruit is because of that. All your nutrients, everything you need for life, is a gift from God.

When you do not honor this gift, then it seems that pruning is called for.

Prayer for the Day: *Life of all who live, when I decide to grow apples and you want grapes, help me get back on track sooner rather than later. Amen.*

Week 26
Thursday

John 15:1-8

Do you fight with every fiber of your being against the possibility that you might receive some pruning and maybe even deserve to be pruned? Do you just not like where these words of Jesus are taking you? More and more, you may agree with the twins, "I don't want Jesus in my heart."

Verse six certainly does not help much. *Whoever does not abide in me is thrown away like a branch and withers; such branches are gathered, thrown into the fire, and burned.* Here you want to say, "Let's just skip over this verse, okay?" But wait a minute. Jesus has already said in verse three that you have been cleansed. *You have been cleansed.* All this pruning will not kill you or destroy you. This pruning gives you life more joyful and abundant than you can ever imagine.

Jesus reminds you in verse six about how painful life without faith can be. Maybe there have been times in your life that without faith, you would not have made it. Maybe there's been more than one occasion when you wanted to cry out to God, "I believe that what I am going through, hurtful though it is, is part of my path that you are leading me on. I believe with every fiber of my being that you are guiding my journey. But right now, I need a sign!!!" Think about things in your life that would have been so much worse without your faith. How would you have gotten through without your friends in the faith, without your church, without your assurance that God's love was surrounding you even in the midst of the pain?

Prayer for the Day: *Thank you, dear Lord, for being with me in those tough times...even when I'm not always aware of your presence. Amen.*

John 15:1-8

Week 26
Friday

So what does it mean to abide in Christ and for Christ to abide in you? The only way one person can abide in another is when a woman is pregnant. The baby abides in her. All the infant's nutrition and even life depend on the mother. Is your faith growing to this deep kind of attachment to your Lord and Savior? Do you really claim and live out the reality that everything in your life is connected to God and God's creation of you?

The image of God being water and you being a fish helps demonstrate that you cannot live without being in the water. You are in God and God is in you. But the fish is not the water.

There are other ways we can think of Jesus's abiding in us. When you hear the words of the Lord's Supper, "This is my body broken for you; this is my blood shed for the forgiveness of sin," and then share the bread and the wine, you are symbolically taking Jesus into your body. When you absorb the teachings of Jesus, in some way, you "eat" his words. They become part of you. You learn Christ's teachings and pay attention to his commandments and learn from his example so that they are just part of you. You can grow into this life of faith so that maybe one day, you can't breathe or think without the love of God resonating in and through you.

Jesus also abides in you through the Spirit. When you pay attention to the Spirit's guidance, wisdom, and advocacy, you experience Christ abiding in you.

When you as a follower of Jesus love others, care for those in need, live your faith rather than just talk about your faith, you demonstrate that you abide in Christ and that Christ abides in you. Because your love is grounded and fed by the true vine, you are empowered to love those who are unlovable, to forgive those who need forgiveness, to offer mercy to those who may not deserve it.

Prayer for the Day: *Lover of my soul, fill my life with overflowing love that I share with all those I connect with each day. Amen.*

Week 26 **John 15:1-8**
Saturday

Verse seven then says that *If you abide in me, and my words abide in you, ask for whatever you wish, and it will be done for you.* Have you prayed for things that have not happened? This verse is *not* saying that you will have a magic wand to wave to get whatever you want. What it *is* saying is what a preacher said: "God always answers prayer. Sometime the answer is "yes", sometimes it is "no", sometimes it is "maybe", and sometimes it is "not yet'. As you think about this promise in the context of Christ abiding in you and you abiding in Christ, then your prayers will align with the requests that Jesus himself would make. Your prayers would not be for glorifying yourself but for glorifying God. Your prayers would be less about relieving your pain and more about being part of the Creator's magnificent plan. Your prayers would be less petty and more full of the promises of God. When you are attached as a branch to the vine, you can only ask for things that benefit the entire plant. You love your fellow branches as you love yourself. You are so connected that you can only pray as Christ would have you pray. Then of course, the prayer will be granted.

The final verse of this passage is, *My father is glorified by this, that you bear much fruit and become my disciples.* This is salvation: being part of the vine is release from bondage, it's returning from exile, it's escape from peril, it's connecting to Jesus because he is the way. Your transformation allows you to bear much fruit and to become disciples of your loving Jesus, your God.

Prayer for the Day: *May I abide in Christ and may Christ abide in me. I will experience salvation, transformation because I am not separated from you, my loving God. Amen.*

Week 27
Mark 7:24-30; Matthew 15:21-28

From there he set out and went away to the region of Tyre. He entered a house and did not want anyone to know he was there. Yet he could not escape notice, 25 but a woman whose little daughter had an unclean spirit immediately heard about him, and she came and bowed down at his feet. 26 Now the woman was a Gentile, of Syrophoenician origin. She begged him to cast the demon out of her daughter. 27 He said to her, 'Let the children be fed first, for it is not fair to take the children's food and throw it to the dogs.' 28 But she answered him, 'Sir, even the dogs under the table eat the children's crumbs.' 29 Then he said to her, 'For saying that, you may go—the demon has left your daughter.' 30 So she went home, found the child lying on the bed, and the demon gone.

Jesus left that place and went away to the district of Tyre and Sidon. 22 Just then a Canaanite woman from that region came out and started shouting, 'Have mercy on me, Lord, Son of David; my daughter is tormented by a demon.' 23 But he did not answer her at all. And his disciples came and urged him, saying, 'Send her away, for she keeps shouting after us.' 24 He answered, 'I was sent only to the lost sheep of the house of Israel.' 25 But she came and knelt before him, saying, 'Lord, help me.' 26 He answered, 'It is not fair to take the children's food and throw it to the dogs.' 27 She said, 'Yes, Lord, yet even the dogs eat the crumbs that fall from their masters' table.' 28 Then Jesus answered her, 'Woman, great is your faith! Let it be done for you as you wish.' And her daughter was healed instantly.

Week 27   Mark 7:24-30; Matthew 15:21-28
Sunday

These passages are ones preachers would like to avoid. Bible commentators see it as extremely difficult, rigid, and even distressing. Jesus seems uncompassionate to this woman's distress. Many people don't like the Jesus this passage seems to show. But because this shows up in lectionary readings, try not to avoid this uncomfortable story. You are not to stop from seeking to find God's truth.

If you are not Jewish, that makes you Gentile. As a Gentile, you certainly *want* the story to end like it does, where a Gentile child, one who lives in the region of Tyre, is cured of her demons. However, *how* that happens is discomforting.

You may choose to agree with some commentators who believe the story was placed in the scriptures at a later time. *Or* you might argue that the story is authentic, but that Jesus was speaking with a smile on his face, or he was simply testing the woman's sincerity. *Or* you could accept the story as it stands in all its harshness, as Douglas Hare does when he suggests that possibly Jesus was a "Jewish man of his day, chauvinistic toward woman and non-Jews" (*Matthew: Interpretation*, p. 177).

This particular story of Jesus's changing his mind was told not once, but twice. *And* this is not the only changing-mind story in the gospels. Jesus himself told a story in Luke 18:1-8 about the widow who kept begging the judge for justice against her opponent. Finally, the judge states: "Though I have no fear of God and no respect for anyone, yet because this widow keeps bothering me, I will grant her justice, so that she may not wear me out by continually coming" (Luke 18:4-5). The judge changed his mind!!!

Prayer for the Day: *Confusing God, maybe it's not you who's confused but me. Open my ears and heart so I may hear your word for me. Amen.*

Mark 7:24-30; Matthew 15:21-28

Week 27
Monday

Hmmm. Changing God's mind. Before going too far down that path right now, consider Mark and Matthew versions of the story bit by bit. Look at their similarities and their differences.

From there [Gennesaret] Jesus set out and went away to the region of Tyre [and Sidon]. He entered a house and did not want anyone to know he was there. Yet he could not escape notice (Mark 7:24 with Matthew references in brackets).

Jesus left Gennesaret, according to Mark, and went to the coast over in Philistia...Gentile country. Bible scholar Paul Minear points out that "this is the first certain reference in Mark to a ministry beyond the bounds of Jesus's own people" (Paul S. Minear, *Mark, The Layman's Commentary*, p. 87). Philistia... Gentile country. Do you wonder why Jesus left his own country? Did he go to be safe where few people knew him... as when celebrities go to deserted islands where paparazzi are not likely to find them? Did he go away simply to rest like when you get away from the phone and social media and cut off your computers? Did he go for privacy as in a retreat with his disciples before the journey to Jerusalem? The only thing you know from Mark is that *he could not escape notice* (Mark 7:24).

Can you imagine Jesus's frustration and fatigue? Maybe there are times when you must get away from your everyday world. Maybe you sit in a park, mute your phone, and listen to soothing music. You hope that when you return, you will be able to focus and work with energy and commitment. Was Jesus the same way? The gospels report that he tried to get away from the crowds but usually they found him.

Prayer for the Day: *God of the Sabbath, there are times when I need to get away. Thanks for showing me through Jesus that's a worthy thing to do. Amen.*

Week 27   Mark 7:24-30; Matthew 15:21-28
Tuesday

The story unfolds:
A woman whose little daughter had an unclean spirit immediately heard about him (Mark 7:25). Mark treats the woman kindlier than Matthew. Mark says the woman is "Gentile, of Syrophoenician origin" rather than Matthew's rather pejorative label of "Canaanite" which was like calling her a half-breed. Her appearance to the group with Jesus went against cultural norms. Mary Anne Tolbert explains that any public display of a woman was strongly discouraged. The mother was obviously so desperate that she did not care about her shame caused by speaking directly to Jesus rather than allowing a man to speak for her. Her love for her child drove her to behavior which caused some to think she was a slave or a prostitute (Mary Ann Tolbert, Women's Bible Commentary, Mark, pp. 268-269). The mother's daughter had an unclean spirit, whatever that entailed. In Mark 5, a man with an unclean spirit sounded very much as if he were mentally ill. He walked around the graveyard, howling and bruising himself with stones. Maybe that was what afflicted the daughter. Whatever the daughter's ailment, the mother made a spectacle of herself out of her love of her child.

She came and bowed down at his feet ... She begged Jesus to cast the demon out of her daughter (Mark 7:26). Matthew says she started shouting and cried out to Jesus, *Have mercy on me, Lord, Son of David; my daughter is tormented by a demon.... She came and knelt before him, saying, "Lord, help me!"* (Matthew 15:22-25).

People who are parents, grandparents, or great-grandparents can feel this mother's pain and fear. Had they been in the same situation, with little hope for the healing of their child and someone, anyone, offered hope, they would do whatever they could to secure that chance for their child.

You may know that you are ordinarily a gentle, calm, law or rule-abiding person until your loved one is at risk. Then you will fight tooth and nail. You understand this mother's action.

Prayer for the Day: *God of all, inspire me with this mother's actions so I may fight hard for justice for ALL people. Amen.*

Mark 7:24-30; Matthew 15:21-28

Week 27
Wednesday

Jesus's response is difficult to understand: *Let the children be fed first, for it is not fair to take children's food and throw it to the dogs* (Mark 7:27). Matthew makes Jesus sound harsher: *I was only sent to the lost sheep of the House of Israel* (Matthew 15:24). Jesus, in effect, called this desperate woman a dog. She was a Gentile, which to Israelites, were dogs by comparison to God's chosen people. To be fair, Jesus did use the term for "dog" which indicated a house pet rather than the term for a stray. Nevertheless, he called her and her child dogs. This was not the only time when Jesus spoke words which sound harsh. Once he said, *Follow me, and let the dead bury their own dead* (Matthew 8:22). And then when told his family was outside, Jesus said, *Who is my mother, and who are my brothers?* (Matthew 12:48).

Jesus, the man of love and compassion, Son of God, refused this woman's request and in a manner that sounds at least tepid if not contemptuous. Jesus turned his back on the pleas of the mother. Why? Scholars have argued about this for centuries. What is important is to acknowledge that Jesus refused to help this woman and at least part of his reason was because she was not Jewish. She was not one of his kind of people.

The disciples, according to Matthew's version, added insult when they repeatedly said, *Send her away, for she keeps shouting after us* (Matthew 15:23)

It's painful to acknowledge that sometimes you simply want to get rid of pests. You do not want to help them. You want to get rid of them.

One minister needed help in how to handle requests from people who showed up at the church on Sunday mornings. An usher proposed that he would lock the door, sit beside it, and only allow the right people into the building. Another minister sheepishly acknowledged that if a beggar came up to him in the church yard, he would reach into his pocket and give whatever money he happened to have on him at the time so the person would just go away. There's the reality of mass shooters entering the worship space. Some congregations have uniformed guards present. These are legitimate issues to wrestle with.

And his disciples came and urged him, saying, Send her away, for she keeps shouting after us (Matthew 15:23).

To the disciples, she was a nuisance, something to be gotten rid of as quickly as possible.

Prayer for the Day: *Savior, show me where I see people only from their outside appearance and not from their innermost selves. Amen.*

Week 27
Thursday

Mark 7:24-30; Matthew 15:21-28

But then the woman does an amazing thing. She uses Jesus's own words, his own metaphor, and comes back at him with an argument. She *argues* with Jesus. *Sir, even the dogs under the table eat the children's crumbs* (Mark 7:28). She points out that the Messiah's concern was surely for more than his own people. Actually, she is pulling truths from the ancient scriptures. Elijah lived for a time with the foreign widow of Zarephath and her son in Sidon. Their meal jar and oil jar never emptied while there was a drought (I Kings 17:8-24). In Isaiah 40, the prophet proclaimed that the glory of the Lord shall be revealed, and *all* people shall see it together.

Jesus himself had chastised the religious rulers for caring more about the rules than the people. Maybe this mother reminded Jesus that what he preached for others, he needed to hear for himself. She was sharp. She was quick. She was focused on getting help for her daughter. And she dared to dispute Jesus, the Savior of the world!

Jesus then said to her, For saying that, you may go—; the demon has left your daughter (Mark 7:29). Matthew adds, *Woman, great is your faith! Let it be done for you as you wish* (Matthew 15:28). Mark concludes: *So she went home, found the child lying on the bed, and the demon gone* (Mark 7:30).

Jesus changed his mind! A mere woman, a foreign nobody, argued with him and he changed his mind. In Mark's version of the story, nothing is even said about her faith. Jesus simply says that for saying what she did, she could go home happy. She went home and found her daughter healed. Her life was transformed.

Prayer for the Day: *God of healing, help me be bold in asking for healing for whoever needs it. Amen.*

Mark 7:24-30; Matthew 15:21-28

Week 27
Friday

What in the world do you do with this Syrophoenician woman? What do you do with the woman who aggravated the judge until he gave her what *she* wanted, demonstrating single-minded persistence resulting in a change of mind? Is this a blueprint for how you can get God to change God's own mind? Most likely not. However, there are things to apply to your own life and faith development.

One thing you can note is that changing God's mind involved deep feeling and clear focus on someone other than yourself. The mother begged God for someone she loved. She was willing to debase herself for her beloved child. She fell down before Jesus and did not care if everyone in the world thought she was a prostitute. She did not think of her position, her image, or her reputation when she sought out Jesus. She thought only about her beloved daughter.

Can you be that totally other-focused? You may pray for another to get well but when you're honest, it may be because you are tired of taking care of the person or you can't stand your own sense of failure or inadequacy when you see them suffer. Your love may not be pure. Your love may be affected by your own needs. So, the first thing to note is the mother's total focus was not on herself but on her daughter. Nevertheless, you can be totally loving, totally other-focused and your loved one will not be healed. There's no explanation for why or why not.

Prayer for the Day: *Dear God, I want to be unselfish and passionate in my prayers for others. Strengthen me. Amen.*

Week 27
Saturday

Mark 7:24-30; Matthew 15:21-28

Another thing to pay attention to is that the mother believed what she had heard about Jesus. She believed that Jesus could heal her daughter. Who knows how much or even what she had heard but she acted on the information she had? She followed her hunch... maybe her God-given intuitions. She was so convinced in the truths of what she had heard that she argued with God. Can you say your belief is that deep and solid? Somehow, she knew that God's love was what her daughter needed, and she took a huge chance on that belief. Somehow, she was certain that what she wanted was in God's plans. The second thing then is that *that* woman believed in her heart what she'd heard about Jesus.

A third thing is that God is in relationship with you and is even willing to interchange with you on your level. God is not always a distant God. God is sometimes, as seen in Jesus, very human, even to the point of arguing with you and being chastised by you. The God who knew you before you were created in your mother's womb is right here on your level—as well as high and lifted up beyond your wildest imaginings. The psalmists and Job in the Old Testament knew that the God you worship can be present with you even when you are being your most aggravating and accusing. That can be comforting. The third thing, then, is God is right here, saving you right here.

In this story you see Jesus in his full humanity...a little snippy and irritable. And even so, with the driving force of love on the mother's part, Jesus himself responds as you yearn for God to respond...with love and compassion and healing. He does not respond as his disciples expect him to. He responds as God, his Father, leads him to. He responds as a savior, someone who leads you to transformation.

Prayer for the Day: *God of grace, thank you for stories like this one that keep me on my toes and keep me from claiming that I have full knowledge of you and your ways. I rest in the assurance that you love me and care for me even when that is not immediately apparent. And that is good news indeed. Amen.*

Week 28
Luke 15:1-10

Now all the tax-collectors and sinners were coming near to listen to him. 2 And the Pharisees and the scribes were grumbling and saying, 'This fellow welcomes sinners and eats with them.'

3 So he told them this parable: 4 'Which one of you, having a hundred sheep and losing one of them, does not leave the ninety-nine in the wilderness and go after the one that is lost until he finds it? 5 When he has found it, he lays it on his shoulders and rejoices. 6 And when he comes home, he calls together his friends and neighbours, saying to them, "Rejoice with me, for I have found my sheep that was lost." 7 Just so, I tell you, there will be more joy in heaven over one sinner who repents than over ninety-nine righteous people who need no repentance.

The Parable of the Lost Coin

8 'Or what woman having ten silver coins, if she loses one of them, does not light a lamp, sweep the house, and search carefully until she finds it? 9 When she has found it, she calls together her friends and neighbours, saying, "Rejoice with me, for I have found the coin that I had lost." 10 Just so, I tell you, there is joy in the presence of the angels of God over one sinner who repents.'

Week 28   Luke 15:1-10
Sunday

You know, a lot of people really did not like Jesus. He angered people. And when you're honest, you may have to say that, had you been alive at that time, Jesus may have angered you. After all, the people who really had trouble with Jesus, who grumbled about him, were the good church people ...the Pharisees and the scribes. They were the people who were diligent in following the teachings of scripture as they understood them. They were the people who prayed a lot. They were the people who were scrupulous about keeping the faith. They were holy people. They knew God and worshiped God and set an example for others about how to be good religious people. And they really did not like Jesus.

Jesus did not meet their understanding of what a good church person did and said and was. This passage is a prime example of how Jesus did not fall in with the party line for appropriate behavior for a person of faith. In verse 2, the scribes and Pharisees grumbled and complained that Jesus *welcomes sinners and eats with them.*

Now on the surface to 21st century Americans, eating with sinners does not seem so bad. But to a Middle Easterner, this was a major break with appropriate behavior. In the east, invitations for dining together went to those one wanted to honor. It indicated peace, deep fellowship, and forgiveness. Sharing a meal meant sharing life. A nobleman might feed any number of lesser needy persons as a sign of his generosity, but he did not eat with them. But because Jesus was eating *with* the sinners, he was hosting them, he was welcoming them as equals.

Prayer for the Day: *Holy Spirit, Advocate, embolden me to ignore social customs when they inhibit your love for me and others. Amen.*

Luke 15:1-10

**Week 28
Monday**

Jesus was criticized for his table customs: He ate with tax collectors and called tax man Matthew to be a disciple (Luke 5:29-32). Tax collectors were local citizens working against their own people when collecting for the Romans. They lined their own pockets and were hated.

The people Jesus was with included rascals, scoundrels, and people who were generally detested by the "good people." Sinners were coming near to listen to Jesus. Sinners were not simply people with a lifestyle problem. They were people who had been kicked out of the synagogue because of their violations of the Mosaic law.

He was at table when the woman washed his feet with her tears and dried them with her hair (Luke7). Fred Craddock points out that "Table fellowship and Sabbath observance were identification marks for a community struggling to maintain identity among many foreign and hostile influences. What was eaten and with whom one ate were critical questions…When the critics [said] of Jesus that he [ate] with anyone, they were saying that he violated the sacred distinctions as to *who is and who is not within the covenant fellowship*" (Fred Craddock, *Luke, Interpretation*, p.103).

No wonder the religious elite were horrified that Jesus was eating with these sorts of people. And so, to respond to their grumblings, Jesus simply tells a story about a lost sheep. Once again, Jesus horrifies the holy leaders. When he says, "Which one of you, having a hundred sheep…" he is comparing them to shepherds. Now you may not have a problem with being called a shepherd. You may have a good feeling for shepherds. You may put them out every year at Christmas with your manger scenes. You know that Moses was a shepherd. King David was a shepherd as a youth. But real-life shepherds at that time were considered unclean. So, Jesus was asking the Pharisees to consider themselves as unclean people. He was asking them to put themselves in the shoes of someone who was so unlike their image of themselves that they could not believe it. Who would Jesus use to shock us that way? Sewer workers? Homeless people? Terrorists?

Prayer for the Day: *Father, who and where is the person I am to reach out to today? Amen.*

Week 28
Tuesday

Luke 15:1-10

The story continues. One hundred sheep were in the shepherd's care. With this many sheep there were probably other shepherds as well helping to care for the flocks that were owned by a number of families. These shepherds were part of the extended families and were responsible for the well-being of their community's economic stability. So, while the shepherd was out looking for that one lost sheep, the other shepherds probably took the other 99 sheep home and told the families what had happened. The shepherd had to find the lost sheep alive or if dead, had to bring back the sheep's body to prove that he had not sold it.

So, Jesus insulted the Pharisees by eating with sinners and tax collectors and adds insult to injury when he tells a story in which he asks them to imagine themselves as shepherds. This is not simply a children's story about a little lamb who was scared and lost and then was found and could go home. What is Jesus teaching about the triune God?

A word that is repeated in three of the four verses of this parable is "joy" or "rejoice." First there is joy when the shepherd finds the sheep. There is joy when the shepherd returns to the village with the sheep. And there is rejoicing in heaven over a repenting sinner.

The shepherd rejoiced when he found the sheep, the sheep that he had lost. Kenneth Bailey says that the verbs used indicate that the shepherd lost the sheep. The sheep did not simply wander off. The shepherd lost it and went to find it. Bailey says that this is a minor turn of phrase, (Kenneth E. Bailey, *Poet and Peasant*, p. 149) but this detail opens a vista on the triune God. Assuming the shepherd is pointing to God's activities with human beings, then when you stray or get lost, God seems to accept responsibility for your being lost and then for finding you and bringing you back, for saving you.

Prayer for the Day: *Searching God, thank you for finding me whenever I'm lost, even though I do not realize that I'm lost. Amen.*

Luke 15:1-10

Week 28
Wednesday

When a good boss has an employee who is not functioning up to capacity or expectations, she looks to see where she has not provided adequate teaching, guidance, clarification of the task, or nurture for the employee to do the job well. God queried, "They still are lost from me. What else do I need to do?" God in Jesus, said, "Here, I'll show you how to love me and how to love each other."

Even when the sheep was found, the shepherd still had a lot of work to do. A lost sheep may lie down helplessly and refuse to budge. The shepherd must carry it over long distances. What kinds of distances does God carry sinners? Sometimes you are caught using other people for your own selfish reasons, or hurting other people, or ignoring God and God's good gifts. Do you acknowledge what you have done, that you are lost? When you are lost, do you simply sit down and deny that you did anything? Do you deny that you are in the wrong? Do you refuse to ask forgiveness or to offer forgiveness? Do you simply sit and stick out your lip and pout and cross your arms and say, "Not me. It wasn't me. I did not do it. No way, not me."

The parable says that even when you act that way, even when you are that way, God comes looking for you anyway. You don't have to do one thing. God comes looking. No matter how awful you are. And God rejoices when you are found.

The rejoicing happens even when the shepherd knows that finding the sheep is only the first step. Even so, the shepherd rejoices. The shepherd still faces the burden of restoration. He will have to pick up the sheep, hoist it on his shoulders and carry it, maybe for miles, and maybe over very rough terrain. What a comfort. Your restoration, your salvation, does not depend on your actions. The hard journey back is handled by God, your savior, redeemer, creator, comforter. God, the one who created you, knows that you will lose your way. Your awesome God finds ways to redeem you, to save you. Through your loving Creator's actions, you are led back to who you are to be.

Who might be some of your God-given shepherds who are carrying you back to the welcoming fold? Who might you need to be a shepherd for? Who needs your shoulders?

Prayer for the Day: *Loving God, help me be a good shepherd to those who need help. Amen.*

Week 28
Thursday

Luke 15:1-10

The shepherd carries the sheep on his shoulders all the way back home. And when he returns to the village, with the sheep alive on his shoulders, the whole community rejoices. Now, there is a practical side to their rejoicing. The lost sheep would have meant lost revenue. A lost shepherd would have meant a lost laborer. But the lost sheep was found and was restored. What pleasure to every person in the village! When there was a recovery of a lost sinner to the community, there was rejoicing, not the murmuring or grumbling that the Pharisees did. They could not imagine a God like that…a God who actually searched for people who were not the "right people," a God who searched for people who were sinners.

And then Jesus repeated the message of God's rejoicing by telling yet another story, the story of a woman who lost a coin in her home. This story is a twin to the parable of the lost sheep. The Pharisees would not have liked to consider themselves a woman any more than they would have liked to be a shepherd. Once again, the woman lost the coin just like the shepherd lost the sheep. She searches and searches until she finds it. The coin was important in that money was scarce in a culture that was largely self-supporting …growing its own food and making its own cloth. She rejoices when she finds the coin. In this parable she did not have to do any work to restore the coin, except to reattach it to either her headdress or her necklace. Once again, the community rejoices with her. By now the community is probably singing with her, "I've got joy, joy, joy, joy down in my heart, down in my heart, down in my heart…"

Prayer for the Day: *God of joy, thank you when I've got joy in my heart, my life, my soul. Amen.*

Luke 15:1-10 **Week 28**
Friday

There is one other interesting lesson that Jesus teaches about our loving God when he tells these stories. He teaches about repentance. The last line of the found sheep parable says, *There will be more joy in heaven over one sinner who repents than over ninety-nine righteous persons who need no repentance* (Luke 15:7). The found coin parable ends with: *There is joy in the presence of the angels of God over one sinner who repents* (Luke 15:10).

"What did the sheep and the coin do to repent?" Kenneth Bailey points out that "the sheep does nothing to prompt the shepherd to begin his search except to become lost...Here, 'being found' is equated with 'repentance'" (Kenneth Bailey, *Poet and Peasant*, p. 155).

This is radical stuff. This is a radically different understanding of repentance. These parables indicate that repentance is God's good gift given to you to restore you to community. These parables demonstrate that repentance is accomplished, your transformation happens, when God or people acting on God's behalf seek those who are lost. These parables call followers to eat with sinners as equals and so restore them to God's community, to help them be transformed.

Prayer for the Day: *God of my soul, transformation in my life is a mighty thing. May I hold it close and rejoice. Amen.*

Week 28
Saturday

Luke 15:1-10

What is this teaching calling you to do? To ignore other people and their behavior and pretend that it doesn't exist? To sit back and let God do it all and if people are not restored to God's community of faith, then it is God's fault and not yours? Some people may choose to see it that way. Or are you to become God and take on all the burden of restoring someone, to call them to repentance, to make sure that you bring them to righteousness, so that you can make God happy? Are you to attack people with the good news of the gospel? Certainly some faithful Christians sometimes see it that way.

Or are you to yearn to join in the rejoicing when someone is brought back to the fold by God? The bringing back may come through a direct miracle as when someone picks up a Bible in a motel room and the words read illuminate the dark corners of a hurting life. The bringing back may come because you befriend someone who feels worthless, and you treat them as worthy. The bringing back may come because you invite someone to church, and they experience the holiness and love of God while there. The bringing back may come because you cared enough to let someone know that they had other options for their life and that you would still be there for them whatever they decided. The bringing back may happen because you pray to God to use you in the lives of the people you meet that day, and you touch someone's life, and you will never know it.

As you think of ways that God has brought you back through the loving acts of people who were God's angels for you, who were shepherds in your life, who searched diligently for you until you were found, you will discover other ways for you to be a shepherd. You will find more ways of helping to bring others back to joy. Jesus is calling us to rejoice with him and to be involved in his work.

You have a choice. You can rejoice or you can grumble. Which do you choose?

Prayer for the Day: *Good shepherd, lead me to places and people who may need a shepherd. Amen.*

Week 29
Acts 10:1-33

In Caesarea there was a man named Cornelius, a centurion of the Italian Cohort, as it was called. 2 He was a devout man who feared God with all his household; he gave alms generously to the people and prayed constantly to God. 3 One afternoon at about three o'clock he had a vision in which he clearly saw an angel of God coming in and saying to him, 'Cornelius.' 4 He stared at him in terror and said, 'What is it, Lord?' He answered, 'Your prayers and your alms have ascended as a memorial before God. 5 Now send men to Joppa for a certain Simon who is called Peter; 6 he is lodging with Simon, a tanner, whose house is by the seaside.' 7 When the angel who spoke to him had left, he called two of his slaves and a devout soldier from the ranks of those who served him, 8 and after telling them everything, he sent them to Joppa.

9 About noon the next day, as they were on their journey and approaching the city, Peter went up on the roof to pray. 10 He became hungry and wanted something to eat; and while it was being prepared, he fell into a trance. 11 He saw the heaven opened and something like a large sheet coming down, being lowered to the ground by its four corners. 12 In it were all kinds of four-footed creatures and reptiles and birds of the air. 13 Then he heard a voice saying, 'Get up, Peter; kill and eat.' 14 But Peter said, 'By no means, Lord; for I have never eaten anything that is profane or unclean.' 15 The voice said to him again, a second time, 'What God has made clean, you must not call profane.' 16 This happened three times, and the thing was suddenly taken up to heaven.

17 Now while Peter was greatly puzzled about what to make of the vision that he had seen, suddenly the men sent by Cornelius appeared. They were asking for Simon's house and were standing by the gate. 18 They called out to ask whether Simon, who was called Peter, was staying there. 19 While Peter was still thinking about the vision, the Spirit said to him, 'Look, three men are searching for you. 20 Now get up, go down, and go with them without hesitation; for I have sent them.' 21 So Peter went down to the men and said, 'I am the one you are looking for; what is the reason for your coming?' 22 They answered, 'Cornelius, a centurion, an upright and God-fearing man, who is well spoken of by the whole Jewish nation, was directed by a holy angel to send for you to come to his house and to hear what you have to say.' 23 So Peter invited them in and gave them lodging.

The next day he got up and went with them, and some of the believers from Joppa accompanied him. 24 The following day they came to Caesarea. Cornelius was expecting them and had called together his relatives and close friends. 25 On Peter's arrival Cornelius met him, and falling at his feet, worshipped him. *(cont'd next page)*

Week 29   **Acts 10:1-33**
Sunday

Maybe it's a function of getting older. Some things that seemed so important in youth no longer are attention grabbing. There was a time when suits were the appropriate attire for the office. No longer! In fact, the pandemic reduced the need to go to an office. Maybe you believed that if you followed the rules, then life would be smooth and easy. Ha! Did you believe all kinds of things about Jesus and the Bible and God and the Holy Spirit that have begun to change, to open up in new significant ways?

In some ways these changes, changes that are growth in your emotional, mental, physical, and spiritual life are a bit scary. Maybe that's a kind of unlearning, a kind of letting go so God can move into the cracks in your life. When one is less well-fortified, new ideas can be allowed. God seems to be finding those cracks and moving right in.

And…truth be told…the current situation in the world causes many to rethink things. What was before may never be the same again. No one could ever have imagined that the world would be shut down because of a virus. People with light skin did not believe that the country would be torn apart again with racial tensions. There are so many things that have changed for everyone in the world in the last few months and years.

The world has turned upside down…from external happenings as well as possible internal changes. You are having to unlearn some things. And you are having to learn new things.

Prayer for the Day: *Beloved, you know that I am not a fan of change. Help me embrace the unlearning you place before me. Amen.*

---

26 But Peter made him get up, saying, 'Stand up; I am only a mortal.' 27 And as he talked with him, he went in and found that many had assembled; 28 and he said to them, 'You yourselves know that it is unlawful for a Jew to associate with or to visit a Gentile; but God has shown me that I should not call anyone profane or unclean. 29 So when I was sent for, I came without objection. Now may I ask why you sent for me?'

30 Cornelius replied, 'Four days ago at this very hour, at three o'clock, I was praying in my house when suddenly a man in dazzling clothes stood before me. 31 He said, "Cornelius, your prayer has been heard and your alms have been remembered before God. 32 Send therefore to Joppa and ask for Simon, who is called Peter; he is staying in the home of Simon, a tanner, by the sea." 33 Therefore I sent for you immediately, and you have been kind enough to come. So now all of us are here in the presence of God to listen to all that the Lord has commanded you to say.'

Acts 10:1-33

Week 29
Monday

Peter, good old Peter, the rock on which Jesus said he would build his church, was confronted with a major unlearning experience.

Peter became a major player in the new and developing process that was becoming the church of Jesus Christ. He was established in Jerusalem which kind of makes sense because in the Jewish mind, Jerusalem was considered the center for faith because that's where the Temple was. It was where sacrifices were made. It was where faithful people came at least once in their lifetime. It was where Jesus came at a young age and astounded the scribes and scholars of the Temple. Jerusalem was where Jesus was killed. Jesus told the disciples after his resurrection to not leave Jerusalem (Acts 1:4).

So, in many ways, Peter was still enmeshed in the faith and ways of being in which he had been raised. He knew that Gentiles were not people to connect with. Remember the woman at the well in Samaria? Jesus was having a significant conversation with her even though she was a woman and a Samaritan, considered to be unworthy by other Jewish people. The scripture says, *Just then the disciples came. They were astonished that he was speaking with a woman, but no one said, "What do you want?" or "Why are you speaking with her?"* (John 4:27). Because the disciples were astonished, they likely were thinking these questions even if they didn't speak them aloud.

Prayer for the Day: *Merciful God, show me where I am enmeshed in ways of thinking that I need to release to grow in my relationship with you and others. Amen.*

Week 29
Tuesday

Acts 10:1-33

It's important to remember that Peter and even Paul were not trying to begin a new religion. They were trying to reform Judaism. It was later before the term "Christian" was used. So, in those early days of the Church, the old rules of Jewish purity still remained in the minds and hearts of many of the followers of Christ. That's just the way it was for Peter. Why question something he was so comfortable with? Yes, he was a follower of Christ, and yes, he knew the ways of formal religion. He and the other disciples were no longer wandering around the countryside following Jesus. They were now located in Jerusalem, as Jesus had instructed them to be.

Peter knew the ways to divide people into groups. There were the Jews, but even with them there were subcategories. There were the scribes, Pharisees, and priests—those with both secular and religious power. There were the Jewish peasants and there were the Jewish tradespeople. These all were welcomed in the synagogues. Then there were the God-fearers. These were people who were not Jewish; they had not been circumcised; but they kept the Jewish purity laws, and worshiped the Jewish God, Yahweh. They were allowed into the synagogue. Then there were the Gentiles. They were "those people." They were unclean, not to be interacted with. They were just wrong. After everything Jesus had gone through, Peter knew he needed to protect the Jesus story from people such as the Gentiles.

By being circumcised, by eating only kosher foods, and by keeping other rules, Peter was doing his best to be the Rock on which the Church of Jesus Christ would be built. He was maintaining walls to keep those people out!!!

This may all sound very comfortable to you. You know who to keep out. You know who is not like you. You know what faith means and that those who do not think or believe like you are not welcomed, even though church signs all over the country say, "All are welcomed."

And the reality is, just as Peter probably accepted the food laws and circumcision laws without question, you, too, accept things without question because that's just the way it is.

Prayer for the Day: *God of vision, open my eyes to your inclusive ways. Amen.*

Acts 10:1-33

Week 29
Wednesday

Everyone has a fund of knowledge based on age, education level, gender, skin color, socioeconomics, where one lives, and life experiences. And you tend to hang out with people who share more of your fund of knowledge. You worship together, you socialize together, you are educated more or less the same way, you live in the same communities. Because most everyone you know shares your basic of fund of knowledge, you may think if a person does not, then that person doesn't have any common sense. Something must be wrong with him/her/them.

However, people with different life experiences have different funds of knowledge. For example, people who are female have a different fund of knowledge that those who are male. Would you agree? People with light skin have a different fund of knowledge that those with darker skin.

So, Peter's fund of knowledge, even though expanded by following Jesus and listening to his teachings, was rooted in traditional Judaism.

That is until Peter was visited by God in what the Bible describes as a trance, something that happened when Peter was in deep prayer while on the roof of the house where he was staying.

Prayer for the Day: *Rabbi, show me more about my own fund of knowledge so I can learn about my blind spots when interacting with others. Amen.*

Week 29   **Acts 10:1-33**
Thursday

Peter had a vision while he was waiting on his meal to be prepared and brought to him. Maybe it was hunger? Even so, no matter how the trance came upon him, he knew that it was from God. He saw all kinds of animals and heard the words, *Kill and eat* (Acts 10:13). But Peter knew there were foods forbidden to Jewish people, foods that were not kosher, foods such as pork, shrimp, shellfish and many types of seafood, most insects, scavenger birds, and various other animals (Leviticus 11). The dietary rules were never intended to apply to anyone other than the Israelites. The purpose of the food laws was to make the Israelites distinct from all other nations. Peter knew he was to be set apart.

But God had other plans. Peter heard, *What God has made clean, you must not call profane [unholy]* (Acts 10:15).

And then the representatives of Cornelius, a *Roman* soldier, came to see Peter and asked him to visit their boss.

To give Cornelius his due, even though he was Roman and part of the occupying force in Israel, he was known to be a God-fearer, someone who adhered to the Jewish understanding of holy without following all the rituals and customs such as circumcision and some of the dietary laws. In Peter's mind, though, Cornelius was unclean, impure.

Let this sink in. In Peter's *mind*, Cornelius was *unclean*.

Prayer for the Day: *Loving God, break open my heart to those I consider unclean. Amen.*

Acts 10:1-33

Week 29
Friday

Okay, imagine that you are Peter but now in this year. Who in your mind is unclean? You only have to answer that question in your heart, not aloud to anyone unless you want to. This acknowledgment is between you and God until/unless you choose to do something with your insight.

It was not that long ago in history that white people would not eat in the same restaurant, at the same lunch counter as black people. When you look at recent news reports, entire groups of people have been considered unclean by churches, communities, politicians, the country. Here are just a few: immigrants, people in the LGBTQ community, people of African descent, people of the opponent's political party, etc. Even when you know to be polite to people in any of these groups, when you're deeply honest with yourself, you may realize that your politeness is only a cover for how you really feel.

That's when this scripture passage gives you a forehead slap with the words, WAKE UP. God reminds you that God created humankind in God's own image. This means, in some ways, that God is not like the picture you had of God as a child. Did you see God as an old man with a white beard sitting on a throne in heaven? Being created in God's image means that God looks like the immigrant child who has been separated from his mother. God looks like the non-white man that you crossed the street to avoid. God looks like the politician you cannot stand. God looks like all those folks that you would rather not have to be around. God looks like people whom you were raised to avoid, or to raise your eyebrows for, or to whisper about.

So, Peter, with God's push, went to Cornelius. Peter said, *You yourselves know that it is unlawful for a Jew to associate with or visit a Gentile; but God has shown me that I should not call anyone profane or unclean* (Acts 15:28).

GOD HAS SHOWN ME THAT I SHOULD NOT CALL ANYONE UNHOLY OR UNCLEAN.

Prayer for the Day: *Oh my God, I confess today that I call people unholy or unclean. Shake me up and cleanse my heart. Amen.*

Week 29
Saturday

Acts 10:1-33

This is a major unlearning. So many ideas and concepts and judgments and presuppositions are deeply embedded in everyone. God is saying *that* is no longer acceptable. God let Peter know that. God is calling you today to know that.

Can you let your heart be broken? Not broken to smithereens but broken so the love of God can seep in deeper, and you will want to let go of your ideas about who is holy and who is not? Who is clean and who is not? Can you allow yourself in your maturity to let go of some of those lessons you learned in your family, your school, your community, and even your church?

Can you allow your heart to warm in ways that are important to God? Can you allow your heart to question some of your long-held beliefs? Can you allow yourself to embrace your community with all its messiness, its differences, as well as its longing to be loved, healed, and embraced?

Peter was changed when he trusted God's voice that he heard in his trance. After he met with Cornelius, he preached a powerful sermon. Listen carefully to what the scripture says: *The circumcised believers who had come with Peter were astounded that the gift of the Holy Spirit had been poured out even on the Gentiles* (Acts 10:45).

Astonishment: God loves THOSE people, those people whom you thought God could never love and if God could not love them, then you did not need to love them either. God LOVES THOSE people.

But truth be told, things did not go so well for Peter when he returned to Jerusalem. *So when Peter went up to Jerusalem, the circumcised believers CRITICIZED him, saying, 'Why did you go to uncircumcised men and eat with them?'* (Acts 11:2).

When you move beyond your old ways of thinking and being and doing, when you let go some of the lessons and beliefs of your younger self, when you allow God to break open your heart in new ways, people who care about you, people who say they love you may push back hard. You are no longer the same person they thought they knew. You are no longer the person they helped create you to be. You are becoming more of the person who God is creating you to be. You are becoming more the person who you know deep in your heart you are meant to be.

Prayer for the Day: *God of new days, I am in the process of unlearning. Thanks be to you, O loving God. Amen.*

Week 30
Jonah 3:1-4:4

Chapter 3

The word of the Lord came to Jonah a second time, saying, 2 'Get up, go to Nineveh, that great city, and proclaim to it the message that I tell you.' 3 So Jonah set out and went to Nineveh, according to the word of the Lord. Now Nineveh was an exceedingly large city, a three days' walk across. 4 Jonah began to go into the city, going a day's walk. And he cried out, 'Forty days more, and Nineveh shall be overthrown!' 5 And the people of Nineveh believed God; they proclaimed a fast, and everyone, great and small, put on sackcloth.

6 When the news reached the king of Nineveh, he rose from his throne, removed his robe, covered himself with sackcloth, and sat in ashes. 7 Then he had a proclamation made in Nineveh: 'By the decree of the king and his nobles: No human being or animal, no herd or flock, shall taste anything. They shall not feed, nor shall they drink water. 8 Human beings and animals shall be covered with sackcloth, and they shall cry mightily to God. All shall turn from their evil ways and from the violence that is in their hands. 9 Who knows? God may relent and change his mind; he may turn from his fierce anger, so that we do not perish.'

10 When God saw what they did, how they turned from their evil ways, God changed his mind about the calamity that he had said he would bring upon them; and he did not do it.

Chapter 4

But this was very displeasing to Jonah, and he became angry. 2 He prayed to the Lord and said, 'O Lord! Is not this what I said while I was still in my own country? That is why I fled to Tarshish at the beginning; for I knew that you are a gracious God and merciful, slow to anger, and abounding in steadfast love, and ready to relent from punishing. 3 And now, O Lord, please take my life from me, for it is better for me to die than to live.' 4 And the Lord said, 'Is it right for you to be angry?'

Week 30
Sunday

Jonah 3:1-4:4

Are you or do you know people who are avid fishermen and fisherwomen? When someone calls to go fishing, the person is ready to go…whenever possible. Real fisher enthusiasts have many, many…many rods, reels, and other fishing stuff. So, any scripture which has fish in it is one they can connect to.

If people know anything about Jonah, it is usually the part about the big fish…or a whale…and that's about it. They know Jonah was swallowed by a fish and lived to tell the tale. Children's Bible story books sometimes have a picture of a cartoon whale with Jonah looking puzzled standing in the whale's open mouth. Even though this is primarily what people know about Jonah, the point of the story is *not* that Jonah spent time in the belly of a big fish. The point of the story is about the relationship between God and Jonah and indeed, even between God and the rest of the world.

Prayer for the Day: *Jesus, you called disciples to be fishers of people. Is this something you want for me? Amen.*

Jonah 3:1-4:4

Week 30
Monday

Before you get too far into the story, there are some details that will help you understand more clearly. There *was* a real person named Jonah mentioned in II Kings 14:25 as the son of Amittai, a prophet from Gathhepher. The particular name, Jonah, is used in this passage because the name means "dove" which was often a way that Israel was described. Here's an example of dove meaning Israel from Psalm 74:18-19 when the psalmist pleads with God: *Remember this, O Lord, how the enemy scoffs, and an impious people reviles your name. Do not deliver the soul of your dove to the wild animals; do not forget the life of the poor forever.* When you read about the *man* Jonah in the story, you are likely reading a story about Israel and God.

God is definitely a central character in the story. There are 39 references to the deity in the 48 verses of the book (James Limburg, *Interpretation, Hosea-Micah*, p. 138).

The city mentioned in the story is Nineveh in Assyria. The Assyrians were the ones who conquered the Northern Kingdom, Israel, in 722 B.C.E. and carried the people off into exile. They almost succeeded in capturing Jerusalem some years later. Listen to how the prophet Nahum described Nineveh [in Nah. 3:1, and 19.] *Ah, City of bloodshed, utterly deceitful, full of [things to plunder] booty! There is no assuaging your hurt, your wound is mortal. All who hear the news about you clap their hands over you. For who has escaped your endless cruelty?* Nineveh was a wicked city. It was located on the Tigris River in present-day northern Iraq.

This passage is a story, not historical fact. You can know this because the very first Hebrew word of the story is *vayehi* (vay-a-hee) which may be translated, "and it happened" or "it came to pass" or even "once upon a time" which signals the beginning of a particular type of literature: a narrative or story (Limburg).

Prayer for the Day: *God of presence, I love a good story. Help me truly hear your truths in this one. Amen.*

Week 30   **Jonah 3:1-4:4**
Tuesday

God told Jonah to go to Nineveh and call the residents to repentance. You already know what a wicked city Nineveh was. It was a mortal enemy of the Israelites. It had destroyed the Israelites' way of life when it hauled the leading citizens off into exile. When Jeremiah talked about another exile, he used language such as being "crushed," being "swallowed...like a monster," being eaten as a delicacy and then "spewed out" (Jeremiah 51:43) There were no kind feelings for the city of Nineveh and its inhabitants. The Israelites knew that the Ninevites were *not* God's people.

And it is to these awful people, these vile people, these enemies, that God instructed Jonah to go.

Well, what would you do? Would you do exactly what Jonah did and run the other way? Jonah definitely did not want to be a prophet to *those* people. What rational person would want to call such a people to repentance? They certainly deserved whatever of God's wrath they experienced. They were the enemies of Israel so, of course, they had to be God's enemy. Going to preach to them could mean only one of two things. 1. You would die 2. They would change and be saved. Neither of those alternatives was appealing *at all*.

So, Jonah hopped a boat going to Tarshish that was going the opposite direction... away from Nineveh. Listen to the descents which Jonah takes as he flees, runs away from God's relationship. Jonah goes *down* to Joppa, he goes *down* into the hold of the ship, he goes *down* into the sea. What a wonderfully descriptive way of talking about what happens, what you experience, what you feel when you run away from God, when you run away from what God is offering you when you run away from what God is asking of you. You descend.

Prayer for the Day: *Holy God, sometimes I, too, just want to run away from you, from my responsibilities, from everything. Hold me close during those times, even though I may not appreciate it then. Amen.*

Jonah 3:1-4:4

Week 30
Wednesday

Jonah is on the ship and a big storm comes up. The sailors (who are not "Israelites," therefore understood by the listeners to the story to not be the chosen of God) are afraid. Each of the sailors cried to the god whom they worshiped. They turned to *their* deity as they understood that god. So, they prayed while emptying the cargo into the sea in the hopes of survival. Where was Jonah during all this? He was asleep in the hold of the ship. The Hebrew word indicates he was in a deep, unconcerned sleep. He seemed ready to die rather than do what God was telling him to do. The captain alerted Jonah to the danger and urged him to call upon his god just as all the sailors were calling upon theirs.

The sailors wanted to know who was responsible for this god-given calamity and so they used the ancient method of casting lots. And of course, the lots indicated that Jonah was the source of their problems. They asked, *Tell us why this calamity has come upon us. What is your occupation? Where do you come from? What is your country? And of what people are you?* (Jonah 1:8). Jonah answered, *I am a Hebrew* (Jonah 1:9).

Ah, now the listeners to the story know that Jonah was an insider, one of them. Jonah added, *I worship the Lord, the God of heaven who made the sea and the dry land* (Jonah 1:9). Well, this confirmed that indeed Jonah was the cause of the storm at sea. It was his God, the one who made the sea, who was threatening their safety. Jonah mentioned that he was fleeing from his God. The men then naturally asked, "What in the world have you done?"

There was more discussion and Jonah told the sailors to throw him overboard to appease the God of the sea. But they kept trying other methods to save the ship and their lives. Finally, they realized that they probably were going to have to sacrifice Jonah to save the rest of them. Even so, they operated with very high morals. They did not want to shed an innocent man's blood, so they prayed to Jonah's God that they not be guilty and thus perish. They threw Jonah overboard and worshiped the Hebrew God, the God of Jonah. The former outsiders were now insiders and Jonah... well... Jonah was outside.

Prayer for the Day: *O God who made the sea and dry land, you are awesome and strong. Amen.*

Week 30
Thursday

Jonah 3:1-4:4

In the mercy of God, God protected Jonah in the sea and brought him to dry land. It was impossible to escape God's love. Paul says it beautifully in Romans 8:38: *For I am convinced that neither death nor life, nor angels, nor rulers, nor things present, nor things to come, nor powers, nor height, nor depth, nor anything else in all creation, will be able to separate us from the love of God in Christ Jesus, our Lord.*

God says again, *Jonah, go to Nineveh, that great city, and proclaim the message I tell you* (Jonah 3:2).

So, Jonah goes. He goes through the motions, without passion or imagination. His sermon consists of eight words: *Forty days more, and Nineveh shall be overthrown* (Jonah 3:4). But this turned out to be the most successful sermon ever given. The entire large city repented. The king himself led the fast. He decreed that even the animals would be involved in the change of heart, mind, and soul that was happening in his city. The king proclaimed that "all shall turn from their evil ways and from the violence that is in their hands." And God saved the city.

Prayer for the Day: *Savior, your ways are not my ways. Thanks be to you, O God. Amen.*

Jonah 3:1-4:4

**Week 30
Friday**

Now wouldn't you think that a preacher would be absolutely thrilled when something like that happened? But no, Jonah was angry. He was mad. He was *not* happy. And the listeners of the story would probably have gasped in horror that their enemy, their tormentor, those outsiders would have been saved.... loved.... honored by their God. How dare God love their enemies! My enemies are supposed to be God's enemies.... RIGHT? RIGHT? This is NOT how the story is supposed to end.

Jonah lashes out in his anger: *O Lord! Is this not what I said while I was still in my own country? That is why I fled to Tarshish at the beginning; for I knew that you are a gracious God and merciful, slow to anger, and abounding in steadfast love, and ready to relent from punishing* (Jonah 4:2).

Jonah as much as said, "If they're in on your love and grace and mercy, I'm out." He asked God to kill him. And then he went out of the city, sat down, and pouted. God interacted with Jonah some more.

God asks Jonah a powerful question: *And should I not be concerned about Nineveh, that great city, in which there are more than a hundred and twenty thousand persons who do not know their right hand from their left, and also many animals?* (Jonah 4:11).

And God said, "And should I not be concerned about Nineveh?" Could we just as easily insert, "And should I not be concerned about Moscow or China or North Korea or Iraq?"

Prayer for the Day: *O my God, I'm with Jonah in not believing you care for my enemies. Really? That's all I have to say today. Amen.*

Week 30 **Jonah 3:1-4:4**
Saturday

The Jonah story has a powerful impact.

God has power over land and sea; the Lord is creator of all. *All* people command God's interest. God's grace and love and forgiveness are as available for the sailors or the people of Nineveh as they are for Jonah and his people. Your political enemies are not God's enemies. People you disagree with about social and moral and church issues are not God's enemies. People whom you would like to ignore are not ignored by God. God is Lord of all, and the people of Nineveh had a change of heart, mind, and soul.

You might be called stubborn and callous when you avoid sharing your understanding of God who is gracious and merciful, slow to anger, and abounding in steadfast love, and ready to relent from punishing. You are not true to God's calling when you run the other way from acknowledging God's mercy. God's mercy is for those whom you like and well as for those who have done you wrong. God is bigger than any of your limited definitions about who is in and who is out. God's mercy led to a change of heart in the people of Nineveh.

What a message the story of Jonah calls you to share. That no matter who you are, that no matter what you have done, that no matter how evil you are, that no matter how far you have descended, that no matter what you think of another, God is calling to you, offering love and mercy and grace and forgiveness and changes in your heart. The story of Jonah points out that the love is God is already present in your life and in the lives of your enemies. All you and they need to do is receive it.

And God said, "And should I not be concerned about Nineveh?" If God is concerned about the city, then what is your part in that concern? If they're in, will you stay as well or will you say, "Then I'm out!"

Prayer for the Day: *God of steadfast love, I truly want to be in even when it's uncomfortable because of who "they" are. So…you really love them, too? Amen.*

Week 31
Joshua 1:1-9

After the death of Moses the servant of the Lord, the Lord spoke to Joshua son of Nun, Moses' assistant, saying, 2 "My servant Moses is dead. Now proceed to cross the Jordan, you and all this people, into the land that I am giving to them, to the Israelites. 3 Every place that the sole of your foot will tread upon I have given to you, as I promised to Moses. 4 From the wilderness and the Lebanon as far as the great river, the river Euphrates, all the land of the Hittites, to the Great Sea in the west shall be your territory. 5 No one shall be able to stand against you all the days of your life. As I was with Moses, so I will be with you; I will not fail you or forsake you. 6 Be strong and courageous; for you shall put this people in possession of the land that I swore to their ancestors to give them. 7 Only be strong and very courageous, being careful to act in accordance with all the law that my servant Moses commanded you; do not turn from it to the right hand or to the left, so that you may be successful wherever you go. 8 This book of the law shall not depart out of your mouth; you shall meditate on it day and night, so that you may be careful to act in accordance with all that is written in it. For then you shall make your way prosperous, and then you shall be successful. 9 I hereby command you: Be strong and courageous; do not be frightened or dismayed, for the Lord your God is with you wherever you go."

Week 31 Sunday — Joshua 1:1-9

Memory is an odd thing. For example, if you were asked to tell about your sixteenth birthday, what kinds of things would you remember? Did you have a party? Did you have a cake? Did everyone forget your birthday?

People tell stories about World War II, college, or former athletic glory days. When they tell these stories of remembered events, are their tales true? Yes...and no. They remember what they choose and forget all the rest. They fill in details that may or may not have been accurate. They color their stories to make them look as good as they remember they were. But did the events happen as they said they did? If someone took a video, is what is seen on the screen what they said happened? No. That's just the way things are. Things in your past become part of your legend, your story, your history. You don't lie. You just don't tell the actual facts because everyone has a different understanding and remembrance of what the facts were.

Well, this is the way the book of Joshua is. It was written 600 years after the events it is telling about. The sagas were meant to help the people of Israel remember who and whose they were after they had been carted off into exile. Just like we tell the story of great-great-great-great-great grandfather who was a Revolutionary war soldier, they told the stories of how they ended up in Palestine and what God expected of them. They needed to understand how in the world they were now living away from home. They needed a framework to hold themselves together. Thus the book of Joshua. Were the stories historically accurate? Archeological work seems to say no. Were the stories true as guides to the work of God in the lives of people who were living in a strange land? Absolutely.

Prayer for the Day: *God of history, help me find my place in your actions and stories. Amen.*

Joshua 1:1-9

**Week 31
Monday**

Some of the framework of this remembered story harkens back to the Exodus stories and history. The river Jordan parted for the Israelites to enter Canaan just as the Red Sea parted for the people to leave Egypt. Joshua was confronted in Jericho by a man with a sword who claimed to be the commander of the army of the Lord, in other words, a holy person. This emissary told Joshua to remove his sandals because the ground was holy. This sounds a lot like Moses and the burning bush. The men were all circumcised since that ritual had been abandoned after Egypt. Rahab's scarlet rope identifying her house as one to be protected in the fall of Jericho harkens back to the blood spread on the door lintels to protect the Hebrews during the Passover. After crossing over the Jordan, the people once again ate food of the land and no longer ate manna.

Mary Mikhael (*Joshua: A Journey of Faith*, Horizons Bible Study, 2009-2010) says that the book of Joshua is rich in profound truths, but skimpy on actual historical details. She argues that to look at the book as a factual war history lays the groundwork for continuing turmoil in the Middle East. Unfortunately, many people have erroneously used the book of Joshua to justify all the fighting and killing that continues in that part of the world. A book that sings of the glory of one people who annihilate another...all at God's command...is not really helpful for those seeking peace and inclusion.

Prayer for the Day: *God of peace, help me see beyond the immediate story to what is truly Your Story. Amen.*

Week 31   **Joshua 1:1-9**
Tuesday

Even the book of Joshua includes people who were not those called Jewish. Rahab the harlot was Canaanite. She and her family were spared because of her actions on behalf of the spies that Joshua sent ahead. The Gibeonites, another Canaanite tribe, were spared through some skillful trickery and negotiating.

Some people claim that the political wars of the Middle East today are synonymous with the fighting listed in Joshua. This is erroneous for several reasons. As already mentioned, one is because the book was written some 600 years after the fact and was written in exile. Additionally, the exact boundaries of the lands claimed today as given by God are actually unclear and inconsistent in Joshua and in other Old Testament books. Furthermore, there is indication in Genesis that *owning* land and *living on* the land are not the same thing. For example, Abraham, the father of these multitudes, did not *own* the land that God gave to him. He had to purchase a grave site for his wife Sarah. Realizing this, you can consider that maybe the land called *Holy* is a land of promise rather the promised land. The vision for the region is for promise, where all people can live in security and health, freedom and faith, a land where God is held as both the God of the universe and the God of the heart, a land where visions, dreams, and promises are fulfilled in the grace and wisdom of God.

And in the final analysis, the book is not really about the land or the people but about God.

Prayer for the Day: *God of Promise, help me not confuse my ideas of promise with yours. Amen.*

Joshua 1:1-9

Week 31
Wednesday

In the story of Joshua, there you meet a God who keeps promises. In the book of Exodus, Moses received a promise that God would *bring [them] up out of the misery of Egypt, to the land of the Canaanites, the Hittites, the Amorites, the Perizzites, the Hivites, and the Jebusites, a land flowing with milk and honey* (Exodus 3:17). In Joshua's closing speech before he dies, he reminds the people of the kept promise: *And now I am about to go the way of all the earth, and you know in your hearts and souls, all of you, that not one thing has failed of all the good things that the Lord your God promised concerning you, not one of them has failed* (Joshua 23:14).

As someone who worships a God who keeps promises, how well do you model that behavior? Do you keep promises? You are a *maker* of promises... to your employer, your spouse, your friends, your children, and your extended family. Do you sometimes make promises to someone just to make them go away? You have no real intentions of fulfilling the promise. Have you ever told someone you want to get together for lunch with them and then do not follow through? Someone once said that every time you promise something, it takes a bit of energy from you. If you keep promising and not fulfilling those promises, then you become weaker and weaker. When you fulfill a promise, then you replenish your energy.

Do we keep our promises to respect others? To love others? To care about God, others, ourselves, and the world?

Do you keep the promise to care for the earth and all the creatures in it? Do you keep promises only when it is convenient for you to do so? Do you honor God with your kept promises?

You worship a God who keeps promises. What a life-giving, wonderful gift that is!

Prayer for the Day: *Amazing God, thank you for the many gifts that you promised and then fulfilled. Amen.*

Week 31
Thursday

Joshua 1:1-9

God of kept promises is also concerned about right living and justice. Cities of refuge are described in chapter 20 of Joshua. Mary Mikhael describes these cities that were set aside as "asylum cities for anyone who accidentally killed a person without the intention of murder... By fleeing to one of these cities a person was safe from any avenger who might be in pursuit until a fair trial could be conducted by the elders of the city. All Israelites and strangers dwelling among them were afforded such protection" (Mary Mikhael, *Joshua: A Journey of Faith,* Horizons Bible Study, 2009-2010, p. 71). With a city of refuge, revenge was halted.

Just think about that. When someone was accidentally killed, the person involved was protected from irate, angry, and grieving family members and friends by going to a city of refuge. Eventually the situation got straightened out sanely and without violence. Wouldn't that be a wonderful thing to have? When revenge is in open season, one death is avenged by another death that leads to another retribution death that leads to yet another death...on and on...until ultimately no one is left.

When you lay awake at night and revisit a hurtful event over and over and plan what you might do the next time you encounter the person, are you living with a revenge attitude or a receptive attitude? A receptive attitude remembers that you worship a God of grace and justice.

Wouldn't it be lovely if there was a form of cities of refuge to run to when you knew that you had hurt someone with your words or your actions. Possibly people who have hurt you might benefit from a city of refuge to avoid your wrath or your cold silence. Stretch the concept of cities of refuge even farther and consider the suicide bombings, the terrorist attacks, and random acts of violence that color much of your world. How much of that is revenge-based? When will people ever learn that violence breeds violence, that war means killing, no matter how well someone defines the rationale for war? In Joshua, a book that describes a lot of killing and conquering, you discover these pearls of peace, cities of refuge.

Prayer for the Day: *Jesus, is it possible for my heart to be a kind of refuge for someone? Amen.*

Joshua 1:1-9

Week 31
Friday

The prophets reinforced this idea of a God of justice. Isaiah first wrote these words that were later spoken by Jesus in Nazareth: *The spirit of the Lord is upon me because the Lord has anointed me; he has sent me to the oppressed, to bind up the brokenhearted, to proclaim liberty to the captives, and release to the prisoners; to proclaim the year of the Lord's favor* (Isaiah 61:1-2).

If you meet a God of justice in the claiming of the land of promise, if the prophets proclaimed God's justice, and if Jesus lived and breathed God's justice, then how might you join in God's activity and create pockets of justice ...cities of refuge... for people in your communities? Where can you create places of safety, health, healing? Where are the opportunities for breathing space in the aftermath of tragedy? Where, when, and how can you demonstrate that you are indeed a follower of the triune God? Would you be willing to set aside your desire for revenge in order to give God's grace time to show through our darkness? Could you trust God's justice rather than believing that justice is yours to bring forth?

God is also a God of covenant. Joshua says: *But just as all the good things that the Lord your God promised concerning you have been fulfilled for you, so the Lord will bring upon you all the bad things, until he has destroyed you from this good land that the Lord your God has given you* (Joshua 23:15). Joshua explains God's responsibilities when he speaks for God saying: *I have allotted to you as an inheritance for your tribes those nations that remain, along with all the nations that I have already cut off, from the Jordan to the Great Sea in the west. The Lord your God will push them back before you and drive them out of your sight and you shall possess their land, as the Lord your God promised you* (Joshua 23:4-5). But then Joshua continued, *If you transgress the covenant of the Lord your God, which he enjoined on you, and go and serve other gods and bow down to them, then the anger of the Lord will be kindled against you, and you shall perish quickly from the good land that he has given you* (Joshua 23:15-16).

Prayer for the Day: *God of justice, guide me in a life of justice. Amen.*

Week 31   **Joshua 1:1-9**
Saturday

And the peoples' responsibilities?

1. *Be very steadfast to observe and do all that is written in the book of the law of Moses* (Joshua 23:6).

2. *Be very careful… to love the Lord your God* (Joshua 23:11).

3. *Revere the Lord and serve God in sincerity and in faithfulness; put away the gods of your ancestors… and serve the Lord* (Joshua 24:14).

Do you live as a person of the covenant? What gods do you worship? Material goods? Prestige? Power? Security? Your family? Your contacts? Do you really love the Lord? Do you live as a person who has been given life and grace by your God to live as a shining example for the entire world? Do you believe that how you live matters to God? When people see how you live and talk and share and interact with others, do you demonstrate that you live in a covenanted relationship with your holy God or do others wonder if you live in covenant with other gods?

No matter how you remember the details and tell the story of God's amazing interactions with humanity throughout the ages, you profess that you worship a God who keeps promises, who is passionate about justice, and who has given you a covenant. Are you prepared to join Joshua when he says, *But as for me and my household, we will serve the Lord* (Joshua 24:15).

Prayer for the Day: *Crucified and risen Messiah, in your strength may I say "Me, too" with your help and people such as Joshua to guide my steps. Amen.*

Week 32
Ezekiel 37:1-14

The hand of the Lord came upon me, and he brought me out by the spirit of the Lord and set me down in the middle of a valley; it was full of bones. 2 He led me all round them; there were very many lying in the valley, and they were very dry. 3 He said to me, 'Mortal, can these bones live?' I answered, 'O Lord God, you know.' 4 Then he said to me, 'Prophesy to these bones, and say to them: O dry bones, hear the word of the Lord. 5 Thus says the Lord God to these bones: I will cause breath to enter you, and you shall live. 6 I will lay sinews on you, and will cause flesh to come upon you, and cover you with skin, and put breath in you, and you shall live; and you shall know that I am the Lord.'

7 So I prophesied as I had been commanded; and as I prophesied, suddenly there was a noise, a rattling, and the bones came together, bone to its bone. 8 I looked, and there were sinews on them, and flesh had come upon them, and skin had covered them; but there was no breath in them. 9 Then he said to me, 'Prophesy to the breath, prophesy, mortal, and say to the breath: Thus says the Lord God: Come from the four winds, O breath, and breathe upon these slain, that they may live.' 10 I prophesied as he commanded me, and the breath came into them, and they lived, and stood on their feet, a vast multitude.

11 Then he said to me, 'Mortal, these bones are the whole house of Israel. They say, "Our bones are dried up, and our hope is lost; we are cut off completely." 12 Therefore prophesy, and say to them, Thus says the Lord God: I am going to open your graves, and bring you up from your graves, O my people; and I will bring you back to the land of Israel. 13 And you shall know that I am the Lord, when I open your graves, and bring you up from your graves, O my people. 14 I will put my spirit within you, and you shall live, and I will place you on your own soil; then you shall know that I, the Lord, have spoken and will act, says the Lord.'

Week 32
Sunday

Ezekiel 37:1-14

The book of Ezekiel is definitely not G-rated. Roughly the first 24 chapters are prophecies of *doom* to the people of Israel because of their worshiping other gods and committing sins that probably should not be mentioned from the pulpit at church especially when there are children present. The second half of the book, Chapters 25-48 have prophecies of hope, relating to the time after the fall of Jerusalem in 587 B. C.

The setting of the book is after the death of King Josiah when all the religious reforms he had implemented during his reign have fallen by the wayside. The Assyrians who had captured Israel were losing their strength. Some people in Jerusalem were trying to make friends with the Egyptians but that did not work out so well. Nebuchadnezzar and the Babylonians captured Jerusalem and took all the leadership into captivity. In the book of Ezekiel, sabers were rattling all around people who were not keeping God's commandments.

When you read the book of Ezekiel, you will notice vivid imagery. Do you remember the spiritual song, Ezekiel Saw the Wheel? It begins with Ezekiel saw the wheel / Way up in the middle of the air/Ezekiel saw the wheel/ Way up in the middle of the air/ And the little wheel run by faith/ And the big wheel run by the grace of God/ A wheel in a wheel/ Way up in the middle of the air.

That's how the book begins with the call of Ezekiel—wheels within wheels up in the air.

Prayer for the Day: *God of vision, help me enjoy the imagery of this story while I learn its truths. Amen.*

Ezekiel 37:1-14

Week 32
Monday

Even though there is a lot of doom and gloom in the book, it is important to realize that the reason God lifted Ezekiel up as a prophet was to warn the people. God loved them and did not want them destroyed. God opened the door for repentance and life to all who were willing to enter. So even though Ezekiel told of dire consequences which indeed came to pass...captivity, destruction of home and Jerusalem, famine...Ezekiel was also a prophet of love and hope. One commentator called him a "herald of divine love for each person" (William Hugh Brownlee, *Ezekiel, Interpreter's Concise Commentary*, Abingdon Press, Nashville, 1983, p. 237).

When Ezekiel told the people about the images that he saw from God depicting what was going to happen, he listed their sins, things such as worshiping in places other than Jerusalem and the Temple, worshiping idols, adultery, oppression of others, robbery, holding back food for the hungry, refusing to clothe the naked, taking interest on loans, injustice, and ignoring God's ordinances. This list sounds rather contemporary, doesn't it?

Ezekiel proclaimed God's words: *If the wicked turn away from all their sins that they have committed and keep all my statutes and do what is lawful and right, they shall surely live; they shall not die. None of the transgressions that they have committed shall be remembered against them; for the righteousness that they have done they shall live. Have I any pleasure in the death of the wicked, says the Lord God, and not rather that they should turn from their ways and live?* (18:21-23).

Prayer for the Day: *Holy Spirit, move in me to show me where I ignore your love for me and that I need to pass along to others. Amen.*

Week 32
Tuesday

Ezekiel 37:1-14

After getting through the first 24 chapters where God yearns for the people's repentance from their sinfulness. the second half of the book has more scenes of hope and other powerful images or visions.

Do you know the spiritual that was inspired by the imagery of the passage about the valley of dry bones? *Dem Bones, Dem Bones, Dem Dry Bones*: Ezekiel connected dem dry bones / Ezekiel connected dem dry bones/ Ezekiel in the Valley of Dry Bones/Now hear the word of the Lord/ Toe bone connected to the foot bone/ Foot bone connected to the heel bone and on and on.

Now to the scripture.

Because Ezekiel was preaching to the people as a whole and also to them as individuals, you can consider this passage as pertinent to the church as a whole and to you as an individual.

When you think about the future of the Church, you may begin to wonder if it is indeed becoming a pile of dry bones. Denominations are shrinking. Many congregations are aging in that the average age of members is 65. The vitality of a church is not dependent on the number of members or the size of the budget, but small churches have to do ministry in ways differently than larger churches can. Especially when a congregation once had a large membership, being small may begin to seem like being in the valley of dry bones.

Large congregations, too, may begin to look like the valley of dry bones when they become focused on marketing the church and forget about saving grace. When a church begins to look and feel more like a YMCA, Rotary Club, or rock concert, then is it in danger of becoming a pile of bone that are dry from lack of deep spiritual roots in the triune God?

Do you as an individual sometimes feel as if you're just dry bones? Maybe you've lost your energy, your feeling of purpose for your life, or your hope. You may have suffered loss, grief, pain, despair, or disillusionment. Possibly you feel as if you have no future. You feel you are just a pile of dried-up old bones. You can understand this image of the Valley of Dry Bones.

Prayer for the Day: *Most caring God, how wonderful it is to realize that you understand feelings of being nothing but a bag of dried-up old bones. Thank you. Amen.*

Ezekiel 37:1-14

Week 32
Wednesday

Ezekiel, under God's direction, began prophesying to the bones. Lo and behold, there was a rattling, and they became zombies. Okay, maybe not zombies—but the description sounds kind of like zombies. Once again, very current, isn't it? The bones pulled together and pulled flesh and muscle onto the skeletons.

Those dry bones pulled it together. Some churches are trying to offer all the programs that they did when the church was twice its size. They are spending money from contingency funds just to keep the staff at the levels they had when the church had more members. Some churches are trying to be all things to all people. The church looks alive… but is it really?

The larger congregation has lots of activities for people of all ages. The name of Jesus is mentioned often but the teachings of Jesus, the mission of Jesus, may be rarely seen. The churches look alive…but are they? Are they just pretending to be alive? Are they zombie churches? Churches of the Undead?

This stage is where you may stop as an individual. You get through your loss, your struggles, and your challenges. You get up in the mornings, you go through the motions of life, and you say the right words, but you just *look* alive. You don't *feel* alive. You are dead inside. You sit in front of the television, tablet, phone, or the computer, you medicate yourself, you lash out at others in your frustration, but you are not alive in the way you want to be. You are simply bones with flesh and muscle but certainly no life.

Prayer for the Day: *Merciful God, I lift up to you today all those who feel like zombies. Help me know how to reach out and be the answer to the prayers I make. Amen.*

Week 32
Thursday

Ezekiel 37:1-14

Thank God, the vision does not stop there. God says, *I am going to open your graves, and bring you up from your graves, O my people… I will put my spirit within you, and you shall live* (Ezekiel 37:12-14).

Life comes to those bones from the Spirit breathing life into those reconstituted bodies. The Spirit of God dwells within the bodies and they are alive! Hallelujah!

When churches and you as an individual seek to listen to God's spirit that is dwelling in them and you, congregations and you experience life!

How do you know when you are living a spirit-filled life, being part of a spirit-filled church? How do you know that you are not a zombie worshiping with other zombies?

There's a church camp song titled "Spirit of the Living God." The words help you think deeply about the Spirit of God. They are: "Spirit of the Living God, Fall afresh on me; Spirit of the living God, fall afresh on me. Melt me, mold me, fill me, use me. Spirit of the Living God, fall afresh on me" (Words and music by minister from Tarboro, NC. *Glory to God, The Presbyterian Hymnal,* Westminster John Knox Press, 2013, #288). The words, "Spirit of the Living God," immediately tie you into your loving God. "Melt me, mold me, fill me, use me."

Prayer for the Day: *Spirit of the living God, fall afresh on me. Melt me, mold me, fill me, use me. Amen.*

Ezekiel 37:1-14

Week 32
Friday

You can look at yourself and how the Spirit moves in your life. You can explore how the gifts or talents given to you by God help you participate in God's kingdom, thereby making a difference in your world.

Evelyn Underhill, in her book *The Spiritual Life*, says that "if we desire a simple test of the quality of our spiritual life, a consideration of the tranquility, gentleness and strength with which we deal with the circumstances of our outward life will serve us better than anything that is based on the loftiness of our religious notions, or fervor of our religious feelings" (*A Guide to Prayer*, quoted in Reuben P. Job and Norman Shawchuck, *A Guide to Prayer for Ministers and Other Servants*, The Upper Room, Nashville, TN, 1983, p. 209)

What wonderful terms: tranquility, gentleness, and strength as a measure of the quality of your spiritual life. Do congregations make decisions, take actions, share fellowship in ways that bring tranquility, gentleness, and strength…or do they bring strife? In your personal life, do your decisions and actions and relationships bring you tranquility, make you gentle with yourself and others, and give you a sense of inner strength…or do they tear you up inside?

Prayer for the Day: *Blessed Lord, I want to live and act with tranquility, gentleness, and strength. Amen.*

Week 32
Saturday

Ezekiel 37:1-14

God knew you and mightily loved you from before you were in your mother's womb. God is still breathing life into your dry bones and you are a partner in creating your life with divine guidance. God gives all you need to walk the path which the Spirit is guiding you along. You may wish that you had a road map for that journey. But if you had known *then* what you know *now*, you may never have taken that first step. You might have been scared, overwhelmed, or reluctant. Maybe you would have been content with being bones held together with muscle and covered with skin. All you are asked to do is feel your lungs expand with that first spirit-infused breath. Then you can take that first step. It does not matter if you get it right or not. You'll keep having opportunities to be alive with your holy God…in your life, in the lives of your family members, in the lives of others in your community, your church, and your world.

What you can do for others is to listen and help them discover their God-instilled tranquility, strength, and gentleness. You as a follower of Jesus Christ can offer your presence to your sisters and brothers. You can ask questions which help you and others to grow in grace. You can support others when they and you are stepping out in ways that are uncomfortable or scary. You can offer your love and your prayers.

When you do that, when you are walking in God's light, when you are aware of the spirit breathing in you, when you trust your life to your triune God, when you really live as a resurrection, Spirit-filled person, then you live in hope. You are guided and graced by the Holy Spirit… What more do you need?

You are not a pile of dry bones. You are not a zombie. You are a hope-filled child of God, infused by the Holy Spirit into new life.

Prayer for the Day: *God, I'm not a zombie! I am your hope-filled, spirit-infused follower. Hallelujah! Amen.*

Week 33
Amos 5:21-24

21 I hate, I despise your festivals,
   and I take no delight in your solemn assemblies.
22 Even though you offer me your burnt-offerings and grain-offerings, I will not accept them; and the offerings of well-being of your fatted animals I will not look upon.
23 Take away from me the noise of your songs;
   I will not listen to the melody of your harps.
24 But let justice roll down like waters,
   and righteousness like an ever-flowing stream.

Week 33
Sunday

Amos 5:21-24

Righteousness is one of those words that is used a lot in the Bible. Unfortunately for many people, it has negative connotations. Marcus Borg suggests terms people often hear when they hear the word "righteous." "[H]olier-than-thou, judgmental, [condemning], hypocritical...legalistic, moralistic, full of themselves...and arrogant" (Marcus Borg, *Speaking Christian*, p. 133).

The people who may pop into your mind when you hear "righteous" may likely be more pompous than righteous. Julia Cameron, in her book "*God is No Laughing Matter,*" caricatures some of these folks when she calls them "Very Spiritual People." She says, "You can tell when you've met one of these officially spiritual types because they won't laugh no matter what. At best they smile thinly...They talk in low, sweet, soft, gentle monotone voices until you want to pinch them or tickle them or hit them with a baseball bat" (p 26-27). Even though she admits it's a terrible thing to say, she thinks "they are pretty mean and controlling and passive aggressive."

Another understanding of the word righteous seems to support what is often called the prosperity gospel. If you are righteous, if you do what is right, if you are good, then you prosper. You have all the financial resources and things that you want, beyond what you need.

Many people would likely proclaim that they do not think that way. Yet when you bemoan a loss, saying something such as, "What did I do to deserve this?" Or why is this happening to me?" you are pulling on the false belief that if you do good, if you are righteous, you are rewarded. AND you define what the reward should be.

Prayer for the Day: *Loving God, help me enfold true righteousness. Amen.*

Amos 5:21-24 **Week 33**
Monday

Jesus refutes the linkage of wealth and walking his Way when he says things such as *Children, how hard is it to enter the kingdom of God! It is easier for a camel to go through the eye of a needle than for someone who is rich to enter the kingdom of God* (Mark 10:24-25). Or when he told the parable of the guy with the bigger and bigger barns who died that very night when God called him a fool for laying up treasures for himself and not being rich toward God (Luke 12:13-22).

Timothy was warned by his mentor of the *depraved in mind and bereft of the truth, imagining that godliness is a means of gain* (I Timothy 6:5).

So, righteousness is not tied with monetary rewards.

Some people think righteousness is seen by how active one is in church. There are many people in congregations who set up and serve in worship, music, youth programs, building and grounds maintenance, meals of fellowship and support, cards, maintaining our social media, to name just a few. However, doing "church right" does not make anyone righteous.

Prayer for the Day: *Holy God, help me not confuse serving in the church with serving you. Amen.*

Week 33   **Amos 5:21-24**
Tuesday

I hate, I despise your festivals, and I take no delight in your solemn assemblies. Even though you offer me your burnt offerings and grain offerings, I will not accept them…Take away from me the noise of your songs; I will not listen to the melody of your harps. But let justice roll down like waters, and righteousness like an everflowing stream (Amos 5:21-24).

So here is what righteousness really means: God wants and is passionate about justice and righteousness. Letting justice roll down like waters is a parallel thought to righteousness like an everflowing stream. The ancient writers often used parallels in scripture to reinforce a single idea. So, justice is righteousness and righteousness is justice.

The term "faith" can unfold when you use the word "trust" in its place. Does your heart and mind expand when asked, "Do you have trust in the Lord Jesus Christ?" rather than asking you, "Do you have faith in the Lord Jesus Christ?"

"Believe" becomes rich when you switch to "belove." A question used all the time for confirmation, joining the church, and baptism is "Do you believe that Jesus is your Lord and Savior?" Listen how that question opens up when you change the language just a bit: "Do you belove Jesus as your Lord and Savior?"

Prayer for the Day: *God of justice and righteousness, I trust you. I belove you. Amen.*

Amos 5:21-24

**Week 33
Wednesday**

The concept of righteousness opens when you switch the word justice.

Try a word switch with a couple of the beatitudes to help expand your understanding and use of the word righteous.

(Matthew 5:6) *Blessed are those who hunger and thirst for righteousness, for they will be filled.* What happens to your understanding when you hear: Blessed are those who hunger and thirst for justice, for they will be filled.

(Matthew 5:10) *Blessed are those who are persecuted for righteousness.* Blessed are those who are persecuted for justice.

Marcus Borg says that "people are seldom persecuted for behaving in accordance with a strict individual moral code. But people are often persecuted because of their passion for justice" (Borg, *Speaking Christian*, p. 139).

In just a few verses below the end of the beatitudes, Jesus says, *For I tell you, unless your righteousness exceeds that of the scribes and Pharisees, you will never enter the kingdom of [God].* Matthew 5:20). So try, "Unless your justice exceeds that of the scribes and the Pharisees, you will never enter the kingdom of God."

The Biblical meaning of justice is not what many people think of when they hear the word "justice." They think of the criminal justice system. You do something wrong. You are punished. You get what you deserve. This is punitive justice. This justice maintains law and order. The order often seems to be created by powerful and wealthy people for the way "the world" should be. It is often unjust, and full of self-interest. There are multiple examples of the fall-out of this kind of justice on the nightly news, with demonstrations from various sides of any issue, increased mass killings, and decisions made or not made in legislative bodies.

And yet, humanity needs law and order because it is necessary when humans live together. People need ways to protect themselves and each other. One cannot imagine society without this kind of justice. Moses in the wilderness knew this truth when he came down from the mountain with rules for living together as God's people: Don't kill, don't steal, etc.

Prayer for the Day: *Jesus, my Messiah, save me from false understandings of what justice truly is meant to be. Amen.*

Week 33
Thursday

Amos 5:21-24

There's a deeper kind of Biblical justice. It's called distributive justice. It is best illustrated by Psalm 24 which begins with: *The earth is the Lord's and all that is in it.* Since everything is God's then you are to distribute the gifts, wealth, benefits as God would distribute the many blessings that abound. Are the systems structured so that everyone benefits, so no one gets more than necessary, and no one gets less?

Charity and justice are not the same. Charity comes from a position of wanting to do "good." Charity allows you to help from a position of wealth, strength, or correctness. When you offer charity, you decide what, when, how, and to whom you will give. It allows you to share something with someone, but you do not have to connect with him or her in any way.

When you take your used clothes to a helping agency, you know the clothes will be given to someone in need or sold to help support the agency's programs. When you give this way, you don't have to worry about the fit of the coat or even the condition of the coat you donate. We sometimes assume that if someone is cold, any old coat will do. You *never* have to move from your comfort or security when you offer charity to someone. You can help and not be touched in any kind of deep, spiritual way. You give to meet a specific need—food, clothing, rent money, homes, etc. From a charity standpoint, you do not question deeply why the person needs your used coat, your bag of groceries, or your financial gift. You simply meet the immediate need.

Justice on the other hand, asks why the person cannot afford to purchase his or her own coat. What is going on within the family so they cannot afford their rent? Justice can go even further by asking risky questions such as:

- "Why does our community allow employers to pay service workers so poorly they cannot afford adequate shelter, or clothe their children?"
- "Why is our community putting up so much housing for people who can pay $1,000 or more a month in rent and not building housing for people for whom $500 or less a month is a stretch?"
- "What is it about our own community that makes it more difficult for a child born into poverty to have less of a chance to move out than in many, many other communities in our country?"
- "What is it about the color of people's skin that makes life so fearful for so many?"

Prayer for the Day: *Giving God, help me always remember the difference between charity and justice. Both are essential. Just don't let me confuse them with each other. Amen.*

Amos 5:21-24

**Week 33
Friday**

In understanding biblical justice, the justice that Jesus called for, you want for others what you want for yourself, and you work to make that happen. Jesus's pronouncement of the two most important commandments helps you move from charity to justice. He said, *You shall love the Lord your God with all your heart, and with all your soul, and with all your mind, and with all your strength... You shall love your neighbor as yourself* (Matthew 22:37-39). Wanting for our neighbor exactly what we want for ourselves helps us understand justice... righteousness (Adapted from BLT, *Loving Our Neighbor*, pp 167-168).

Marcus Borg explains: "The indictment of injustice continues throughout the New Testament. [Jesus, Paul, and others] stood against the Roman Empire because of its injustice and violence. Many of them were killed by the authorities—not because they advocated charity and taught individual righteousness and the way to heaven. People do not get martyred for that. Why would the authorities care? Rather, they were killed because those in power perceived their message and passion to be a threat to 'the way things were'—that is, to the way the wealthy and powerful had structured the world to garner most of society's resources for themselves" (Borg, *Speaking Christian*, 138).

God's distributive justice is for everyone. Righteousness as justice tells you not only what you should seek and be about but also shows you more about God. God is gracious and compassionate. God's passion is that everyone is treated as God's beloved family.

Prayer for the Day: *God of steadfastness and encouragement, I want to love you with all my heart, soul, mind, and strength but I need you in my life to guide me. Amen.*

Week 33
Saturday

Amos 5:21-24

Try out this fantasy as you think about this passage from Amos:

Sometimes I wish there was a room for people to visit. This room is filled with different masks. Some masks are faces of children. One visage looks like the model for an ad for senior citizens' cruises. Another is lined and well-worn. One's hair is well-coiffed. Another's hair is frizzy and straggly.

There are masks of men's faces, women's faces, children's faces, androgynous faces. Masks are European, African, Asian, Native American, Middle Eastern, and South and Central American. One group of masks are faces of people who are homeless or very poor. Another group has faces showing the benefits of money, good nutrition, and appropriate cosmetics.

There are masks for Presbyterians, Baha'is, Baptists, Pentecostals, Catholics, New Agers, Unitarians, Mormons, Moslems, Sikh, Methodists, Buddhists, Hindus, and all other faiths. There are masks for straights and LGBTQx, for educated and uneducated, rich, poor, loved, and battered.

There are thousands of masks in this room. Every one of us is required to go into the room and put on whatever mask the attendant gives to us. The choice is the attendant's, not ours. For the next thirty days, we become whoever our mask tells us we are.

If you had to feel the feelings of someone else or live the realities of another person for an entire month, how would your world be different? (The fantasy is adapted from BLT, *Loving Our Neighbor*, p. 168)

Prayer for the Day: *Faithful God, may justice roll down like waters and righteousness like an everflowing stream in my life. Amen.*

Week 34
Matthew 5:1-12

When Jesus saw the crowds, he went up the mountain; and after he sat down, his disciples came to him. 2 Then he began to speak, and taught them, saying:

3 "Blessed are the poor in spirit, for theirs is the kingdom of heaven.

4 "Blessed are those who mourn, for they will be comforted.

5 "Blessed are the meek, for they will inherit the earth.

6 "Blessed are those who hunger and thirst for righteousness, for they will be filled.

7 "Blessed are the merciful, for they will receive mercy.

8 "Blessed are the pure in heart, for they will see God.

9 "Blessed are the peacemakers, for they will be called children of God.

10 "Blessed are those who are persecuted for righteousness' sake, for theirs is the kingdom of heaven.

11 "Blessed are you when people revile you and persecute you and utter all kinds of evil against you falsely on my account.

12 "Rejoice and be glad, for your reward is great in heaven, for in the same way they persecuted the prophets who were before you."

Week 34
Sunday

Matthew 5:1–12

This week's readings pull heavily from Loving Our Neighbor: A Thoughtful Approach to Helping People in Poverty, *Beth Lindsay Templeton, Chapter One.*

The Beatitudes are about much more than an individual's faith development. They teach that when you share in the life of someone who is struggling and witness that person overcoming tremendous obstacles, you celebrate.

To understand this kind of celebration, consider the Greek word *makarios* which can be translated "blessed," "lucky," or "happy." The full intent of *makarios* describes a kind of joy that is permanent, that holds a deep secret. *Makarios* is not dependent on what is going on in your external world. It is within you, internal—a gift from God. It is blessing in the fullest sense of the word.

Jesus describes different ways in which people experience this kind of permanent joy.

Matthew 5:3: *Blessed [makarios / permanently joyful] are the poor in spirit, for theirs is the kingdom of heaven.* "Poor in spirit" does not describe people who are depressed or lethargic. Remember that Jesus was speaking Aramaic with roots in the Hebrew language. Deuteronomy 8:11–20 helps capture the Hebrew sense of "poor in spirit." *Take care that you do not forget the LORD your God, by failing to keep his commandments, his ordinances, and his statutes, which I am commanding you today.* After telling what God had done in leading them out of Egypt, it says, *When you have eaten your fill and have built fine houses and live in them ... and your silver and gold is multiplied, ... then do not exalt yourself, forgetting the LORD your God ... But remember the LORD your God, for it is he who gives you power to get wealth* (Deuteronomy 8:12–14, 18). "Poor in spirit" refers to people who are dependent on God's grace, not on their own accomplishments and their own accumulation for security. Material things mean nothing. God means everything.

Can you honestly claim that things mean nothing to you? How much time and energy do you spend fretting about what you have? Does it need repair? Where will you put it? You fret about what you don't have. "I need another "whatever. Every other church has a van, a gym, a state-of-the-art nursery...whatever. *We need one too!* You live and act sometimes as if things mean everything and God means nothing. It is a myth that possessing more and more things will make you happy.

This first Beatitude points to the fact that you are totally dependent on God. And when you claim and live that reality, you have permanent joy.

Prayer for the Day: *God of each moment, help me remember that in you I have everything that's truly important. Amen.*

Matthew 5:1–12

Week 34
Monday

Gandhi was persecuted when he stood up for people to be treated fairly. Martin Luther King Jr. was assassinated when he stood up against racism and war. Nelson Mandela served prison time for standing up against apartheid. Ordinary people in the struggle against societal ills are labeled "crazy," "nuts," "extremist," "anti-Christian," etc. Standing up for what is right and just is not easy but does offer *makarios*, deep, permanent joy according to Jesus.

When your faith influences and permeates every fiber, impulse, and act, you may be compelled to say unpopular things, take unpopular stands, or speak God's truth as you understand it to people who love lies. Jesus says that those scary actions are the actions of deep, abiding, permanent joy.

The Beatitudes turn everything upside down. This world says to let the chips fall where they may, to ignore others because they get what they deserve, to live insulated lives, and to get others before they do unto you. Jesus sits and teaches just the opposite. Jesus tells that living in his way, walking his path, following him as Lord and Savior, and being his disciple is where you discover permanent joy. When you reach out, when you care, when you work for the good of others, when you live as Jesus challenges you to live, you experience the reality of *makarios*: deep, abiding, and permanent joy.

Matthew 5:4: *Blessed* [makarios / permanently joyful] *are those who mourn, for they will be comforted.*

Isaiah 61:1-4 tells about the oppressed, the brokenhearted, the captives, and the prisoners. Mourning here refers to those who mourn the devastation of Israel. They mourn the Israelites' disobedience, which brought about their captivity. When you look beyond yourself, you can mourn the conditions facing people in your community who are oppressed, brokenhearted, captive, or prisoners.

With this beatitude, you look beyond yourself and see all the other people. You mourn what is happening to them: lack of food and medical care, living in houses that are not fit for your dog, not being able to provide adequately for their families, even though they are working 60 or more hours a week. You mourn a world where violence is the primary tool for solving conflicts and problems. You mourn the devastation from hurricanes, fires, or earthquakes. You mourn your apathy when you detach from others.

When you mourn, people can relate to you in your full humanity. When others mourn, you can empathize with them and begin to understand some of their pain. When we are open to the vulnerability of the world, we will experience deep, abiding joy.

Prayer for the Day: *God of the downtrodden, help me be vulnerable to others who are hurting. Amen.*

Week 34 — Tuesday
Matthew 5:1–12

Matthew 5:5: *Blessed* [makarios / permanently joyful] *are the meek, for they will inherit the earth.*

Meek does not mean being a doormat. Because you are a recipient of God's love and grace, even though undeserved, you too can be loving and gracious to others. Aristotle described meekness as that center point between too much and too little anger. Gandhi said meekness was the power of love called *soul force*. In your meekness, you know that you are not God. You do not have to dominate the world.

Being meek means that when you meet someone seeking your assistance, in whatever form, you can be kind and gracious. When you choose to be in relationship with people who are different from you, you choose to honor the gifts they exhibit. You acknowledge that you do not know what it feels like to live in their skin, to have experienced the conditions of their lives or to know the best solutions for next steps. You know you care and that you're willing to walk alongside others, learning from them as they learn from you.

Matthew 5:6 *Blessed* [makarios / permanently joyful] *are those who hunger and thirst for righteousness, for they will be filled.*

This is yearning for social justice—for righteousness. This is not simply: "Wouldn't it be nice if we built a Habitat house, if we opened a medical clinic, if we had a letter-writing campaign to increase funding for childcare?" All these things are important. However, this verse speaks of hungering and thirsting.

Hungering is more than needing an afternoon snack to get you through to dinnertime. Hungering is about that feeling one gets when the money runs out before the month runs out and there is no food in the house. Hungering is about having a bloated belly and bugged-out eyes because you have not had a square meal in weeks. Do you have that kind of yearning for social justice? Do you thirst for justice like someone stranded in the desert thirsts for water? Do you thirst for a world where everyone can meet his or her needs and where all can reach the full potential God created in them? Do you have that gut kind of yearning for righteousness?

Do you act on your feelings of disgust when you learn of injustices, or do you simply say, "That's awful," and forget about it the next day? Do you really hunger and thirst for the well-being of everyone in your own community?

Prayer for the Day: *Confronting God, these verses are challenging. However, I want to be engaged in your world with the Beatitudes' depth of love and concern. I want to experience deep, abiding joy, like Jesus describes. Amen.*

Matthew 5:1–12

Week 34
Wednesday

Matthew 5:7 – *Blessed* [makarios / permanently joyful] *are the merciful, for they will receive mercy.* Are you beginning to see a pattern here? When you are poor in spirit, you acknowledge your total dependence on God. You mourn as you see the pain and devastation in the world. In meekness you realize you have all and none of the solutions for others. With intense yearning, you hunger for healing in the world. And then you offer mercy, God's steadfast loving-kindness, that reaches out to everyone, deserving and undeserving.

Mercy is not an attitude: "Oh, I feel compassion for you." No, mercy is action. You put yourself in the other's place to try to see, taste, touch, hear, and smell the world as he or she does. You try to see life as another might see it.

Mercy tempers your sense of righteousness. Without mercy you may try to deal with your hunger and thirst for righteousness by being ruthless, aggressive, or violent. Being merciful reminds you that the kingdom of God is in God's hands, not yours. You can admit that God has indeed been merciful with you, even when you did not deserve it. As you live in God's grace, you can offer that same kind of freedom, accountability, and love to another of God's beloved children.

Sometimes people have said that they do not want to reach out to others. They don't want to help people who made bad choices that led to their current condition. Yes, people do make bad choices. Doesn't everyone? Mercy says that maybe, just maybe, you can reach out yet one more time, offer an alternative to previous bad decisions, and love with both wisdom and compassion so a person can grow into a healthier way of living.

Prayer for the Day: *Merciful God, help me be merciful to others as you have been merciful to me. Amen.*

Week 34 — Thursday — Matthew 5:1–12

Matthew 5:8: *Blessed* [makarios / permanently joyful] *are the pure in heart, for they will see God.*

Being pure in heart follows naturally when you no longer yearn for things, when you are able to mourn, when you hunger for what is right because you are full of mercy and see others as beloved people of God. Psalm 24:3–4 states, *Who shall ascend the hill of the* LORD? ... *Those who have clean hands and pure hearts, who do not lift up their souls to what is false, and do not swear deceitfully.* The pure in heart, according to the psalmist, are not only people who are innocent of moral failures but who are also free of evil intentions. The Hebrews believed the heart to be the seat of will, so being pure in heart meant simply having purity of will.

When conversing with dedicated people of faith who ask about the wisdom of giving money to people who come up to them on the street asking for a handout, a poverty advocate asks them why they give money. With reluctance, they often acknowledge they give because they want the person to go away, they are afraid, or they feel guilty. They admit that their response is not in the manner which Jesus teaches. They are acting not with a pure heart but rather from an impulse that is guarded and protected.

Prayer for the Day: *Protector of all who trust, help me see where my heart and will are not aligned with purity as you define it. Amen.*

Matthew 5:1–12

Week 34
Friday

Matthew 5:9: Blessed [makarios / permanently joyful] *are the peacemakers, for they will be called children of God.*

You now know you are dependent on God. You see the pain in the world around you. You yearn for a world where everyone enjoys the full knowledge and benefit of God's love. You are merciful toward those with whom you disagree or who frustrate you or who challenge you in a variety of ways. Now what?

You do something about all that. You make peace. You don't *keep* peace. You make it. You do that hard work of reconciling hostile individuals or situations. You strive to return good for evil and to love those you do not like. You painstakingly build bridges when every fiber of your being would rather build walls.

Peacemaking is hard work. It is much harder than keeping peace. Keeping peace often allows secrets to continue wreaking their havoc in their dark hiddenness. Keeping peace means that people "play nice" to each other's face and knife each other in the back through phone calls or parking-lot meetings or e-mail messages or letter campaigns. Yes, making peace is harder. When you are a peacemaker, you have permanent, deep, and abiding joy—according to Jesus.

Prayer for the Day: *God of peace, help me be a peacemaker...not a peacekeeper. Amen.*

Week 34
Saturday

Matthew 5:1–12

Matthew 5:10–11: *Blessed* [makarios / permanently joyful] *are those who are persecuted for righteousness' sake, for theirs is the kingdom of heaven. Blessed are you when people revile you and persecute you and utter all kinds of evil against you falsely on my account.*

People who love as God loves, who are dependent on God, who allow the woes of the world to penetrate their innermost being, and then choose to do something about it are likely to experience discord, antagonism, hatred, ostracism and, yes, even death. Look what happened to Jesus. Jesus is not telling you to do anything he did not do.

Gandhi was persecuted when he stood up for his people in India to be treated fairly as valuable human beings. Martin Luther King Jr. was assassinated when he stood up against racism and war. Nelson Mandela served decades of prison time for standing up against apartheid in South Africa. Ordinary people who stand up for fair housing, public transportation, health care for all, and equitable wages and join the struggle against societal ills are labeled with "crazy," "nuts," "extremist," "anti-Christian," and lots of other negative epithets. Standing up for what is right and just is not easy but does offer a state called *makarios*, deep, permanent joy according to Jesus.

When you take your faith seriously, when you choose to let your faith influence and permeate every fiber, impulse, and act, you may be compelled at times to say unpopular things, to take unpopular stands, or to speak God's truth as you understand it to people who love living with lies. Jesus tells you that those actions that scare you are the very actions of deep, abiding, permanent joy.

These teachings of Jesus simply do not make sense in the rational ways of thinking in the 21st century. These Beatitudes turn everything upside down. This world says to get what you can. If others are poor, that's not your fault. You work hard, and since they are poor, they must not work. Your world says to pay attention to me and mine. We can ignore people who are poor or needy. The needs of others are not your concerns. Your world says to let the chips fall where they may, to ignore others because they get what they deserve, to live insulated lives behind gates, and to get others before they do unto you. These are the teachings of this world.

Jesus sits and teaches just the opposite. Jesus says that living in his way, walking his path, following him as Lord and Savior, and being his disciple is where you discover permanent joy. When you reach out, when you care, when you work for the good of others, when you live as Jesus challenges you to live, you experience the reality of *makarios*: deep, abiding, and permanent joy. Do you dare believe that?

Prayer for the Day: *God of vision, turn me upside down! Amen.*

Week 35
Psalm 103:1-14

1 Bless the Lord, O my soul,
 and all that is within me,
 bless his holy name.
2 Bless the Lord, O my soul,
 and do not forget all his benefits—
3 who forgives all your iniquity,
 who heals all your diseases,
4 who redeems your life from the Pit,
 who crowns you with steadfast love and mercy,
5 who satisfies you with good as long as you live
 so that your youth is renewed like the eagle's.

6 The Lord works vindication
 and justice for all who are oppressed.
7 He made known his ways to Moses,
 his acts to the people of Israel.
8 The Lord is merciful and gracious,
 slow to anger and abounding in steadfast love.
9 He will not always accuse,
 nor will he keep his anger for ever.
10 He does not deal with us according to our sins,
 nor repay us according to our iniquities.
11 For as the heavens are high above the earth,
 so great is his steadfast love towards those who fear him;
12 as far as the east is from the west,
 so far he removes our transgressions from us.
13 As a father has compassion for his children,
 so the Lord has compassion for those who fear him.
14 For he knows how we were made;
 he remembers that we are dust.

Week 35
Sunday

Psalm 103:1-14

How do you bless God? Most of your ideas about blessings may be about what you get. People ask God to give divine favor as when they bless a house, for example. You may sometimes use it as a hope for protection or nurture as in the southern phrase, "Bless your heart."

Maybe you sometimes see it as the opposite of a curse. If the team doesn't win—in other words if it's cursed with turnovers, injuries, and just bad luck. When it wins, it must be blessed. Sometimes blessing is used as a physical action as when the Pope makes the sign of the cross over an individual or a multitude.

When children are taught to "say the blessing," they usually are told to be grateful for the food, for the people who prepared it, and for those who made it possible for everyone to be together to share the meal.

It seems that generally, people think of blessings as something good coming to them.

What good could you offer to God? How do you bless God?

Prayer for the Day: *Awesome God, so how do I bless you? I guess I'll have to think on this. Amen.*

Psalm 103:1-14

Week 35
Monday

This psalm begins with a personal call to bless God. *Bless the Lord, O my soul, and all that is within me bless God's holy name* (Psalm 103:1). Whoa… blessings, looking to God, remembering God, holding up God as more than ordinary is to be done with all that is within me? All that is within me? Does that include the mean things I've done that I regret or things I did that harmed someone? Does all that is within me mean any illnesses that I am dealing with personally or that I am struggling with because of a loved one's health issues? Does all that is within me mean blessing God even when I feel I'm in a black hole and the darkness is overwhelming? Does all that is within me mean when I feel that no one really loves me for who I am rather than who they think I am? Does this mean blessing God when I'm aware of all the aches and pains and regrets I gather as I add years to my age?

The Psalmist's resounding answer is Yes!!! Blessing the Lord with all that is within you means all those things.

Prayer for the Day: *Loving God, how can all that is within me bless you? I guess I have some growing to do. Amen.*

Week 35
Tuesday

Psalm 103:1-14

The language of this poem continues (Psalm 103:3-5): *[The Lord] forgives all your sins,* (the mean things you've done that you regret or that harmed someone)

> *heals all your diseases,*
> *redeems your life from the Pit,* (that black hole and overwhelming darkness)
> *crowns you with steadfast love and mercy,* (love no matter what)
> *and renews your youth* (pains and regrets do not have the last word).

And then to really emphasize this, the psalmist uses the word ALL four times in five verses: ALL that is within me…ALL God's benefits…ALL your iniquity…ALL your diseases.

As these truths sink in, then you might be tempted to stand up, twirl around, sing, shout, and in general demonstrate that you are blessing the Lord with everything that is in you.

But you might not do these things.

Prayer for the Day: *God, in my heart, I'm singing, jumping, and shouting. Just not out loud. But I know you hear me anyway. Amen.*

Psalm 103:1-14

**Week 35
Wednesday**

But what about that phrase, "Heals all your diseases." You know that all illnesses are not healed, so what does this mean? The psalmist, too, knows that life for humans is finite. Listen to this: *For God knows how we are made…and remembers that we are dust. As for mortals, they flourish like a flower of the field…but the steadfast love of the Lord is from everlasting to everlasting* (Psalm 103:14, 17). Both things are true. It's a paradox.

Scriptures are full of paradoxes. A paradox is when two things are equally true, but they seem to be saying the opposite. For example: Jesus is human. Jesus is God. How can that be? You cannot explain that, but you know it to be true. God heals all diseases and God knows you are dust.

And yet, how do you trust that God heals all diseases when you've had family members and friends die of illnesses before they'd lived their three score and ten years? Disease in the ancient world was looked at very differently from how illness is understood today. One of Job's friends best helps with this insight. Friend Eliphaz told Job that he must have sinned to have all these illnesses and losses. He continued, *Think now, who that was innocent ever perished?* (Job 4:7). Bildad believes that Job's ancestors must have done something terribly wrong. He said, *Does God pervert justice? Or does the Almighty pervert the right?* (Job 8:3). In the ancient world, illness was not known as viruses and bacteria, poor nutrition, harmful environment, and bad lifestyle decisions.

Because people were getting sick and dying during the pandemic, you may need to allow for a time that "healing all our illnesses" may remain in the mystery category and that illness is not God's choice for us.

A God who heals all illnesses must want you to be healthy…in your lifestyle, in how you care for your home, the Earth, in how you care for those who do not have some of the advantages that you take for granted. A God who values your health must think that compassionate and skilled medical personnel and staff are a gift. When you value your own health as well as the health of all living beings—human and nonhuman… then you bless God.

Prayer for the Day: *God of healing, thank you that you created my body so that cuts heal, bones reset, and my muscles work. Amen.*

Week 35
Thursday

Psalm 103:1-14

The psalmist deepens your understanding of this God you are to bless. Verse 9 states that God *will not always accuse, nor will the Lord keep his anger forever.* God will not always accuse…this indicates that the people of Israel, the intended audience for this psalm, must have experienced accusations from God. When people read the prophets: Isaiah, Jeremiah, Hosea, and others they certainly hear God's statements of judgement and accusations. Hear Jeremiah 14:10: *Truly they have loved to wander, they have not restrained their feet; therefore, the Lord does not accept them, now he will remember their iniquity and punish their sins.* But you know that God did not keep this kind of anger forever. How do you know that? Because you are still here.

The psalmist also reminds that God does not punish you to the extent that punishment is warranted. Verse 10 states that God does not punish according to your sins nor repay you according to your iniquities. Thanks be to God for that. Praise God.

A God who forgives all your iniquities seemingly would like for you to try to live without iniquities. This is sometimes hard when you fall into the traps of "This is how it's done, this is what people want, this is how I was raised," when you buy into power and pushing. On and on. You fall into iniquities because you do not consider if and how your routines might *not* align with the Jesus Way. When you consciously walk the Jesus Way, you bless God.

Prayer for the Day: *God of forgiveness, as you forgive me, may I forgive others. Amen.*

Psalm 103:1-14 **Week 35**
Friday

In Psalm 103:15-22, you discover that this God is so awesome, so much more than you can get your mind and heart around that the psalmist lets you know that the entire world, indeed the entire universe blesses your Lord. Angels, all God's hosts, the entire dominion, bless God.

Then this triumphant song, this psalm, closes with *Bless the Lord, O my soul*.

This brings you back to how do you bless God? The psalmist seems to lead to an even deeper understanding of how you bless God, beyond praise, thanks, worship, and singing.

A God who asks you to remember all your benefits must want you to acknowledge that everything you have and are comes from God. People rarely remember this. Folks are proud of what *they* have accomplished. When you live your life with gratitude and mindfulness acknowledging that God is above you, below you, behind you, in you, and beside you, then you bless God.

A God who redeems you from the Pit calls you to reach out to those who are in deep pain. You allow space for people to share their distress. Alcoholics and Narcotics Anonymous are wonderful examples of blessing God in the way members support each other.

Prayer for the Day: *Holy Spirit, let all that is within me bless your holy name. Amen.*

Week 35
Saturday

Psalm 103:1-14

Can you fully incorporate into your heart, mind, and soul that your God crowns you with steadfast love and mercy? This crown allows you to live as a royal king, queen, princess, or prince who graciously cares for others and for the world. That's what good royalty does. They spread love and mercy throughout their kingdom. That's how you bless God.

A God who can renew your youth like an eagle's must want you to live well until you die. This God must value the wisdom, the insights, and the value of older people. You can claim that you are vital, whether you're young, old, or in in the middle. This is how you bless God. You live well the moments of your life, so you reflect God's love on others.

So how do you bless God? You bless God with how you live, move, and have your being. You thank God with your heart, soul, mind, and strength. You trust God to keep all the promises…even when you're not sure how that can and will happen. You live as a person who follows Jesus on the wondrous and mysterious way ahead of you.

You bless God and all that is within you blesses God's holy name.

Prayer for the Day: *God of blessing, I want to bless you with how I live my life. Amen.*

Week 36
Letter to Philemon

Paul, a prisoner of Christ Jesus, and Timothy our brother, to Philemon our dear friend and co-worker, 2 to Apphia our sister, to Archippus our fellow-soldier, and to the church in your house: 3 Grace to you and peace from God our Father and the Lord Jesus Christ.

4 When I remember you in my prayers, I always thank my God 5 because I hear of your love for all the saints and your faith towards the Lord Jesus. 6 I pray that the sharing of your faith may become effective when you perceive all the good that we may do for Christ. 7 I have indeed received much joy and encouragement from your love, because the hearts of the saints have been refreshed through you, my brother.

8 For this reason, though I am bold enough in Christ to command you to do your duty, 9 yet I would rather appeal to you on the basis of love—and I, Paul, do this as an old man, and now also as a prisoner of Christ Jesus. 10 I am appealing to you for my child, Onesimus, whose father I have become during my imprisonment. 11 Formerly he was useless to you, but now he is indeed useful both to you and to me. 12 I am sending him, that is, my own heart, back to you. 13 I wanted to keep him with me, so that he might be of service to me in your place during my imprisonment for the gospel; 14 but I preferred to do nothing without your consent, in order that your good deed might be voluntary and not something forced. 15 Perhaps this is the reason he was separated from you for a while, so that you might have him back for ever, 16 no longer as a slave but as more than a slave, a beloved brother—especially to me but how much more to you, both in the flesh and in the Lord.

17 So if you consider me your partner, welcome him as you would welcome me. 18 If he has wronged you in any way, or owes you anything, charge that to my account. 19 I, Paul, am writing this with my own hand: I will repay it. I say nothing about your owing me even your own self. 20 Yes, brother, let me have this benefit from you in the Lord! Refresh my heart in Christ. 21 Confident of your obedience, I am writing to you, knowing that you will do even more than I say.

22 One thing more—prepare a guest room for me, for I am hoping through your prayers to be restored to you.

23 Epaphras, my fellow-prisoner in Christ Jesus, sends greetings to you, 24 and so do Mark, Aristarchus, Demas, and Luke, my fellow-workers.

25 The grace of the Lord Jesus Christ be with your spirit.

Week 36
Sunday

Letter to Philemon

Based on Marcus Borg and John Crossan, *The First Paul*, pp. 34-42 (Note: The section on dominance is heavily dependent on Gray Temple, "Theological Perspective, Philemon," *Feasting on the Word, Year C, Vol. 4*, pp. 40-42)

The Apostle Paul is known for his letter writing. He is credited with more letters in the New Testament than scholars believed he personally wrote. The consensus is that Paul definitely wrote seven of the epistles. They are: Romans, I & II Corinthians, Galatians, I Thessalonians, Philemon, and Philippians. Scholars are divided about Ephesians, Colossians, and II Thessalonians. Those definitely *not* written by Paul are I & II Timothy and Titus. This is helpful because some subjects are treated differently in the letters fully attributed to Paul than they are in the other letters. For example, I Timothy 6:1-2 states: *Let all you who are under the yoke of slavery regard their masters as worthy of all honor.* He says, *Slaves must serve [their masters] all the more, since those who benefit by their service are believers and beloved.*

Unfortunately, the First Timothy reading was used by the church to endorse and uphold slavery. In Paul's letter to Philemon, you see a new thing regarding slavery. Paul does not speak against the Roman institution of slavery. However, he does speak to the relationship of one slave—Onesimus, one owner—Philemon, and Paul himself. He addresses this relationship in light of the love of Jesus Christ and who this Christ is in the lives of all three men.

Prayer for the Day: *Creator God, open my mind to having my mind changed by you. Amen.*

Letter to Philemon   **Week 36**
         Monday

In his letters, Paul often uses the blessing *Grace and peace from God our Father and the Lord Jesus Christ* (verse 3) making it very clear that he is writing not on his own authority but as an agent of Jesus Christ.

Of the seven authentic letters by Paul, this is the only one written to an individual. Even though it was personal, it was not meant to be private. Paul also sends greetings to Apphia and Archippus, leaders of the house church that meets in Philemon's home. Since Philemon provides the space in his house for a church, he obviously is a man of means, someone of status. If Philemon actually does what Paul in Christ is asking, he, as a wealthy man, could lose status.

The heading of Paul's letter begins with, *Paul, a prisoner of Christ Jesus* (verse 1). Normally Paul identifies himself using the phrase, "I Paul, an apostle of Jesus Christ." It seems that his imprisonment is a key part of understanding this letter. In verse 13, Paul wrote, *I wanted to keep Onesimus [the slave owned by Philemon] with me, so that he might be of service to me in your place during my imprisonment for the gospel*...which actually means "in my chains." Agrippa was another man imprisoned about the same time. In his writings about his imprisonment, he reports that a prisoner might have someone, possibly even a Roman centurion, chained to him so the prisoner could bathe every day, receive visitors, and have other bodily comforts. Because of this practice, Paul was able to write letters and receive support and assistance from fellow Christians.

Prayer for the Day: *Holy God, may I hear your voice through Paul's words. Amen.*

Week 36
Tuesday

Letter to Philemon

Paul thanks God for Philemon's faith and for how Philemon has refreshed the hearts of the saints. He identifies Philemon as a co-worker (verse 1) and partner in the gospel (verses 6, 17). Paul even claims Philemon as his brother (verses 6, 17) and his son (verse 10). He acknowledges that Philemon has hosted Paul and they will soon again be able to share hospitality. Paul and Philemon obviously had a warm relationship in Christ.

After the thanksgiving, you begin to see a master communicator at work. As Philemon is basking in the accolades of co-worker, partner, brother, he then reads: *For this reason, though I am bold enough in Christ to command you to do your duty, yet I would rather appeal to you on the basis of love—and I, Paul, do this as an old man, and now also as a prisoner of Christ Jesus* (verses 8-9).

How can Philemon not possibly do his duty…which he will discover shortly in the letter…when Paul is clearly doing his? Paul is not just a prisoner. He's a "prisoner of Christ Jesus." And he's an old man!

Prayer for the Day: *God of wisdom, I want to explore the difference between actions inspired by wisdom and those done for duty. Amen.*

Letter to Philemon　　　　　　　　　　　　　　　**Week 36**
　　　　　　　　　　　　　　　　　　　　　　　　　　Wednesday

Paul begins his appeal for Onesimus who is now like a son to Paul even though he is a slave owned by Philemon. Onesimus has been caring for Paul during the imprisonment. Paul mentions that Onesimus was formerly useless to Philemon. Why was he useless? That is not known.

However, Roman law allowed a slave to flee to temples of refuge or to a friend of the owner to beg for intercession and mercy. Onesimus must have been in serious trouble with his owner because he not only ran away but ran to a Roman prison. He must have indeed been desperate.

Interestingly, the name, Onesimus, means *useful* in Greek so the useless person to Philemon is now the useful person to Paul.

But now the pagan slave, Onesimus, has become a Christian convert. What is Philemon's duty? What is he to do? Take Onesimus back as a forgiven and now Christian slave? Give him to Paul as Paul's own slave?

Prayer for the Day: *Creator of all, living with you sometimes places me in a dilemma. I trust you will guide me through the process. Amen.*

Week 36
Thursday

Letter to Philemon

Paul first clarifies that he's not asking Philemon to leave Onesimus with him, enslaved or free. He writes, *I am sending him, that is, my own heart back to you. I wanted to keep him with me, so that he might be of service to me in your place...but I preferred to do nothing without your consent, in order that your good deed might be voluntary and not something forced* (verses 12-14).

Paul professes his love of Onesimus as his own heart. That's what you might say as a parent or grandparent of one of your children... of my own heart. Paul continues with something that sounds almost like: "Onesimus was here to help me. Where were you dear brother?" Paul again mentioned being in prison. And then he planted the seed for Philemon to act voluntarily rather than being forced. Paul wants Philemon to free Onesimus because of faith and not from enforced obedience to Paul.

This is unheard of. Can Philemon be expected to receive his slave without inflicting the punishment to which he is legally entitled? How could Philemon exert his legal rights if Paul considers Onesimus his son? One would certainly not beat Paul's son! But Onesimus is a slave, a Christian slave, but still a slave. No one would chastise Philemon for beating this slave. Well, maybe Jesus the Christ might have problems. After all, Jesus broke social conventions all the time. He reached out to the underdog. He refused to be limited by class distinctions, disabilities, societal rules. He died on the cross for challenging the status quo, the Roman imperial government, and the elite religious leadership.

Paul elaborates: *Perhaps this is the reason he was separated from you for a while, so that you might have him back forever, no longer as a slave but more than a slave, a beloved brother—especially to me but how much more to you, both in the flesh and in the Lord* (verses 15-16). And now Paul has upped the expectation. If Onesimus is welcomed as a brother in the Lord, then...all bets are off. One treats a brother well. One loves a brother. One embraces a brother no matter what is past. Brothers in the Lord means treating that brother as one would treat Jesus!

Now the ups and down of the letter become quite clear. Paul wants Philemon to welcome Onesimus back physically, socially, spiritually, and theologically.

Prayer for the Day: *Surprising God, you make life challenging to me when I'd rather do what is socially acceptable rather than where you will lead me. Amen.*

Letter to Philemon **Week 36 / Friday**

And just in case Philemon has not yet been convinced, Paul adds: *So if you consider me your partner, welcome him as you would welcome me. If he has wronged you in any way, or owes you anything, charge that to my account. I, Paul, am writing this with my own hand: I will repay it* (verses 17-19).

Paul sounds confident in what he thinks Philemon's response will be. He calls Philemon, brother, and uses phrases such as *I am writing to you, know you will do even more than I say* (verse 21). And Paul does throw in a little guilt just in case Philemon is not yet convinced. Paul reminds him that Philemon owes Paul. For what, who knows? His life? His relationship with Jesus Christ? Whatever it is, it reminds Philemon how deep the bond between him and Paul is. And therefore, how deep the bond between Philemon and Onesimus is called to be.

Paul is confident that Philemon will do what Paul in Christ asks and even more. He also lets Philemon knowing he's coming for a visit. Now if you were Philemon, what would you do? Try to save face with your business and social colleagues or demonstrate to Paul that you are indeed a true disciple of Jesus Christ? Will you as Paul says, "Refresh your heart in Christ?"

Gray Temple in his theological perspective in *Feasting on the Word*, Year C explains that Paul used a process of non-dominance throughout this entire letter. Jesus, too, taught a refusal to dominate other people, even when it is easy to do sometimes. This seems to be the lesson for today, God's new thing.

Non-dominance: Paul trusted Philemon to give the God-given response to the situation with Onesimus, to receive one who had been a disobedient slave as a spiritual equal, a son, a brother. Paul clearly indicated that he did not expect Philemon to resort to the cultural expectations of prestige, discrimination, and violence that the current structure allowed and even encouraged. But the decision was always Philemon's.

Prayer for the Day: *My Lord and my guide, help me release my need for dominance so I may walk your way. Amen.*

Week 36
Saturday

Letter to Philemon

Non-dominance is radical teaching. Choosing non-dominance is almost unheard of in today's world. No matter where you stand on the issue of gun laws, guns are symbols of dominance. People carry guns for a variety of reasons. But…guns get bigger and bigger, they are easier and easier to obtain, and more and more people have guns. If your gun is not as rapid fire, accurate, and long range as the other person's, then that person has dominance over you. And you see the evidence of guns being part of the national culture with murders, mass shootings, use of guns when other means might accomplish a better result, and general fearfulness in society.

Paul counsels with language such as *"no longer a slave [but] a beloved brother."* This is the language of non-dominance. Paul's willingness to reimburse Philemon indicates that the scales can be balanced. Non-dominance is a radical consideration.

Paul's trust in God is so deep that he is able to discern the love of God in every circumstance, even imprisonment. He writes almost as if he's residing in a hotel penthouse rather than a prison. He depends on the love of God that he shares with Onesimus and with Philemon to be the guiding force, not dominance.

Paul challenges Philemon to allow God to move even deeper into his life with Jesus so that he is not guided by respectability, by cultural expectations. Paul counts on Philemon to be moved by what is just and what is right.

Not participating in dominance and thwarting another person's trying to dominate you or anyone else is ultimately healing and empowering. It is choosing to say that you are a child of God, and the other person is a child of God. In God you will find ways to be brother and sister. This may be all pie in the sky. Or it may be God's deepest desire for how God's children created in God's image are to live and move and have life. God's new thing calls you to put aside your old ways of interacting with others and to explore the wonder of living in a world where you see *everyone* as your sibling.

Prayer for the Day: *God, I have a question. If I received such a letter from Paul about a challenge for my own hidden and maybe nor so hidden tendencies for dominance, how would I respond? I'll have to think about that one. Amen.*

Week 37
Ephesians 2:1-10

You were dead through the trespasses and sins 2 in which you once lived, following the course of this world, following the ruler of the power of the air, the spirit that is now at work among those who are disobedient. 3 All of us once lived among them in the passions of our flesh, following the desires of flesh and senses, and we were by nature children of wrath, like everyone else. 4 But God, who is rich in mercy, out of the great love with which he loved us 5 even when we were dead through our trespasses, made us alive together with Christ—by grace you have been saved—6 and raised us up with him and seated us with him in the heavenly places in Christ Jesus, 7 so that in the ages to come he might show the immeasurable riches of his grace in kindness towards us in Christ Jesus. 8 For by grace you have been saved through faith, and this is not your own doing; it is the gift of God—9 not the result of works, so that no one may boast. 10 For we are what he has made us, created in Christ Jesus for good works, which God prepared beforehand to be our way of life.

Week 37
Sunday

Ephesians 2:1-10

For the next few weeks, the readings will look at certain things that people of faith are encouraged to do. No one typically commits to all but each person has gifts uniquely suited to one or more of the calls of faith. You'll explore these "calls" so you can discover which one(s) speak to you. They are: proclaim the gospel, take care of God's children with nurture and fellowship, worship God, pay attention to Truth, promote social justice, and demonstrate God's kingdom to the world.

So...Proclaim the gospel.

When some people hear the word "proclamation," they picture a guy, always a guy, in funny pants and a shirt with voluminous sleeves with a feather in his cap blowing a very long trumpet with a banner hanging off it. After getting everyone's attention, then he, or someone else on the platform, shouts the proclamation...the news that something of great importance is about to happen. Maybe the king is getting married or maybe a curfew is being put into place. Proclamation is a clear declaration of something.

Proclamation also indicates that your message of great importance is not whispered or mumbled but is told with conviction and strength.

In this case, the clear something you are to proclaim is the gospel.

Prayer for the Day: *Dear God, during this time of learning more about your expectations for people of faith, guide my discernment process. Amen.*

Ephesians 2:1-10

Week 37
Monday

If someone asked you what exactly is meant by gospel, what would you say? Would you begin quoting scripture? You might use John 3:16: *For God so loved the world that he gave his only begotten Son that whosoever believed in him should not perish but have everlasting life.* Would you begin by telling stories of Jesus? You might talk about Jesus's acts of healing or feeding large crowds. You might say that Jesus died a horrible death but then was raised from the dead. Would you begin telling personal stories about how your faith, your walk with God, has affected your very being?

Christians talk about "the gospel" all the time. But what *exactly* does it mean?

Paul in his letter to the Ephesians can help your understanding. Paul begins by telling who people were before they learned about the Lord Jesus Christ. He says: *You were dead through trespasses and sins in which you once lived* (Ephesians 2:1). He spends the next verses explaining what he means by that. This is the "before" picture. He talks about the desires of flesh and senses. These are not a list of specific actions or thoughts. This is about how you live, how your life is guided, to whom you give your allegiance.

Prayer for the Day: *Loving God, help me see where my allegiance is focused on things and people and values who are not you. Amen.*

Week 37
Tuesday

Ephesians 2:1-10

When Paul talks about flesh, he refers to how you allow your world, your culture to guide you or influence you. And in reality, you are often not even aware of how you are affected by this world. For example, studies have shown that if people watch a lot of killings on television, or in movies or games, they are less likely to be affected by real life murders. They/you are guided, led by unconsidered media saturation. People are guided by love of property values and so NIMBYism (not in my backyard) will rear its nasty head.

Humans are led by various addictions: alcohol, drugs, sex, food, gaming, material goods, and any other activities or substances that people use to avoid the joys and pains of living in this world.

When you are honest with yourself, you are aware that powers other than your Lord Jesus Christ often lead you and guide you in ways that you accept and may not even be aware of. As scripture has said, *We all have sinned and fallen short of the glory of God* (Romans 3:23).

Either you or friends or family members may suffer extremely because of some of these powers that are controlling your thoughts and actions and your sense of who you are. You are unable to make good decisions. You cause harm to yourself or others. We are consumed by wrath, to use Paul's language.

Prayer for the Day: *Yikes, God, through Paul you tell it like it is. Help me to ponder these things and not simply let them slip by me. Amen.*

Ephesians 2:1-10

Week 37
Wednesday

When Jesus cast out the demons from a man, he first asked the demons what their name was. Maybe you, too, are called to name your own demons, your own ways of falling into alternative routes to make you feel good. Maybe you are to meditate on your own ways of living *following the desires of the flesh and senses* (Ephesians 2:3).

Bible commentator, Adam Eckhart, points out even the church is a fallen institution made up of fallen individuals. Together members can help each other discern the powers that control. Congregations can learn to listen to God for guidance rather than to the siren voices of effectiveness, church growth, and greater influence.

Because God has made you and all other people, according to verse 10 in the passage, then "any substance, idea, or institution that competes with God's title as source and sustainer in effect opposes God" (Adam E. Eckhart, *Feasting on the Word*, Year B, Vol. 2, p. 112)

Prayer for the Day: *God of truth, help me see ways that I follow my own desires and not yours. Amen.*

Week 37
Thursday

Ephesians 2:1-10

On your own, you cannot conquer the powers of the world, the subtle and not-so-subtle things, thoughts, and activities that pull you away from your centeredness on God. You can't. Even Jesus was victim of the powers of the world…the political world and the religious world when he was tried, tortured, and hanged on a cross where he died. But, the powers that killed Jesus did not have the last word. Jesus was raised from the dead. You cannot explain the hows of that miracle, but you can stand in awe that your God does not allow the powers of the world to have the last word.

Fortunately, the passage does not stop with the "BEFORE." Paul says, *But…but God, who is rich in mercy, out of the great love with which he loved us even when we were dead through our trespasses, made us alive together through Christ* (Ephesians 2:4).

So even though you can be a victim to following other voices, God loves you so much that God lifts you up. By grace you have been saved. This is the good news. This is the gospel you are to proclaim.

Prayer for the Day: *Jesus my savior, help me proclaim that by grace I am saved. By grace others are saved. Amen.*

Ephesians 2:1-10

**Week 37
Friday**

You cannot conquer the powers of this world. You often cannot even recognize some of the powers. You are so immersed as a society in certain ways of seeing and thinking that you are not even aware. For example, many people with light skin are just now beginning to realize how much light skin has provided them a bubble to ignore inequities, injustice, and inequalities that people of color have known all along. People are becoming awake. The opening of hearts and eyes are God's doing.

Certainly, the passage says that you yourself cannot save yourself from your blindness, your sins, your trespasses. You frequently cannot even acknowledge them, see them, or claim them. But God…but God…saves you. You can begin to put your life into God's hands. You respond to the love of God by loving God back. You trust God so much that you give your life to that love. When you follow the nudge to trust God, you discover amazing things. God loves you! God wants for you the wholeness that humanity experienced in the Garden of Eden. God wants you to live freely, not consumed by the world's messages but embraced by love that loves you just as you are…even in your waywardness. God wants you to allow the wind of the Spirit to blow you to new paths that you never even knew about, much less expected.

Prayer for the Day: *Holy Spirit, you love me!!! You love me just as I am!!! You call me to respond by loving you back. Holy smoke!!! Amen.*

Week 37
Saturday

Ephesians 2:1-10

This sense of being saved from the weights you've been carrying around is not your own doing. It is God's doing. It is not anything you can do on your own. If that were so, you would boast and boast and boast. Many people who are recovering addicts will proclaim that as often as they tried to quit the drugs, the alcohol, the other addictions, that they could not until they admitted they were powerless over the substance or actions. They turned their lives to the higher power, a power they discovered had been there all along, waiting and leading them to the new life offered through AA or other such programs. They experienced the reality that *by grace, you have been saved, and this is not your own doing* (Ephesians 2:8).

You likely have your own experiences of knowing the grace of God in totally unexpected ways. You may be able to look back at your life and realize that but for the grace of God, your path might have been very different.

The passage does not stop there, however. Yes, you live in a fallen state of not being whole and healthy and complete. Yes, you participate in systems, including the church, that can follow voices other than that of your Creator, Savior, and Comforter to guide and inspire you. Yes, God through great love, grace, and mercy holds you tight and loves you and helps release the bonds that bind you. But then what? Is all that done just to give you a better life?

No. All this happens so you can participate in God's activities in the world. You reach out. The passage says you are created as a new creature for good works. You do not sit around "being manipulated by numerous forces" (Ian S. Markham, *Feasting on the Word, II B*, p. 114). You are engaged in the life and actions of Jesus the Christ. You are a recipient of absolutely everything!!! You respond by getting involved with others, proclaiming the good news of the gospel. You shout that in Jesus Christ you are forgiven. You connect with the fallen world to help open eyes to the newness that God is providing for everyone. You challenge the systems that continue to manipulate people into giving up lives of joy and wholeness. You join with love and exuberance to share the gifts that you have been given.

You proclaim the gospel for the salvation of humankind!

Prayer for the Day: *Loving God, help me proclaim your saving love and grace wherever, whenever, and in whatever manner I can. Amen.*

Week 38
Acts 5:1-11

But a man named Ananias, with the consent of his wife Sapphira, sold a piece of property; 2 with his wife's knowledge, he kept back some of the proceeds, and brought only a part and laid it at the apostles' feet. 3 'Ananias,' Peter asked, 'why has Satan filled your heart to lie to the Holy Spirit and to keep back part of the proceeds of the land? 4 While it remained unsold, did it not remain your own? And after it was sold, were not the proceeds at your disposal? How is it that you have contrived this deed in your heart? You did not lie to us but to God!' 5 Now when Ananias heard these words, he fell down and died. And great fear seized all who heard of it. 6 The young men came and wrapped up his body, then carried him out and buried him.

7 After an interval of about three hours his wife came in, not knowing what had happened. 8 Peter said to her, 'Tell me whether you and your husband sold the land for such and such a price.' And she said, 'Yes, that was the price.' 9 Then Peter said to her, 'How is it that you have agreed together to put the Spirit of the Lord to the test? Look, the feet of those who have buried your husband are at the door, and they will carry you out.' 10 Immediately she fell down at his feet and died. When the young men came in they found her dead, so they carried her out and buried her beside her husband. 11 And great fear seized the whole church and all who heard of these things.

Week 38
Sunday

Acts 5:1–11

Note: The following story of Sapphira and Ananias originally appeared in Templeton, *More Conversations on the Porch*, 2014.

People of faith are encouraged to take care of God's children with nurture and fellowship. One couple, Sapphira and Ananias, *did not* do that. They were members of an early Christian community where everything was held in common. No one claimed private ownership (Acts 4:32). Listen to Sapphira tell their story in her own words.

"My name is Sapphira. If you know anything about me, it's probably not good. I certainly am not proud of what I did.

"My name, Sapphira, means beautiful. Many told me when I was growing up that my name was appropriate. More than once, someone said, 'What a beautiful child.' My parents beamed because they expected that I'd be able to make a very successful marriage.

"When it came time for me to wed, Ananias approached my parents. At that time, I did not know his name. I peeked at him from behind a curtain and was certain I'd never seen him before. I knew that I would have remembered him because I certainly liked what I saw. He was pleasing to the eye. The quality of his robe indicated that he was a man of means. In a moment, I wanted more than anything to be this man's wife. I knew that my beauty would be an asset to him. I also considered that he'd be able to keep me in a fine manner. He would provide lovely gifts to me that would only enhance my beauty.

"I could not hear all the conversation. I knew that my father and Ananias discussed my dowry and the marriage terms. My father related the entire conversation to me after the marriage arrangement had been finalized. He said that Ananias participated in a group that met in Jerusalem where Peter, a man known to be a disciple of Jesus, and James, the brother of Jesus, regularly taught and preached. Ananias wanted to make sure that my father did not object to his practices of faith. My father was never a very religious man. All he could see was the obvious wealth that his future son-in-law had. He said he had no objections to his daughter marrying a Jew who had joined this particular sect. After all, the name Ananias meant 'Yahweh is gracious.'"

Prayer for the Day: *Lord God almighty, the heavens declare your glory. May I always see that in all your creation. Amen.*

Acts 5:1–11   Week 38 / Monday

Sapphira continues: "The wedding celebration was wonderful. People partied long and with enthusiasm. Everyone complimented my parents on the auspicious marriage that their daughter had made. My wedding clothes were made of the finest materials available. I truly lived up to my name and made my family very proud.

"My marriage to Ananias was everything I had hoped for. He gave me beautiful things to wear and for our home. He bought property to enhance our holdings. I was very proud to be his wife. I was a little concerned about his involvement in this Jerusalem group. They were very serious about what they believed. All kinds of people began joining the meetings. I was not sure about some of the people who came, especially peasants and slaves. I was even a little suspicious of the man, Peter. I had heard that he had once been a fisherman. I could certainly believe that because of the dialect he spoke and the way he dressed. The group was very important, however, to my husband, so I went along.

"One thing I liked about this gathering was that I was able wear my beautiful clothes to be seen and admired. I tried to act humble on the outside but inside I glowed with the appreciation I thought the others felt. I believed that some of them were even jealous because their clothes were not as nice as mine."

Prayer for the Day: *Jesus, help me see where I am proud and ignorant of others. Amen.*

Week 38
Tuesday

Acts 5:1–11

"As this sect grew, it became known as a church—not a synagogue. I didn't care. Church…synagogue…it all seemed the same to me until the group made a significant change in how they took care of each other. All the believers decided that no one would claim private ownership of anything. What belonged to one belonged to everyone. They committed to providing for everyone in the church so that no one needed anything. People began selling some of their land and even their homes in order to give the proceeds to the church leaders whom they called apostles.

"Well, I thought this was going too far. I wasn't about to give up my pretty things. People admired me, I thought, and I said so to Ananias.

"He replied, 'My beautiful wife. I love you dearly. You are the rose of Sharon and a lily of the valley to me. However, I must tell you that people do not admire your beauty when you come into the gathering spot with all your finery. They see you as haughty and proud. They question if you are a true believer. Some even have suggested that you should stay home and not attend the meetings with me.'

"When Ananias said those cruel things to me, I burst into tears and ran from the room. I picked up a pottery bowl and slammed it to the floor where it broke into as many pieces as there are stars in the sky. I was hurt and angry. All my life I had lived with my beauty and the privileges it had given to me. I feared that Ananias would ask me to give up everything. I had to think what could be done about this change of circumstances."

Prayer for the Day: *God of all good gifts, are there things that I am holding onto that get in the way of my relationship with you and other people? Amen.*

Acts 5:1–11

Week 38
Wednesday

"Later when Ananias joined me on our pallet, I turned away from him and refused to talk with him. I did this for several days and nights while I thought about what I could do. Surely there had to be a middle ground, where I could keep some of my pretty things and we could also provide for believers in the congregation.

"I could tell that Ananias was torn. He wanted to spoil me, his beautiful wife, but he was also growing deeper and deeper into the message being preached by the apostles. He believed that Jesus had been raised from the dead and was the long-awaited messiah. He believed we were to obey everything that Jesus taught and that meant caring for the oppressed, the outsider, and the downtrodden.

"All my pouting and crying could not change his mind. He said his faith was too strong to ignore the teachings of the apostles. He also said, however, that he loved me with all his heart and that he wanted us to be happy like we used to be.

"I could tell that my distance was not pleasing to my husband, and I was scared. What if he decided to put me aside because I was not being the wife he wanted?"

Prayer for the Day: *Sometimes God, the battle within about what I want and think I deserve and what you want for me is very strong. Amen.*

Week 38   Acts 5:1–11
Thursday

Sapphira explains: "I decided to prepare a dinner of Ananias's favorite foods. He was suspicious because I had been unkind to him for several days. When he had completed his sumptuous meal, I said, 'My husband, I have not been a good wife. I have been thinking only of myself. I have ignored those poor believers who also are part of the Jerusalem church.'

"Ananias looked at me with curiosity and then a relieved smile. He said, 'You really mean that? If so, I've been thinking about selling that last piece of property I bought and then giving the proceeds to the church.'

"That was not exactly the way I had expected the conversation to go. I bowed my head, I think with a look of humility, and cleared the remains of the meal away. That night we once again slept as husband and wife. Well, I did not sleep. I lay awake thinking about what my next move could be.

"In the morning, I arose early. I dressed carefully, not too fancy and not too dowdy. I greeted my husband with a beautiful smile. I said, 'Dear husband, does the church require that you give everything to it? If so, what happens when we give away all your wealth? Will we become one of the families that the church has to take care of? This does not sound prudent. You owe it to the church to not become a burden on it. You want to be able to provide for the believers who need help. When you give away everything, you will no longer be able to fulfill this obligation.

"He looked at me and said, 'You are not only beautiful, but you are also very wise. I will indeed sell the land that I chose. However, so that we will not become destitute and become a burden on the church for our livelihood, I will keep a portion for us.'

"I cast my eyes down and said, 'Dear husband, what did I do to marry such a brilliant and compassionate man as you?'

"By the end of the week, Ananias had completed the transaction. He was excited to be able to provide so generously for the church with the portion of the proceeds he was planning to lay at the apostles' feet. Almost immediately, he delivered the money to the church.

Prayer for the Day: *God of truth, someone once said that rationalizations are just rational lies. Help me be truthful. Amen.*

Acts 5:1–11   **Week 38 / Friday**

"I was not there but knowing my husband as I do, I think he expected to be applauded for his magnificent gift. Ananias had not yet returned home, but I could not wait to experience what I assumed was Peter's happy reaction. I went to see the apostle and found out that Ananias had been there three hours earlier. I was confused about why he had not come back home to give me the good news himself. I decided that he must have had other business and that he planned to share Peter's joyful pleasure with me that evening.

"When I saw Peter, I was genuinely confused when he said, 'Tell me whether you and your husband sold the land for such and such a price' (Acts 5:8). I thought that Ananias had already been to the church until I heard Peter's question to me.

"I answered, 'Yes that was the price.' I glowed with pride at the amount that Ananias and I had agreed we would give to the believers.

"Then Peter said, 'How is it that you have agreed together to put the Spirit of the Lord to the test? Look, the feet of those who have buried your husband are at the door, and they will carry you out' (Acts 5:9).

"I could hardly take in the shock of my husband's death before I, too, collapsed and died."

Prayer for the Day: *Life of the world, help me be truthful with you… and myself. Amen.*

Week 38   **Acts 5:1–11**
Saturday

Sapphira continued with her story, after admitting that she had indeed died then.

"As much as I do not want to admit it, our deaths were the right thing to have happened. At first, we rationalized how we could keep some of the money. To our way of thinking, we believed we were extremely generous while making sure that we did not end up destitute. We convinced ourselves of the rightness of our decision. Have you ever done that? Convinced yourself that a bad decision was actually the correct one?

"And we lied. We lied, not just to Peter but to God. We under-declared the proceeds we got from the sale of the land. We were wrong. As believers, we were to think of others. How many times had the conversation included the teaching of Jesus to love the Lord our God with all our hearts, souls, minds, and strength, and our neighbors as ourselves? I did not love my neighbors. I only loved myself, and of course, my husband.

"Some people believe our treatment was harsh. After all this time, I do not think so. In order to preach and spread the gospel, the church truly needed the support of everyone who had resources. Our deceit hindered that work. I'm not sure that I could have ever given joyfully. I was too spoiled. But our deaths did serve as an example. People got scared. I honestly do not think we died because we did not give our all, but because we lied about it. Sure, we may have been ostracized if Ananias announced that he was not going to sell any of his property. He could have explained our decision with our rationalization that the congregation might need the sale more later on. We lied. We pretended that we'd given our all to the apostles for the preaching of the gospel, when we had not.

"When I think about how beautiful my life could have been had I been able to devote my entire being to the way of Jesus, rather than to the surface beauty that I thought was so important, I grieve all that I missed."

As you allow Sapphira's story to sink into your being, these questions may begin to lay on your heart. You may want to discuss them with your close friends, family, or your church family. Certainly bring your answers to the questions to God.

Shelter, nurture, and spiritual fellowship of the children of God. How is God nudging you?

Prayer for the Day: *Spirit, my advocate, show me where I fall short of nurturing and caring for others. Amen.*

Week 39
Isaiah 6:1-8

In the year that King Uzziah died, I saw the Lord sitting on a throne, high and lofty; and the hem of his robe filled the temple. 2 Seraphs were in attendance above him; each had six wings: with two they covered their faces, and with two they covered their feet, and with two they flew. 3 And one called to another and said:

"Holy, holy, holy is the Lord of hosts;
the whole earth is full of his glory."

4 The pivots on the thresholds shook at the voices of those who called, and the house filled with smoke. 5 And I said: "Woe is me! I am lost, for I am a man of unclean lips, and I live among a people of unclean lips; yet my eyes have seen the King, the Lord of hosts!"
6 Then one of the seraphs flew to me, holding a live coal that had been taken from the altar with a pair of tongs. 7 The seraph touched my mouth with it and said: "Now that this has touched your lips, your guilt has departed and your sin is blotted out." 8 Then I heard the voice of the Lord saying, "Whom shall I send, and who will go for us?" And I said, "Here am I; send me!"

Week 39
Sunday

Isaiah 6:1-8

It is likely that worship is one of the first things people think of when they think of church. People will often ask, "Who's the preacher there?" So even that question about the name of the minister alludes to the primary functions of many clergy: preaching and planning and leading worship.

Isaiah had an amazing worship experience one day. He was most likely of the upper class of Judah with social position. He likely was a prophet or priest associated with the Temple. One morning he arrived at the Temple. Maybe he'd had a bad night. Maybe the neighbor's dog had barked all night. Maybe his favorite robe had snagged on the branch just outside his door. Maybe he was hoping that his time at the Temple would be better than the night before.

When he entered this holy place, he was met with a scene that we would have labelled today as one with amazing technological special effects. The experience unfolds.

Prayer for the Day: *God of wonder, open my full self to the experience of worshiping you. Amen.*

Isaiah 6:1-8

Week 39
Monday

When you enter the space with Isaiah, you see a throne floating up about four feet from the ceiling. It was not there the last time you were in this space. Then you realize that the Lord God Almighty is sitting on this throne. The sight is too wondrous for you. The light is too bright, the colors too vivid, the fear too intense. You cannot look at the throne, so you look at the floor. All you can see on the floor are the ends of God's robes. Everywhere you look, you see robes. You are actually standing on them.

Then you hear a noise and look up again. But this time you see four awesome creatures attending God. You can hardly describe how they look. They seem kind of like snakes…but maybe they look more human? They each have six wings. They use one set for flying, keeping them near the ceiling and the throne. They use two wings to cover themselves since they aren't wearing any clothes. They use the third pair to cover their faces. Maybe they know that they are too scary or too glorious to be looked at.

You have come into the presence of God. In a usual Sunday morning worship service, this would be a call to worship which signifies that you have entered the sacred space for worship.

Since you are still speechless, the seraphim take over singing *Holy, holy, holy is the Lord of Hosts, the whole earth sings of God's glory* (Isaiah 6:3). The voices of the seraphim are so lusty that the walls of the space shake and then… smoke billows in…clouds and clouds of smoke. There is so much smoke that you can hardly see anything.

If you sing the opening hymn on Sunday morning, does your song of praise overwhelm you like the seraphim's singing does? All your senses may not be on alert. Isaiah may have had ears blasted with the seraphim's voices of praise. His sense of touch was alert with the feel of the robes. Smell was triggered with the smoke. Does your worship ever connect three of your senses in this powerful way? With hearing? Touch? Smell?

Prayer for the Day: *God Almighty, I confess that my worship is often lukewarm at best. Amen.*

Week 39   **Isaiah 6:1-8**
Tuesday

If God were to appear to you in the same way as God appeared to Isaiah, you likely would join with Isaiah and exclaim: *Woe is me! I am lost, for I am a person of unclean lips, and I live among a people of unclean lips; yet my eyes have seen the King, the Lord of hosts!* (Isaiah 6:5).

When one comes into the presence of God, this may be the only appropriate response. In the face of God, you realize how little and insignificant you really are. This kind of fear and this kind of pain of seeing yourself as God sees you is not pleasant by any stretch of the imagination. This kind of sincere confession, this way of seeing yourself as you really are rather than trying to convince the world who you think you are is wrenching.

In today's worship services, members may offer prayers of confession. Once you acknowledge that you are who you are and that you have not always been a prime specimen of a loving, caring, faithful person, you realize that God has other things in store for you.

Isaiah does not leave the scene. God does not stop with smells and singing seraphim. God recognizes the agony that Isaiah is in and cleanses him, forgives him. The seraphim take live coals from the altar and touch Isaiah's lips and says, *Now that this has touched your lips, your guilt has departed, and your sin is blotted out* (Isaiah 6:7).

After the Prayer of Confession in contemporary worship services, the people hear the assurance of pardon. You learn that you are *not* what you seem. In God's eyes, you are more than who you think you are. In Christ you are infused with forgiveness and made clean. Your sin is blotted out. No matter what you have done, God in Christ can make you whole. No matter that your life is not smooth and easy, you can be whole through God's healing touch. You recognize that you are forgiven only because God has deemed you special…not because of anything you have done yourself. Through confession and pardon, you are made ready for the next step in this holy drama.

Prayer for the Day: *God of forgiveness, thank you for seeing me as special no matter what. Amen.*

Isaiah 6:1-8 **Week 39 / Wednesday**

After the entrance into God's presence, the songs of praise, the confession of sin and declaration of pardon, then comes the holy challenge. *Who will go for us?* (Isaiah 6:8). You look around the room where you've witnessed God and the seraphim. There is no one else. Only you. What else can you say? *Here am I. Send me* (Isaiah 6:8). In gratitude for the actions of God, you say, almost without thinking, "Here am I, send me." In God's presence, there are no other words but "Here I am."

So, you hear God's word. In contemporary worship, there are readings of scripture and the preaching of the word. You listen to what God is saying to you today. You focus on how you glorify God today because of what you have heard. You wonder how you can become more the person God is calling you to be. You listen for what you are being called to release so you can fully experience the love, the presence, the wonder of your Creator, Redeemer, and Comforter.

In current worship services, there are a variety of ways to respond to "Here I am, send me." It may be by giving gifts of talent, time, and treasure. It may be through special commissioning of youth as they leave for mission trips. "Send me" could involve training for special tasks in the church or community or accepting leadership roles in the congregation. To the question, "Who shall I send?" people respond in various ways, "Here I am, send me." And then they and you are sent out with blessing.

When people come together, they enter the holy presence of God. There may be only two or three of you, but together you worship and experience the wonder and glory of your God. You respond in praise and thanksgiving.

Prayer for the Day: *Calling God, help me respond with an open heart with "Here I am, send me." Amen.*

Week 39   **Isaiah 6:1-8**
Thursday

Worship is about coming to God and God's coming to you. People come to worship in person or via social media. People come to see those folks they care about. Some come to be inspired by the music. Others say they come to get prepared for the week. Worshipers come to learn more from the scriptures.

You also worship because it helps you put your focus on God. During your everyday life, you may forget to talk with God. You may not find time to read your Bible or inspirational readings. You may not choose to listen to books or music that put you in touch with the Holy One. But when you come to a place of worship, you can pay attention to God…sometimes.

You worship because worship matters to God. Joshua 24:19 says that God is a jealous God when you worship anything or anyone other than God. God created you and desires that this wonderful creation pay attention to God's overwhelming love and offer it back with praise, prayer, singing, and immersion in God's word.

You worship because it helps you get out of the way. Worship changes you. You try to give up trying to *do* church and learn to *be* church. You try to see the world as God wants you to see it rather than as you are accustomed to seeing. You strive to live as a follower of Jesus the Christ, and not a follower of the principalities and powers of your world.

Prayer for the Day: *Fountain of life, I did not realize that worship is about you and not me! Help me to immerse myself into the experience of worship wherever and whenever it may be. Amen.*

Isaiah 6:1-8   **Week 39 / Friday**

You worship because it involves some personal sacrifice. Sometimes you must put aside your own feelings and try to feel as Jesus would feel. You give up some of your otherwise planned time to focus on being present to God in your worship. You acknowledge that all your time, all the days of your lives, are a gift from God. So, you focus on giving God glory and your attention rather than ruminating on how great...or awful...you are.

You worship in the face of pain and loss. Maybe you've heard people say, "If I did not have God in my life, I do not know how I could have gotten through this event in my life." In those painful times, it is when you move closer to God rather than away from God that you begin to experience some peace...often peace that passes your understanding.

You worship because you celebrate who God is and what God is doing and has done. The psalms remind of this aspect of worship. Hear these words from Psalm 100: *Make a joyful noise to the Lord, all the earth. Worship the Lord with gladness; come into his presence with singing...Enter his gates with thanksgiving, and his courts with praise. Give thanks to him, bless his name. For the Lord is good; his steadfast love endures forever, and his faithfulness to all generations* (Psalm 100:1-2, 4-5).

When you come together with others in worship, the image of God in the Temple reminds you that God is watching you. You come together not to be entertained but to show God your love, your willingness to look at yourself through God's lenses, your commitment to hearing God's word for you *this* day, and your response to what God is, and who God is in your life. When you enter the temple, you experience the awe-filled wonder of God in God's glory.

At least sometimes you do. Sometimes you just show up and experience nothing out of the ordinary. However, it may be foolhardy on your part to be nonchalant about coming to worship. If you never expect anything amazing to happen, nothing amazing may ever happen for you. But who can tell? Did Isaiah expect what he encountered?

Prayer for the Day: *Holy God, with gladness I accept the gift of this day. May I use it well. Amen.*

Week 39
Saturday

Isaiah 6:1-8

You may come to a place of worship week after week and never see a throne or seraphim. But if you come knowing that God fills the place, you may, in the secret places in your heart, step into Isaiah's shoes.

And once you, like Isaiah, are aware you are indeed in the presence of God Almighty, then what shall you do but sing praises to God, offer prayers of praise, show with your whole countenance that you are about holy business. As you join with others in song and prayer, you can listen for seraphim voices as undercurrents to human voices singing and praying. You can join joyfully in telling the mighty deeds of a loving God and a God who is present with you even now.

You can confess your sin and your failures and your shortcomings, knowing that a loving God is here waiting to get your attention with forgiveness and healing. The pain of confession and the forgiveness that is experienced after the shedding of your layers to become who you really are, can open you in worship to hear God's call upon your life.

So, when you are asked, "Whom shall I send," you can say, "Here I am; send me. Send me to whomever and wherever you want me to go." Because now you go with yourself heightened by the presence of the Lord, high and lifted up, with your praises to God, with your heart lightened from your confessions, with yourself made whole because God has made you that way, released into your full humanity, and by your wholehearted response in giving your very soul, your life, your all.

Of course, you want to participate in this. Of course, you want to invite others to join you in this amazing experience.

Prayer for the Day: *Blessed assurance, I want to join with others in the glory and challenges of worshipping you and experience the gifts you offer in that time. Amen.*

Week 40
2 Timothy 3:14-4:5

Chapter 3

14 But as for you, continue in what you have learned and firmly believed, knowing from whom you learned it, 15 and how from childhood you have known the sacred writings that are able to instruct you for salvation through faith in Christ Jesus. 16 All scripture is inspired by God and is useful for teaching, for reproof, for correction, and for training in righteousness, 17 so that everyone who belongs to God may be proficient, equipped for every good work.

Chapter 4

In the presence of God and of Christ Jesus, who is to judge the living and the dead, and in view of his appearing and his kingdom, I solemnly urge you: 2 proclaim the message; be persistent whether the time is favourable or unfavourable; convince, rebuke, and encourage, with the utmost patience in teaching. 3 For the time is coming when people will not put up with sound doctrine, but having itching ears, they will accumulate for themselves teachers to suit their own desires, 4 and will turn away from listening to the truth and wander away to myths. 5 As for you, always be sober, endure suffering, do the work of an evangelist, carry out your ministry fully.

Week 40   **2 Timothy 3:14-4:5**
Sunday

Followers of Christ are admonished to preserve the truth. As soon as you read the word "truth," you may hear Pilate asking Jesus at his trial, "What is truth?" This passage in the book of 2nd Timothy will help with that.

The setting is a letter from Timothy's mentor in ministry. Historically, this mentor is claimed to be Paul, but the best scholarship declares that this was not written by Paul but by someone writing much later. So, you can name the writer, The Mentor. This letter to Timothy carried instructions for him to *do your best to present yourself to God as one approved by him, a worker who has no need to be ashamed, rightly explaining the word of truth* (2 Timothy 2:15).

So how does this happen?

The first thing Timothy is reminded of is the importance of *relationship*. The Mentor says, *Continue in what you have learned and firmly believed, knowing from whom you learned it* (2 Timothy 3:14). Timothy knew his teachers. The "whom" in Greek is plural, letting you know that Timothy had several teachers. His learning did not happen in a vacuum. It occurred among various people.

Prayer for the Day: *In the beginning was the Word and the Word was with God and the Word was God (John 1:1). Help me hear your Word to me in all its forms. Amen.*

2 Timothy 3:14-4:5 **Week 40 / Monday**

Do you remember some of the important lessons in your life, whether they happened in a classroom, in a church, in your family, or in casual situations? Did the lessons that stuck involve just head learning or also heart learning? Most likely when you need to receive some correction, you are much more likely to accept it when you trust the person who is trying to help you grow. Could you hear a lesson better because of the person the teacher was? Sometimes you learn from someone who does not even know he or she was teaching you in the moment.

A minister told the story about being taught by a cashier who was checking her out at a K-Mart. The pastor did not know the two already had a relationship. The checkout line was long. The minister was getting very aggravated. She really wanted to say something to the people in line ahead of her who were taking so long in their transactions. Even though she never said anything, looking back she was sure her body language spoke volumes. When she finally reached the register to check out, the clerk said, "I really appreciated the sermon you preached at my church on Sunday." The pastor sheepishly said, "Thank you" and once her transaction was completed, she hightailed it out of the store. What a lesson for her to realize that one never knows when a careless action may be a terrible witness of one's faith in God to someone else!

Sometimes the lessons come from someone because you realize you want to do just the opposite. For example, a young father once said that when he's unsure what to do in a given situation, he thinks what *his* father would do and then he does the opposite. This father-son relationship was obviously one that taught...and probably in ways that no one would hope for in their own relationships.

Prayer for the Day: *Rabbi Jesus, help me know that I teach others even when I'm unaware. May I always be a good teacher. Amen.*

Week 40 **2 Timothy 3:14-4:5**
Tuesday

The Mentor reminds Timothy of the importance of the sacred writings that he has studied since his childhood. These writings for Timothy would have been what Christians call the Old Testament. The New Testament did not exist as you know it until centuries later. But these sacred writings were God-breathed.

When the lessons you teach your children, youth, and adults are God-breathed, then you are even more powerfully in a relationship...a relationship with your holy God as well as the people you are teaching or who are teaching you.

O. Hallesby in his book *Prayer* helps us grasp the reality of God-breath. He writes: "The air which our body requires envelopes us on every hand. The air of itself seeks to enter our bodies and, for this reason, exerts pressure on us. It is well known that it is more difficult to hold one's breath than it is to breathe. We exercise our organs of respiration, and air will enter forthwith into our lungs and perform its life-giving function to the entire body. The air which our souls need also envelopes all of us at all times and on all sides. God is round about us in Christ on every hand...All we need to do is open our hearts" (Quoted in Rueben P. Job and Norman Shawchuck, *A Guide to Prayer for Ministers and Other Servants*, Upper Room: Nashville, 1983, p. 17)

So God-breathed holy writings can fill you, can inspire you, can lead you to do a thorough job as God's servant.

Prayer for the Day: *Holy Spirit, fill me. Amen.*

2 Timothy 3:14-4:5 **Week 40 / Wednesday**

People approach the same scriptures and come out with vastly different interpretations. Who is listening to the God-breathed words and who is listening to human breathed words?

The Mentor moves from the importance of relationships and God-breathed sacred writings to relying on sound principles.

There are some principles for Biblical interpretation that can help you deal with problems when you're talking with others about controversial issues. These principles help you converse, not determine who is going to win.

The first one: **Scripture interprets scripture**. If you believe a passage is saying to stone a sinner, what might scripture say about such a situation in another place? Might forgiveness be a more fully Biblical interpretation? A corollary to this is to be in conversation with people who are different from you…people who may see scripture in a different way, whose context for God-breathed holy writings may be different.

The next interpretation principle is **the Christ principle**. "This Christological principle has been especially helpful [when] the church has struggled with contemporary issues such as women's place in the church and society, [the ordination of people who are gay], justice for the poor and oppressed, and treatment of others who have been forgotten or oppressed" (Shirley Guthrie, *Always Being Reformed*, p. 27). In today's language, this is WWJD, What would Jesus do?

The third interpretation principle is **the Law of Love**. "It is not possible to love people who are different from us without getting to know them, listening to and learning from them, and willing only their good whether or not we agree with what they believe, say, and do" (Guthrie, p. 28)

The fourth interpretation principle is the **rule of faith**. The Spirit is for everyone, not just for one or a few. When you "listen carefully and respectfully to the consensus of the church concerning what scripture requires us to believe and do…[you] are more likely to avoid confusing the guidance of the Spirit with [your] own personal and social biases" (Guthrie, p. 28).

The last principle is **respect for literary and historical context**. What was going on in the land and culture when this passage was originally written? How would the original audience have heard this?

As you rely on sound principles, you are more likely to encounter the truth in the God-breathed writings you encounter. Some of those writings may come from secular sources. You can determine if they are indeed God-breathed for you at that particular time by thinking about the law of love, the Christological principle, etc.

Prayer for the Day: *God of the holy scriptures, thank you for these guides to interpretation. May I use them well. Amen.*

Week 40
Thursday

2 Timothy 3:14-4:5

The Mentor exhorted Timothy in one last teaching: To remain steadfast. Hear again the Mentor's words, this time from the Contemporary English Version, *So with God and Christ as witnesses, I command you to preach God's message. Do it willingly…point out their sins. But also cheer them up, and when you instruct them, always be patient* (2 Timothy 4:1-2).

These words are for all disciples. You are to share willingly God's message in ways that are right for you and for the person with whom you are sharing. *Sometimes* you might even choose to use words. Pointing out sins might be a bit tricky. One nonprofit that works with people who are unhoused and/or with low resources might ask a program participant who was making bad choices, "And how's that working out for you?" This method allows the person to assess the outcomes of actions without someone pointing them out.

Prayer for the Day: *Holy counselor, when I feel I must point out something to someone as they journey the road of faith, help me be gracious and kind…and always listen. Amen.*

2 Timothy 3:14-4:5 **Week 40 / Friday**

You are to cheer people up…not with platitudes but with love and presence and gentleness and even sometimes…silence. And you wrap all this up with patience…as you share God's actions in your life, as you help others to acknowledge their own sins, and as you cheer them up.

The Mentor continues: *The time is coming when people won't listen to good teaching. Instead, they will look for teachers who will please them by telling them only what they are itching to hear. They will turn from the truth and eagerly listen to senseless stories* (2 Timothy 4:3). Has the Mentor been watching television and reading social media posts? This part of the Mentor's teaching is certainly contemporary! There is hardly any issue that does not have adamant people on both sides who believe they are right.

But the Mentor goes on to say, *You must stay calm and be willing to suffer. You must work hard to tell the good news and to do your job well* (2 Timothy 4:5 CEV).

Stay calm.
Be willing to suffer.
Tell the good news.
Do the job well.

The God who breathes into the written word is the only one who can enable you to teach, reprove, correct, and train for righteousness with yourself and others. Only until God breathes into words, can anyone use the words to find life. Without God's breath, the words often read as "do's," "don'ts," mere history, or lyrical language. They offer no hope for life.

Prayer for the Day: *God of guidance, help me work hard to tell the good news and to do my job well. Amen.*

Week 40 **2 Timothy 3:14-4:5**
Saturday

This God is a living God who is calling you to be God's new creation. God's word, the Scriptures, is your rule, your truth, your description of how life in God's kingdom is and will be. You can use Scripture to discover who God is and what it means to relate to this living God. Your focus remains on the life-breathing God…your Truth with a capital T.

If someone were to ask you, "Do you believe in the Bible?" theoretically you could answer "No." Your faith is in Jesus the Christ, in our triune God, not in a book. Shirley Guthrie, theologian and seminary professor reminds: "God…*not* the Bible, rules and judges and helps, and saves us…We believe the Bible just when we do not believe IN the Bible but in the living, acting, speaking God to whom the biblical writers introduce us" (Guthrie, *Christian Doctrine*, p. 82). God—creator, redeemer, comforter, Father, Son, and Holy Ghost—is your truth, your life, your faith.

Truth is when you study the scriptures and thoroughly know them. Truth is knowing your teachers with whom you form God-breathed relationships. Truth is using principles for interpreting these God-breathed words because people do not always agree on the answer to Pilate's question, "What is truth?" And truth is remaining steadfast as these words are breathed into you so you can carry out your individual ministries fully. Preservation of the Truth. May it be so.

Prayer for the Day: *Living God, help me seek your truth always and share it whenever the opportunity arises. Amen.*

Week 41
Luke 4:16-30

16 When he came to Nazareth, where he had been brought up, he went to the synagogue on the sabbath day, as was his custom. He stood up to read, 17 and the scroll of the prophet Isaiah was given to him. He unrolled the scroll and found the place where it was written:

18 'The Spirit of the Lord is upon me,
   because he has anointed me
      to bring good news to the poor.
He has sent me to proclaim release to the captives
   and recovery of sight to the blind,
      to let the oppressed go free,
19 to proclaim the year of the Lord's favour.'

20 And he rolled up the scroll, gave it back to the attendant, and sat down. The eyes of all in the synagogue were fixed on him. 21 Then he began to say to them, 'Today this scripture has been fulfilled in your hearing.' 22 All spoke well of him and were amazed at the gracious words that came from his mouth. They said, 'Is not this Joseph's son?' 23 He said to them, 'Doubtless you will quote to me this proverb, "Doctor, cure yourself!" And you will say, "Do here also in your home town the things that we have heard you did at Capernaum."' 24 And he said, 'Truly I tell you, no prophet is accepted in the prophet's home town. 25 But the truth is, there were many widows in Israel in the time of Elijah, when the heaven was shut up for three years and six months, and there was a severe famine over all the land; 26 yet Elijah was sent to none of them except to a widow at Zarephath in Sidon. 27 There were also many lepers in Israel in the time of the prophet Elisha, and none of them was cleansed except Naaman the Syrian.' 28 When they heard this, all in the synagogue were filled with rage. 29 They got up, drove him out of the town, and led him to the brow of the hill on which their town was built, so that they might hurl him off the cliff. 30 But he passed through the midst of them and went on his way.

Week 41
Sunday

Luke 4:16-30

Another thing that people of faith are encouraged to do is promote social righteousness.

The passage can be rather intimidating. Jesus talks about working with people who are poor. Then he reminds people that Elijah and Elisha worked with folks who were not the right people. And with that, his friends and neighbors want to throw him over a cliff!

What in the world made the people react that way?

Luke 4:16-30 says that Jesus, filled with the Spirit, returned to Galilee. Marcus Borg talks about Jesus being a *spirit person*. By this he means that "at the center of Jesus's life was a profound and continuous relationship to the Spirit of God" (*Meeting Jesus Again for the First Time*, Harper-San Francisco, 1995, p. 36).

So out of this relationship with God, this spirit-filled Jesus confronted the very basis of Judaism as it was being practiced in his day.

Prayer for the Day: *Strong God of grace, I yearn for a continuous relationship with you...sometimes. Amen.*

Luke 4:16-30

**Week 41
Monday**

The primary focus shaping the Jewish social world at that time was *Be holy as God is holy* (Leviticus 19:2). This understanding led to a purity system which, according to Marcus Borg, "established a [continuum]... of people ranging from the pure through varying degrees of purity to people on the margin, to the radically impure. One's purity status depended to some extent on birth...But [the]... degree of purity or impurity also depended on [a person's] behavior. Those who were carefully observant of the purity codes, [those who kept all the do's and don'ts], were the 'pure,' of course. The worst of the non-observants were 'outcasts.'... The effect of the purity system was to create a world with sharp social boundaries: between pure and impure, righteous and sinner, whole and not whole, male and female, rich and poor, Jew and Gentile...At the center of the purity system were the temple and the priesthood. Moreover, the income of both temple and priests (and Levites) depended upon the observance of purity laws by others.... So temple and priesthood had economic as well as religious interests in the purity system" (Marcus Borg, *Meeting Jesus Again for the First Time*, pp. 50-52).

If you want to understand the purity code with its many do's and don'ts, read the book of Leviticus. Certainly, parts of it are still used to tell people how and how not to live and act.

Into this system Jesus modeled another focus: *Be compassionate as God is compassionate* (Luke 6:36). In both Hebrew and Aramaic, the word for "compassion" is connected with the word "womb." When people share the same womb, there is compassion. There is love because the people are related. They are and have been connected personally.

Often the Hebrew words for *compassion* and *compassionate* are translated into English as *mercy* and *merciful*. In English *mercy* and *merciful* often suggests an over-under relationship. One is merciful to someone who really deserves punishment. Compassion suggests something else. To paraphrase William Blake, mercy wears a human face, and compassion a human heart.

With Jesus's message and activity of "*Be compassionate as God is compassionate*," he shattered boundaries. "Whereas purity divides and excludes, compassion unites and includes. For Jesus, compassion had a radical sociopolitical meaning" (Borg, *Meeting Jesus Again for the First Time*, p. 58).

Prayer for the Day: *Compassionate God, help me love others as if we shared the same mom and grew up together. Amen.*

Week 41
Tuesday

Luke 4:16-30

In the Luke passage, Jesus says he is anointed in the Spirit to bring good news to the poor, to proclaim release to the captives and recovery of sight to the blind and to let the oppressed go free. Jesus's listeners were proud of his speaking this way. *Is this not Joseph's son?* (Luke 4:22).

So far, no problem. Being someone with a message about good news to the poor and giving sight to the blind and releasing captives and oppressed people is noteworthy. Others are glad there are people like that around. They do good work. People even give them plaques for their walls, commending them on their service.

But then Jesus said something that really angered the people of his day and is extremely uncomfortable in our day. He told about Elijah and Elisha. Briefly Elijah went to live with a widow who was not one of his people because she lived in Zarephath, outside of Israel. She was totally unclean in any way one could imagine. Elijah revived her son from death, and even though there was a general famine, the *foreign, impure* family that Elijah lived with had an adequate supply of food (I Kings 17:8-24).

For his part, Elisha healed Namaan, a foreigner, of leprosy. Even after Namaan was healed of leprosy he explained to Elisha that he would have to kneel down in the Temple of Rimmon when his boss worshiped there and Elisha said, "Okay" (II Kings 5:1-14).

Jesus went on to say that even though there were many widows in Israel in the time of Elijah, he was sent to the widow in Zarephath. And there were many lepers in Israel, but Elisha cleansed only Naaman, the Syrian.

Both Elijah and Elisha worked with "those people" and God blessed that work!

Prayer for the Day: *God of surprises, help me embrace the idea that you love even those people I do not, those I intensely dislike. Amen.*

Luke 4:16-30

Week 41
Wednesday

The people got angry. They who kept the prevailing religious customs of the land, those who *deserved* to be chosen, those who were good and pure and holy, those who lived by shoulds and oughts, do's and don'ts, were not the people whom Jesus identified as tied to God.

Jesus said Spirit people were those people who were intimately involved with God's compassionate love and who were servants of others. Jesus's call was a call to compassion, a call to servanthood. Servanthood comes through a relationship of equals and is filled with gratitude. Servanthood is not "fixing" the other person who is perceived as broken or who is seen through eyes of judgment. It is not based on inequality or inequity. Servanthood with compassion says that we each came from the same loving womb, and we love and care passionately for our community family.

Prayer for the Day: *Jesus, my savior, help me grasp that in your eyes I am no better than anyone else and no else is better than me. Amen.*

Week 41   **Luke 4:16-30**
Thursday

Servanthood is not the same thing as outreach. Outreach can be described as reaching out to others from where you stand. Servanthood is changing where you stand. The two concepts can appear to be the same because they are often organized in the same manner. At times, if you don't know what you are looking for, outreach and servanthood may even appear to be mirror images of each other.

There is nothing wrong with outreach…sending a check, bringing clothes to the clothing drive, serving soup. A lot of people benefit from outreach. However, in many ways the person giving the outreach benefits more than the person receiving the outreach. And this is because outreach is always connected to charity. Charity is a provision that is given to help the needy. The problem with charity is this: If you are involved in the giving of charity, you get to decide when enough is enough. You get to say, "That's all I am going to give," whether the problem is solved or not. You get to quit. That's outreach. And it's not a bad way of doing things. It's just that the level of outreach is determined by the people who would do the healing. This is almost always determined by a budget, by a particular number of people, and by those people's perception of what has to be done.

If on the other hand, you are the person receiving the charity, you may or may not actually get help that can allow you to emerge from your hurting situation. You may simply end up sleeping under a bridge in a brand new, used-to-belong-to-someone-else coat. Or you may get referred to the new soup kitchen in town when what you really need and want is education or a job so you don't need a soup kitchen.

Outreach is a good thing. It really is. It helps people. It gives a reason, other than worship, to go to church. It brings people together for a cause. It allows people to participate in a ministry that they may otherwise miss. Outreach is a good way for raising money to send a check to an agency that really needs help.

Outreach becomes servanthood when a relationship is established. Servanthood demands that you want for the children of people who are living in poverty exactly what you want for your children. If you want decent education for your children, then you want decent education for children who are poor. If you do not want your children to go without medical care, then you do not want anyone's children to go without medical care.

Prayer for the Day: *Strength of my life, open opportunities for me to build relationships with other people and not just give them things. Amen.*

Luke 4:16-30   **Week 41 / Friday**

Jesus said that God was yearning for love from you like a good mother has for her own child. Jesus who lived in the Spirit demonstrated that you are to mirror that kind of love, that kind of righteousness. That mirroring of God's love, God's compassion, is how you align your heart with the Spirit. The shoulds and oughts, do's and don'ts that you put on yourself and even more important that you put on other people is not living in the image of God's compassion.

A woman during the early years of the AIDS crisis volunteered at a homeless shelter. She was there because she believed that as a Christian, she had a duty to minister to those "unfortunate souls." Hers was a ministry of outreach. One day she was talking with a young man who had full blown AIDS. As she was talking to this man, he started crying as he told her that it had been four years since another person had touched him. Everyone was afraid of him. His tears were tears of death, loneliness, and abandonment. This woman changed during that conversation as she reached up and pulled that young man down in to her lap. She placed his head on her shoulder and rocked him while he cried. She loved him like she would love her own child. She dried his tears and told him that she would be there every Thursday. That's servanthood. Yes, she got him to take a shower, she got him clothing, and she told him where the soup kitchen was. She did all that stuff. But what's important is what she became. She became his friend. She became his family.

Her actions would have flunked her in the purity code test but passed her with flying colors in the compassion test.

Prayer for the Day: *Loving God, thank you for people who show the rest of us how to be truly compassionate and share your love. Amen.*

Week 41
Saturday

Luke 4:16-30

Faith, hope, charity, prayer, love. Where is the challenge if you share these with only those people who look, act, live, and breathe just like you? Making the decision for servanthood is not easy. That's why more people don't do it. That may be why the people wanted to throw Jesus over the cliff. You have to go to places you may not normally go. You have to associate with people you would not normally meet. Sometimes you have to decide if your efforts will help someone move beyond their pain or simply endure it.

No wonder the people wanted to throw Jesus over the cliff. He challenged them to action…even uncomfortable, unpopular, and unexpected action. He dismissed their world view. He called them/you to love. It's so easy to get angry and tell Jesus that he is asking the impossible, that he just doesn't understand. Jesus is calling you to love with every fiber of your being. Jesus is calling you to acknowledge when you say, "Somebody ought to do something," that you are Somebody. Jesus is calling you to be compassionate, to love with God's love. Jesus is asking you to move beyond your own arena and to hurt and laugh and cry and rejoice with people with whom you have no natural ties. And with God's help you can!

Promote social righteousness. Be a spirit-filled person who is compassionate. Let these God words from an unknown writer soak into your spirit: "I love you. I want joy for you. I want you to enjoy life. All I ask of you is that you hold your hands open so that the love I give to you can flow through to others. Love as I love. Be compassionate as I am compassionate. Open your heart so you can relate to everyone with whom you come in contact so that you can feel their heart and their joy, their hopes and their pain. Ask for my Spirit to pray in place of you since you often do not know who or what needs special care. I love you. All I ask is that you love as I love" (author unknown).

Prayer for the Day: *Compassionate God, let me promote social righteousness even when I am threatened with a cliff. Amen.*

Week 42
Matthew 20:1-16

'For the kingdom of heaven is like a landowner who went out early in the morning to hire labourers for his vineyard. 2 After agreeing with the labourers for the usual daily wage, he sent them into his vineyard. 3 When he went out about nine o'clock, he saw others standing idle in the market-place; 4 and he said to them, "You also go into the vineyard, and I will pay you whatever is right." So they went. 5 When he went out again about noon and about three o'clock, he did the same.

6 And about five o'clock he went out and found others standing around; and he said to them, "Why are you standing here idle all day?" 7 They said to him, "Because no one has hired us." He said to them, "You also go into the vineyard." 8 When evening came, the owner of the vineyard said to his manager, "Call the labourers and give them their pay, beginning with the last and then going to the first."

9 When those hired about five o'clock came, each of them received the usual daily wage. 10 Now when the first came, they thought they would receive more; but each of them also received the usual daily wage. 11 And when they received it, they grumbled against the landowner, 12 saying, "These last worked only one hour, and you have made them equal to us who have borne the burden of the day and the scorching heat."

13 But he replied to one of them, "Friend, I am doing you no wrong; did you not agree with me for the usual daily wage? 14 Take what belongs to you and go; I choose to give to this last the same as I give to you. 15 Am I not allowed to do what I choose with what belongs to me? Or are you envious because I am generous?" 16 So the last will be first, and the first will be last.'

Week 42 **Matthew 20:1-16**
Sunday

People of faith are called to exhibit the kingdom of heaven to the world. Jesus uses in his teaching a lot of images about the kingdom of heaven or as some gospel writers say, the kingdom of God. In chapter 13, Matthew uses a string of parables that begin with "The kingdom of heaven is like…" The kingdom of heaven is like someone whose wheat field was contaminated with deliberately sown weeds; the kingdom of heaven is like a mustard seed; like yeast; like a treasure hidden in a field; like a merchant in search of fine pearls; like a fishing net that catches every kind of fish; and on and on.

This parable begins with: *For the kingdom of heaven is like a landowner* (Matthew 20:1). This immediately lets you know that the central character of this story is God, here depicted as a landowner.

But another interesting aspect of Matthew's use of this parable is its placement in his gospel. In chapter 19 just before this parable in chapter 20 is the story of the rich young ruler who was a rule keeper and left in grief when Jesus told him to give his money to the poor.

After that episode, the disciples wondered aloud, "Then who *can* be saved?" And Peter, good old Peter, said, "Look, we have left everything and followed you. What then will we have?" Peter implies that because of the disciples' longevity with the master, they expected a decent reward. Chapter 19 closes with these words. *But many who are first will be last, and the last will be first* (Matthew 19:30). Those similar words end our parable in Matthew 20:16: *So the last will be first, and the first will be last.* And then again in chapter 21, the same thought appears after the mother of James and John asks Jesus to put her sons on his left and right when Jesus comes into his kingdom. Jesus says, *Whoever wishes to be great among you must be your servant and whoever wishes to be first among you must be your slave* (Matthew 21:26-27). In all three of these instances, Jesus turns the expected order of things upside down.

Prayer for the Day: *Holy God, you continue to turn what's assumed upside down. Help me sort through this. Amen.*

Matthew 20:1-16

Week 42
Monday

With this background, now look more closely at this parable of the workers in the vineyard. When you listened to it, was your immediate first reaction, "That's not fair. The people who worked the longest should have been paid more or those who worked less should have been paid less." In our world with our individual sense of justice, this parable is an affront. Those who put in the most work should get the most glory. Some congregations play this out when the long-time members and the newcomers in the church disagree on what should happen within God's house of worship. Churches may shrivel and die because members cannot figure out how to honor the past while adopting new ideas or ways of thinking and doing things. It's just not fair.

Advocating for fairness is admirable. It is not fair for people who have rented their home for 30 years or more to be given 45 days to move because a developer has purchased their house from the landlord. It is not fair that people work long hours and do not earn enough to take care of their families. It's not fair that people come out of prison having paid the price for their crime and no landlord will rent to them and no employer will hire them.

For people who value fair, this is a Jesus story that makes them squirm. Can you just throw it out, ignore it, even though it teaches you about the kingdom of heaven which you are told to exhibit? Well, you could. But then are you truly striving to be a disciple of Jesus and to learn what he is trying to teach you?

Prayer for the Day: *Beloved, help me grasp that "fair" is not always your way. Amen.*

Week 42
Tuesday

Matthew 20:1-16

Looking more closely: When the vineyard owner went out at 6 a.m., he hired workers who were standing in the marketplace. These were guys who had no regular employer. They came to the market with their tools and waited and hoped that someone would hire them. If not, their family might not eat. Maybe they are like contemporary day laborers who gather hoping that someone will come by to hire them for the day.

The owner and the laborers agreed on the usual daily wage. Some translations say a drachma. The pay was perfectly normal. It was a wage that was not too little and certainly not too much. A drachma provided for just one day, just getting by. The workers likely were pleased that they had been chosen while others continued to stand in the marketplace and hope.

About nine o'clock, the owner was back at the marketplace. He saw others standing "idle" as the passage says. They were idle? Why? Was it their fault? Were they not there for the 6 am pick up? Were they there and no one chose them? For whatever reason, they were still there, standing, hoping someone would want them to work that day so they and their family could eat. The owner said, *I will pay you whatever is right* (Matthew 20:4).

Uh-oh. There are assumptions going on here. How do you define "whatever is right"? Is it a full day's wage? Is it adjusted for the lost three hours? Is the landowner honest? Will he think that what is right is piddling or even nothing at all? At this point, nobody but the landowner knows what will happen.

The same scene happens again at noon and at 3:00. *Why are you standing here idle all day?* (Matthew 20:6).

Because no one has hired us (Matthew 20:7).

Go into the vineyard and I will pay whatever is right (Matthew 20:4).

At 5:00, once again the landowner came to the marketplace and asked the people who were standing there, *Why are you standing here idle all day?*

It is amazing that the day laborers were still there and still standing under a blazing sun. By 5:00, you may have given up hope and gone back home. You would be dreading having to tell your family that you had not been able to work that day and so had no money for supper. But no, the workers in Jesus's story were still there. And here comes this landowner willing to give at least an hour's worth of work. That was certainly better than nothing at all.

Prayer for the Day: *Kingdom God, your ways are not my ways. I want to believe that is good but sometimes…well you, know, God. Amen.*

Matthew 20:1-16

Week 42
Wednesday

By the end of the day the vineyard was full of workers. Maybe the harvest was plentiful and the landowner needed all those workers. Did he not hire enough at 6 a.m.? If so, why not? Did he realize there were people who still wanted to work and so he gave them work, even when he didn't really need them? For whatever reasons known only to the landowner, he kept bringing more and more workers to the vineyard.

And then when it came time to pay the workers, the prudent thing would have been to pay the first hired first. They had agreed on a day's wage, a drachma. Those hired at 9:00 would be paid a bit less since they worked a bit less. Wages would be paid in that diminishing manner. Or if the intention was to pay everyone the same, then begin with the first hired, pay them their drachma, send them on their way, and then continue. That way those paid first would not know that those paid last got a drachma, too.

But Jesus does not tell the story that way. The owner instructed the pay master to pay the usual daily wage, a drachma, to those hired last. That way those hired first knew, *knew* that they had worked harder and received the same amount as those who worked for an hour, when the sun was no longer blazing.

They grumbled. Is that a nice, Biblical way of saying they got really mad and cussed?

Prayer for the Day: *Dearest Lord Jesus, I just don't understand. Amen.*

Week 42
Thursday

Matthew 20:1-16

The first hired workers compared themselves to the last hired. The act of comparison to another is always dangerous for those who struggle to be followers of Jesus. If you compare yourself to *that* person over there, you will decide that he's better, smarter, better looking, or more Christian than you are. OR you will think you are better, smarter, better looking, or more Christian than he is. When you compare yourself to another you may decide that God loves you better or, heaven forbid, God loves the other person better than you. Or what if you compare yourself to your spouse, a teacher, a grandparent and decide that your children must love that parent, teacher, grandparent better than you? Does that affect how you love your child? Does that move you to do things that are not true to who you are just so you'll "win"? Does comparing yourself to someone else affect how you see yourself? Do you see who you truly are, or do you see yourself through *your* definition of another person? Do you see yourself as God sees you or do you see yourself by some external measuring process?

The games of win-lose that people play a lot, maybe even daily, are not healthy for human beings and children of God. They are not how the kingdom of heaven works. Comparing yourself to someone else just to make you feel better about yourself is not true. Your sense of strength, gentleness, and tranquility comes from your relationship with the holy God and the person that God's spirit leads you to discover within. You do not learn about yourself by deciding that you are better than someone else. Nor do you learn who you are by deciding you are worse than someone else.

Prayer for the Day: *Dear God, help me know who I am without needing to compare myself to anyone else. Amen.*

Matthew 20:1-16

Week 42
Friday

Those first hired may remind you a bit of the older son in the parable of the Prodigal Son where the son who stayed home and worked renounced the father and the father's joy upon the wayward son's return. Comparing the father's reaction between his sons was certainly not healthy for the elder brother.

Then Jesus gives the words of the landowner who depicts God. The landowner says, *Friend, I am doing you no wrong; did not you agree with me for the usual wage?* (Matthew 20:13). Maybe the worker hangs his head so he would not have to look at the landowner. He *would* have to agree with the rationality of the comment, but in his mind he's likely saying, "Yes, but…" The landowner continues, *Take what belongs to you and go; I choose to give to this last the same as I give to you* (Matthew 20:14).

This is God's way, not your way. How you are rewarded is decided by God and not by what *you* think *you* earned. When you allow that concept to soak in, are you relieved? You do not have to earn or fret about receiving God's favor. This is a wonderful message you can exhibit to the world.

Prayer for the Day: *God of good gifts, help me accept your way, not mine. I do not have to fret about earning your favor. Amen.*

Week 42   Matthew 20:1-16
Saturday

The landowner continues: *Am I not allowed to choose to do what I choose with what belongs to me? Or are you envious because I am generous?* (Matthew 20:15).

This part can be hard when you realize that God loves people you find unlovable or when a person does not follow God as you believe that person should.

Upon hearing this parable, a woman related this story. She said, "There was a person I was very concerned about. I'll call her Janet. I wanted Janet to experience the kind of relationship I had with God. I thought if she could just connect with God in the way I understood connection, she would feel more satisfied about her life, would find an inner strength to hold onto, and could live with hope in the midst of the unhappy issues that came her way. I prayed and prayed to God to bring Janet into a nurturing relationship where she knew and depended on the steadfast grace and love of our Lord.

"One day an insight, a truth, holy words came into my mind. What I heard was, 'I love Janet as much as I love you. How I love her may be different from how my relationship is with you, but I am in her life, and I love her as I love you.'"

From your point of view, the first shall be first and the last, last. But that's not God's way. In God's, there may be no first and last. There's just everybody, surrounded by a God who loves you, no matter what, and cares for you, no matter what. That's a huge truth to wrap your mind around. You want to know, like Peter, James, and John, if you have earned your place. You learn that the answer to that is No, you can never earn God's steadfast love. It is pure gift even when you show up at the last hour! And what an amazing truth to share with the entire world in every way you can!!! And when you do that, you exhibit the kingdom of heaven to the world.

Prayer for the Day: *God of steadfast love, I can never earn your love and you love me steadfastly. Thank you. Amen.*

Week 43
Genesis 12:1-9

Now the Lord said to Abram, 'Go from your country and your kindred and your father's house to the land that I will show you. 2 I will make of you a great nation, and I will bless you, and make your name great, so that you will be a blessing. 3 I will bless those who bless you, and the one who curses you I will curse; and in you all the families of the earth shall be blessed.'

4 So Abram went, as the Lord had told him; and Lot went with him. Abram was seventy-five years old when he departed from Haran. 5 Abram took his wife Sarai and his brother's son Lot, and all the possessions that they had gathered, and the persons whom they had acquired in Haran; and they set forth to go to the land of Canaan. When they had come to the land of Canaan, 6 Abram passed through the land to the place at Shechem, to the oak of Moreh. At that time the Canaanites were in the land. 7 Then the Lord appeared to Abram, and said, 'To your offspring I will give this land.' So he built there an altar to the Lord, who had appeared to him. 8 From there he moved on to the hill country on the east of Bethel, and pitched his tent, with Bethel on the west and Ai on the east; and there he built an altar to the Lord and invoked the name of the Lord. 9 And Abram journeyed on by stages towards the Negeb.

Week 43
Sunday

Genesis 12:1-9

A long time ago in a faraway place lived a man and his wife. The man's name was Abram. He lived a good life. He was the eldest son of his father, Terah (The family had some repute because they could trace their ancestry back to Shem, second son of Noah who built the ark per instructions from God.) As the eldest son, Abram inherited his father's lands, herds, and servants. As eldest son, he was also responsible for other members of his family.

Abram's wife's name was Sarai. She was a good companion, a beautiful woman with a sense of humor, a wife totally devoted to her husband. Abram was extremely pleased with his wife in all respects except one: she could give him no children. And so, in some ways Abram looked on the son of his brother as his son. His nephew's name was Lot.

In all respects Sarai and Abram were a great couple. They had everything going for them. Their friends and neighbors held them in awe, even though they were childless.

But then something changed. No one who knew Abram could figure out what happened. Abram began to talk about leaving. Everyone was aghast, especially Sarai. She could not believe what he was saying. He was abandoning his responsibilities in Haran; he was asking her to leave the comfortable life she'd always known; he was expecting her to join him willingly and with a sense of excitement. It was unheard of that anyone, especially the oldest son, would leave his land, much less his friends and family and neighbors. This just was not done.

Prayer for the Day: *God of the journey, sometimes you call me to leave what feels comfortable. Help me be brave when that happens. Amen.*

Genesis 12:1-9   **Week 43**
                                                                                                                Monday

Abram told Sarai that his God had promised to make him a great nation and would bless him. Sarai thought that her husband's God had not told *her* these things. She wondered if Abram was simply making all this up or if he truly had had a direct encounter with the Holy One.

The couple began packing up their household belongings, instructing their servants, and saying goodbye. To many people who asked Abram, "Why are you doing this?" he replied, "I'm not sure. It's just something I know I have to do." But at night, he whispered again to Sarai that God had spoken to him.

Lot, too, decided for his own reasons, to leave with his uncle Abram and Sarai and accompany them on this adventure with its rich promises. He and Abram worked side by side checking strappings and food supplies. Abram shared with his nephew the promises that God had made. He said that God would lead them to another country. This was the first time that Lot learned that Abram did not even have a destination in mind. Abram told Lot that God was going to make him a great nation. Abram? Abram and Sarai had no children. And Abram and Sarai were already OLD. Abram also said that God had promised well-being, security, prosperity, and prominence. Lot questioned Abram about how and when all these things were going to happen. Abram never gave satisfactory answers. His explanations always ended with "The Lord commanded, and the Lord has promised. That I believe."

The two families became wanderers, claiming land that God told Abram was his. They stopped and built an altar at Shechem in Canaan. The place was holy to the Canaanites. When Sarai asked why Abram wanted to build an altar there, he told her that his God had revealed that this land, Canaan, would be the land of Abram's descendants. Sarai did not know whether to shout for joy or scream with hysteria. She had left her home for a land which would be given not to her but to her children which she didn't have. What a barren, hopeless situation. From there they moved to the hill country east of Bethel and built another altar. By stages they moved to the Negeb. They held onto the promise that Abram would be a great nation and would be blessed. As much as Sarai hoped the blessing would begin and she'd become pregnant, nothing happened.

Prayer for the Day: *God of promises, help me live with your promises and know that your timing is not mine. Amen.*

Week 43
Tuesday

Genesis 12:1-9

Neither Abram nor Sarai felt very blessed. The land that supposedly was theirs to claim was not rich and fertile. The more they traveled, the more sand they seemed to eat and the less food they were able to gather. Because of a famine, Abram decided they would travel to Egypt, where he would get herds and slaves.

Once again, Abram astounded Sarai. As they got close to Egypt, Abram said to Sarai, "Sarai, you are so beautiful. I love you dearly. I need you to help me with one small thing." He wanted her to pretend to be his sister. He feared that if Pharaoh knew that Sarai was Abram's wife, Pharaoh would kill Abram to get Sarai as his own.

The plan worked. Because of Pharaoh's pleasure with Sarai, he gave Abram, her "brother," sheep, oxen, male and female donkeys, male and female slaves, and camels. Then plagues hit Pharaoh's house, and he suspected that everything was not as Abram presented it. Pharaoh did not kill Abram and Sarai but told them to leave along with all the magnificent gifts he'd given to them. Lot and Abram parted ways.

Prayer for the Day: *God my delight, today I can only say your name and hold onto you as Creator, Redeemer, and Sustainer, Father, Son, and Holy Spirit. Amen.*

Genesis 12:1-9

**Week 43
Wednesday**

Abram and Sarai returned to the Negeb, the place between Bethel and Ai but this time they were very rich. Abram lived by God's guidance. The couple kept trying to figure out how God's promises were being fulfilled. When Abram was 99 years old, God changed his name to Abraham, meaning father of many nations. Twenty-five years after leaving that faraway place they had called home, when there was absolutely no way God's promises could be fulfilled because Abraham was now 100 and Sarai, now called Sarah, was barren, they had a baby son, whom they named Isaac.

This story has been known as a story of faith. In the book of Romans, the great faith of Abraham is extolled: *Abraham believed God, and it was reckoned to him as righteousness* (Romans 4:3). In Hebrews 11:8: *By faith Abraham obeyed when he was called to go out to a place which he was called to receive as an inheritance; and he went out, not knowing where he was to go.*

How does this story seem to you? As you move further and further into the vision of allowing God's spirit to direct your life, you too are called to step out in faith. You may move in ways that are frightening or confusing as you listen to the wind of God moving in you. You too may experience being called by God to leave security, comfort, and familiarity and go to another place. Even if you are not called to physically pack up your belongings, you may be called to move from safe, secure, familiar ways of thinking or doing things to other, new, sometimes more costly, or at least more Spirit-led ways of living or thinking.

Prayer for the Day: *God, are you calling me to move into unfamiliar places? Amen.*

Week 43
Thursday

Genesis 12:1-9

Will you believe that God is leading you to think in fresh ways about how you grow and nurture your discipleship? Will the Spirit blow you in different ways as you consider your call to serve in your family, your community, and your world? Will Jesus pull you to embrace prayer in your life as he did? Where will God lead you in ways that you cannot even imagine right now? Will you become known as a model of great faith?

The story of Abram and Sarai leads you to realize that the promises of God may occur in the midst of those who practice more effective and more attractive ways. Abram could have argued that he would be more effective, more vital if he remained in Haran and tended his flocks and his family. He needed to take care of his responsibilities as others defined those responsibilities. But Abram listened to the voice of God and not the voices of well-meaning and influential people, including his family and friends.

Faith for Abram meant believing in the promises of God with no visible evidence. There are times when you are called to step out in faith, in trust, to do something that seems right even though you may not even be sure what that is. Some theologians call that a "leap of faith." It's only in looking back that you can say, "Yes, God led me and I followed."

Prayer for the Day: *There are times, O Holy One, when you call me to step out in faith, in trust, to do something that seems right even though I may not even be sure what that is. Help me walk in trust. Amen.*

Genesis 12:1-9

Week 43
Friday

In taking this journey, Abram and Sarai departed from security. How often do you not get involved, not speak out, not be there for someone because getting involved, speaking out, not being there may cost you financially, may threaten your reputation, may make you uncomfortable? Choosing to allow God's spirit to power your life is frightening when you've done fairly well handling it on your own. You know security when you do things the way you've done them all along. You know security when you count on things coming back like they were before the pandemic, before rising prices, war, mass killings. You feel secure when you have an agenda and follow it rather than allowing gaps that may be filled in fresh, sacred ways. You like knowing what's going on. That's security. Abram, the great model of faith, left security to follow God's lead.

Abram's and Sarai's faith journey shows something that you may not like. The fullness of God's promise did not happen in their lifetimes. Yes, they had a son. Yes, they received lands and wealth, but the great nation took generations to be fulfilled. There were several generations before the descendants of Abram ended up in Egypt and then even more generations before they left. And there was at least one more generation before they even began to claim Canaan as the land of promise.

Prayer for the Day: *God, you know I'm not very patient. Help me trust in your promises. Amen.*

Week 43   **Genesis 12:1-9**
Saturday

People yearn for instant gratification. Take a pill now to stop the pain. Solve the problems now. Make a buck now. Solutions now!!! If you try something new and it doesn't work like you wanted it to, then you cast it aside. Some things require simmering to come to fruition. Some things get pushed before their time has come. Sometimes God's time is not your time. Time is so important to you. But is time as we understand it important to God?

The Iroquois have a tradition that helps you get beyond your need for solutions, fulfillment, gratification NOW. They ask, "What will be the effect of this decision on the people who live seven generations hence?"

Abram and Sarai lived their lives in tune with God's word, whether they completely understood it or not. Maybe this world chooses silence, ideology, or propaganda rather than the word of God. Maybe in fear and doubt, the world listens to weak voices, speeches with innuendos rather than true power. Nevertheless, God's word breaks all these barriers. God's word is the life-giving word to listen to.

Abram and Sarai, stepping out in faith, followed God's leading, in ways they often did not understand. Abraham and Sarah, faithful people, ancestors in faith did not always get it right. However, they showed what living in faith looks like. They showed that others may offer enticing diversions from your faith. They demonstrated that when you follow that nudge of faith, you land right in God's love. They point out that in leaving your security you discover a life which is full and blessed beyond your wildest imaginings. They show you that God's promises are fulfilled in your life and in the lives of your children. And glory be to God, they show you that God's word leads you to faithful actions even when you don't know where you're headed.

Prayer for the Day: *Holy God, I want to be ready to travel with Abraham and Sarah in faith. Amen.*

Week 44
Genesis 16:1-15; 21:8-21

Now Sarai, Abram's wife, bore him no children. She had an Egyptian slave-girl whose name was Hagar, 2 and Sarai said to Abram, 'You see that the Lord has prevented me from bearing children; go in to my slave-girl; it may be that I shall obtain children by her.' And Abram listened to the voice of Sarai. 3 So, after Abram had lived for ten years in the land of Canaan, Sarai, Abram's wife, took Hagar the Egyptian, her slave-girl, and gave her to her husband Abram as a wife. 4 He went in to Hagar, and she conceived; and when she saw that she had conceived, she looked with contempt on her mistress. 5 Then Sarai said to Abram, 'May the wrong done to me be on you! I gave my slave-girl to your embrace, and when she saw that she had conceived, she looked on me with contempt. May the Lord judge between you and me!' 6 But Abram said to Sarai, 'Your slave-girl is in your power; do to her as you please.' Then Sarai dealt harshly with her, and she ran away from her.

7 The angel of the Lord found her by a spring of water in the wilderness, the spring on the way to Shur. 8 And he said, 'Hagar, slave-girl of Sarai, where have you come from and where are you going?' She said, 'I am running away from my mistress Sarai.' 9 The angel of the Lord said to her, 'Return to your mistress, and submit to her.' 10 The angel of the Lord also said to her, 'I will so greatly multiply your offspring that they cannot be counted for multitude.' 11 And the angel of the Lord said to her, 'Now you have conceived and shall bear a son; you shall call him Ishmael, for the Lord has given heed to your affliction. 12 He shall be a wild ass of a man, with his hand against everyone, and everyone's hand against him; and he shall live at odds with all his kin.' 13 So she named the Lord who spoke to her, 'You are El-roi'; for she said, 'Have I really seen God and remained alive after seeing him?' 14 Therefore the well was called Beer-lahai-roi; it lies between Kadesh and Bered.

15 Hagar bore Abram a son; and Abram named his son, whom Hagar bore, Ishmael.

8 The child grew, and was weaned; and Abraham made a great feast on the day that Isaac was weaned. 9 But Sarah saw the son of Hagar the Egyptian, whom she had borne to Abraham, playing with her son Isaac. 10 So she said to Abraham, 'Cast out this slave woman with her son; for the son of this slave woman shall not inherit along with my son Isaac.' 11 The matter was very distressing to Abraham on account of his son. 12 But God said to Abraham, 'Do not be distressed because of the boy and because of your slave woman; whatever Sarah says to you, do as she tells you, for it is through Isaac that offspring shall be named after you. 13 As for the son of the slave woman, I will make a nation of him also, because he is your offspring.' 14 So Abraham rose early in the morning, and took bread and a skin of water, and gave it to Hagar, putting it on her shoulder, along with the child, and sent her away. And she departed, and wandered about in the wilderness of Beer-sheba.

15 When the water in the skin was gone, she cast the child under one of the bushes. 16 Then she went and sat down opposite him a good way off, about the distance of a bowshot; for she said, 'Do not let me look on the death of the child.' And as she sat opposite him, she lifted up her voice and wept. 17 And God heard the voice of the boy; and the angel of God called to Hagar from heaven, and said to her, 'What troubles you, Hagar? Do not be afraid; for God has heard the voice of the boy where he is. *(cont'd next page)*

Week 44
Sunday

Genesis 16:1-15; 21:8-21

Based on "Hagar" from Templeton, *Conversations on the Porch*.

Imagine that you're sitting on a screen porch. The chair cushions are flat in places. The wind chimes tinkle as the breeze plays with the pipes. The three-story magnolia tree embraces the porch with its wide, old branches. This seems to be a sacred place where souls are nurtured, and people find their way. As you sit on the porch, you realize that someone is on the porch with you, rocking with you. Hagar announces herself.

Just some background about Hagar: Hagar was Sarai's slave brought from Egypt. Sarai sent Hagar to Abram. Whatever child Hagar had would belong to Sarai and Abram because Hagar belonged to Sarai. After she became pregnant, Hagar ran away and encountered God. Then she returned to Sarai to give birth to her son, Ishmael. After Sarai's son, Isaac, was born, Hagar was banished. The Lord came to her again for her and Ishmael's protection.

Back to the porch. You greet your visitor. "Hello, Mistress Hagar. You saw the Lord. You bore both blessing and curse because of your relationship with Abraham, Sarah, and Ishmael. What path are you calling us to?"

Hagar speaks. "I fear you. People who befriended me have turned out not to be my friends. I have been a pawn in other peoples' plans. That is not a comfortable place to be. I was used as a slave; I was used by Abram so he could have an heir; I was used by Sarai so she could give her husband a child. Used!

"To them I was a nobody, property, a thing. Abram and Sarai did not even call me by my name! I was simply a way for them to get what they wanted.

"Please don't use people as I was used. I wanted Sarai and Abram to recognize that I was still a person with hopes and dreams of my own. I had visions for my life which were bigger than being used by them, bigger than being their servant. I performed menial jobs in taking care of Sarai. I wanted her to appreciate my service to her. I needed her to acknowledge how I had helped her have the life of her choosing. I yearned for her to recognize my dignity. When she did not, well then, I regret to say, I developed an attitude with her.

"Please, please do not use people as I was used."

Prayer for the Day: *Dearest Lord, awaken me to acknowledge those people who make my life what it is: cashiers, dishwashers, childcare workers, servers, and many, many others. Amen.*

---

18 Come, lift up the boy and hold him fast with your hand, for I will make a great nation of him.' 19 Then God opened her eyes, and she saw a well of water. She went, and filled the skin with water, and gave the boy a drink.

20 God was with the boy, and he grew up; he lived in the wilderness, and became an expert with the bow. 21 He lived in the wilderness of Paran; and his mother got a wife for him from the land of Egypt.

Genesis 16:1-15; 21:8-21

Week 44
Monday

Hagar continues: "I cannot say that my life was totally bad. I gave life to my darling Ishmael. Even though his existence caused me to be cast away, I still am proud of him and who he became. He married a lovely girl from Egypt!

"Because of my love of and for Ishmael, I remind you to look for God's blessing even when life demeans you and people mistreat you. If you cannot immediately see the good in your situation, keep looking.

"It took me a while to see how blessed my life had become after I was exiled from Sarai and Abram. I finally realized I was no longer a slave! I was on my own in the wilderness. That was scary and depressing at first. I thought both my child and I were going to die from dehydration. I did not know where to turn.

"When the Lord of Abram and Sarai came to me in the desert, called me by name (something neither of them ever did), comforted and supported me, I was frightened. Then I was angry. Then I was encouraged. Then I had hope. Then I knew that Ishmael and I would survive. That was when I realized what a gift I had with my freedom and my son. So, remember. Bad situations can lead to good.

"My son, Ishmael, lost his birthright. As Abram's first born, he should have received his father's blessing. Sarai made sure that that did not happen. For that I will not forgive Sarai.

"On the other hand, when we were sent away, Ishmael no longer had to bow down to his father. He was no longer the son of a slave, since I was no longer in slavery! Ishmael was freed to find his own way, which he did. He sired the people who worship Allah, the followers of Islam.

"At first, I thought all was lost. But because the Lord of Sarai and Abram watched over us, we more than survived. We thrived!"

Prayer for the Day: *God of the past, present, and future, keep reminding me that this too shall pass...whatever "this" is. Amen.*

Week 44
Tuesday

Genesis 16:1-15; 21:8-21

Hagar's narrative continues. "I have two other lessons for you to consider. The first is one I do not like to admit. I *never* forgave Sarai. She had Isaac and was honored along with Abram. I, however, was a nobody who wandered in the wilderness after being exiled. Once she sent me away, Sarai forgot about me. I, unlike Sarai, was not remembered kindly in the history of the Christian church. As far as Sarai was concerned, I no longer existed. But she definitely existed for me. Every day I fed my hatred of her. I drank deeply of my bitterness.

"Now... I can see that my hatred of her did not affect her at all. I was affected. I became a bitter woman. I hope you will seek to forgive those who have wronged you, not for the other person's sake but for your own. My life would have been more joyful and satisfying if I could just have forgiven her.

"My other lesson is to know that God is always with you. When my life looked the bleakest, God showed up in the most amazing ways. When other people intend to do you harm, God can help you see possibility and claim hope. God can come to you in ways most appropriate for you."

Prayer for the Day: *Blessed Savior, help me forgive others as well as myself. Amen.*

Genesis 16:1-15; 21:8-21 — Week 44, Wednesday

Hagar proclaims, "I am a strong woman. God came to me in a strong and direct way when I was feeling most defeated. Trust that God can do the same for you in ways which are utterly right for you.

"I do not wish my path on you. Even so, I would not trade my path. I encountered the holy God in an amazing manner. I have Ishmael. I thrived! Ultimately, what more could I ask? "

And then she leaves the porch.

Does Hagar's journey find resonance with you? If so, what good news it is to know that God was with Hagar even when she thought that all was lost.

It is most profound that God called her by name and she called God by name!!! Certainly, Abraham and Sarah did not honor her with her name, according to the scripture. To be called by name meant that the other person knew you intimately and had some deep and profound connection with you. Your name was part of your essence. When your central reason for existence changes, then your name changes. You may have known Jimmy who is now Jim or James. Abram became Abraham, Sarai became Sarah, Saul became Paul. When you learn the correct pronunciation of someone's name, you honor them, you value their personhood, and their culture. Your name is you in many ways.

You may relate somewhat to that when you try to decide what to name a baby (or a puppy). What do you want the name to signify? Who do you want to honor when naming? How do you want this child to be known as an adult? How traditional, ordinary, unusual do you want this person's name to be?

Prayer for the Day: *Yahweh, I confess that I do not often try to learn how to correctly say another's name, especially when the person has a different ethnic heritage than mine. Help me honor the other's personhood by trying harder. Amen.*

Week 44
Thursday   **Genesis 16:1-15; 21:8-21**

Name also involves the sentiments which are sometimes attached to labels. Think of all the labels that you wear, that you ascribe to others, that you embrace, that you hate. Labels may be names such as teacher, doctor, PaPa, Mimi, Dad, Mom, daughter, son, etc. The labels applied to you can either be absorbed in negative ways or you can use them as catalysts for change. Some labels inspire you to grow into them so you can merit that positive view which someone has of you. Some labels have to be shrugged off so that their destructive energy does not infiltrate your very being. Knowing the labels helps you understand the power of the name within the context of your story.

God's knowing Hagar's name meant that God knew her. This may mean that God knew her hopes, her dreams, her pain, her struggles, her joy, her despair. If this is so, then that means you need withhold nothing from your Holy God. You were known, as Jeremiah says, even before you were in your mother's womb. And if God loves you and knows you and cares for you, then as followers of this God, you too are involved in holy activity when you love and know and care for all of God's other creations.

What a shame that does not happen. Do you cast off, dismiss, the Hagars in your own life? Are you cast off as Hagar by others in your life?

Prayer for the Day: *Precious Lord, forgive me when I label another with judgment and little compassion. Help me be more aware. Amen.*

Genesis 16:1-15; 21:8-21 **Week 44**
                                  Friday

What is even more astounding is that Hagar calls God, El Roi. She herself calls God by name. Not even Moses got away with this. Moses asked God, "What shall I tell the people your name is?" Tell them, "Yahweh" or "I am who I am" or "I will be who I will be." If anyone knew God's name, then it should have been Moses. But Moses did not. Hagar did. She is the only person in the entire Hebrew scripture who called God by name.

She knew the God of Abraham by name. She knew the essence of God. She had a deep and profound connection with God. Who would have guessed? People seem to expect those who know God intimately to look and smell and act like saints. Hagar certainly does not fit the usual description of a holy person. There is no record of her quoting scripture or of going on mission trips (voluntarily) or of giving large sums of money for God's work. You do not know whether she was liberal or conservative. You only know that she saw God and lived. God knew her and she knew God. Through her, a great nation was founded.

Hagar's story is one of triumph out of tragedy. It is a story of God's compassion to redeem the wrongs brought on by humanity's cruelty to each other. Her story is one of hope in the midst of evidence to the contrary. It is a story of intimacy and love in the midst of hatred and fear. It is a story that reminds you that ultimately what is right wins.

Prayer for the Day: *Holy Comforter, I live in the midst of such a love story that is life. Thank you. Amen.*

Week 44 **Genesis 16:1-15; 21:8-21**
Saturday

This 13th century prayer could easily have been written by Hagar:

> Lord, because I am the lowliest of creatures,
> You have raised me to Yourself.
> Lord, because I have no earthly treasures,
> You have poured upon me heavenly wealth.
> Lord, because I am dressed in the grey rags of flaws,
> You have clothed me in the pure white robe of grace.
> Lord, because I desire the merest hut for my home,
> You have welcomed me to Your eternal place.

Mechthild of Magdeburg, Germany, c 1212-1280

Prayer for the Day: *Today Lord, I pray the prayer of Mechthild of Magdeburg. Amen.*

Week 45
Genesis 22:1-14

After these things God tested Abraham. He said to him, 'Abraham!' And he said, 'Here I am.' 2 He said, 'Take your son, your only son Isaac, whom you love, and go to the land of Moriah, and offer him there as a burnt-offering on one of the mountains that I shall show you.' 3 So Abraham rose early in the morning, saddled his donkey, and took two of his young men with him, and his son Isaac; he cut the wood for the burnt-offering, and set out and went to the place in the distance that God had shown him. 4 On the third day Abraham looked up and saw the place far away. 5 Then Abraham said to his young men, 'Stay here with the donkey; the boy and I will go over there; we will worship, and then we will come back to you.' 6 Abraham took the wood of the burnt-offering and laid it on his son Isaac, and he himself carried the fire and the knife. So the two of them walked on together. 7 Isaac said to his father Abraham, 'Father!' And he said, 'Here I am, my son.' He said, 'The fire and the wood are here, but where is the lamb for a burnt-offering?' 8 Abraham said, 'God himself will provide the lamb for a burnt-offering, my son.' So the two of them walked on together.

9 When they came to the place that God had shown him, Abraham built an altar there and laid the wood in order. He bound his son Isaac, and laid him on the altar, on top of the wood. 10 Then Abraham reached out his hand and took the knife to kill his son. 11 But the angel of the Lord called to him from heaven, and said, 'Abraham, Abraham!' And he said, 'Here I am.' 12 He said, 'Do not lay your hand on the boy or do anything to him; for now I know that you fear God, since you have not withheld your son, your only son, from me.' 13 And Abraham looked up and saw a ram, caught in a thicket by its horns. Abraham went and took the ram and offered it up as a burnt-offering instead of his son. 14 So Abraham called that place 'The Lord will provide'; as it is said to this day, 'On the mount of the Lord it shall be provided.'

Week 45 **Genesis 22:1-14**
Sunday

Isaac's parents, Abraham and Sarah learned of Isaac's birth when three men visited Abraham and Sarah by the oaks of Mamre. One of them said, *I will surely return to you in due season, and your wife Sarah shall have a son* (Genesis 18:10). The passage goes on to say that Sarah was old, advanced in age, certainly too old to have a baby. But God said to Abraham…note God, the Lord, spoke and said, *Is anything too wonderful for the Lord? At the set time I will return to you, in due season, and Sarah shall have a son* (Genesis 18:14). God went on to say that Abraham would become a great and mighty nation, and all the nations of the earth would be blessed by him (Genesis 18:18). In chapter 21, God told Abraham that *through Isaac* offspring would be named for the patriarch. These offspring included nations and kings. God told Abraham the descendants would come through Sarah. It is very clear that God gave Isaac to Abraham and Sarah so that Abraham's descendants would be great in number.

Prayer for the Day: *God of Abraham, Sarah, and Isaac, your actions are too wonderful for words. Praises to you. Amen.*

Genesis 22:1-14   **Week 45**
    Monday

Now you come to God's test. Note, this scenario was totally in God's control. This test was designed by God. This test of Abraham seems unbelievable. Here was this child of promise and God was testing Abraham to see if he could and would kill this special offspring. The language here lines out the drama. God tells Abraham to take his son, and then to underscore how important this boy is to Abraham, the passage says, take your son, your *only* son, Isaac (no nameless kid here), *whom you love*, and offer him as a sacrifice.

This testing God does not sound like the God you talk about all the time. This does not sound like the God you worship and glorify. This God, this God, your God, tests his most faithful follower. Is God really not sure about Abraham's faith? Is it like when God allowed Satan to test Job, a blameless and upright man who feared God? Is it like God's own self and the test of the cross?

Are you uncomfortable thinking about having faith in a God who might ask you to give up, to release, to kill someone whom you love. Not only that, but you may also be extremely unhappy about having to choose between a God and a beloved child or grandchild. How in the world could a loving God ask such a thing? Unfortunately, you must allow that question to shimmer in the air because this scripture does not give you the explanation about your God that you crave.

Prayer for the Day: *God, how could you? Would you ever ask these kinds of things of me? Amen.*

Week 45 **Genesis 22:1-14**
Tuesday

Obedient Abraham prepared for the journey that God told him to take. *This* journey was not like the one when he left the land of Ur for the land of Haran. *That* journey required him to leave everything and everyone he loved to follow this God to the land that God promised. *After that* journey Abraham had fully tasted the bounty of God to whom he'd dedicated his life. He now had land, livestock, grains, a wife, and a son. But on *this next* journey, Abraham was being asked to give up this most precious son. How can that be?

Abraham, Isaac, and two young men began the journey. They loaded up the donkey with the firewood for the sacrificial fire. When Abraham drew near to the place that God had indicated to him, he told the two young men, *Stay here with the donkey; the boy and I will go over there; we will worship, and then we will come back to you* (Genesis 22:5). Note that Abraham said, "We will come back to you." Is it possible that he knew that God would intervene and that he would not have to make the awful journey by himself after slaying his son? Did he trust God so devoutly that he *knew*, he knew that God's promise of great nations through Isaac would somehow come true, even though all evidence pointed elsewhere? The passage does not explain except to put words into Abraham's mouth saying, "We, meaning my son and I, will come back to you."

If this were a movie, you'd be horrified to see that Isaac was required to carry the firewood himself...the very firewood on which he'd be burned as a sacrifice. The boy and his father chatted. *Isaac said to his father, "Father!" and Abraham answered, "Here I am, my son"* (Genesis 22:7). Isaac noted that they had wood but no lamb for the offering. Abraham said, *God himself will provide the lamb for a burnt offering, my son* (Genesis 12:8). This statement is two-edged. God had indeed provided Isaac as gift to both Abraham and Sarah. Was Isaac to be the offering provided by God? Or could Abraham still be trusting God so deeply that he *knew*, he knew that God would provide a lamb? You don't know at this point in the story the true explanation. All you know is that Abraham seems intent on doing what God required as part of this test.

Prayer for the Day: *Father God, give me the faith of Abraham. Amen.*

Genesis 22:1-14

Week 45
Wednesday

Abraham lays the wood for a fire and then binds Isaac. As he was raising his arm with the knife to kill his son, the angel of God said, "Abraham, Abraham!" and he said, "Here I am." Wait, where have you heard those words before? "Here I am." Those are the exact words that Abraham said to his son while they were walking with the wood for the fire and now he says them to the messenger of God.

This little detail is fascinating. "Here I am." You hear those words in other scriptures. When the Lord asks *Whom shall I send, and who will go for us?* Isaiah says, *Here I am; send me!* (Isaiah 6:8). Mary says to the angel of the Lord, *Here I am, the servant of the Lord; let it be with me according to your word* (Luke 1:38). Other people in scripture also uttered those words: Esau when his father Isaac called to him, Jacob when he wrestled with the angel of the Lord, Joseph when his brothers tricked him to come to them so they could kill him, Moses at the burning bush, Samuel when answering God but thinking it was Eli, and Ananias when told to open Paul's eyes. There were others as well. Almost every one of these instances involved a life changing encounter with God. Moses became the leader of his people, Mary became the mother of Jesus, Samuel became the great prophet and king maker, Isaiah became an important prophet whose words foretold the suffering servant and the coming of the Messiah better than anyone, and Paul received his literal as well as his spiritual sight and spread the gospel.

Prayer for the Day: *Source of all true joy, when you ask "Whom shall I send?" give me the strength and commitment to answer, "Send me." Amen.*

Week 45
Thursday
Genesis 22:1-14

It seems that when a person says, "Here I am," those words can be truly life changing, especially when said to God. Is it possible that all you have to do is show up and be willing to follow where God leads…no matter how scary and impossible that thought may be? Abraham says, "Here I am" on the way to sacrifice his son, his heir, the one who was supposed to make Abraham's family as numerous as the stars. Abraham says again, "Here I am" and hears the words that he's to spare his son. When you say, "Here I am" who knows what may happen in your relationship with God? Will God test you? Will God provide for you? The passage says, "Yes" to both questions. God will test you… and God will provide for you.

This is so challenging to get your mind around. How can God be both the God who tests as well as the God who provides? Theologians through the centuries have certainly tried to unravel this puzzle. How can God be both?

Do you remember what God told Moses to say to the people when they asked what God's name was? God said, Yahweh, which is often translated as "I am who I am." "I will be who I will be." "I was who I was." God refuses for anyone to domesticate the Lord. God is both tester and provider.…as Abraham discovered.

Prayer for the Day: *Lord Jesus, I trust that you will provide when you call me to unknown opportunities. Amen.*

Genesis 22:1-14

Week 45
Friday

When Abraham lifted his arm with his knife in his hand, God responded: *Do not lay your hand on the boy or do anything to him; for now I know that you fear God, since you have not withheld your son, your only son, from me* (Genesis 22:12). From this passage, it seems that God did not know how Abraham would behave. God was not absolutely certain of Abraham's faith. In the first verse of our passage, God tested Abraham. In verse 12, God responds, "Now…now I know…"

You may be saying in your mind, but God already knew. That's not how the scripture tells the story. God says, "Now I know…" Abraham showed up. Abraham was willing to hand over the son that God had given him. Did Abraham trust so deeply that he believed he'd have another son to carry out God's promises? Did he believe that God would indeed provide the ram that was caught in the brambles? Did Abraham act blindly or in the full light of God's graciousness to him? Who knows?

Nevertheless, the story had a happy ending. Isaac was unloosed from the ropes that bound him. He and his father slaughtered the ram and sacrificed it according to the rituals that had been laid down. Abraham called the place "On the mount of the Lord it shall be provided."

Prayer for the Day: *Holy God, I trust you hold me in the palm of your hand. Amen.*

Week 45
Saturday

Genesis 22:1-14

This is more than an ancient story. It is more than a story that points you to the cross when *God's* only son was killed. This is a story that calls to you when you are bold enough to listen.

In the gospel of Matthew, when Jesus's mother and brothers were standing outside to talk with him, Jesus replied, *Who is my mother, and who are my brothers?...Here are my mother and my brothers! For whoever does the will of my Father in heaven is my brother and sister and mother* (Matthew 12:48-50). Jesus reinforces the Genesis passage that family, as dear and important and cherished as they are, are not as important to you as God and your relationship with God.

Does this cause you to roll your eyes? Can you believe what she said, that God is more important than you, your spouse, your children, your grandchildren, or your great-grandchildren?

Do you have great difficulty believing that God might ask you to give up family in order to prove your faith? That's what this story says…but wait. Abraham just had to show up…here I am… be prepared to do God's calling… and God provided. God did not take Isaac from Abraham. In some ways, this test made Isaac even more special because God provided a way for Isaac to live yet again.

Is that what you can do…just show up and be willing to follow your God wherever that may lead? That's quite a challenge, isn't it? And yet, this passage says that God provides. Your willingness is part of your own test for the strength of your faith. God did not allow Abraham to do the gruesome task. God provided bountifully a ram, not a lamb, but a full-grown sheep. That ram was tangled in the brush and so must have been there for a while. Why did Abraham not see that ram? Could it be because he was so intent on doing what he believed God was asking him to do? God intervened in Abraham's focus with an angel. An angel! Don't you wish that you could have an angel speak and stop you from doing something wrong?

This passage raises a lot of questions. And yet you have a powerful story that even when God tests you, God provides a way out for you. You have to show up and listen and follow wherever God is leading you. That's the power of faith, and that's the power of God to whom you offer all praise and glory.

Prayer for the Day: *Father God, help me show up and follow wherever you are leading. Amen.*

Week 46
Genesis 25:19-34

19 These are the descendants of Isaac, Abraham's son: Abraham was the father of Isaac, 20 and Isaac was forty years old when he married Rebekah, daughter of Bethuel the Aramean of Paddan-aram, sister of Laban the Aramean. 21 Isaac prayed to the Lord for his wife, because she was barren; and the Lord granted his prayer, and his wife Rebekah conceived. 22 The children struggled together within her; and she said, 'If it is to be this way, why do I live?' So she went to inquire of the Lord. 23 And the Lord said to her,

'Two nations are in your womb,
  and two peoples born of you shall be divided;
one shall be stronger than the other,
  the elder shall serve the younger.'

24 When her time to give birth was at hand, there were twins in her womb. 25 The first came out red, all his body like a hairy mantle; so they named him Esau. 26 Afterwards his brother came out, with his hand gripping Esau's heel; so he was named Jacob. Isaac was sixty years old when she bore them.

27 When the boys grew up, Esau was a skillful hunter, a man of the field, while Jacob was a quiet man, living in tents. 28 Isaac loved Esau, because he was fond of game; but Rebekah loved Jacob.
29 Once when Jacob was cooking a stew, Esau came in from the field, and he was famished. 30 Esau said to Jacob, 'Let me eat some of that red stuff, for I am famished!' (Therefore he was called Edom.) 31 Jacob said, 'First sell me your birthright.' 32 Esau said, 'I am about to die; of what use is a birthright to me?' 33 Jacob said, 'Swear to me first.' So he swore to him, and sold his birthright to Jacob. 34 Then Jacob gave Esau bread and lentil stew, and he ate and drank, and rose and went his way. Thus Esau despised his birthright.

Week 46   **Genesis 25:19-34**
Sunday

This family is very interesting! Abraham is the grandfather of twin brothers, Esau and Jacob. Abraham with God's leading, left his ancestral home, suffered famine, went down into Egypt where the twins' grandmother, Sarah, was passed off to Pharaoh as Abraham's sister. Pharaoh sent Abraham and Sarah away with slaves, animals, and many riches. Late in life, Sarah gave birth to the twins' father, Isaac... a total surprise. She knew that Abraham was supposed to be the father of great nations but without children, she didn't see how that could happen. So, she gave Abraham her slave Hagar who bore a son, Ishmael, Isaac's older half-brother. Hagar and Ishmael were sent away to protect Abraham's legacy to Isaac. The second born son, Isaac, therefore, received the blessing and birthright. Even that seemed in jeopardy because God told Abraham to kill Isaac as a sacrifice, but once again God intervened, and Isaac was saved to become the next in line for this promised great nation.

So that his son would not marry a Canaanite woman, Abraham sent a servant to find the wife that God had in mind for Isaac. The servant prayed for a sign. Sure enough, Rebekah responded as the girl who fulfilled the sign that the servant asked of God. Not only did she offer water to men and camels, she was also *very fair to look upon* (Genesis 24:16), and was pure *as no man had known [her]*. She even offered the hospitality of her father's home when she said, without being asked, "*We have plenty of straw and fodder and a place to spend the night*" (Genesis 24:25).

So, *Isaac brought Rebekah into his mother Sarah's tent. He took her and she became his wife; and he loved her* (Genesis 24:67). But no children came. Once again, the promise of a great nation seemed in doubt. Isaac prayed to God for his barren wife to have a child. The Lord granted his prayer. Rebekah became pregnant with not one but two children. The scripture indicates a difficult pregnancy saying *the children struggled together within her* (Genesis 25:22). Can you imagine her complaining, "God, why in the world did I want so badly to be pregnant? These babies are tearing my insides apart. Oh, God, please help me get through this." And God said, *Two nations are in your womb, and two peoples born of you shall be divided; the one shall be stronger than the other, the elder shall serve the younger* (Genesis 25:23). With the luxury of hindsight, you can see that Rebekah was given a hint about what would ultimately happen.

Prayer for the Day: *God of history, guide me today. Amen.*

Genesis 25:19-34

Week 46
Monday

The twins were born, first Esau and then Jacob. Even at birth, they were physically different. Esau was red and very hairy, and Jacob must not have been. He came out holding onto Esau's foot. Some commentators suggest that Jacob was already trying to usurp Esau's place. Or just maybe Jacob, having spent nine months with his brother, was just trying to keep up, to make sure that he did not get left behind.

A grandmother of twins remarked after thinking about this story with a 21st-century perspective, that it did not seem fair that a matter of minutes... at the most... determined who got the birthright and the blessing. The children had shared everything to the point of their birth. But because of Esau's being born first, he, by all rights, got the prizes. But after their birth, the children received different things from their parents. Isaac's favorite child was Esau. As the scriptures describe him, Esau was a man's man...a hunter and hairy. He could bring his father food from his hunts. Rebekah's favorite was Jacob, who liked to stay close to home.

In today's way of thinking, not God's, Esau was the obvious choice for all good things. He was first-born, he was a skilled hunter, and he was his father's favorite. As you think about Esau, consider all those people who by virtue of birth, skin color, gender, socioeconomic situation, or education believe they, too, deserve all the good things life has to offer. Do you simply take it for granted that life is good, and you will be blessed with riches? You do not question your right to power, possessions, or prominence. They are simply yours. You may act as if it's the second- or third-born's fault when they don't have such blessings. Some people who may be Esaus in life have never known the challenges of not being blessed, of not having opportunities, or of not getting more than their fair share.

By the reality of being the first to come out of the womb, Esau was the one who was destined to receive all the family's riches and hopes. Esau might be that person today who says, "I'm a self-made person. If I can do it, why can't that person over there who lives in poverty?"

Jacob, the second-born...by just minutes, did not hunt. He liked to stay close to home. Some might even have made fun of him since he didn't do the manly kinds of things that his brother did. Later he had to work years and years for Laban, his father-in-law-to-be, for his wives, Leah and Rachel, but at this point, you just know that he stayed close to mom.

Prayer for the Day: *Giver of life and health, help me see where I take for granted things that I did not earn but received at birth. Amen.*

Week 46   **Genesis 25:19-34**
Tuesday

If you've ever watched twins play, you can assume that Esau and Jacob played together. Hopefully they learned to share and to take turns. They probably were at times each other's best friends and worst enemies. They were twins after all, never knowing what life was like without the other one there. So, when Esau came in from hunting and smelled the food that Jacob was cooking (Why was Jacob cooking in the first place? That's what the women did. He really did not fit the role of a manly man, did he?), imagine that Esau, in his hunter's kind of way, retorted, "Let me have some of that red stuff, for I am famished." Have you exaggerated a bit when you want to let others know what you've been doing? "I've been working in the yard all day long and I just don't have the energy to prepare dinner." or "I've been slaving away all week at the office. I need a break. I'm not going to church." Or kids coming in saying, "I'm starving!" when they ate just an hour ago.

Even though Jacob has often been described as a schemer, these are two brothers who have spent their entire lives together, vying for the other parent's love, and trying to best each other. So, when Esau retorts, "I'm famished," then Jacob can easily come with "What will you give me for it?" except he says, "Sell me your birthright." And in the way that brothers banter, Esau says, "Well, I'm dying anyway, so what does it matter. Okay, you got it." "Swear." "I swear."

This was more than boys bantering. Walter Brueggemann says that this was giving away a birthright. This was giving away... without much thought... "security, prosperity, fertility, and land" (Brueggemann, *Genesis, Interpretation*, John Knox Press; Atlanta, 1982, p. 219). This was taking care of short term wants without thought for the future. Uh, oh. Esau may once again remind you of yourself: taking care of short term wants without thought for the future. Using up vital resources now without a thought to the impact on the planet earth or the future of generations who follow. Spending now because you have money without counting how your consuming may be affecting people who live in another hemisphere.

Prayer for the Day: *God of past, present, and future, may I not carelessly use resources today that hurt the future for me and others. Amen.*

Genesis 25:19-34

**Week 46
Wednesday**

The story continues. Esau married two Hittite women. Since the scriptures say that Esau's wives made life bitter for Isaac and Rebekah, he must have acted once again on his immediate desires without thought for the future and God's great promise of descendants as numerous as the stars. On the other hand, Rebekah sent Jacob to her brother, his uncle Laban, to find wives within the family constellation. He married Leah and Rachel, fathered 12 sons and one daughter. His sons became the 12 tribes of Israel.

But before he left, his mother helped Jacob get his father's blessing by tricking the old blind man into believing that he was Esau, his father's favorite. And so Jacob ended up with both birthright and blessing, just like Rebekah was told before the twins were born when God said, "Two nations are in your womb…the one shall be stronger than the other, the elder shall serve the younger."

This story is packed with drama. It could serve well as a model for studying family systems, sibling rivalry, and recurring themes from one generation to the next. But if that was all it was, it would not be in the scriptures. This story is more importantly about who God is, what God's promises look like, and how God acts.

Prayer for the Day: *Holy Spirit, be with me today, whatever it may bring. Amen.*

Week 46
Thursday
Genesis 25:19-34

Throughout the Abraham saga, humans tried to make God's promises of land and descendants come to pass. Sarah used Hagar to produce a child. Sarah got pregnant through God's intervention. God revealed Rebekah to be Isaac's wife but no children were born until Isaac asked God for them. Twins were born but the one who seemed to have it all was not the child that God had chosen to carry forth the family promise. And so it goes on and on throughout the Bible. God doesn't owe anyone anything. Whatever you receive is God's gift...free, not earned; through grace, not gratuity.

This is uncomfortable especially when you are blessed by your birth and the circumstances into which you've found yourself. You may be Esau. You do what's right. You provide for your family. You may be the child who is the favorite. You are certain that life as you have known it is yours because you deserve it. You are... in some ways...the first born...by virtue of your skin color, your nationality, your gender, or your education. Even when you may experience setbacks, you assume, for the most part, that they are temporary. God will bless you because you are one of the world's first born.

But God reminds that the first will be last, that the second born will get the birthright and blessing, that your advantages are not yours to claim as a right but God's to give as pure grace.

When you want to align yourself with God and God's will, you will look around for those who are not getting their share of security, prosperity, fertility, and land. You will reach out to help the second-born of this world claim their share of the good gifts of God. Those folks may not fit your definitions of who or what they should be. They may not fulfill your understandings of a work ethic like Esau did. They may not have what it takes...privileges granted by birth... like Esau did. They may be willing to be sneaky and possibly manipulative like Jacob was. They may not fit your perceptions of people who should receive your help, your partnership, your compassion, or your commitment. But they fit God's perceptions. And that's what matters. As God told Moses, *I will be gracious to whom I will be gracious, and I will show mercy on whom I will show mercy* (Exodus 33:19).

Prayer for the Day: *Loving God, help me see those who are not getting justice and then help me find ways to do something about it. Amen.*

Genesis 25:19-34   **Week 46**
                                                                                                                 Friday

One other uncomfortable thing this passage may be calling all those Esaus to...So that Jacob could thrive as God had desired and promised, Esau had to give up his birthright and blessing. Esau gave up...even willingly... because he was hungry...the birthright to which he was born.

What a hard message this is to hear. But Jesus, himself, in the parable of the two sons, reminded us that the father loved both sons. Nevertheless, Esau needed to relinquish what was legally and rightfully his by human law as part of God's promises being fulfilled. God through Rebekah even used trickery to make this happen. Esau and his Hittite wives did not end up with the heritage and lineage of the 12 tribes of Israel, King David, and the rest of the genealogy of Jesus. But they did not do poorly for themselves when they established a nation called the Edom. And in God's time, Esau and Jacob were eventually reconciled.

Questions to ponder:

Can you listen with ears tuned and seek with your heart primed by God and not by your assumptions of how things are supposed to be?

Are you really willing to live in the promises of God even when doing so goes against all that you believe are the "right and fair" ways of the world?

Are you willing to relinquish the things you think you value most in order to live in the promises, grace, hope, joy, and future that God is holding out to you?"

Are you? Can you?

Yes. With God's help.

Prayer for the Day: *God of my ancestors, tune my ears and prime my heart so I can follow where you lead. Amen.*

Week 46   **Genesis 25:19-34**
Saturday

God's promise to grandfather Abraham was of land and descendants. Throughout the saga, *humans* tried to make God's promises come to pass. Sarah passed off Hagar to produce a child. God intervened and Sarah got pregnant. God revealed Rebekah as the woman to be Isaac's wife but even though it was a match made in heaven, no children were born until Isaac asked God for them. Twins were born but the one who seemed to have it all was not the child that God had chosen to carry forth the family promise. And so it goes on and on throughout the Bible. Walter Brueggemann has written, "Promise requires an end to grasping and certitude and an embrace of precariousness. It is only God who gives life. Any pretense that the future is secured by rights or claims of the family is deception" (Genesis, *Interpretation*, p. 214). In other words, God doesn't owe anyone anything. Whatever you receive is God's gift—free, not earned; grace, not gratuity.

And this revelation about how God can work makes you uncomfortable especially when you are blessed by virtue of your birth and the circumstances into which you've found yourself. You may be Esau, more often than not. You are the older brother in the parable Jesus told about the two brothers, the parable that is often called the Prodigal Son. You do what's right. You provide for your family. You are the adult sibling who cares for aging parents. You may be the child who is the favorite. You are certain that life as you have known it is yours because you deserve it. You are, in some ways, the first born—by virtue of your skin color, your nationality, your gender, or your education. Even when you may experience set-backs of unemployment, illness, or other distresses, you assume, for the most part, that they are temporary. You will be on your feet again. God will bless you because you are one of the world's firstborn.

Prayer for the Day: *Loving God, help me remember that I am not any more special to you than any of your other children. I do not earn your love. It is pure gift. Amen.*

Week 47
Genesis 45:1-15

Then Joseph could no longer control himself before all those who stood by him, and he cried out, 'Send everyone away from me.' So no one stayed with him when Joseph made himself known to his brothers. 2 And he wept so loudly that the Egyptians heard it, and the household of Pharaoh heard it. 3 Joseph said to his brothers, 'I am Joseph. Is my father still alive?' But his brothers could not answer him, so dismayed were they at his presence.

4 Then Joseph said to his brothers, 'Come closer to me.' And they came closer. He said, 'I am your brother Joseph, whom you sold into Egypt. 5 And now do not be distressed, or angry with yourselves, because you sold me here; for God sent me before you to preserve life. 6 For the famine has been in the land these two years; and there are five more years in which there will be neither ploughing nor harvest. 7 God sent me before you to preserve for you a remnant on earth, and to keep alive for you many survivors. 8 So it was not you who sent me here, but God; he has made me a father to Pharaoh, and lord of all his house and ruler over all the land of Egypt. 9 Hurry and go up to my father and say to him, "Thus says your son Joseph, God has made me lord of all Egypt; come down to me, do not delay. 10 You shall settle in the land of Goshen, and you shall be near me, you and your children and your children's children, as well as your flocks, your herds, and all that you have. 11 I will provide for you there—since there are five more years of famine to come—so that you and your household, and all that you have, will not come to poverty." 12 And now your eyes and the eyes of my brother Benjamin see that it is my own mouth that speaks to you. 13 You must tell my father how greatly I am honoured in Egypt, and all that you have seen. Hurry and bring my father down here.' 14 Then he fell upon his brother Benjamin's neck and wept, while Benjamin wept upon his neck. 15 And he kissed all his brothers and wept upon them; and after that his brothers talked with him.

Week 47   **Genesis 45:1-15**
Sunday

On one level, the Joseph saga explains how the Hebrews ended up in Egypt, enslaved by Pharaoh, and were led to safety by Moses acting as God's emissary. But the primary focus of the story is how God works out God's purposes even when it looks as if everything is going down the tubes. Here's a brief review of how the story got to this point.

Abraham's grandson Jacob wanted to marry Rachel but his future father-in-law, Laban, told him he had to work for seven years for Rachel's hand. Jacob complied with Laban's demands. What else could he do? But Laban proved to be a scoundrel for on the long-awaited wedding day, he substituted Rachel's older sister, Leah, under the wedding veils. What an unwelcome surprise for Jacob. Laban said, "No problem. Work for me another seven years and Rachel will be yours." So Jacob worked another seven years and along the way picked up another two wives. Needless to say, all was not well with all the wives and children vying for center stage in Jacob's life.

All in all, Jacob had 12 sons and one daughter. The youngest two were his favorites since they were the sons of his favorite wife, Rachel. Their names were Joseph and Benjamin. Joseph especially was the apple of his father's eye. Jacob even gave Joseph a special coat. Earlier translations said the coat had many colors. More recent scholarship says that the coat had sleeves. No matter what the distinction was, the gift made the other brothers jealous. Joseph did not do anything to improve his relationship with his older brothers. In fact, from a family dynamics point of view, he did everything he could to fan his brothers' jealousy. Listen to the dreams that he told his brothers: He said, *"There we were, binding sheaves in the field. Suddenly my sheaf rose and stood upright; then your sheaves gathered around it and bowed down to my sheaf"* (Genesis 37:6-7). On another occasion he shared this dream: *"The sun, the moon, and eleven stars were bowing down to me"* (Genesis 37:9).

Prayer for the Day: *Most loving God, thank you for this day. May I use it well. Amen.*

Genesis 45:1-15

Week 47
Monday

Jacob sent Joseph out to check on the brothers as they were tending the flocks. When they saw him coming toward them, at first, they decided to kill him. Who wouldn't after his sharing his dreams? But Reuben talked the brothers into throwing Joseph into a pit. He planned to rescue his little brother later on. They took Joseph's despised coat and threw him into a pit. Then at brother Judah's suggestion without Reuben's knowledge, they decided to sell him to a passing Ishmaelite caravan. They took the coat and smeared it with blood and told their father that Joseph had been eaten by wild animals. That's how Joseph ended up in Egypt.

Joseph was bought by Potiphar, a captain of Pharaoh's guard. In that household, Joseph excelled in management and leadership. But sexual harassment was prevalent even in that time. The Bible says: *Now Joseph was handsome and good-looking. And after a time his master's wife cast her eyes on Joseph and said, "Lie with me"* (Genesis 39:6-7). Joseph refused and refused. One day though, she made advances when there were only the two of them in the house. Joseph was so scared that he ran from the house with Potiphar's wife holding onto his garment. She, by this time was tired of being denied, so she decided to get even. She announced that Joseph had been coming on to her. How dare he since he was a trusted employee of her husband! Joseph was thrown in jail.

But the scriptures say: *The Lord was with Joseph and showed his steadfast love; God gave him favor in the sight of the chief jailer* (Genesis 39:21). Joseph was given responsibility in jail and handled it well. At one point, Pharaoh's cup-bearer and his chief baker were thrown into the same prison. They each had a dream. Joseph said to them, *"Do not interpretations belong to God? Please tell them to me"* (Genesis 40:8). So, they did, and Joseph interpreted the dreams. His interpretations came true. The cup-bearer was restored to Pharaoh's house and the baker lost his head…literally.

Prayer for the Day: *Dearest God, help me trust that you in all things. Amen.*

Week 47
Tuesday
Genesis 45:1-15

Eventually Pharaoh, too, had a dream that confused him and that he wanted and needed interpretation with. Finally, the cup-bearer remembered Joseph and told Pharaoh about him. Joseph's jail time was over. The Pharaoh's dreams indicated that there were going to be seven years of plenty and seven years of famine. Pharaoh said, *"Since God has shown you all this, there is not one so discerning and wise as you. You shall be over my house, and all my people shall order themselves as you command; only with regard to the throne will I be greater than you"* (Genesis 41:39-40). Pharaoh even changed Joseph's name to Zaph'-e-nath-pa-ne'-ah and gave him a wife with whom he had two sons, Manasseh and Ephraim. Joseph took charge and assured that there would be grain stored for the years of famine.

In fact, the famine did come, and Jacob became hungry and decided to send all of his sons except Benjamin to Egypt to buy grain. Joseph recognized his brothers at once, but they did not recognize Zaph-e-nath-pa-ne'-ah. Joseph played mental games with them to determine what kind of people they had become in the intervening years. He kept Simeon locked up and told the brothers to return to Canaan to their father and to bring back Benjamin. The brothers realized that their current anguish was a direct result of what they had done years ago to a brother but as they discussed the situation among themselves, they did not know that very brother, Joseph, was standing in front of them and could understand every word they were saying. When they returned to Jacob, they did not want to risk Benjamin's life but when they needed grain yet again, they had no choice but to return to Joseph with Benjamin. Joseph toyed with them one more time but when Judah pleaded for the release of their youngest brother, Joseph broke down and revealed his identity, which is where our passage today picks up.

Joseph makes this powerful speech: *"I am your brother, Joseph, whom you sold into Egypt. Do not be distressed, or angry with yourselves, because you sold me here; for God sent me before you to preserve life… God sent me before you to preserve a remnant on earth, and to keep alive for many survivors. So, it was not you who sent me here but God…"* (Genesis 45:5-8)

Prayer for the Day: *God of wonder, you work in mysterious ways your wonders to behold. Thanks be to you. Amen.*

Genesis 45:1-15

Week 47
Wednesday

Once you discover the words of Genesis 50:20: *Even though you intended to do harm to me, God intended it for good*, which in Genesis 45:5 says, *You sold me here but God sent me before you to preserve life*, you may find comfort and freedom beyond belief. During those times when on the surface, it appears that everything is going wrong, God is working out God's own purposes, even if you can't see it at the time.

Walter Brueggemann, Old Testament scholar and retired professor of Columbia Seminary, helps explain why Joseph's speech so moving emotionally as well as so instructive to faith. He says that this "narrative asserts that God's purpose is finally sovereign. It will not be questioned or altered. It may be held in abeyance, but it works with and through every human action. [God's purpose] makes use even of the dark side of human action and planning" (*Genesis, Interpretation Commentary*, p. 347).

Sometimes it is hard to believe that God is at work in the world. You see or you experience hurt and pain and killing and hatred and violence. You do not affirm that God causes these things. You *can* affirm that God can use these horrors to work out God's will in your world and in your lives. This story does not explain why God does that. It is stated matter-of-factly and bluntly by Joseph that, paraphrasing his words: "You decided to sell me into slavery but from God's perspective God sent me to Egypt." Now Joseph may have wished that God had used a different means of transportation and process. Nevertheless, Joseph was in the right place at the right time and this was God's doing.

Prayer for the Day: *Amazing God, you are working your purpose out even when I'm not aware of it. Amen.*

Week 47   **Genesis 45:1-15**
Thursday

Walter Brueggemann also points out "the sovereign character of God's purpose can create a real newness.... a freshness that negates the past, redefines the present, and opens the future" (Genesis, *Interpretation*, p. 357). It is God's activity that allows Jacob's family to begin again...12 brothers, not 11, who are united in their love of their father and in wanting the family to survive. The arrogant younger brother breaks down in tears and the older brothers value the love and care of family.

What a message for peoples who are fighting each other...in the middle East, Afghanistan, eastern Europe, Central America, between vaccinated and unvaccinated, between Jews, Christians, and Moslems, between people who are black, white, brown, and other hues of beautiful color, between spouses, sisters and brothers, church members, work mates, neighbors. That the action of God can make a new reality...negating the past, redefining the present, and opening the future is good news indeed.

This passage also assures that God is passionate about grace. Joseph repeats three times that God had acted for life. He says: "*God sent me before you to preserve life* (Genesis 45:5)...*to preserve a remnant on earth...to keep alive for you many survivors*" (Genesis 45:7). In Ezekiel 18:32, God says, "*For I have no pleasure in the death of anyone... Turn, then, and live.*"

Sometimes you may clutch life, you hold onto what you believe is life giving, and ignore the life that God's grace is holding out to you, is beckoning to you, is leading you to. Martin Luther King, Jr. knew this when he said, "I still believe that standing up for the truth is the greatest thing in the world. This is the end of life. The end of life is not to be happy. The end of life is not to achieve pleasure and avoid pain. The end of life is to do the will of God, come what may."

There are people in our communities who cannot leave the life they know of drugs or of violence because that is all they have ever known. They settle for what is. They cannot imagine that life could be beautiful and loving and life giving instead of life threatening. For those who must leave their families, get new friends, move from their bad neighborhoods, learn new patterns of thinking, develop new ways of relating to others, they fear all the promises of life and grace. The Joseph story asserts that God's gracious love and commitment to life makes such miracles possible. That's why you are called to engage with them because you too, believe that new life is possible.

Prayer for the Day: *Gracious God, I choose to believe that new life is possible. Help my unbelief. Amen.*

Genesis 45:1-15   **Week 47**
                                                                                                 Friday

You might like to linger on, analyze and explain, but the Bible usually does not do so. It reveals that God acted and that's that. Biblical narrative gives you thoughts to ponder. And isn't that often the way you see God's action in your life? You are not aware of it until you look back and realize that God has acted. You may not have had a clue about the direction of your life but when you look back, you can see God's footprints in the sand carrying you.

A public speaker said that one of her jobs in the past was to go into the homes of total strangers and "take charge" by teaching a group some basic crafting skills. She had no clue that this little business she did to pay her light bill was teaching her valuable skills for her career in the public eye.

She said she was by nature an introvert. Making herself go into unknown territory, be friendly, and assume responsibility for the evening's activities taught her how to go into unknown venues and speak, prepared her for all her public appearances, and built skills for teaching others through her workshops and keynote addresses. God's actions were certainly hidden to her and very mysterious, but she relates that she can look back in awe at God's gracious love and care.

Prayer for the Day: *Challenging God, help me to say yes to those things that are of your doing for leading me into my future. Amen.*

Week 47   **Genesis 45:1-15**
Saturday

There's an old story you've probably heard of the man who proclaimed his close relationship with God. His town was flooded, and the water kept rising closer and closer to his house. The rescue squad came by in a bus and told him that everyone on his street was being asked to evacuate the premises. He said, "Thank you, but no. God will save me." The water kept rising. People came by in a boat and offered to take him to safety. He said, "Thank you, but no. God will save me." The water kept rising. He was sitting on his roof when a helicopter came by. A guy leaned out and, on a bullhorn, called, "Grab onto the ladder that we are dropping." He said, "Thank you, but no. God will save me." Finally, the water overtook him and he drowned. When he got to heaven he was sputtering and shaking water off him. He went before God and demanded, "Where were you? I had faith in you. All my life I have said that you would take care of me. Where were you? Why did you let me drown?" And the Lord said, "I sent a bus, a boat, and a helicopter for you." God's solution was not the one the man had planned.

"Probably every day of our lives, our plan goes awry. Often, we have counted heavily on a particular outcome. We generally assume we have all things under control and know exactly what's best for us...But such is not the case. There is a bigger picture than the one we see. The outcome of that picture is out of our hands. Our vision is limited, and...divinely so. However, we are able to see all that we need to see, today. And more important, if we can trust our guidance [from God], we can begin to see how each day fills in a shade more of the bigger picture of our lives. In retrospect we can see how all events have contributed, in important ways to [our lives.] Where today's events are leading, we can't know, for certain, but we can trust the divine plan" (*Each Day a New Beginning, Daily Meditations for Women, Hazelden, Sept. 8*)

The story of Joseph and his family and his God is profound in that it affirms that God's purpose is finally sovereign even while working in human time with human beings. God's purpose can create a real newness; God's purpose is utterly gracious; God's purpose is hidden and mysterious; and God's purpose is worked out in concrete history. What a wondrous God! Amen. and Amen.!

Prayer for the Day: *Wondrous God, help me to trust that my life is in your hands. Amen.*

Week 48
Psalm 85

1 Lord, you were favourable to your land;
   you restored the fortunes of Jacob.
2 You forgave the iniquity of your people;
   you pardoned all their sin. Selah.
3 You withdrew all your wrath;
   you turned from your hot anger.

4 Restore us again, O God of our salvation,
   and put away your indignation towards us.
5 Will you be angry with us for ever?
   Will you prolong your anger to all generations?
6 Will you not revive us again,
   so that your people may rejoice in you?
7 Show us your steadfast love, O Lord,
   and grant us your salvation.

8 Let me hear what God the Lord will speak,
   for he will speak peace to his people,
   to his faithful, to those who turn to him in their hearts.
9 Surely his salvation is at hand for those who fear him,
   that his glory may dwell in our land.

10 Steadfast love and faithfulness will meet;
   righteousness and peace will kiss each other.
11 Faithfulness will spring up from the ground,
   and righteousness will look down from the sky.
12 The Lord will give what is good,
   and our land will yield its increase.
13 Righteousness will go before him,
   and will make a path for his steps.

Week 48
Sunday

Psalm 85

As we approach the end of the year—either by calendar or in this book, a time of waiting and expectation begins.

Art Linkletter had a program on television decades ago where he asked children questions just to see what their responses might be. Those poignant, insightful, and often embarrassing comments ended up in a book he titled, *Kids Say the Darndest Things*. That title can aptly apply to questions children ask about God, heaven, and other things holy. A seven-year-old girl lost her beloved dachshund, Belle. Knowing that her Sunday school teacher had also recently lost her dog, Georgia, she began asking about both dogs being in heaven. The teacher said that God loves dogs and so she has to believe that God continues to love our dogs after their death. That was as far as the teacher intended to go. But children being children, the little girl asked, "Teacher, Georgia and Belle did not get along when they were alive. Do you think they still fight in heaven?"

Okay, now, this is a test. How would you answer that question?

Prayer for the Day: *God, give me answers when children seek knowledge about you. Amen.*

Psalm 85

Week 48
Monday

This psalm speaks to the questions that young girl asked and a whole lot of other things you wonder about when you think about who God is and who you are as a follower of God.

The first three verses of Psalm 85 remember what God did in ancient times. God was favorable to the land. Most likely that means that the crops succeeded, rain fell in appropriate amounts, and the land thrived. God restored the fortunes of Jacob. In other words, the people remembered when life was good. They were positive *that* good life was a gift from God.

During the shutdown time with Covid 19, you may have begun to remember the "good ole days" pre-Covid. You may have thought that everything before the pandemic was good and right. Of course, you may acknowledge that you remember selectively the things of the past. But you hold onto what was right with the world a long time ago, much as the psalmist does.

The psalm says that God forgave the iniquity of God's people. Well, at least the people admitted that they had not always lived as God wanted them to, *and* they knew that God had forgiven them, even when they may not have deserved it. God withdrew God's anger.

Do you wonder what that anger may have been about? If you choose to read this psalm as a contemporary writing and you say, "God, you withdrew all your wrath from us," what actions that are not pleasing to God might you be referring to? To the way people abuse the planet? To abandonment of people who live or flee from war torn countries? To how you hurt people you love most by ignoring them or abusing them verbally, emotionally, or physically? To how certain groups of people are always tormented, blamed, or attacked just because of the color of their skin, their choice of religion, or other reasons? To how your myths and prejudices affect your judgment and compassion? To the reality that poverty exists in this the wealthiest country in the world, and children cannot get adequate medical care? To violence being the first choice for dealing with conflict or disagreement? To how people focus on themselves to the detriment of everyone else in the world? Do these things make God angry? Should they make God angry with you?

Prayer for the Day: *God of steadfast love, rend my heart by showing me how I anger you. Amen.*

Week 48
Tuesday

Psalm 85

Verses 4-7 continue with the theme of God's anger. Interestingly these verses are excluded from the prescribed pulpit reading of this psalm. But without them, the rest of the psalm can become a little too clichéd, too sweet, too weak. The psalmist highlights the fact that God *is* angry with God's people. Might God be angry with you? If God is truly the Lord and desires for you to love God and follow what God has taught you through the prophets and especially through Jesus, then when you fail to care for others, when you neglect those abandoned in your society—those called widows, sojourners, and orphans in the Bible—when you do not share your God-given gifts, when you abandon God's ways of living for ways of your own choosing, when churches become social clubs rather than the body of the living Christ, when you find other gods to worship—gods named workaholism, technology devices, consumerism, and many others—then... God may be truly angry with you.

You know God is a God of steadfast love...*and* your God gets angry with you when you reject that love in all the ways you do that. Parents or grandparents understand that juxtaposition of love and anger. They love their children and grandchildren. They get angry with them when they do something dangerous or harmful or disrespectful. They love them and correct them out of that love. And yes, they get angry because they want so much more for them...because they love them.

Prayer for the Day: *Most merciful, I claim that when I sometimes feel your distance or anger, that may be a time when you are acting most for my benefit. Amen.*

Psalm 85

Week 48
Wednesday

Along with the psalmist, you can acknowledge God's anger and seek God's forgiveness. Listen to the psalmist's words: *Will you be angry with us forever? Will you not revive us again? Show us your steadfast love, O Lord, and grant us your salvation* (Psalm 85:5). When you experience those times where things are not going well for you, your church, your community, or your world, you can come to God—even in those times—and ask for God's intervention on your behalf, even if what you need intervention from may be God's own anger against you.

The prophets certainly understood God's anger. The prophet Isaiah says: *Comfort my people, says your God. Speak tenderly to Jerusalem, and cry to her that she has served her term, that her penalty is paid, that she has received from the Lord's hand double for all her sins* (Isaiah 40:1).

So, after acknowledging God's anger, the psalmist begs, *Let me hear what God the Lord will speak, for he will speak peace to his people* (Psalm 85:8). And what you hear about God's peace, God's salvation, is surely some of the most beautiful imagery in all of scripture.

Listen again not only with your ears but also with your heart to this from Psalm 85:10-11.

> *Steadfast love and faithfulness will meet;*
>
> *Righteousness and peace will kiss each other.*
>
> *Faithfulness will spring up from the ground*
>
> *And righteousness will look down from the sky.*

Prayer for the Day: *Most Holy God, may I embody love and faithfulness meeting, righteousness and peace kissing each other. Amen.*

Week 48 Psalm 85
Thursday

Psalm 85 "offers a vision of salvation and God's intention for this world that stretches from earth to heaven and back again" (Talitha Arnold, *Feasting on the Word*, Year B, Vol. 1, Westminster Press, 2008, p. 34). This salvation is for all who turn to God in their hearts (verse 8). The verse does not define people by skin color, socioeconomics, intelligence, political persuasion, or any other human category that is used to divide people. The verse is inclusive to those who *turn in faithfulness and trust in God...who turn to God in their hearts* (Psalm 85:8).

Steadfast love and faithfulness will meet. The Hebrew word for steadfast love is *hesed*. No single word in English captures *hesed*. Translators use words like "kindness," "loving-kindness," "mercy," "loyalty." Perhaps "loyal love" is close.

Hesed is one of the richest, most powerful words in the Old Testament. It reflects the loyal love that God has...for God's own people...and the kind of love that we, God's people, should have for one another. It is not a "mood." *Hesed* is not primarily something people "feel." Steadfast love is a verb, not a noun. It is something we DO for other people who have no claim on us.

So steadfast love and faithfulness meet. Righteousness and peace will kiss each other.

Righteousness is a word thrown around in church a lot. But most people struggle to define what it means. It can be another term for shalom, where everyone has what he or she needs to live fully the life that God is creating. A shalom world, a righteous world is a world where no one has too much, and no one has too little. It encompasses the idea that what you want for you and yours, you also want for them and theirs even when they and theirs are very different. If you want a safe home for you, then you want that for them. If you want release from fear, then you want that for them. If you want a full tummy, then you want that for them. And you strive to help that happen. That's righteousness.

You see this embodiment of right living...righteousness...kiss peace. That picture makes sense. If everyone has what he or she needs for healthy life in body, soul, and spirit, then war, violence, and brutality are not necessary. Hatred finds no place to put down roots. A kiss becomes as normal as breathing. To kiss someone means standing face to face and being very close. Peace reigns.

Prayer for the Day: *God of my salvation, thank you for the beautiful imagery of what your world can look like with righteousness, peace, faithfulness, and steadfast love. May it be so. Amen.*

Psalm 85

Week 48
Friday

Faithfulness will spring up from the ground…so the earth is involved in this salvation that God is calling forth. Righteousness will look down from the sky. The heavens, to quote another psalm, are telling the glory of God. Salvation is not just for an individual. Salvation is described as where people live in and with steadfast love, have deep care for each other, are faithful to God and each other, and seek right relationships here and around the world. The whole universe is involved.

You can hear an echo of the angels' words to the shepherds, Glory to God in the highest and on earth, peace, goodwill to all. Maybe you could commit to memory this vision where, again from verses 10-11:

Steadfast love and faithfulness will meet;
Righteousness and peace will kiss each other.
Faithfulness will spring up from the ground
And righteousness will look down from the sky.

This is the message of the Christ whose birth will soon be celebrated. You are not waiting just for a babe to be born. You are waiting for the world that Jesus showed, where death is no more, where there is no mourning and crying. A world where pain will be no more. This is salvation…where Jesus showed us what righteousness, faithfulness, and steadfast love look like. Where the first become last, the tax collector is one of the inner circle, the woman who bled could reach out and be healed, the hungry were fed, the powers were chastised, the children were welcomed. This is salvation of the world for whom Christ died.

Prayer for the Day: *God of the weak, surround me with the message of steadfast love during the next few weeks so I do not get ground up in the "Christmas Machine." Amen.*

Week 48
Saturday

Psalm 85

The psalm's description of salvation is more than words that you say. This salvation is about the actions that you do, how you live, how you love. "When steadfast love and faithfulness meet in our lives, when righteousness and peace embrace in our business practices, our family relations, or our nation's policies, God's salvation is at hand. When we work for justice, we make way for God in our world" (Talitha Arnold, "Pastoral Perspective, Year B, Advent II, Ps. 85:1-2, 8-13, *Feasting on the Word*, p. 36).

So…will Georgia and Belle get along in heaven? Yes, because of God's kind of peace.

The last verse of this psalm is: *Righteousness will go before him, and will make a path for his steps* (Psalm 85:13). This path is the path that God walked in the Garden of Eden, the path that Jesus, the Messiah walked as a human on earth showing you how to live, and is the path that has been blazed in the crucifixion and resurrection for you to walk as God's faithful person who lives with steadfast love, righteousness, faithfulness, and peace. *Righteousness will go before him, and will make a path for his steps.*

Prayer for the Day: *God of salvation, help me live and act and think and feel with faithfulness, steadfast love, righteousness, and peace. Amen.*

Week 49
Luke 1:68-79

68 Blessed be the Lord God of Israel, for he has looked favourably on his people and redeemed them.
69 He has raised up a mighty saviour for us in the house of his servant David,
70 as he spoke through the mouth of his holy prophets from of old,
71 that we would be saved from our enemies and from the hand of all who hate us.
72 Thus he has shown the mercy promised to our ancestors, and has remembered his holy covenant,
73 the oath that he swore to our ancestor Abraham, to grant us
74 that we, being rescued from the hands of our enemies, might serve him without fear,
75 in holiness and righteousness before him all our days.
76 And you, child, will be called the prophet of the Most High; for you will go before the Lord to prepare his ways,
77 to give knowledge of salvation to his people by the forgiveness of their sins.
78 By the tender mercy of our God, the dawn from on high will break upon us,
79 to give light to those who sit in darkness and in the shadow of death, to guide our feet into the way of peace.

Week 49   **Luke 1:68-79**
Sunday

Zechariah was married to Elizabeth, a cousin of Mary, mother of Jesus. Zechariah and Elizabeth had a decent life. They kept all the commandments and regulations of the Lord. Zechariah was a respected priest in the Temple. There was joy in their lives because they kept God's law. They were well-to-do since he was a priest and she was descended from Aaron, the brother of Moses. Elizabeth was not totally happy because she could not bear a child. A time or two when she thought she was pregnant, her heart would soar. But then she would discover that she was not going to be a mother.

Even though Elizabeth was married to a well-respected man, she was seen as a failure because she could not give him children. Her wonderful husband, Zechariah, did not have the full status he so richly deserved because he had no heir.

Elizabeth finally reconciled herself to her inadequacies. She was getting past the age of childbearing. She contented herself with caring for others who needed mothering. Zechariah would let her know of some special need in the community so she could reach out to the person or family, trying to show God's love and care for them (Templeton, *Conversations on the Porch*, p. 93-94).

Little did she know how things were going to change for her and her husband.

Prayer for the Day: *God of miracles, prepare my heart for the birth of your Son. Amen.*

Luke 1:68-79

**Week 49
Monday**

One day Zechariah was serving in the Temple. As was the custom, lots were drawn to see which priest would be honored and allowed to enter the sanctuary. Zechariah's lot was drawn. He entered and offered incense. While he was inside, the entire assembly of people was outside praying. But then something strange happened. Zechariah saw an angel of the Lord standing to the right side of the altar of incense. Needless to say, he was terrified. Fear overwhelmed him.

The angel said, *Do not be afraid, Zechariah, for your prayer has been heard. Your wife Elizabeth will bear you a son, and you will name him John* (Luke 1:13).

Zechariah's eyes got huge. He gulped. As he tried to catch his breath, he heard the angel continue. *You will have joy and gladness, and many will rejoice at his birth, for he will be great in the sight of the Lord. He must never drink wine or strong drink; even before his birth, he will be filled with the Holy Spirit* (Luke 1:14). Zechariah tried to absorb everything the angel was telling him.

The angel continued: *He will turn many of the people of Israel to the Lord their God. With the spirit and power of Elijah he will go before him, to turn the hearts of parents to their children, and the disobedient to the wisdom of the righteous, to make ready a people prepared for the Lord* (Luke 1:16-17).

Then Zechariah found his voice. He asked, *How will I know that this is so? For I am an old man, and my wife is getting on in years* (Luke 1:18).

The angel replied, *I am Gabriel. I stand in the presence of God, and I have been sent to speak to you and to bring you this good news. But now, because you did not believe my words, which will be fulfilled in their time, you will become mute, unable to speak, until the day these things occur* (Luke 1:19-20).

Prayer for the Day: *God, as I move into the days of hope, waiting, joy, and peace during this time of preparing for my Lord's birth, warm my heart with the awesomeness of what is happening. Amen.*

Week 49
Tuesday

Luke 1:68-79

Zechariah stayed in the sanctuary longer than was customary because of his conversation with the angel. The people outside wondered what was causing the delay. When Zechariah finally emerged and could not speak, they realized that he had seen a vision. As much as he tried to speak to tell them the amazing message he had received, he could not. When he finished his priestly obligations, he went home.

Elizabeth did indeed become pregnant. For nine months, Zechariah had time to ponder what he'd heard from the angel. He studied the stories, prophecies, and traditions of Elijah since the angel said that Elijah's spirit and power would lead his son. The tradition taught that Elijah returned to children and old people alike. He gave wings to people's imaginations. Elijah was seen in the Jewish culture as necessary hope and the reality of fantasy. Zechariah, of course, knew these things about the prophet Elijah.

Elie Wiesel said that "[Elijah] was tough, fierce, cruel, irascible, inflexible, …a destroyer of false idols and their worshipers…He reject[ed] weaknesses and compromises…His mission [was] to punish complacent kings and their flatterers, to bend the vain and encourage the humble, to show the great how small they are, and the mighty how vulnerable they are…He unmask[ed] hypocrisy and falsehood" (Elie Wiesel, *Five Biblical Portraits*, University of Notre Dame Press: London, 1981, pp 41-42).

This *is* the man whose spirit and power the angel Gabriel said would lead Zechariah's son. Was this who Zechariah's son would be?

Prayer for the Day: *God of wonders, remind me that you are with me no matter what. Amen.*

Luke 1:68-79

**Week 49
Wednesday**

Zechariah also pondered the prophet Isaiah's words: *A voice cries out: "In the wilderness prepare the way of the Lord, make straight in the desert a highway for our God. Every valley shall be lifted up and every mountain and hill be made low... Then the glory of the Lord shall be revealed, and all people shall see it together, for the mouth of the Lord has spoken"* (Isaiah 40:3-5).

Randle Mixon suggests that Zechariah, whose name means "God remembered," had time to "consider the entire course of his life—his faithful service as a priest, his faithful love for Elizabeth, this faithful belief that God would redeem his people. He [had] time to consider the long arc of his life and how it has been disrupted by the sudden appearance of the holy at a time and in a manner he was not expecting" (Randle R. Mixon, *Feasting on the Word, Year C, Vol 1*, p. 37).

For all the months of Elizabeth's pregnancy, Zechariah thought of these things. He tried to let Elizabeth know some of what was happening in his heart and soul, but no speech made that difficult. However, she understood that she was going to have a son whose name would be John.

Prayer for the Day: *God of silence, bring me to the silence of contemplation to consider who you are in my life and what you are calling me to do and be. Amen.*

Week 49
Thursday

Luke 1:68-79

When it came time for the birth, everyone rejoiced with Elizabeth and Zechariah over God's mercy to them. On the eighth day, the naming and circumcising day, the people gathered there pronounced that the child's name would be Zechariah, after his father which was the custom. But Elizabeth challenged them by saying, "*No, he is to be called John*" (Luke 1:60). The crowd would not be swayed by Elizabeth's announcement and so they gestured to Zechariah for him to confirm that his son would bear *his* name. Zechariah asked for a tablet. He wrote: "His name is John." The people were truly amazed. This just was not done. But then Zechariah discovered that he could once again speak. The first words out of his mouth were praise for God. The people whispered among themselves about this newborn child. Who was he? Who would he become? He was obviously chosen by the Lord God. But for what? For whom?

The story was eventually told over and over until it reached the entire hill country of Judea.

Zechariah was filled to overflowing with the power of God's Spirit. The formerly speechless man was now full of exaltation. He sang of God's favorable connections with his people in the past as he redeemed them.

Zechariah was filled with praise of King David, chosen by God to save them from their enemies and from the hand of all who hated them. He sang of God's mercy to their ancestors of old, God's holy covenant, of being rescued from the hands of enemies. He demonstrated he wanted to serve his God without fear, in holiness and righteousness in all the ways of his life.

Prayer for the Day: *God of Elizabeth and Zechariah, may I join with them in celebrating the gifts of life you provide. Amen.*

Luke 1:68-79   **Week 49 / Friday**

This new father was overcome with joy and praise to the God who had made all this happen. Can you relate to this kind of joy? Have you ever been overwhelmed with how God has been evident in your life, in the lives of your foremothers and forefathers, your world? Or are you so numbed with the news you absorb, the grind of getting through each day, the tedium of life itself, that this kind of singing is beyond anything you can imagine? Taking time…or having time forced upon you…to be still and know that God is God…can be a true gift.

Maybe Zechariah's time of silence gave him time and pause to remember… to remember the God he served as priest, to revel in the reality that he was about to be a father, to go back to ancient texts and remind himself again of how God had been with God's people even when it did not seem that way.

Zechariah's response to the return of his voice certainly reinforces that he'd been given a tremendous blessing by God because then he moves into a prophecy about his son, this wonderful gift from God. He says that his son John will be called a prophet of the most high. This John is the man who baptized Jesus. In many ways this John introduced Jesus to the populace. He truly was a prophet for the Savior of the world.

Prayer for the Day: *God of all possibilities, help me to believe that. Amen.*

Week 49
Saturday

Luke 1:68-79

Zechariah foretold that his son would go ahead of the Lord to get everything ready for him. He said, *"You will tell [the Lord's] people that they can be saved when their sins are forgiven"* (Luke 1:76-77 CEV).

And then Zechariah gives words for you to hold onto. He said: *God's love and kindness will shine upon us like the sun rises in the sky* (Luke 1:78 CEV). Just as the sun rises every single day, God's love and kindness will be with you. Sometimes you will not see it just like some days you cannot see the sun, but you know it is there…because there is some light even on the darkest days.

And Zechariah has obviously experienced some of the darkest days because he ends his song with: *On us who live in the dark shadow of death this light…[this light, Jesus the Light of the World, this light] will shine to guide us into a life of peace* (Luke 1:78-78 CEV).

This is a needed message. You need to know that God is with you. You need to know that someone can be interrupted in going about everyday responsibilities and learn that God has unbelievable plans that you could never imagine. You need to be silenced for a time, especially during this season, to meditate on what faith means to you, and what faith means in your life. You need to patiently wait for a gestation time for a new thing of God to come to pass. You need to trust the Spirit that what seems at first frightening can turn out to be amazing not only for yourself but even for the entire world. You need to stand against the popular opinions of those who tell you the son's name is Zechariah when you know it is John. You need to sing your praises to God for God's amazing care. You need to affirm your children by acknowledging that God has plans for each one of them. You need to find the Zechariahs and Elizabeths in your life, in yourself.

Imagine that *this* is the Moment
of holy in-breaking,
because it is.
It always is.
Imagine that *this* is the One
for whom we yearn,
because it just might be.
It really might be.
This may be the Moment,
this may be the One
that will split your heart wide open.
Be ready.

*Used with permission, Elaine Nocks, 2019

Prayer for the Day: *Beloved God, I need to know that you are with me. Help me wait patiently for a gestation time for your new thing in my life to come to pass. Amen.*

Week 50
Luke 1:46-55

46 "My soul magnifies the Lord,

47 and my spirit rejoices in God my Saviour,

48 for he has looked with favour on the lowliness of his servant. Surely, from now on all generations will call me blessed;

49 for the Mighty One has done great things for me, and holy is his name.

50 His mercy is for those who fear him from generation to generation.

51 He has shown strength with his arm; he has scattered the proud in the thoughts of their hearts.

52 He has brought down the powerful from their thrones, and lifted up the lowly;

53 He has filled the hungry with good things, and sent the rich away empty.

54 He has helped his servant Israel, in remembrance of his mercy,

55 according to the promise he made to our ancestors, to Abraham and to his descendants for ever."

Week 50
Sunday

Luke 1:46-55

In using a compilation of various versions and paraphrases of this passage, you may be able to hear it a bit differently this time. Mary sings:

> v. 47 I'm bursting with God-news;
>   I'm dancing the song of my savior God (m)
> v. 48 God cares for me, his humble servant.
>   From now on, all people will say God has blessed me (c)
> v. 49 For you, the Almighty, have done great things for me,
>   and holy is your name, set apart from all others (i & m)
> v. 50 Your mercy, O God, reaches from age to age
>   for those who are in awe of you (i & m)
> v. 51 You have bared your arm and shown your strength,
>   to scatter those who are proud in their conceit (c & i)
> v. 52 You have knocked tyrants off their high horses
>   and put humble people in places of power (m & c)
> v. 53 You have filled the hungry with good things
>   while you have sent the rich away empty (i)
> v. 54 You have come to the aid of Israel, your servant,
>   mindful of your mercy—(i)
> v. 55 the promise you made to our ancestors—
>   to Sarah and Abraham and their descendants forever (i)
>
> m = Eugene H. Peterson, *The Message*
> c = *The Contemporary English Version*
> i = Priests for Equality, *The Inclusive New Testament*

Prayer for the Day: *God of good news, I too want to burst with joy from your love, grace, and forgiveness. Amen.*

Luke 1:46-55   **Week 50**
Monday

The setting for the song is Mary's visit to Elizabeth. Mary went to her cousin after learning that she was to give birth to the Son of the Most High. Elizabeth confirmed what the angel Gabriel had told Mary.

Don't you sometimes look for an Elizabeth in your own life...someone who will confirm what you believe in your inmost heart? Sometimes you know on a deep level what God is calling you to do but you are afraid to fully embrace that call. You try to talk yourself out of it. You convince yourself that you are foolish to even be thinking that way. You list all the roadblocks for why you cannot pursue the dream which God has planted in your innermost being. You, too, yearn for someone to help you take that next challenging step. You can be Elizabeth for another while you discern who can be Elizabeth for you.

Prayer for the Day: *Jesus, please send me an Elizabeth. Amen.*

Week 50
Tuesday

Luke 1:46-55

The first three verses sing of Mary's joy in what God has done and is doing in her life. Listen again to the exhilaration. *"I'm bursting with God-news. I'm dancing the song of my Savior God. God cares for me... From now on, all people will say God has blessed me... The Almighty has done great things for me."* Her joy invites you to jump up from your chair, to start moving your body to music which you hear in your heart, and to sing of your love for God and God's love for you.

Or maybe you do not feel that way? Maybe you are such a product of the "whatever" culture that you hear the words and think, "That's nice" and continue your life... all the while missing the point.

Why in the world is Mary so full of joy and praise? She has been told that she is going to have a baby in a most unusual way. Her betrothed, Joseph, is not going to be the baby's father. When she begins showing her condition, the gossips are going to have a field day. She has left her own home in the early days of her pregnancy and traveled to the hill country to be with her cousin Elizabeth, who, surprisingly, as it turns out, is also pregnant. Mary may have been experiencing morning sickness since she was in her first trimester. Why is she so happy?

Prayer for the Day: *God of joy, thank you for those times of unexplained delight. Amen.*

Luke 1:46-55

Week 50
Wednesday

Even though Elizabeth confirmed what Mary already knew, even though Mary now knew that she was not crazy…her joy still seems over the top for the situation. That is, until you look at the next verses. God scattered those who are proud, knocked tyrants off their high horse, put humble people in places of power, filled the hungry with good things, sent the rich away empty.

Mary sees those very things happening in her own life. She was lowly. She was already engaged to Joseph. She had never borne a child. She was not learned in the scriptures. Why in the world would God choose someone such as she to be the mother of God's son? It made no sense. It was the craziest thing that could have happened…to think that God would choose to come into the world the way all humans did…through childbirth as a baby…being vulnerable, immature, with wet swaddling cloths. And yet that is the very thing that God had announced would happen.

God's choosing to come into the world as the baby of a peasant family was as ridiculous as the hungry being fed and the powerful being toppled. In her own life, Mary was experiencing a complete toppling of the natural order, of the way things should be. She was literally experiencing in her body a reversal of the general expectations of the world. These kinds of things were not supposed to happen, and especially not to someone who had no position, no authority, no prestige. When the realization of all this hit her, what else could she do but sing and dance? "I'm bursting with God-news. I'm dancing the song of my Savior God."

Prayer for the Day: *God of all possibilities, help me believe that. Amen.*

Week 50
Thursday

Luke 1:46-55

OK, that's Mary. But what about you? You may already enjoy that kind of relationship with your Holy God. Or you may yearn for such feelings to well up in you. Wouldn't you love to have that same kind of ecstatic experience with your God?

Look back at verses 51-53, this time using the New Revised Standard Version. *God has shown strength with his arm; [God] has scattered the proud in the thoughts of their hearts. [God] has brought down the powerful from their thrones and* [has] *lifted up the lowly; [God] has filled the hungry with good things, and* [has] *sent the rich away empty.* All of these verbs are past tense, as if they have already happened!

What a puzzle. You know that tyrants still rule. You know that people are still hungry. You know that rich people are not empty, and that lowly people are still lowly. So why in the world does Mary sing as if all these things have already happened for everyone? She, indeed, has experienced for herself a reversal in the way things normally are. But what about you and everyone else?

Prayer for the Day: *God who overcomes death, life, angels, rulers, things present, things to come, powers, heights, depths, and everything else in all creation: sometimes I need a sign. Is there a possibility that you can provide assurance for me? Amen.*

Luke 1:46-55   **Week 50**
      Friday

To help with your understanding, here is a small lesson about Biblical interpretation here. There is a verb tense in Greek for which there is no English translation. That tense is called aorist. It is a past tense verb, but it does not carry the idea of being only in the past once and forevermore. Here's an illustration. If you have children, you loved them when they were born. But you continued to love them as they grew. You still love them and will continue to love them until the day that you die. You used the aorist tense when you said you loved your children when they were born, listeners would have known that you have loved them, you love them now, and you will continue to love them in the future.

The verbs in Mary's song are in aorist tense. God has already done all these things. God is doing these things now and will continue to accomplish all these things.

Mary's song leads you to look at God's activity so you can claim for yourself what God values for God's world. God values lowly people and hungry people. Uh-oh. That may leave you and most of your friends and colleagues out. God does not place much value on powerful people or rich people. You really are in trouble.

Prayer for the Day: *Creation yearns for your light to renew us once again. I beg for your presence. I crave tangible evidence of peace and hope. I hunger for your joy that is greater than my understanding. I await your coming. Please hurry. Amen.*

Week 50   **Luke 1:46-55**
Saturday

Now at this point in this discussion, you might write a check or call your broker and give a hefty sum of money to help the lowly and hungry. You might even decide to give one day of your holidays to help others. All that is commendable. But that is not what this song, or indeed even the whole of the gospel, is about. It is not about doing one's duty. It is not about acting from guilt. It is not about giving a proportional share of your income. All that is a wonderful first step. But that is not what you are really called to do.

Back to Mary's exultation. "I'm bursting with God-news. I'm dancing the song of my savior God." This is not about duty. This is not about figuring out if the tithe comes from the before tax or after-tax income. This is about a wonderful, magnificent, astounding personal relationship with the Lord God Almighty. And how does that happen? Look again at the song. When the proud are no longer proud in and of themselves, when the tyrants are no longer tyrants, when people who are low are now visible and acknowledged, when the rich no longer define themselves by what they have, when people's stomachs are filled every day. This is how you are in relationship with God.

How much plainer can it be? Jesus said, *"Truly I tell you, just as you did it to one of the least of these who are members of my family, you did it to me"* (Matthew 25:40).

This song is not about guilt or pressure to write an end-of-the-year check. This passage is about pure, unadulterated, gleeful joy which happens in God's world… where everyone has what he or she needs, where society has a healthy balance to it. The marvelous thing is that God is already bringing these things to happen. What good news for those who suffer and are heavy laden. God is giving them rest and will continue to give them rest. What good news for those without power. God has, is, and will give them power.

Prayer for the Day: *My source and my end, thank you for the myriad ways you let me know you are in me, around me, beside me, in front of me, behind me, and under me. You are my source and will be my end, now and forever. Amen.*

Week 51
Psalm 80:1-7, 17-19

Give ear, O Shepherd of Israel, you who lead Joseph like a flock!
You who are enthroned upon the cherubim, shine forth
2 before Ephraim and Benjamin and Manasseh. Stir up your
    might, and come to save us!
3 Restore us, O God;
    let your face shine, that we may be saved.

4 O Lord God of hosts,
    how long will you be angry with your people's prayers?
5 You have fed them with the bread of tears,
    and given them tears to drink in full measure.
6 You make us the scorn of our neighbours;
    our enemies laugh among themselves.
7 Restore us, O God of hosts;
    let your face shine, that we may be saved.

17 But let your hand be upon the one at your right hand,
    the one whom you made strong for yourself.
18 Then we will never turn back from you;
    give us life, and we will call on your name.
19 Restore us, O Lord God of hosts;
    let your face shine, that we may be saved.

Week 51
Sunday
Psalm 80:1-7, 17-19

If you've been reading these devotionals on a calendar year basis, you may wonder why this psalm appears here, as we move toward Christmas. It just doesn't ring of Christmas cheer. Instead, it is a psalm where the people feel abandoned by God. Listen to the psalmist's words: *You make us the scorn of our neighbors; our enemies laugh at us* (Psalm 80:6).

Three separate times in this reading are the words, *Let your face shine, that we may be saved* (Psalm 80:3, 7, 19).

Obviously, people believed that they needed saving. But from what? Who knows? But you may know some folks who would love to be saved from all the Christmas hope, peace, joy, and love. If that describes someone you know, then this psalm can be a balm to their spirit because the people of Israel also called out to God for God's salvation. They believed that God's face would shine on them. They trusted God even in the midst of their sense of abandonment. You can pray that people you care about, too, will find God's love in the midst of this time that may be painful for them. You can yearn for them to get through the holiday and find comfort in some way, maybe by your reaching out to them or by their reaching out to someone. Hopefully, they will discover God's love in unexpected ways and in unexpected places.

Maybe you will find ways to be with people who experience this time of the year as painful. Pray that you will accept their feelings and not try to wrap them up into bright paper and tinsel. The pain this psalm talks of is very real, and you need to be aware of that in yourself, your family, churches, community, and friends.

Prayer for the Day: *God of hope, the song Blue Christmas reminds me that there are people you care about who need reminding of that by me and others. Amen.*

Psalm 80:1-7, 17-19   **Week 51**
                                                                                                Monday

Yes, this psalm powerfully articulates the reality of the feelings of "being abandoned by God." Wouldn't be nice to move on to the joy and love of the season? Don't you want to be filled with Christmas cheer and good feelings?

Of course, but that is not faithful to this reading. E. Lane Alderman, Jr. says that the people of this psalm tell of "experiencing the misery of life without God, an unsustainable life in which every other relationship is out of joint" (Pastoral Perspective, *Feasting on the Word*, Year 1, Vol. 1, p. 85). And honestly, haven't you felt this at some time?

Possibly even Mary and Joseph felt this on their trip from Nazareth to Bethlehem.

Prayer for the Day: *God of presence, I am so glad that the scriptures tell of people feeling abandoned by you like I do sometimes. I guess those feelings are acceptable? Amen.*

Week 51   **Psalm 80:1-7, 17-19**
Tuesday

Join the weary couple as they make their journey to the town of Joseph's birth to register for taxation purposes. Listen in on the conversation between the couple. Mary is speaking to Joseph.

"Oh, husband. I am so tired. My back hurts. I am exhausted from sitting on this donkey for such long hours. Help me down so I can walk alongside of you for a while. This baby is kicking hard, and maybe if I walk, I can find some comfort.

Joseph helps Mary to her feet. He stands by her as she regains her balance. Lines of worry cross his forehead. He knows that her time must be near, and they still have much distance to cover before they arrive in Bethlehem. The journey has been so tedious and could not have come at a worse time.

Prayer for the Day: *Holy Savior, knowing Mary and Joseph as real people and not pictures on a Christmas card or figurines under the Christmas tree is heart-opening for me. Thank you. Amen.*

Psalm 80:1-7, 17-19   **Week 51**
Wednesday

As Joseph and Mary begin to walk in front of the donkey, Joseph muses. He thinks, "I wish I could believe that the dream I had about Mary was as fresh for me today as it was when I first dreamed it. I had learned that Mary was pregnant, and I knew that I was not the father. However, I care deeply for this young girl and wanted to do the honorable thing by her. I decided I would quietly put her away. I could have had her stoned, but I could not abide the thought of my sweet Mary...I cannot even finish that thought. It is too painful. And then I had that dream where the angel told me, *Joseph, son of David, do not be afraid to take Mary as your wife, for the child conceived in her is from the Holy Spirit. She will bear a son, and you are to name him Jesus, for he will save his people from their sins* (Matthew 1:20-21). At the time the dream seemed so real. I believed that this child Mary is carrying was truly sent to me by God. How that happened I cannot explain but I was certain that I would become the father of this son and raise him according to the prophets' teachings. I would teach him how to be a good carpenter. I would be a good father to the boy.

"But now, now, I'm not so sure. We've been walking along this road. I'm tired. I'm remembering the disorientation we experienced when it became evident that Mary was with child. I remember how our neighbors whispered about us, and some even scorned us. We certainly did not tell them that we each had been visited by angels. They did not and do not understand what is happening to us. *We* do not really understand what is happening to us.

"And God, I don't understand all this either. Where are you? Aren't you supposed to be taking care of us? Why do we have to walk this long journey from Nazareth to Bethlehem just at the very time when this child you tell me is yours is to be born? I don't understand. I feel as if you have been feeding us with bread of fears and filled our cups with tears. Mary certainly is weepy, but I've been told that women can get this way when they are pregnant. O God, shine your face on us that we may be saved."

Prayer for the Day: *Loving God, amid times of confusion, thank you for encouraging me to bring those feelings to you. Amen.*

Week 51   **Psalm 80:1-7, 17-19**
Thursday

The couple continued to walk along, sharing water from their bag and eating a little bread when they stopped to rest. They shared food with some of their companions, each family providing what they could: bread, wine, figs, cheese, or whatever other meager items they may have had. The women travelers were especially kind to Mary because they could see how uncomfortable she was.

Mary did not complain aloud but she pulled into herself with her thoughts. She was ready for this baby to be born, but she certainly did not want her son to be born on the side of the road. She too wondered about the visit from the angel. Was it truly real? Had she only imagined it?

As she walked, Mary tried to remember all the angel's words to her: *He said, Greetings, favored one! The Lord is with you. Do not be afraid, Mary, for you have found favor with God. And now, you will conceive in your womb and bear a son, and you will name him Jesus. He will be great and will be called the Son of the Most High, and the Lord God will give to him the throne of his ancestor David. He will reign over the house of Jacob forever, and of his kingdom there will be no end* (Luke 1:28, 30-34).

For nine months, Mary had a lot to ponder. On the journey, Mary knew that she had no more clue about her future than any other mother has about the future when discovering that she is pregnant. As the miles passed, Mary wondered, "Why was I chosen for this responsibility? Do I believe that I have been honored... or punished? What does it mean to be the mother of the Son of the Most High? What is going to happen between Joseph and me? How in the world do you train someone to become the heir to the throne of David? What is God asking me to do? Why is God asking me to do this? Is there any way to say *no* to God? Where is God now? Is God on this road with us? I don't feel the presence of the Most Holy One. I simply feel weary and weepy."

Prayer for the Day: *Most wondrous God, fill me with peace...not anxiety; joy...not cattiness; love...not judgment; compassion...not hurry; hope...not resignation; faith...not abandonment. Amen.*

Psalm 80:1-7, 17-19

Week 51
Friday

And then the thought crossed Mary's mind that giving birth to the Son of the Most High might mean the circumstances for the birth would be vastly different than what they actually turned out to be. Having the Son of God on the side of the road or even in a barn? Outrageous! Mary wondered again if she had had some fantastic dream and that her understanding of the specialness of her baby was only a figment of her imagination. She knew that she already desperately loved her son, but she was confused about so much else.

Mary remembered the laughter of the neighbors. She had many moments when she wondered where God was. She would sometimes walk away from the village so she could look at the shepherds in the far field. She well understood the psalmist's plea to God, the Shepherd of Israel. She yearned for God's might to save her and her family. But at times, she felt that God had turned away.

After a while, Mary asked Joseph to stop once again so she could rest. She looked up at her husband with both fear and faith in her eyes. Joseph realized that the baby's movements must be making Mary very uncomfortable. He gazed at her with a full heart. He pleaded with God using the ancient words of the psalmist. He prayed: *Let your hand be upon the one at your right hand, the one whom you made strong for yourself. Then we will never turn back from you; give us life, and we will call on your name* (Psalm 80:17-18).

As he helped Mary settle once again on the donkey, she said with tears in her eyes, "My dear husband, I have to believe that with you and God, this journey will turn out okay. God will give us life in the form of our son, a boy whom we'll call Jesus. Beyond that, I do not know what the future holds for us, but I know that God's face will shine on us. We'll see God's light when we first look at the face of our baby boy. We will be saved because of who God is."

Companions on the journey chatted with the couple as they traveled on the road. They sensed that something was special about Mary and Joseph. Yes, they were obviously country people. Yes, they were tired. Yes, Mary was especially anxious because she knew that her time was near. Yes, they seemed distracted at times. But there was something…something about this couple as they walked toward their future.

Prayer for the Day: *O Lord God of hosts, restore me. Let your light shine, that I may be saved. Amen.*

Week 51
Saturday   Psalm 80:1-7, 17-19

Today you are challenged to think about how you love, especially those people for whom God seems absent. In this time in history, there are people wandering roads far from their homes because of political reasons, just as Joseph and Mary had to do. There are people who yearn for God's light to shine on them. You may seek God's light in your own life.

In just a few days, Christmas will celebrate Love becoming human, in the form of a baby. You can seek to love others as you would love this baby—a baby, who needs to be fed, cuddled, kept clean and warm. You will welcome this child once again into your life. In welcoming *this* child, you can welcome all children, rich and poor, with different colors of skin, and with varying capabilities. You can be part of God's love as you allow that love to reflect from your own face and be revealed in your own ways of reaching out to the Christ child and all children.

If you but look, you will find God's light shining in your life, leading you on your own journey to Bethlehem where the love of God becomes absolutely, positively real for you. You can experience God's love and know that you are living in the fullness of life beyond your wildest imagination. You will know that your good shepherd is protecting you and saving you. You will know… you *will* know that you will have life abundant.

Prayer for the Day: *Restore me, O Shepherd of Israel: let your face shine, that I may be saved. Amen.*

Week 52
Luke 2:1-7

In those days a decree went out from Emperor Augustus that all the world should be registered. 2 This was the first registration and was taken while Quirinius was governor of Syria. 3 All went to their own towns to be registered. 4 Joseph also went from the town of Nazareth in Galilee to Judea, to the city of David called Bethlehem, because he was descended from the house and family of David. 5 He went to be registered with Mary, to whom he was engaged and who was expecting a child.

6 While they were there, the time came for her to deliver her child. 7 And she gave birth to her firstborn son and wrapped him in bands of cloth, and laid him in a manger, because there was no place for them in the inn.

Week 52
Sunday

Luke 2:1-7

In just a few days, you will celebrate the coming of the baby Jesus. How do you welcome Christ into your life?

Jesus was hardly welcomed even prior to his birth. When Mary and Joseph went to the innkeeper, they were told there was no room in the inn.

When James Welch was pastor at MacPherson Presbyterian Church in Fayetteville, NC, he told this story of a nativity play performed by the first graders. The children had practiced their lines and had finally gotten their bathrobes tied so they would not trip over them. The head dresses were a little off balance. The room was filled with expectant parents, grandparents, and church members who remembered their own performances years ago in their youth. They watched the children go through the pageantry of the Christmas story. But during this performance, the story took a twist. "When Joseph came into the inn and asked if there was room, the little boy playing the innkeeper replied, 'You're lucky. We just had a cancellation'" ("Proclaiming the Good News of God's Peace," *2000 Advent Devotions*, Presbyterian Peacemaking Program).

Prayer for the Day: *God of Love, help me make room for you amidst all the activities of the holiday. Amen.*

Luke 2:1-7 Week 52
Monday

Your first reaction to this version of the nativity story may be: "All right, the holy family finally gets out of the night air and into shelter." And then…then listen to the real message in the child's response, "You're lucky. We just had a cancellation."

Is this how you welcome Christ into your life? "You're lucky, Christ. We just had a cancellation." Do you allow Christ in only when you have a cancellation? Only when you can make room in your life?

In the Gospel of John (5:40-43), Jesus says scathing words for those around him and for us. He says, *"You refuse to come to me to have life. …I know that you do not have the love of God in you."* It's horrifying that Jesus might even *think* that you don't have the love of God in you, much less say it. And yet when you are honest, you acknowledge that Christ is lucky *if* you have time to give to him. Because of work, family, holiday preparations and celebrations, financial headaches and so on, there is simply no time to fully allow Christ to come in. Most often you are one of the ones telling Christ there is no room in the inn. Jesus the Christ, Lord of the Universe, is simply not very lucky with you very often.

Prayer for the Day: *Blessed one, forgive me for being too busy for you. Amen.*

Week 52   **Luke 2:1-7**
Tuesday

So how can you increase your "hospitality quotient"? How can you show that you love God? How can you demonstrate that you want to embrace this baby who will grow to adulthood for your salvation? How can you celebrate Christmas in your heart, your home, your life?

First, you ask yourself if you really want God to dwell in your life. Your obvious answer is "Yes, of course, I want Jesus in my life. Jesus is already in my life. What a silly question." But if you dare ask that question again and think about the consequences of your answers, you may be a little more hesitant in your reply. In I Thessalonians 3:12-13, Paul says, in the earliest writing we have in the New Testament: *"May the Lord make you increase and abound in love for one another and for all, just as we abound in love for you."*

May the Lord make you increase and abound in love for one another and for all...

Psalm 25:10 reinforces with: *All the paths of the Lord are steadfast love and faithfulness, for those who keep his covenant and his decrees.*

There's a Beatles song "All You Need Is Love." And that's what love of God calls you to: love, love, love, love, love.

Prayer for the Day: *God of love, that's what I want to do: love, love, love, love. Amen.*

Luke 2:1-7

Week 52
Wednesday

The love of God is not a valentine kind of love or the love spoken of in cute Christmas cards. God's kind of loving calls you to love actively...as a choice. To love as God loves is to choose to love people who are unlovable.

Will Campbell was a Baptist minister, author, country farmer, and also the model of the character Pastor Will B. Dunn in the old comic strip Kudzu. He astounded everyone when he reached out to the Ku Klux Klan in Christian love even when he was opposed to everything they believed in and everything they did to terrorize black people. He said that God created people in the Klan just as God created him and that God demanded that we love. How, he asked, can we expect people to love as God loves if we do not love them?

This kind of love may be a big stretch for you. You just cannot see yourself loving someone who hurts people you love or who can hurt you. It may be *some* comfort to realize that God does not ask you to like "the enemy" but God does ask you to love...to seek for them what you seek for yourself... compassion, acceptance, healing for old and new hurts, people who see through the bad you to the good you.

Prayer for the Day: *Jesus, Messiah, thank you for this day when I remember that you chose to become human like me. What a miraculous and special gift. Amen.*

Week 52
Thursday

Luke 2:1-7

The love that Jesus calls you to is the kind he had when he reached out to the untouchables—the crippled, the disgusting, the poor, the outcasts. The Pharisees constantly contended with Jesus about how he lived out faith. In love he challenged the Pharisees who used rules rather than love as the way to be holy. Jesus even taught one Pharisee, Nicodemus, using perhaps the most popular verse in the Bible: *"For God so loved the world that he gave his only begotten Son, so that everyone who believes in him may not perish but may have everlasting life"* (John 3:16).

Jesus even loved the men on either side of the cross with him as well as his tormentors. Remember that he said, *"Father, forgive them for they know not what they do."* (Luke 23:34).

Prayer for the Day: *Christ, open my heart to reflect your love to others. Amen.*

Luke 2:1-7 **Week 52**
Friday

Love, intentional, deliberate love...an easy concept but not so easy to do. In fact, the only way to love as God desires is to ask God to love through you. Only God can help you find the gleam of divinity in another person, a gleam that you can claim as God's light in that person. Whereas you may see only someone who is filthy or who is hateful, God may see a person who needs a surprise dose of unexpected love. Where you may see only someone who is disgusting, God may see a person who is disgraced, in other words, who is without grace or, more accurately, without the experience of grace.

When you see babies, they are all cute. You ooh and aah over them. No matter what their skin color, their hair color, or what kind of clothes they wear. Some babies with runny noses may not be so cute, but by and large, people love children. You make faces at them in the grocery store or at restaurants. Jesus came as a baby. You see him all cuddled up in his swaddling clothes and you love him. You smile at him hoping that he'll smile back at you. But at some point, all the babies grow up. At what age do you begin hating them? When do they stop being children whom you want to rescue, cuddle, nurture, and teach? When do they become "those people"? When do they become abusers, addicts, gang members, thieves, and all those people whom we label with negative words? What's wrong with human beings that they allow situations that create "those people" out of precious, darling small children? When and how do you decide which of those babies you'll love and which you'll ignore or even despise? When do you choose to no longer love? The Christmas story begins your journey of loving everyone in God's name, with God's help. You may never know when your acts of love, your deliberate decisions, may affect a whole family, a whole congregation, a whole community. You may never know when your efforts to stop the wounding, the abandonment, the abusing, and the demeaning will make a true difference. You may never know for sure when a deliberate decision to love can change you forever. You do know that you want to welcome Christ and for that you are to be a loving person, filled with joy and goodwill. You do know that you want Jesus to know that you love him and that you eagerly anticipate his coming into your life now and every day.

Prayer for the Day: *Empowering God, fill me with your love so I can love and welcome others. Amen.*

Week 52
Saturday

Luke 2:1-7

Here are some ideas to help you be a welcoming innkeeper:

Praying in the morning before getting out of bed is a way of connecting with God. Others pray while going to or from work or when sitting in traffic. Others read meditatively poems, devotions, stories, scriptures, or words in carols. Some see candles of the season and let Christ, the light of the world, paint pictures in their hearts and souls as they focus reflectively. A few minutes of uninterrupted quiet to listen for that holy small voice is a way to show God your love. Others pray a brief prayer for anyone who pops into their minds. For those who have caused you pain, your prayer may be, "God, give them love because I can't" or "God, give them compassion."

You might sit in the darkness of this winter season and dare to look at your own darkness so that the light of the world can illumine what you need to see for your own healing and wholeness. You may begin to see the baby Jesus in the children in your community who are abused or neglected or abandoned and struggle to find ways to care for these kids. If Jesus had been born into such a family, would you not do so? Or you may begin to see that just as homelessness and being refugees was the plight of the holy family, so it is with others in your midst and thus you might choose to make a difference. You might decide that you are going to be a change agent for love and for good in your family, your school, your community, your church, and your workplace. You might shock your friends and family by reaching out with love to someone or to a group whom you have every right to hate.

As you actively love and pray, you are indeed making room in your life for the Christ child. You do not even have to use church words. God is love. This is one of the first truths you may have learned as a child. God is love. Whenever you demonstrate love, you are in God and God is in you. You make a room in the inn. Welcome, God, your room is ready.

Prayer for the Day: *God of relationships, help me be more thoughtful during these winter days about whose I am and how I demonstrate that connection to others. Amen.*

Day 365
Luke 2:21-40

21 After eight days had passed, it was time to circumcise the child; and he was called Jesus, the name given by the angel before he was conceived in the womb.

22 When the time came for their purification according to the law of Moses, they brought him up to Jerusalem to present him to the Lord 23 (as it is written in the law of the Lord, 'Every firstborn male shall be designated as holy to the Lord'), 24 and they offered a sacrifice according to what is stated in the law of the Lord, 'a pair of turtle-doves or two young pigeons.'

25 Now there was a man in Jerusalem whose name was Simeon; this man was righteous and devout, looking forward to the consolation of Israel, and the Holy Spirit rested on him. 26 It had been revealed to him by the Holy Spirit that he would not see death before he had seen the Lord's Messiah. 27 Guided by the Spirit, Simeon came into the temple; and when the parents brought in the child Jesus, to do for him what was customary under the law, 28 Simeon took him in his arms and praised God, saying,

> 29 'Master, now you are dismissing your servant in peace,
>   according to your word;
> 30 for my eyes have seen your salvation,
> 31 which you have prepared in the presence of all peoples,
> 32 a light for revelation to the Gentiles
>   and for glory to your people Israel.'

33 And the child's father and mother were amazed at what was being said about him. 34 Then Simeon blessed them and said to his mother Mary, 'This child is destined for the falling and the rising of many in Israel, and to be a sign that will be opposed 35 so that the inner thoughts of many will be revealed—and a sword will pierce your own soul too.'

36 There was also a prophet, Anna the daughter of Phanuel, of the tribe of Asher. She was of a great age, having lived with her husband for seven years after her marriage, 37 then as a widow to the age of eighty-four. She never left the temple but worshipped there with fasting and prayer night and day. 38 At that moment she came, and began to praise God and to speak about the child to all who were looking for the redemption of Jerusalem.

The Return to Nazareth

39 When they had finished everything required by the law of the Lord, they returned to Galilee, to their own town of Nazareth. 40 The child grew and became strong, filled with wisdom; and the favour of God was upon him.

Day 365
Sunday

Luke 2:21-40

After fulfilling their ritual obligations at the temple, Mary, Joseph, and the baby returned to Nazareth. The child grew and became strong, filled with wisdom, and the favor of God was upon him.

Anna and Simeon are two relatively minor characters in the birth narrative of Jesus. Both of them are old. Their exultations make you question what you believe is normal. But isn't that what often happens when you come into the presence of your God or one of God's representatives? You think that you have the full picture of what it means to be Christian and then someone like Simeon points out that God chooses a whole lot of other people—surprising people. Not just Israelites but Gentiles as well. Not just people with resources, but those without as well. Not just people born in the United States but those in other countries as well. Not just US but also THEM as well.

You may distrust things you cannot prove scientifically or with rational thought, but someone like Anna points out that sometimes God reveals God's truth and grace and love in ways that cannot be explained. Both Simeon and Anna demonstrate that when Jesus comes into your life, things can get turned upside down from what you expect.

When you allow life to be guided by the wind of the Holy Spirit, you may be taken to unforeseen places...which at first just seem wrong or irresponsible. And then you commit to following where God is leading and you exclaim, OF COURSE. You shout along with Simeon and Anna that something, someone amazing has come into your life. Something is coming forth that you expected but never fully believed would happen. You have been blessed even when you were least expecting it. Or maybe Simeon and Anna lead you to live with hope and expectations even when it makes you look crazy to others. But the unexpected seems to be the way Jesus pointed to...healing, challenging the power systems, refusing to defend himself at his trial, rising from the dead.

Prayer for the Day: *God of past, present, and future, on this last day of the year, let me see stars and rainbows and puppies and babies...and you. Always you. Amen.*

Acknowledgments

Books "pop" into my brain and often will not let me go until I've written the last word. The writing of this book happened in some ways like that. On the other hand, it was years in the making. Throughout my ministry, I have had the opportunity to preach in a variety of congregations as a pulpit supply, as a temporary minister while the "regular" minister was on sabbatical or vacation, and at special occasions within congregations. Thus, I've been blessed by many congregations—large, small, medium-sized—who encouraged my preaching and writing skills.

But this book grew out of the interim ministry that I enjoyed with Eastminster Presbyterian Church in Simpsonville, SC. This congregation encouraged me to preach with freedom and creativity. They nurtured my minister's heart and allowed me to be part of their fellowship for 19 months before they called their new pastor. I was encouraged to publish a book of my sermons but that did not grab my soul. Then I decided to try turning the sermons into devotions.

I passed the idea along to my wonderful editor, Vally Sharpe, who encouraged me to move ahead. She especially liked the idea of using the same passage for seven days.

I am fortunate to have friends who ask, "What are you working on now? Are you writing?" Now with this twelfth book, I guess that I can honestly say, "Yes, I'm a writer and I'm working on a writing project."

Thank you to everyone who encourages me to listen to those God-whispers in my life and then to act on them.

About the Author

Beth Lindsay Templeton is a Presbyterian USA minister, poverty advocate and teacher, workshop leader, and writer. She enjoys working with congregations, schools and universities, women's groups, medical personnel, and civic organizations in Greenville, S.C. and around the country.

www.ingramcontent.com/pod-product-compliance
Lightning Source LLC
Chambersburg PA
CBHW050309120526
44592CB00014B/1842